lonely planet

IRELAND'S
BEST TRIPS

34 AMAZING ROAD TRIPS

This edition written and researched by

**Fionn Davenport, Belinda Dixon
Catherine Le Nevez, Oda O'Carroll**

SYMBOLS IN THIS BOOK

✓ Top Tips	📖 History & Culture	📷 Essential Photo
🔗 Link Your Trips	👫 Family	🏃 Walking Tour
💬 Tips from Locals	🍷 Food & Drink	🍴 Eating
↱ Trip Detour	🌳 Outdoors	🛏 Sleeping

📞 Telephone Number	@ Internet Access	📖 English-Language Menu
🕓 Opening Hours	📶 Wi-Fi Access	👪 Family-Friendly
P Parking	✎ Vegetarian Selection	
⊖ Nonsmoking	🏊 Swimming Pool	🐾 Pet-Friendly
❄ Air-Conditioning		

MAP LEGEND

Routes
- ▬▬ Trip Route
- ▬▬ Trip Detour
- ▬▬ Linked Trip
- ▬▬ Walk Route
- ▬▬ Tollway
- ▬▬ Freeway
- ▬▬ Primary
- ▬▬ Secondary
- ▬▬ Tertiary
- ▬▬ Lane
- ▬▬ Unsealed Road
- ▨▨ Plaza/Mall
- ⋯⋯ Steps
-)= = Tunnel
- ▬▬ Pedestrian Overpass
- ▬▬ Walk Track/Path

Boundaries
- --- International
- ---- State/Province
- ⌐⌐⌐ Cliff
- ▬▬ Wall

Population
- ✪ Capital (National)
- ◉ Capital (State/Province)
- ● City/Large Town
- ○ Town/Village

Transport
- ✈ Airport
- +⊕+ Cable Car/Funicular
- P Parking
- +⊕+ Train/Railway
- Ⓣ Tram
- Ⓜ Underground Train Station

Trips
- 1 Trip Numbers
- 9 Trip Stop
- 🏃 Walking Tour
- ↱ Trip Detour

Route Markers
- E44 E-Road Network
- M100 National Network

Hydrography
- ⌒ River/Creek
- ⌒ Intermittent River
- ⌒ Swamp/Mangrove
- ⌒ Canal
- ⬭ Water
- ⬭ Dry/Salt/Intermittent Lake
- Glacier

Areas
- ▨ Beach
- ▨ Cemetery (Christian)
- ⌧ Cemetery (Other)
- ▨ Park
- ▨ Forest
- ▨ Urban Area
- ▨ Sportsground

CONTENTS

Belfast &
the North of
Ireland
p299

Galway &
the West of
Ireland
p231

Dublin &
Eastern Ireland
p35

Cork &
Southwest
Ireland
p159

3

Contents cont.

ROAD TRIP ESSENTIALS

Classic Trips

Look out for the Classic Trips stamp on our favourite routes in this book.

Kenmare River A boat in the river's tranquil waters

WELCOME TO
IRELAND

In all likelihood, you've come to experience Ireland of the postcard. The exquisite peninsulas of the southwest, the brooding loneliness of Connemara and the dramatic wildness of County Donegal. You'll also find it around the lakes of Counties Leitrim and Roscommon and the undulating hills of the sunny southeast.

Scenery, history, culture, bustling cosmopolitanism and the stillness of village life – you'll find all of this along the roads covered by the 34 drives in this book. You'll visit blockbuster attractions and replicate famous photo ops. But there are plenty of surprises too – and they're all within easy reach of each other.

Whether you want to drive through the wildest terrain or sample great food while hopping between spa treatments, we've got something for you. And if you've only got time for one trip, make it one of our eight Classic Trips, which take you to the very best of Ireland. Turn the page for more.

→

IRELAND
Classic Trips

1

What is a Classic Trip?

All the trips in this book show you the best of Ireland, but we've chosen eight as our all-time favourites. These are our Classic Trips – the ones that lead you to the best of the iconic sights, the top activities and the unique Irish experiences. Turn the page to see the map, and look out for the Classic Trip stamp throughout the book.

1 Ireland's Highlights
Brave the elements to get to Skellig Michael, the Unesco World Heritage Site and largest of the Skellig Islands

16 Southwest Blitz Plant a kiss on the famous Blarney Stone at the 15th-century Blarney Castle

29 The North in a Nutshell
See *The Big Fish* sculpture by John Kindness, Queen's Quay, Belfast

STEPHEN SAKS/GETTY IMAGES ©

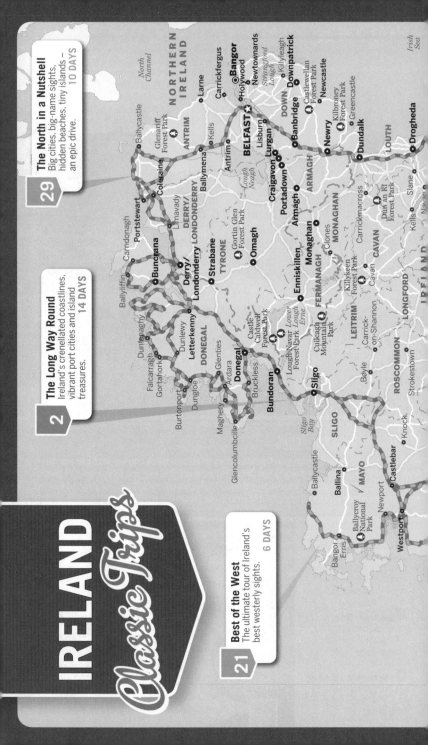

IRELAND
Classic Trips

29 **The North in a Nutshell**
Big cities, big-name sights, hidden beaches, tiny islands – an epic drive. **10 DAYS**

2 **The Long Way Round**
Ireland's crenellated coastlines, vibrant port cities and island treasures. **14 DAYS**

21 **Best of the West**
The ultimate tour of Ireland's best westerly sights. **6 DAYS**

North Channel

Irish Sea

NORTHERN IRELAND

Ballycastle · Glenariff Forest Park · Larne · Carrickfergus · Bangor · Holywood · Newtownards · Carrickfergus · Killyleagh · Downpatrick

Portstewart · Coleraine · Ballymena · Kells · Antrim · **BELFAST** · Lisburn · Lurgan · **DOWN** · Castlewellan Forest Park · Newcastle

Carndonagh · Limavady · Ballymoney · **ANTRIM** · Craigavon · Portadown · Banbridge · Kilbroney Forest Park · Greencastle

DERRY/ LONDONDERRY · Gortin Glen Forest Park · **ARMAGH** · Armagh · Newry · Dundalk

Ballyliffin · Buncrana · Derry/ Londonderry · Strabane · **TYRONE** · Omagh · Enniskillen · Monaghan · **MONAGHAN** · Clones · Carrickmacross · **LOUTH** · Drogheda

Dunfanaghy · Letterkenny · **DONEGAL** · Castle Caldwell Forest Park · **FERMANAGH** · Killykeen Forest Park · **CAVAN** · Dún an Rí Forest Park · Slane

Falcarragh · Gortahork · Dunlewy · Glenties · Lough Navar Forest Park · Lower Lough Erne · Cuilcagh Mountain Park · **LEITRIM** · Cavan · Kells · Navan

Burtonport · Dungloe · Ardara · Bruckless · Donegal · Carrick- on-Shannon · **LONGFORD**

Maghery · **DONEGAL** · Bundoran · Sligo · Boyle · **IRELAND**

Glencolumbcille · **SLIGO** · *Sligo Bay* · **ROSCOMMON** · Strokestown

Ballycastle · Ballina · Knock · Castlebar · **MAYO** · Bangor Erris · Ballycroy National Park · Newport · Westport

Lough Neagh · *Strangford Lough*

1 **Ireland's Highlights**
The best of Ireland's five-star cultural and natural attractions. **7 DAYS**

28 **Tip to Toe**
The ultimate pan-Irish experience. **10 DAYS**

16 **Southwest Blitz**
The best of the southwest coast, countryside and cosmopolitan city life. **4 DAYS**

14 **Ring of Kerry**
Pass jaw-dropping scenery as you circumnavigate the Iveragh Peninsula. **4 DAYS**

22 **Musical Landscapes**
A ride round County Clare's hottest trad music spots. **5 DAYS**

Ireland's best sights and experiences, and the road trips that will take you there.

IRELAND
HIGHLIGHTS

★

Dublin

It's most likely that your Irish visit will begin and end in Dublin, Ireland's capital and largest city by far. On **Trip 1: Ireland's Highlights**, you can visit some of the city's best-known attractions, while **Stretch Your Legs: Dublin** gives you a chance to explore the city in greater depth, especially its rich Georgian heritage.

TRIPS

Dublin Halfpenny Bridge over the River Liffey

Connemara The shore of Kylemore Lake

Connemara

A kaleidoscope of rusty bogs, lonely valleys and enticing hamlets laid across a patchwork of narrow country roads punctuated by the odd inviting country pub: welcome to Connemara, yours to discover on **Trip 23: Mountains & Moors**. Connemara evokes the very best of Irish scenery and the country itself, unsullied by centuries of history and transformation.

TRIPS

Galway

Storied, sung-about and snug, Galway is one of Ireland's great pleasures. So much so that it's full of people who came, saw and still haven't managed to leave. Wander the tuneful streets and refuel in any of the city's great pubs on **Trip 22: Musical Landscapes** – it *could* keep you busy for a month's worth of nights.

TRIPS
1 4 21 22 23 24

Belfast

There's far more to Belfast than its troubled past, as you can discover for yourself on **Trip 29: The North in a Nutshell**. But you can learn about Northern Ireland's recent history on our walking tour, **Stretch Your Legs: Belfast**, on which you'll explore the political murals and peace lines of West Belfast's divided neighbourhoods of the Falls and the Shankill.

TRIPS
2 29 33

Connemara Boats moored at Roundstone Harbour

BEST ROADS FOR DRIVING

R560, County Kerry Drive the spectacular Connor Pass. **Trips** 1 15 21

R115 (Old Military Rd), County Wicklow The loveliest, loneliest road of the east. **Trip** 8

Ring of Kerry Ireland's most famous circular route. **Trips** 1 2 14 16

Beara Peninsula Magnificent views and lovely villages. **Trips** 1 2 18 21

N59, Connemara Mountains, moors and broody boglands. **Trips** 21 23 24 25

Cork

An appealing waterfront location, some of the best food you'll find anywhere in the country, lively craic and a vibrant 'Dublin? Where's that?' dynamic make Ireland's second city, Cork, hard to resist. Foodies can taste the best of the city's (and county's) eateries and markets on **Trip 17: Southwestern Pantry**, and take in the key sites on our designated walking tour.

TRIPS 2 16 17 21

Glendalough View of the ruin's intact round tower

Glendalough

Once one of Ireland's most dynamic universities, the monastic ruins of Glendalough, founded by St Kevin as a spiritual retreat, are now among the country's most beautiful ruined sites. They're easily visited from Dublin on **Trip 3: A Week Around Dublin**. The remains of the settlement (including an intact round tower), coupled with the stunning scenery, are unforgettable, and are the perfect spot for a mountain hike.

TRIPS

BEST TOWNS FOR TRADITIONAL MUSIC

Dingle A handful of bars with nightly music.
Trips 1 2 15 21

Miltown Malbay Come for the Willie Clancy Festival in July.
Trip 22

Ennis The capital of music country. **Trips** 1 22 27

Doolin Three pubs host some of the country's best sessions.
Trips 2 4 22

Dingle Peninsula Slea Head beach

Rock of Cashel The Rock of Cashel overlooks the ruins of the 13th-century Hore Abbey

Dingle Peninsula

It seems that everybody wants to go to Dingle – join them on **Trip 15: Dingle Peninsula**. Luckily, this is one place that transcends the crowds with its allure. Sure you may be stuck behind a bus, but this rocky, striated land has a history as compelling as its beauty, not to mention prehistoric monuments, scenic spots and fabulous pubs.

TRIPS  1 2 15 21

Brú na Bóinne

The vast neolithic necropolis of Brú na Bóinne in County Meath is 600 years older than the pyramids, 1000 years older than Stonehenge, and designed with a mathematical precision that would have confounded the ancient Greeks. You can visit on **Trip 6: Ancient Ireland**, especially to see the simulated winter sunrise that illuminates the main burial chamber.

TRIPS 3 5 6 13

Rock of Cashel

The Rock of Cashel, a highlight of **Trip 20: The Holy Glen**, never ceases to startle when you first see it rising from the otherwise mundane plains of Tipperary. And this ancient fortified home of kings is just the tip of the iceberg, as moody ruins are hidden in the surrounding green expanse, set neatly atop a rock overlooking pretty Cashel town.

TRIPS  6 20 28

Ring of Kerry

Yes, it's popular. And yes, it's always choked with bus traffic, especially in summer. But there are about 1000 reasons why the Ring of Kerry is the tourist charm bracelet it is – and gets its own designated itinerary (**Trip 14: Ring of Kerry**). You'll find most of the reasons around the Iveragh Peninsula just west of Killarney; do it counter-clockwise unless you want to get stuck behind a caravan of tour buses!

TRIPS 1 2 14 16

Giant's Causeway

The grand geological flourish of the Giant's Causeway is Northern Ireland's most popular attraction and one of the world's iconic natural wonders. You can clamber across the 40,000 unique hexagonal basalt columns on **Trip 34: The Antrim Coast.** Decide then whether you prefer the scientific explanation or the far more colourful legend that explains them.

TRIPS 2 29 33 34

(left) **Ring of Kerry** View of the Ring of Kerry from near Waterville

(below) **Giant's Causeway** The basalt columns of the Causeway

Cliffs of Moher

Bathed in the golden glow of the late afternoon sun, the iconic Cliffs of Moher are one of the west coast's splendours. Witnessed from a boat bobbing below or from dry land as you would on **Trip 1: Ireland's Highlights**, the towering stone faces have a jaw-dropping, dramatic beauty that's enlivened by scores of sea birds, including cute little puffins.

TRIPS 1 27

BEST ANCIENT RUINS

Carrowkeel A megalithic tomb atop a scenic hill. **Trip** 26

Dún Aengus A prehistoric fort abutting a sea-lashed cliff. **Trips** 2 4 22 27

Clonmacnoise Ireland's most important monastic university. **Trips** 4 6 7

Loughcrew Cairns A 'forgotten' neolithic passage grave. **Trip** 6

Cruachan Aí Europe's most significant Celtic royal site. **Trip** 6

21

IF YOU LIKE...

Paragliding Killiney Hill, near Dublin

Ancient Monuments

Ireland is old, like older-than-the-pyramids old. Everywhere you go you can find a historic castle, the ruins of a 1500-year-old monastery, or a collection of stones with faded carvings done by prehistoric people so ancient that archaeologists talk of eras rather than centuries.

6 Ancient Ireland The big stars of Ireland's ancient past.

15 Dingle Peninsula Slea Head is littered with prehistoric monuments.

20 The Holy Glen Visit County Tipperary's collection of monastic treasures.

26 Sligo Surrounds A wealth of prehistoric sites within easy reach of each other.

Great Views

What do you fancy? A jagged coastline pounded by the waves? A desolate mountain range with a brooding, low-slung sky? Or perhaps an emerald valley stretched out below you, dotted with clusters of sheep and criss-crossed by stone walls? In Ireland, keep your camera close by.

8 Wicklow Mountains Mountain passes and glacial valleys are the scenic highlights.

14 Ring of Kerry Virtually every corner on this iconic drive reveals a postcard view.

23 Mountains & Moors A trip through broody, beautiful Connemara.

30 Delights of Donegal The stunning scenery of Ireland's northwestern corner.

Hidden Treasures

Exploring the best of Ireland is not just about five-star attractions or the bustling crowds that just won't get out of your perfect picture. Beyond the tourist chart-toppers there's a host of sights and towns that have escaped mass attention, but are no less worth the effort.

9 Carlow Back Roads A marvellous county untouched by mass tourism.

19 Shannon River Route Ireland's mightiest river has a host of little-visited delights.

24 Loughs of the West The west's lesser-known backwaters.

31 Inishowen Peninsula Remote and hard to get to, but worth every effort.

Live music One of Ireland's music pubs

Traditional Music

The west, particularly, is the home of traditional music, and there are communities where it is so woven into the social fabric that it's as important to the people as a decent dinner and a well-poured pint. Whether organised or impromptu, a great traditional session is a highlight of any Irish trip.

15 Dingle Peninsula Forget yourself in one of Dingle's music pubs.

22 Musical Landscapes The best of the west's pubs, venues and music festivals.

29 The North in a Nutshell Visit the home of Enya, Clannad and a whole musical movement.

Good Food

Throughout Ireland, there is abundant evidence of the foodie revolution as local chefs and producers combine international experience with the kind of meals that have always been taken for granted on well-run Irish farms.

11 Wexford & Waterford Parts of west Waterford are a gourmet heaven.

17 Southwestern Pantry County Cork is the flag bearer of the foodie revolution.

18 West Cork Villages Virtually every village in West Cork boasts a good restaurant.

21 Best of the West From Sligo to Kerry, there's great grub to be had.

An Adrenalin Rush

Ireland has myriad ways for you to work up a sweat – from chasing chickens around a farmyard to paragliding off the edge of a mountain.

13 Family Fun From working farms to adventure centres – fun for the whole family.

15 Dingle Peninsula Scuba diving and surfing in the beautiful southwest.

32 Northwest on Adrenalin Get breathless in the sea and up a mountain.

NEED ^{TO} KNOW

CURRENCY
Euro (€) in the Republic, pound sterling (£) in Northern Ireland

LANGUAGE
English, Irish in some areas

VISAS
Generally not required for stays up to three months in the Republic, six months in Northern Ireland

FUEL
Petrol (gas) stations are everywhere, but are limited on the motorways. Expect to pay €1.60 to €1.80 per litre in the Republic, £1.25 to £1.35 in Northern Ireland.

RENTAL CARS
Avis (www.avis.ie)
Europcar (www.europcar.ie)
Hertz (www.hertz.ie)
Thrifty (www.thrifty.ie)

IMPORTANT NUMBERS
Country code (📞353 Republic, 📞44 Northern Ireland)
Emergencies (📞999)
Roadside assistance (📞1800 667 788 in the Republic, 📞0800 887 766 in Northern Ireland)

Climate

Warm to hot summers, mild winters

Belfast
GO May–Sep

Dublin
GO any time; lots of indoor attractions

Galway
GO May–Sep

Killarney
GO May–Sep

Cork
GO May–Sep

When to Go

High Season (Jun–Aug)
» Ireland's weather at its best.

» Accommodation rates at their highest (especially August).

» Tourism peaks in Dublin, Kerry, southern and western coasts.

Shoulder Season (Easter–May, Sep & Oct)
» Weather often good; sun and rain in May.

» 'Indian summers' often warm September.

» Crowds and accommodation rates drop.

Low Season (Nov–Feb)
» Reduced opening hours from November to Easter; some destinations shut down.

» Cold and wet weather throughout the country; fog can reduce visibility.

» Big-city attractions operate as normal.

Daily Costs

Budget: Less than €60
» Dorm bed: €12–€20

» Cheap meal in cafe/pub: €6–€12

» Intercity bus travel: €12–€25 (for 200km journey)

» Pint: €4.50

Midrange: €60–€120
» Double room in a hotel or B&B: €40–€100 (Dublin €60–€130)

» Main course in midrange restaurant: €10–€18

» Car rental: from €40 per day

Top End: Over €120
» Double room in four-star hotel: from €150

» Three-course meal in good restaurant: around €50

» Round of golf at respected course: from €80

Eating

Restaurants From cheap 'n' cheerful to Michelin-starred.

Cafes Perfect for a quick bite.

Hotels Most hotel restaurants cater to outside diners.

Pubs Pub grub is ubiquitous; it's mostly of the toasted-sandwich variety, but a large number of pubs also have full-menu service.

Eating price indicators represent the cost of a main dish:

Republic/ Northern Ireland	
€/£	< €10/£10
€€/££	€11–€20/ £11–£20
€€€/£££	> €20/£20

Sleeping

B&Bs Ubiquitous and varying in standard. Many rural ones only accept cash.

Guesthouses Family homes with boutique-hotel comfort. Most accept credit cards.

Hotels Ranging from local pubs to five-star castles; priced accordingly.

Sleeping price indicators represent the cost of a double room in high season:

Republic/ Northern Ireland	
€/£	< €60/£40
€€/££	€60–€150/ £40–£100
€€€/£££	> €150/£100

Arriving in Ireland

Dublin Airport
Rental cars All the companies well represented.

Taxis To central Dublin €20–€25; 30 to 45 minutes.

Buses Aircoach (€7) serves 18 stops throughout the city.

Shannon Airport
Rental cars All the companies represented.

Taxis To central Limerick or Ennis €35; 45 minutes.

Dun Laoghaire Ferry Port
Buses Public bus (€2.20); about 45 minutes to Dublin's city centre.

DART Suburban rail (€2.50); 25 minutes to city centre.

Taxis To city centre €15–€20; 30 minutes.

Mobile Phones

Phones from most other countries work in Ireland, but attract roaming charges. Local SIM cards cost from €10, SIM and basic handsets around €40.

Internet Access

Most towns have an internet cafe (€4–€8 per hour); wi-fi is free in many hotels and cafes.

Money

Change bureaus and ATMs widely available, especially in cities and major towns. Credit cards accepted in all hotels, many B&Bs and most restaurants.

Tipping

Not required, but 10% to 15% in restaurants; €1 for taxi drivers; €1 per bag for porters.

Useful Websites

Automobile Association (AA; www.aaireland.ie) Breakdown assistance.

Lonely Planet (www.lonelyplanet.com) Destination information, hotel bookings, travellers' forum.

Failte Ireland (www.discoverireland.ie) Official tourist board site.

Northern Ireland Tourist Board (www.nitb.com) Official tourist site.

For more, see Road Trip Essentials (p372).

CITY GUIDE

DUBLIN

Ireland's largest city by far has all the credentials of a capital city: superb restaurants, world-class museums and more nightlife than you could ever use, from theatre to its 1000-plus pubs. Still the sine qua non of the city's social life, these watering holes are the best place to take Dublin's pulse.

Dublin Grafton street mall

Getting Around

The one-way system makes driving in Dublin tricky; the traffic can make it a test of patience. You can walk pretty much anywhere in the compact city centre.

Parking

Street parking is scarce and costly, except on Sundays, when you can park on single-yellow lines. Sheltered car parks (€5 per hour) are your best bet if your hotel doesn't have a car park.

Discover the Taste of Dublin

Temple Bar has the biggest concentration of restaurants, mostly mid-priced and often bland; the best options are on the streets on either side of Grafton St. Top-end spots are around Merrion Sq and Fitzwilliam Sq.

Live Like a Local

Base yourself in a suburb immediately south of the city centre, such as Ballsbridge, Donnybrook or Ranelagh, to experience the best of the city's B&B culture. The little shops and boutiques immediately west of Grafton St are the best for shopping.

Useful Websites

Dublin Tourism (www.visitdublin.com) Sights, accommodation bookings, discounts.

Entertainment.ie (www.entertainment.ie) Comprehensive listings of events and gigs.

Lonely Planet (www.lonelyplanet.com/ireland/dublin) Travel tips, accommodation and a travellers' forum.

Trips Through Dublin: 1 2 4 13

For more, check out our city and country guides. www.lonelyplanet.com

TOP EXPERIENCES

→ Stroll the Elizabethan Cobbles of Trinity College

Ireland's most famous university is also Dublin's most atmospheric bit of city-centre real estate, as well as home to the *Book of Kells*.

→ Discover Ireland's Treasures

The National Museum of Ireland is where you'll find the country's most complete collection of medieval gold work, Celtic design and iconic treasures dating back 2500 years.

→ Indulge Your Thespian Side

From classic plays to experimental new works, the city's theatres have something for everyone.

→ Saunter Through Georgian Squares

The Georgian gems of St Stephen's Green and Merrion Sq are the best spots to catch a bit of urban R & R.

→ Get to Grips with Irish History

The tour of Kilmainham Gaol is a hard-hitting exploration of the country's troubled past.

→ Tap into Your Inner Victorian Botanist

Opened by Dr David Livingstone, the Natural History Museum, aka the 'dead zoo', has preserved its 19th-century spirit – as well as some two million stuffed animals.

→ Grab a Pint in a Traditional Pub

There's nowhere better to sample a pint of Guinness – the 'black stuff' or 'liquid gold' – than in one of the city's many traditional pubs.

Galway Shoppers at a weekend market

GALWAY

Ireland's most bohemian burg has long celebrated difference, which accounts for its vibrant arts scene, easygoing pace and outstanding nightlife. Old-fashioned pubs with traditional sessions, theatres hosting experimental works, designated music venues in thrall to the heartfelt outpourings of the singer-songwriter... It's just another night in Galway.

Getting Around

Traffic in and out of the city centre is a major issue during peak hours. The one-way system and network of pedestrianised streets can make getting around a little tricky.

Parking

Parking throughout Galway's streets is metered. There are several multistorey and pay-and-display car parks around town.

Discover the Taste of Galway

Seafood is Galway's speciality, be it fish and chips, ocean-fresh chowder or salmon cooked to perfection. Galway Bay oysters star on many menus. Pedestrianised Quay St is lined with restaurants aimed at the tourist throngs.

Live Like a Local

Base yourself in the city centre, so that you can take full advantage of the city's tightly packed attractions. The west side, on the far side of the River Corrib, is where you'll find the best concentration of eateries, classic pubs and music venues.

Useful Websites

Discover Ireland (www. discoverireland.ie) Sights, accommodation bookings, discounts.

Galway Pub Guide (www. galwaycitypubguide.com) Comprehensive guide to the heaving scene.

Galway Tourism (www. galwaytourism.ie) Local tourist information.

Trips Through Galway:

1 4 21 22 23 24

BELFAST

Vibrant, confident and fascinating – not words that immediately jump to mind when imagining Belfast. But Northern Ireland's largest city has worked hard to get rid of its reputation as a violence-scarred protagonist of the news, and now offers great museums, fine dining and a wealth of shopping to go with its rich history.

Getting Around

Belfast is easy enough to drive in, with a good road network and signposting delivering you to where you want to go.

Parking

For on-street parking between 8am and 6pm Monday to Saturday, you'll need to buy a ticket from a machine. For longer periods, head for one of the many multistorey car parks that are dotted around the city centre.

Discover the Taste of Belfast

In the evening, the liveliest part of the city centre stretches south of Donegall Sq to Shaftesbury Sq. During the day, many pubs, cafes and restaurants do a roaring trade. South Belfast is also where you'll find some terrific restaurants.

Live Like a Local

Most of Belfast's budget and midrange accommodation is south of the centre, in the university district around Botanic Ave, University Rd and Malone Rd. This area is also crammed with good-value restaurants and pubs, and is mostly within a 20-minute walk of City Hall.

Useful Websites

Belfast City Council (www.belfastcity.gov.uk/events) Information on a wide range of organised events.

Belfast Music (www.belfastmusic.org) Online gig listings.

Belfast Welcome Centre (www.gotobelfast.com) Sights, accommodation bookings, discounts.

Great Belfast Food (www.greatbelfastfood.com) Stay up to date with Belfast's foodie scene.

Trips Through Belfast:

2 29 33

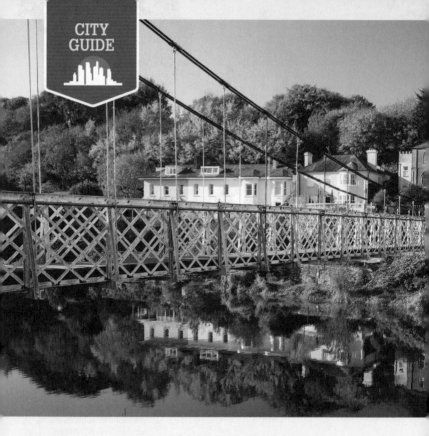

CORK

Ireland's second city is second only in size; in every other respect it considers itself equal to Dublin (or even better). Great restaurants, top-class galleries and a vibrant pub scene lend credence to its claim, while the people are as friendly and welcoming as you'll find anywhere.

Getting Around

Cork's compact centre and easy-to-follow one-way system makes driving a relatively hassle-free experience.

Parking

Streetside parking requires scratch-card parking discs (€2 per hour), obtained from the tourist office and some newsagencies. There are several signposted car parks around the central area, with charges of €2 per hour and €12 overnight.

TRISH PUNCH/GETTY IMAGES ©

TOP EXPERIENCES

➡ **Look Upon Cork**
Wander up through Shandon and
explore the galleries, antique shops
and cafes of the city's prettiest
neighbourhood, perched on a hill on
the northern side of town.

➡ **Eyeball the Best of Irish Art**
The Crawford Municipal Art Gallery
is small, but it's packed with great art
by top Irish names like Jack B Yeats,
Nathaniel Hone, Sir John Lavery and
Mainie Jellett.

➡ **Indulge Your Tastebuds**
Cork's foodie scene is made
famous by its collection of terrific
restaurants, but don't forget the
splendid Victorian English Market.

➡ **Have a Night on the Town**
Atmospheric old pubs, buzzing
music venues and a well-respected
theatre scene make for a memorable
night out.

Cork Daly's bridge over the River Lee

Discover the Taste of Cork
The narrow pedestrianised streets north
of St Patrick's St are packed with cafes
and restaurants, and the place hops day
and night. The English Market is *the*
place for great produce and outstanding
daytime eats.

Live Like a Local
Base yourself in town, as close to St
Patrick's St and the South Mall as
possible. Once you've exhausted the
warren of streets between these two
locations, venture west across the Lee
and wander up to Shandon, where

Corkonians regularly take refuge from
the city below.

Useful Websites
Cork City Tourism (www.cometocork.com)
Sights, accommodation bookings, discounts.

People's Republic of Cork (www.
peoplesrepublicofcork.com) Indie guide to what's
on in Cork.

WhazOn? (www.whazon.com) Comprehensive
entertainment listings.

Trips Through Cork: 2 16 17 21

IRELAND
BY REGION

Framed by rugged coastlines and peppered with breathtaking scenery, Ireland's compact driving circuit could keep you busy for months. Here's your guide to each region and road trips for the best experiences.

Galway & the West of Ireland (p231)

Connemara has a lyrical beauty that drives artists wild, while County Clare is the spiritual home of traditional Irish music. Between them are the Aran Islands, the very definition of windswept and remote. And don't forget Galway city, Ireland's bohemian capital.

Get musical on Trip 22
Go wild in Connemara on Trip 23

Cork & Southwest Ireland (p159)

The Ireland of the postcard and tourist brochures, the southwest's abundance of stunning drives and iconic scenery will leave you spoilt for choice. From the country's most popular drives to untrodden back roads meandering through the region's gourmet heartland, *this* is the Ireland you came to see.

See the best of Cork on Trip 14
Taste gourmet goodness on Trip 17

Belfast & the North of Ireland (p299)

Beyond the best-known driving routes along the Antrim Coast with its cluster of world-class attractions, the north of Ireland is as delightful as it is surprising, whether you're snaking up a meandering mountain pass in Donegal or exploring the fascinating cities of Belfast and Derry/Londonderry.

Take giant footsteps on Trip `34`

Go mountain wild on Trip `30`

Dublin & Eastern Ireland (p35)

A capital city with all the distractions deserving of the title, Dublin can be explored on foot before you set off to experience its surrounding counties. Within an hour's drive of Dublin there are eye-catching Palladian piles, remote mountain passes cutting through gorgeous glacial valleys, and prehistoric monuments of world renown.

Explore ancient Ireland on Trip `6`

Get mountain fever on Trip `8`

Dublin & Eastern Ireland

A SPIDER'S WEB OF ROADS – from motorways to tiny rural routes – spreading from Dublin's city centre transport you to myriad delights and distractions, all within easy reach of Ireland's capital.

Within an hour's drive from Dublin you can find yourself on a lonely mountain pass with only the odd sheep for company, or be transported back 3500 years in time to explore a passage grave built before the pyramids were a twinkle in a Pharaoh's eye.

And just a little further afield is a collection of historic towns, beautiful seaside resorts and a wealth of monastic monuments that all serve to remind you of Ireland's breathtaking cultural patrimony.

Dublin O'Connell Bridge over the Liffey
RICHARD I'ANSON/GETTY IMAGES ©

Dublin & Eastern Ireland

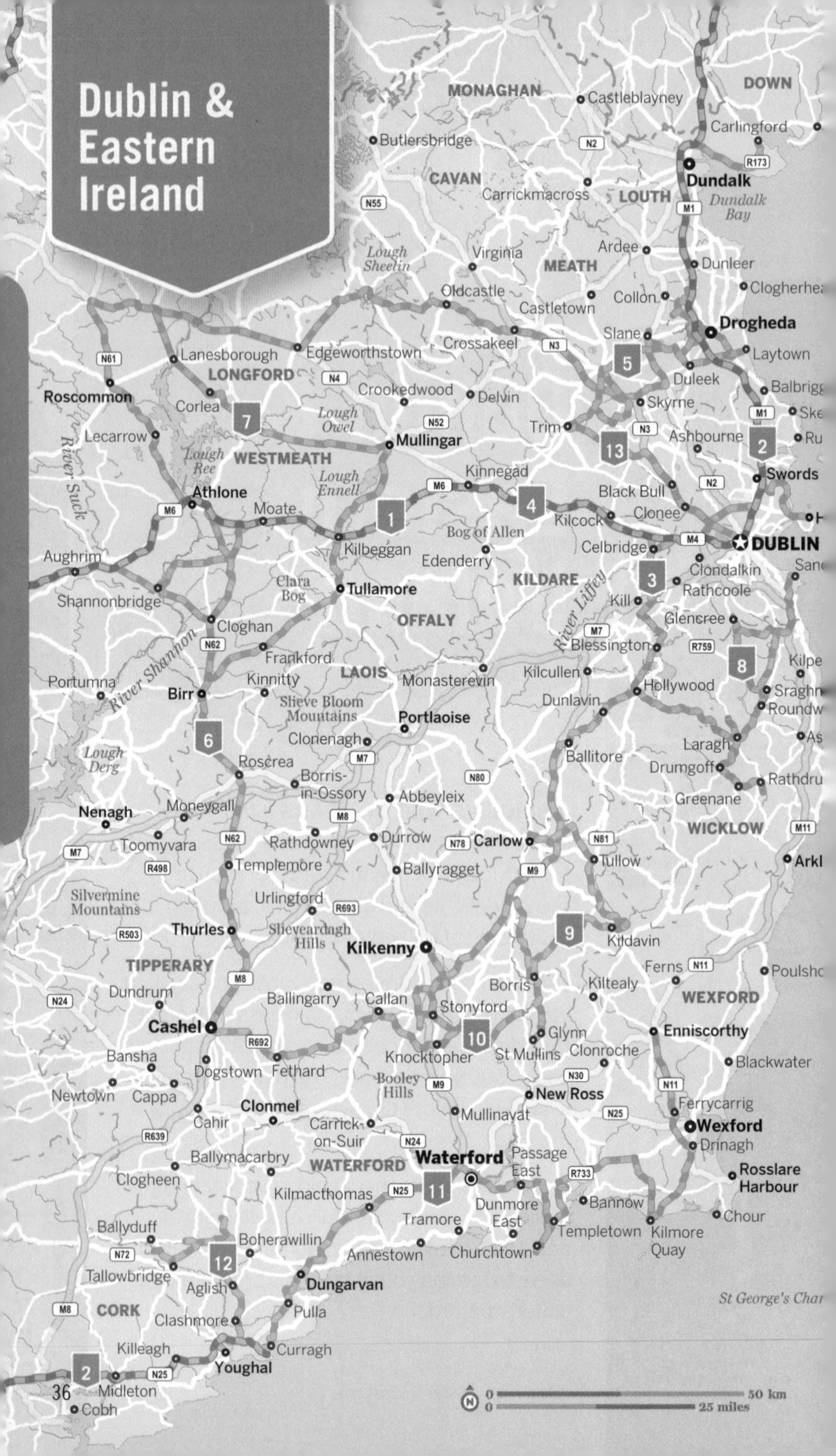

Classic Trip

Ireland's Highlights 7 Days
 1 The best of Ireland's five-star attractions: cultural treasures, stunning scenery and traditional music. (p39)

 Classic Trip

The Long Way Round 14 Days
2 Ireland's crenellated coastlines, vibrant port cities and island treasures – the ideal drive. (p55)

A Week Around Dublin 3 Days
3 Seaside villages, monastic ruins and palatial Palladian mansions. (p69)

East to West 7 Days
 4 Cut across Ireland's midriff, from the capital to Connemara. (p77)

The Boyne Valley 2 Days
 5 A shortish trip that's long on history – from neolithic tombs to bloody battlefields. (p85)

Ancient Ireland 4 Days
 6 Salivate at the thought of exploring 4000 years of history in four days. (p93)

Monasteries, Mountains & Mansions 3 Days
 7 A heritage trip that skirts on and off the beaten path. (p101)

Wicklow Mountains 3 Days
8 Heritage and history along the spine of eastern Ireland's most scenic mountain range. (p109)

Carlow Back Roads 3 Days
9 A trip to uncover the hidden delights of Ireland's second-smallest county. (p117)

Kilkenny's Treasures 3 Days
 10 The very best of a medieval city and its surrounds. (p125)

Wexford & Waterford 5 Days
11 The sunny southeast revealed – from bustling port villages to moody monastic ruins. (p135)

Blackwater Valley Drive 2 Days
12 Follow the river from the sea and discover its hidden treasures. (p143)

Family Fun 3 Days
 13 Adventure, heritage and distractions for the whole family. (p151)

DON'T MISS

Brú na Bóinne
Ireland's most important neolithic monument is a breathtaking feat of prehistoric genius and imagination. Let yourself be wowed on Trips **3 5 6 13**

Dublin
Most visits to Ireland begin and end in the capital, so be a latter-day Dubliner on Trips **1 2 4 13**

Monasterboice
Best experienced on a summer's evening with only crowing ravens for company, contemplate the high crosses and ruins on Trip **5**

Clonegal
An arched stone bridge over a river populated by swans and banked by a multitude of flowers? Visit Ireland's real fairy tale village on Trip **9**

Ballysaggartmore Towers
A Gothic folly in the middle of a forest that is testimony to love's foolish ambition. Let yourself dream on Trip **12**

Dingle Peninsula Breathtaking
mountain views and wild oceans

Ireland's Highlights

1

This trip gives you a glimpse of the very best Ireland has to offer, including the country's most famous attractions, most spectacular countryside, and most popular towns and villages.

TRIP HIGHLIGHTS

km

Dublin
World-class museums, superb restaurants and terrific nightlife

Roundstone

1 START

5

Ennis

460 km

Cliffs of Moher
Majestic sea cliffs rising over 200m from a churning sea

7

Killorglin • Killarney
FINISH
• Kenmare

670 km

Dingle
Traditional pubs, enticing craft studios and music, music everywhere

---

7 DAYS
959KM / 596 MILES

GREAT FOR...

BEST TIME TO GO

April to September for the long days and best weather.

ESSENTIAL PHOTO

The iconic Ladies' View on the Ring of Kerry.

BEST TWO DAYS

The Connemara peninsula and the Ring of Kerry.

1 Ireland's Highlights

Every time-worn truth about Ireland will be found on this trip: the breathtaking scenery of stone-walled fields and wave-dashed cliffs; the picture-postcard villages and bustling towns; the ancient ruins that have stood since before history was written. The trip begins in Ireland's storied, fascinating capital and transports you to the wild west of Galway and Connemara before taking you south to the even wilder folds of County Kerry.

TRIP HIGHLIGHT

1 Dublin

World-class museums, superb restaurants and the best collection of entertainment in the country – there are plenty of good reasons why the capital is the ideal place to start your trip. Get some sightseeing in on our walking tour (see p52) before 'exploring' at least one of the city's storied – if not historic – pubs.

Your top stop should be the grounds of **Trinity College** (🚶 walking tours 01-896 1827; www.tcd.ie; tour €10; ⊘ tours every 30min 10.15am-3.40pm Mon-Sat, to 3pm Sun mid-May–Sep), home to the gloriously illuminated ***Book of Kells***. It's kept in the Old Library's stunning 65m **Long Room** (East Pavilion, Library Colonnades; adult/student/child €9/8/ free; ⊘9.30am-5pm Mon-Sat year-round, noon-4.30pm Sun Oct-Apr, from 9.30am Sun May-Sep).

🍴 🛏 p50

The Drive » It's a 210km trip to Galway city across the country along the M6 motorway, which has little in terms of visual highlights beyond green fields, which get greener and a little more wild the further west you go. Twenty-four kilometres south of Athlone (about halfway) is a worthwhile detour to Clonmacnoise.

2 Galway City

The best way to appreciate Galway is to amble – around Eyre Sq and down Shop St towards the Spanish Arch and the River Corrib, stopping off for a little liquid sustenance in one of the city's classic

LINK YOUR TRIP

17 Southwestern Pantry

From Kenmare, it's a 42km drive south to Durrus and the start of the mouth-watering Southwestern Pantry trip.

18 West Cork Villages

You can explore the gorgeous villages of West Cork from Kinsale.

Classic Trip

old pubs. Top of our list is **Tig Cóilí** (Mainguard St), a fire-engine-red pub that draws them in with its two live *céilidh* (traditional music and dancing sessions) each day. A close second is the cornflower blue **Séhán Ua Neáchtain** (17 Upper Cross St), known simply as Neáchtain's (*nock*-tans) or Naughtons – stop and join the locals for a pint.

✕ 🛏 p50

The Drive » The most direct route to Roundstone is to cut through Connemara along the N59, turning left on the Clifden Rd – a total of 76km. Alternatively, the 103km coastal route, via the R336 and R340, winds its way around small bays, coves and lovely seaside hamlets.

❸ Roundstone

Huddled on a boat-filled harbour, Roundstone (Cloch na Rón) is one of Connemara's gems. Colourful terrace houses and inviting pubs overlook the dark recess of Bertraghboy Bay, which is home to lobster trawlers and traditional *currachs* with tarred canvas bottoms stretched over wicker frames.

Just south of the village, in the remains of an old Franciscan monastery, is Malachy Kearns' **Roundstone Musical Instruments** (www.bodhran.com; Michael Killeen Park; ⏰9am-7pm Jul-Sep, 9.30am-6pm Mon-Sat Oct-Jun). Kearns is Ireland's only full-time maker of traditional bodhráns. Watch him work and buy a tin whistle, harp or booklet filled with Irish ballads; there's also a small free folk museum and a cafe.

The Drive » The 22km inland route from Roundstone to Clifden is a little longer, but the road is better (especially the N59) and the brown, barren beauty of Connemara is yours to behold. The 18km coastal route along the R341 brings you through more speckled landscape; to the south you'll have glimpses of the ocean.

❹ Clifden

Connemara's 'capital', Clifden (An Clochán) is an appealing Victorian-era country town with an amoeba-shaped oval of streets offering evocative strolls. It presides over the head of the narrow bay where the River Owenglin tumbles into the sea. The surrounding countryside beckons you to walk through woods and above the shoreline.

✕ 🛏 p50

The Drive » It's 154km to the Cliffs of Moher; you'll have to backtrack through Galway

CLADDAGH RINGS

Not much remains of Claddagh, a former fishing village that once had its own king, customs and traditions but is now subsumed by the Galway city centre. The Claddagh rings have survived though, as both a timeless reminder of the village as well as a timeless source of profits.

Popular with people of real or imagined Irish descent everywhere, the rings depict a heart (symbolising love) between two outstretched hands (friendship), topped by a crown (loyalty). Rings are handcrafted at jewellers around Galway, and start from about €20 for a silver band to well over €1000 for a diamond-set blinged-up version worthy of Tony Soprano.

Jewellers include Ireland's oldest jewellery shop, **Thomas Dillon's Claddagh Gold** (www.claddaghring.ie; 1 Quay St), which was established in 1750. It has some vintage examples in its small back-room 'museum'.

city (take the N59) before turning south along the N67. This will take you through the unique striated landscape of the Burren, a moody, rocky and at times fearsome space accented with ancient burial chambers and medieval ruins.

TRIP HIGHLIGHT

5 Cliffs of Moher

Star of a million tourist brochures, the Cliffs of Moher (Aillte an Mothair, or Ailltreacha Mothair) are one of the most popular sights in Ireland.

The entirely vertical cliffs rise to a height of 203m, their edge falling away abruptly into the constantly churning sea. A series of heads, the dark limestone seems to march in a rigid formation that amazes, no matter how many times you look.

Such appeal comes at a price: mobs. This is check-off tourism big time and busloads come and go constantly in summer. A vast **visitor centre** (www.cliffsofmoher. ie; admission to site adult/child €6/free; ◷9am-9.30pm Jul & Aug, 9am-7pm May, Jun & Sep, 9am-6pm Mar, Apr & Oct, 9.15am-5pm Nov-Feb) handles the hordes.

Like so many overpopular natural wonders, there's relief and joy if you're willing to walk for 10 minutes. Past the end of the 'Moher Wall' south, there's a trail along the cliffs to Hag's Head – few venture this far.

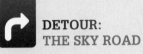

DETOUR: THE SKY ROAD

Start: 4 Clifden

If you head directly west from Clifden's Market Sq you'll come onto the Sky Rd, a 12km route tracing a spectacular loop out to the township of Kingston and back to Clifden, taking in some rugged, stunningly beautiful coastal scenery en route. It's a cinch to drive, but you can also easily walk or cycle it.

The Drive >> The 39km drive to Ennis goes inland at Lahinch (famous for its world-class golf links); it's then 24km to your destination, through flat south Clare. Dotted with stone walls and fields, it's the classic Irish landscape.

---

6 Ennis

As the capital of a renowned music county, Ennis (Inis) is filled with pubs featuring trad music (see the boxed text, p46). In fact, this is the best reason to stay here. Where's best changes often; stroll the streets pub-hopping to find what's on any given night.

If you want to buy an authentic (and well made) Irish instrument, pop into **Custy's Music Shop** (☎065-682 1727; www. custysmusic.com; Cooke's Lane), off O'Connell St, which sells fiddles and other musical items as well as giving general info about the local scene.

✗ ⊨ p50

The Drive >> It's 186km to Dingle if you go via Limerick city, but only 142km if you go via the N68 to Killimer for the ferry across the Shannon estuary to Tarbert. The views get fabulous when you're beyond Tralee on the N86, especially if you take the 456m Connor Pass, Ireland's highest.

TRIP HIGHLIGHT

7 Dingle Town

In summer, Dingle's hilly streets can be clogged with visitors, there's no way around it; in other seasons, its authentic charms are yours to savour. Many pubs double as shops, so you can enjoy Guinness and a singalong among screws and nails, wellies and horseshoes.

✗ ⊨ p51

The Drive >> It's only 17km to Slea Head along the R559. The views – of the mountains to the north and the wild ocean to the south and west – are a big chunk of the reason you came to Ireland in the first place.

LOCAL KNOWLEDGE
CATHY KELLY,
DUBLIN-BASED
BEST-SELLING AUTHOR

The best way to experience Dublin is to get walking – the city is compact so you can walk to most places. Failing that, take a Viking Splash tour (www.vikingsplash.com) in an amphibious vehicle. It's a lot of fun, like being on a school trip again. Be sure to visit the National Gallery, my favourite museum. I love marvelling at the fire inside Caravaggio's *The Taking of Christ*.

Top: Derryanne Estuary near Caherdaniel
Left: Staigue Fort
Right: Clifden village

HOLGER LEUE /GETTY IMAGES ©

ROBERT MCGRATH/GETTY IMAGES ©

❽ Slea Head

Overlooking the mouth of Dingle Bay, Mt Eagle and the Blasket Islands, Slea Head has fine beaches, good walks and superbly preserved structures from Dingle's ancient past, including **beehive huts**, forts, inscribed stones and church sites. Dunmore Head is the westernmost point on the Irish mainland and the site of the wreckage in 1588 of two Spanish Armada ships.

The Iron Age **Dunbeg Fort** is a dramatic example of a promontory fortification, perched atop a sheer sea cliff about 7km southwest of Ventry on the road to Slea Head. The fort has four outer walls of stone. Inside are the remains of a house and a beehive hut, as well as an underground passage.

The Drive » The 88km to Killarney will take you through Annascaul (home to a pub once owned by Antarctic explorer Tom Crean) and Inch (whose beach is seen in *Ryan's Daughter*). At Castlemaine, turn south towards Miltown then take the R563 to Killarney.

❾ Killarney

Beyond its proximity to lakes, waterfalls, woodland and moors dwarfed by 1000m-plus peaks, Killarney has many charms of its own as well as being the gateway to the Ring

45

Classic Trip

of Kerry, perhaps *the* outstanding highlight of many a visit to Ireland.

Besides the breathtaking views of the mountains and glacial lakes, highlights of the 10,236-hectare Killarney National Park include Ireland's only wild herd of native red deer, the country's largest area of ancient oak woods and 19th-century Muckross House (see p171).

🍴 🛏 p51

The Drive » It's 27km along the N71 to Kenmare, much of it through Killarney National Park with its magnificent views – especially Ladies' View (at 10km; much loved by Queen Victoria's ladies-in-waiting) and, a further 5km on, Moll's Gap, a popular stop for photos and food.

---

⑩ Kenmare

Picturesque Kenmare carries its romantic reputation more stylishly than does Killarney, and there is an elegance about its handsome central square and attractive buildings. It still gets very busy in summer, all the same. The town stands where the delightfully named Finnihy, Roughty and Sheen Rivers empty into Kenmare River. Kenmare makes a pleasant alternative to Killarney as a base for visiting the Ring of Kerry and the Beara Peninsula.

🍴 🛏 p51

The Drive » The 47km to Caherdaniel along the southern stretch of the Ring of Kerry duck in and out of view of Bantry Bay, with the marvellous Beara Peninsula to the south. Just before you reach Caherdaniel, a 4km detour north takes you to the rarely visited Staigue Fort, which dates from the 3rd or 4th century.

---

⑪ Caherdaniel

The big attraction here is **Derrynane National Historic Park** (📞066-947 5113; www.heritageireland.ie; Derrynane; adult/child €3/1; 🕙10.30am-6pm Apr-Sep, to 5pm Wed-Sun Oct-late Nov), the family home of Daniel O'Connell, the campaigner for Catholic emancipation. His ancestors bought the house and surrounding parkland, having grown rich on smuggling with France and Spain. It's largely furnished with O'Connell memorabilia, including the restored triumphal chariot in which he lapped Dublin after his release from prison in 1844.

The Drive » Follow the N70 for about 18km and then turn left onto the R567, cutting

---

ENNIS' BEST TRAD SESSION PUBS

» **Cíaran's Bar** (Francis St) Slip into this small place by day and you can be just another geezer pondering a pint. At night there's usually trad music. Bet you wish you had a copy of the Guinness mural out front!

» **Brogan's** (24 O'Connell St) On the corner of Cooke's Lane, Brogan's sees a fine bunch of musicians rattling even the stone floors from about 9pm Monday to Thursday, plus even more nights in summer.

» **Cruise's Pub** (Abbey St) There are trad music sessions most nights from 9.30pm.

» **Poet's Corner Bar** (Old Ground Hotel, O'Connell St) This old pub often has massive trad sessions on Fridays.

» **John O'Dea** (66 O'Connell St) Unchanged since at least the 1950s, this plain-tile-fronted pub is a hideout for local musicians serious about their trad sessions. Gets some of Clare's best.

through some of the wildest and most beautiful scenery on the peninsula, with the ragged outline of Skellig Michael never far from view. Turn left onto the R565; the whole drive is 35km long.

---

12 Portmagee & Valentia Island

Portmagee's single street is a rainbow of colourful houses, and is much photographed. On summer mornings, the small pier comes to life with boats embarking on the choppy crossing to the Skellig Islands.

A bridge links Portmagee to 11km-long **Valentia Island** (Oileán Dairbhre), an altogether homier isle than the brooding Skelligs to the southwest. Like the Skellig Ring it leads to, Valentia is an essential, coach-free detour from the Ring of Kerry. Some lonely ruins are worth exploring.

Valentia was chosen as the site for the first transatlantic telegraph cable. When the connection was made in 1858, it put Caherciveen in direct contact with New York. The link worked for 27 days before failing, but went back into action years later.

The island makes an ideal driving loop. From April to October, there's a frequent, quick ferry trip at one end, as well as the bridge to Portmagee on the mainland at the other end.

DETOUR: SKELLIG MICHAEL

Start: 12 **Portmagee**

The jagged, 217m-high rock of **Skellig Michael** (Archangel Michael's Rock; like St Michael's Mount in Cornwall and Mont Saint Michel in Normandy) is the larger of the two Skellig Islands and a Unesco World Heritage Site. It looks like the last place on earth where anyone would try to land, let alone establish a community, yet early Christian monks survived here from the 6th until the 12th or 13th century. Influenced by the Coptic Church (founded by St Anthony in the deserts of Egypt and Libya), their determined quest for ultimate solitude led them to this remote, wind-blown edge of Europe.

It's a tough place to get to, and requires care to visit, but is worth every effort. You'll need to do your best grisly sea-dog impression ('argh!') on the 12km crossing, which can be rough. There are no toilets or shelter, so bring something to eat and drink, and wear stout shoes and weatherproof clothing. Due to the steep (and often slippery) terrain and sudden wind gusts, it's not suitable for young children or people with limited mobility.

Be aware that the island's fragility requires limits on the number of daily visitors. The 15 boats are licensed to carry no more than 12 passengers each, for a maximum of 180 people at any one time. It's wise to book ahead in July and August, bearing in mind that if the weather's bad the boats may not sail (about two days out of seven). Trips usually run from Easter until September, depending, again, on weather.

Boats leave Portmagee, Ballinskelligs and Derrynane at around 10am and return at 3pm, and cost about €45 per person. Boat owners generally restrict you to two hours on the island, which is the bare minimum to see the monastery, look at the birds and have a picnic. The crossing takes about 1½ hours from Portmagee, 35 minutes to one hour from Ballinskelligs and 1¾ hours from Derrynane.

PHOTOGRAPHY BY PAULOMCCABE/GETTY IMAGES ©

The Drive >> The 55km between Portmagee and Killorglin keep the mountains to your right (south) and the sea – when you're near it – to your left (north). Twenty-four kilometres along is the unusual Glenbeigh Strand, a tendril of sand protruding into Dingle Bay with views of Inch Point and the Dingle Peninsula.

----

⑬ Killorglin

Killorglin (Cill Orglan) is a quiet enough town, but that all changes in mid-August, when the town erupts in celebration for Puck Fair, Ireland's best-known extant pagan festival.

First recorded in 1603, with hazy origins, this lively festival is based around the custom of installing a billy goat (a poc, or puck), the symbol of mountainous Kerry, on a pedestal in the town, its horns festooned with ribbons. Other entertainment ranges from a horse fair and bonny baby competition to street theatre, concerts and fireworks; the pubs stay open until 3am.

Author Blake Morrison documents his mother's childhood here in *Things My Mother Never Told Me*.

Skellig Michael The view from the largest Skellig island

Eating & Sleeping

Dublin ❶

🍴 Green Nineteen   Irish €€

(☎01-478 9626; 19 Lower Camden St; mains
€10-12; ⏱10am-11pm Mon-Sat, noon-6pm
Sun) Proof that good food doesn't have to be
expensive resides in this sleek restaurant that
specialises in locally sourced, organic grub. We
love it, but so does everybody else. Book ahead.

🛏 Number 31   Guesthouse €€

(☎01-676 5011; www.number31.ie; 31 Leeson
Close; s/d/tr from €100/140/240; 🛜) This
elegant slice of accommodation paradise,
designed for his own use by modernist architect
Sam Stephenson (of Central Bank fame – or
infamy), is unquestionably the most distinctive
of Dublin's hotels. Children under 10 are not
permitted.

Galway City ❷

🍴 Quays   Irish €€

(Quay St; mains €12-25; ⏱11am-10pm)
This sprawling pub does a roaring business
downstairs in its restaurant, which has hearty
carvery lunches and more ambitious mains at
night. The cold seafood platter is a symphony of
the bounty from Galway Bay.

🛏 House Hotel   Hotel €€€

(☎091-538 900; www.thehousehotel.ie; Spanish
Pde; r €100-200; 🅿🛜) It's a design odyssey
at this boutique hotel. Public spaces contrast
modern art with trad details and bold accents.

Clifden ❹

🍴 Mitchell's   Seafood €€

(☎095-21867; Market St; mains €15-25;
⏱noon-10pm Mar-Oct) Seafood takes centre
stage at this elegant spot. From a velvety

chowder through a long list of ever-changing
specials, the produce of the surrounding
waters is honoured. The wine list does the food
justice. Book for dinner. (Lunch specials include
sandwiches and casual fare.)

🛏 Dolphin Beach   B&B €€

(☎095-21204; www.dolphinbeachhouse.com;
Lower Sky Rd; r €80-180; 🅿🛜) It's hard to find
the bones of the 19th-century manor house
that forms the basis for this posh B&B set amid
some of Connemara's best coastal scenery. It's
5km west of Clifden.

Ennis ❻

🍴 Rowan Tree
Cafe/Bar   Mediterranean €€

(Harmony Row; mains €7-20; ⏱food 11am-9pm)
On the ground floor of Ennis' new hostel, there's
nothing low-rent about the excellent Med-
accented fare served here. The gorgeous main
dining room has a wondrous old wooden floor
from the 18th century, while tables outside have
river views. The food is locally and organically
sourced.

🍴 Zest   Bakery, Cafe €

(Market Pl; meals €5-10; ⏱8am-6pm Mon-Sat)
A much-welcome addition to Ennis' fresh food
scene, Zest combines a deli, bakery, shop and
cafe. Excellent prepared foods from the region
are offered along with salads, soups and much
more.

🛏 Old Ground Hotel   Hotel €€

(☎065-682 8127; www.flynnhotels.com;
O'Connell St; s/d from €90/140; 🅿@🛜)
Parts of this rambling landmark date back to
the 1800s. The 83 rooms vary greatly in size
and decor – don't hesitate to inspect a few. On
balmy days, retire to tables on the lawn.

Dingle Town ⑦

✗ Doyle's Seafood €€€
(☎066-915 2674; www.doylesofdingle.ie; 4 John St; mains €25-30; ☉dinner) Recently reopened, the scarlet-fronted Doyle's has reconfirmed its reputation for serving some of the best seafood in the area (which in these parts is really saying something). Starters such as tempura of fish, seafood risotto and seafood pie team up with mains such as warm shellfish salad, seafood linguine and lobster.

✗ Out of the Blue Seafood €€€
(☎066-915 0811; The Wood; lunch €10-20, mains €15-30; ☉dinner daily, lunch Sun) 'No chips', reads the menu of this funky blue-and-yellow, fishing-shack-style restaurant on the waterfront. Despite its rustic surrounds, this is Dingle's best restaurant, with an intense devotion to fresh local seafood; if they don't like the catch, they don't open.

🛏 Pax House B&B €€
(☎066-915 1518; www.pax-house.com; Upper John St; s/d from €90/120; P @ ☎ ⏚) From its highly individual decor (including contemporary paintings) to the outstanding views over the estuary from room balconies and the terrace, Pax House is a treat. Choose from cheaper hill-facing rooms, rooms that overlook the estuary, and two-room family suites opening to the terrace. Wi-fi is available in the lounge. It's 1km from the town centre.

Killarney ⑨

✗ Chapter 40 Irish €€
(☎064-667 1833; www.chapter40.ie; Lower New St; mains €22.50-28.50; ☉dinner Tue-Sat) Popular with Killarney's stylish bounders (and chefs on their nights off), this beautiful dining room is all polished wood and cream leather. Starters like grilled polenta with wild mushrooms are followed by classy mains such as pork Wellington with pea and crab salsa. The wines by the glass show a deft hand in the cellar.

🛏 Crystal Springs B&B €€
(☎064-663 3272; www.crystalspringsbb.com; Ballycasheen; d €80-110; P ☎ ⏚) You can cast a line from the timber deck of this wonderfully relaxing riverside B&B or just laze about on the adjacent lawn. Rooms are richly furnished with patterned wallpapers and walnut timber; bathrooms (most with spa baths) are larger than many Irish hotel rooms. The glass-enclosed breakfast room also overlooks the fast-flowing River Flesk. It's about a 15-minute stroll to town.

Kenmare ⑩

✗ Horseshoe Pub €€
(☎064-664 1553; www.horseshoebarkenmare.com; 3 Main St; mains €14.50-26.50; ☉lunch & dinner) Ivy frames the entrance to this gastropub, which has a short but excellent menu that runs from Kenmare Bay mussels in creamy apple-cider sauce to local lamb on mustard mash and Kerry's best burgers.

🛏 Parknasilla Resort & Spa Hotel €€€
(☎064-667 5600; www.parknasillahotel.ie; d from €180; P @ ☎ ☎) This hotel has been wowing guests (including one George Bernard Shaw) since 1895 with its 500 acres of pristine resort on the edge of the village of Sneem and the broad expanse of the Kenmare River separating it from the Beara Peninsula to the south (oh, the views!). Irish hospitality at its very best.

STRETCH YOUR LEGS DUBLIN

Start/Finish Trinity College

Distance 4.9km

Duration 3 hours

Dublin's most important attractions are concentrated on the south side of the Liffey, split between the older medieval town dominated by the castle and the two cathedrals, and the handsome 18th-century city that is a showcase of exquisite Georgian aesthetic.

Take this walk on Trips

Trinity College

Ireland's most prestigious **university** (✏ walking tours 01-896 1827; www.tcd. ie; tour €10; ⏱ tours every 30min 10.15am-3.40pm Mon-Sat, to 3pm Sun mid-May–Sep) is a masterpiece of architecture and landscaping, and Dublin's most attractive bit of historical real estate, beautifully preserved in Georgian aspic.

The Walk » From Trinity College, walk west along Dame St and turn into Dublin Castle.

Chester Beatty Library

The world-famous **library** (www.cbl.ie; Dublin Castle, Cork Hill; admission free; ⏱ 10am-5pm Mon-Fri, 11am-5pm Sat, 1-5pm Sun), in the grounds of Dublin Castle, houses the collection of mining engineer Sir Alfred Chester Beatty (1875–1968). Spread over two floors, the breathtaking collection includes more than 20,000 manuscripts, rare books, miniature paintings, clay tablets, costumes and other objects of historical and aesthetic importance.

The Walk » Exit the castle and walk west; you'll see Christ Church directly in front of you.

Christ Church Cathedral

Its hilltop location and eye-catching flying buttresses make this the most photogenic by far of Dublin's three **cathedrals** (www.cccdub.ie; Christ Church Pl; adult/senior/student €6/4/3; ⏱ 9.45am-6.15pm Mon-Fri, to 4.15pm Sat, 12.30-2.30pm & 4.30-6.15pm Sun mid-Jul–Aug) as well as one of the capital's most recognisable symbols. It was founded in 1030 on what was then the southern edge of Dublin's Viking settlement. The Normans rebuilt the lot in stone from 1172.

The Walk » Go south along Nicholas St (which becomes News St); St Patrick's is 400m along.

St Patrick's Cathedral

It was at this **cathedral** (www. stpatrickscathedral.ie; St Patrick's Close; adult/child €5.50/free; ⏱ 9am-6pm), reputedly, that St Paddy himself dunked the Irish heathens into the waters of a well. Although there's been a church

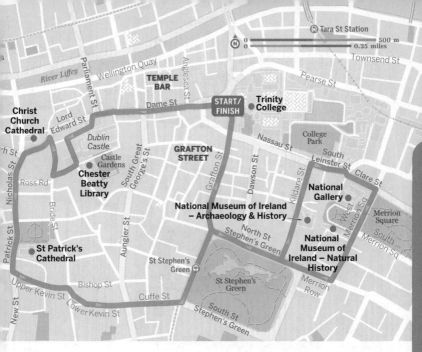

here since the 5th century, the present building dates from 1190 or 1225 (opinions differ).

The Walk » Just south of St Patrick's, turn left onto Kevin St and keep going until you reach St Stephen's Green; turn onto Kildare St.

National Museum of Ireland – Archaeology & History

The star attraction of this branch of the **National Museum of Ireland** (www.museum.ie; Kildare St; admission free; ⏲10am-5pm Tue-Sat, 2-5pm Sun) is the Treasury, home to the finest collection of Bronze Age and Iron Age gold artefacts in the world, and the world's most complete collection of medieval Celtic metalwork.

The Walk » Walk north on Kildare St and turn right on Nassau St, then stay right on Clare St.

National Gallery

A magnificent Caravaggio and a breathtaking collection of works by Jack B Yeats – William Butler's younger

brother – are the main reasons to visit the **National Gallery** (www.nationalgallery.ie; West Merrion Sq; ⏲9.30am-5.30pm Mon-Wed, Fri & Sat, to 8.30pm Thu, noon-5.30pm Sun), but not the only ones. Its excellent collection is strong in Irish art, but there are also high-quality collections of every major European school of painting.

The Walk » Walk south along Merrion Sq W.

National Museum of Ireland – Natural History

Dusty, weird and utterly compelling, and a window into Victorian times, this **museum** (www.museum.ie; Merrion St; ⏲10am-5pm Tue-Sat, 2-5pm Sun) has barely changed since Scottish explorer Dr David Livingstone opened it in 1857 – before disappearing into the African jungle for a meeting with Henry Stanley.

The Walk » Turn right onto Merrion Row, skirt St Stephen's Green and go right into Grafton St to head back to Trinity College.

53

Dublin Full to the brim with art, literature, music and nightlife

The Long Way Round

2

Why go in a straight line when you can perambulate at leisure? This trip explores Ireland's jagged, scenic and spectacular edges; a captivating loop that takes in the whole island.

TRIP HIGHLIGHTS

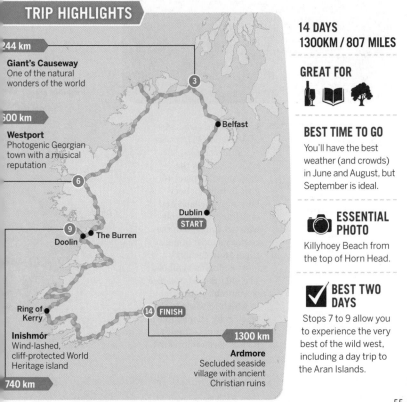

244 km

Giant's Causeway
One of the natural wonders of the world

500 km

Westport
Photogenic Georgian town with a musical reputation

● Belfast

Dublin ●
START

The Burren
Doolin

Ring of Kerry

14 FINISH

Inishmór
Wind-lashed, cliff-protected World Heritage island

740 km

1300 km

Ardmore
Secluded seaside village with ancient Christian ruins

---

14 DAYS
1300KM / 807 MILES

GREAT FOR

BEST TIME TO GO

You'll have the best weather (and crowds) in June and August, but September is ideal.

ESSENTIAL PHOTO

Killyhoey Beach from the top of Horn Head.

BEST TWO DAYS

Stops 7 to 9 allow you to experience the very best of the wild west, including a day trip to the Aran Islands.

2 The Long Way Round

There's a strong case to be made that the very best Ireland has to offer is closest to its jagged, dramatic coastlines: the splendid scenery, the best mountain ranges (geographically, Ireland is akin to a bowl, with raised edges) and most of its major towns and cities – Dublin, Belfast, Galway, Sligo and Cork. Each is worthy of attention, but don't ignore the bits in between.

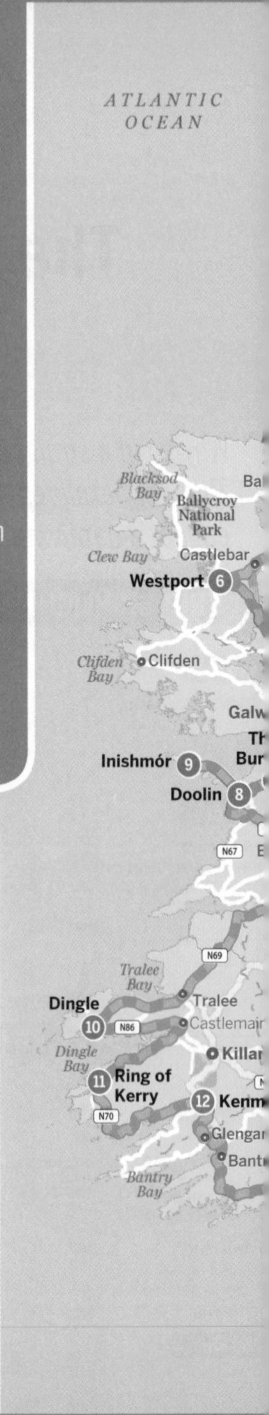

① Dublin

From its music, art and literature to the legendary nightlife that has inspired those same musicians, artists and writers, Dublin has always known how to have fun and does it with deadly seriousness.

Should you tire of the city's more highbrow offerings (see our walking tour, p52), the **Guinness Storehouse** (☑01-408 4800; www. guinness-storehouse.com; St James's Gate Brewery; adult/child/under 6yr €15/11/free, ⊙9.30am-5pm Sep-Jun, to 7pm Jul-Aug) is the most popular place to visit in town; a beer-lover's Disneyland and multimedia bells-and-whistles homage to the country's most famous export and the city's most enduring symbol. The old grain storehouse is a suitable cathedral in which to worship the black gold; shaped like a giant pint of Guinness, it rises seven impressive

(map labels)

ATLANTIC
OCEAN

Blacksod Bay
Ballycroy National Park
Ba
Clew Bay Castlebar
Westport ⑥

Clifden Bay o Clifden

Galw
Th
Inishmór ⑨ Bur

Doolin ⑧

N67 E

Tralee Bay
Dingle ⑩ N86 o Tralee
Dingle Bay Castlemair
⑪ **Ring of Kerry** o Killar
N70 ⑫ **Kenm**
o Glengar
o Bant
Bantry Bay

SCOTLAND

Campbeltown

Giant's
Causeway ③
Ballycastle
*North
Channel*

Dunfanaghy
④
Buncrana
Coleraine
p58

*Rosses
Bay*
N56
N13
Derry
A2
A37
A26

Letterkenny
N56
Ballymena
Larne
A2

Strabane
Antrim
A2

A5

Donegal
Omagh
Belfast ②
Lisburn

*onegal
Bay*
Dromore

N15
Bundoran
Armagh
A4
Banbridge
A1

:o ⑤
Enniskillen
Monaghan
Newry

Ballysadare
7
N3
Dundalk
*Dundalk
Bay*

N4

estown
Longford
Drogheda
*Irish
Sea*

common
N55
Mullingar
M1

m
M6
Swords

linasloe
Athlone
Dublin ① START

Tullamore
Naas
p52
Bray

N65
Birr
M7
Greystones

Portlaoise
Wicklow

Nenagh
M7
Carlow
Arklow

Thurles
Kilkenny
M11

Limerick
28

Tipperary
Cashel
M9
Enniscorthy

Clonmel
New Ross
Wexford

ow
M8
Waterford ◎
Rosslare
Harbour

⑫
Dungarvan
N25

Youghal ⑭ Ardmore
*St George's
Channel*

⑬
N25
FINISH

Cobh

*ATLANTIC
OCEAN*

Ⓝ 0 ▭▭▭▭▭ 100 km
0 ▭▭▭▭▭ 50 miles

storeys high around a
stunning central atrium.

🍴 🛏 p66

The Drive » It's 165km of
motorway to Belfast – M1 in the
Republic, A1 in Northern Ireland
– but remember that the speed
limit changes from kilometres
to miles as you cross into the
North.

----

② Belfast

Once lumped with
Beirut, Baghdad and
Bosnia as one of the
four 'Bs' for travellers
to avoid, Belfast has
pulled off a remarkable
transformation from
bombs-and-bullets
pariah to a hip hotels-
and-hedonism party
town.

There's plenty to
see in Belfast, but
given that 2012 was
the much-trumpeted
centenary of the world's
most famous liner,

S LINK
YOUR
TRIP

**12 Blackwater Valley
Drive**

From Ardmore, it's only 5km
to Youghal, where you can
explore the gorgeous valley
of the Blackwater River.

28 Tip to Toe

Kilmore Quay is
134km east of Ardmore,
where you can pick up the
toe part of this trip and do it
in reverse.

a visit to the Titanic Quarter is a must. It's best done as part of a tour – the reputable **Lagan Boat Company** (☎028-9033 0844; www.laganboatcompany.com) run the excellent **Titanic Tour** (adult/child £10/8; ⏰12.30pm, 2pm & 3.30pm Apr-Sep, 12.30 & 2pm Oct, 12.30 & 2pm Sat & Sun Nov-Mar), which explores the derelict docklands downstream of the weir, taking in the slipways where the liners *Titanic* and *Olympic* were launched, and the huge

dry dock where they could fit with just 9 inches to spare. Tours depart from Donegall Quay near the *Bigfish* sculpture.

If you're keen on learning more about the city's troubled history, take the walking tour of West Belfast (see p328).

✗ 🛏 p66

The Drive » The *fastest* way to the causeway is to take the A26 north, through Ballymena, before turning off at Ballymoney – a total of 100km – but the longer (by 16km), more scenic route is to take the A8 to Larne and follow the coast through handsome Cushendall and popular Ballycastle.

- - - - - - - - - - - - - -

TRIP HIGHLIGHT

❸ Giant's Causeway

When you first see it, you'll understand why the ancients believed the causeway was not a natural feature. The vast expanse of regular, closely packed, hexagonal stone columns dipping gently beneath the waves looks for all the world like the handiwork of giants.

This spectacular rock formation – a national nature reserve and Northern Ireland's only Unesco World Heritage Site – is one of Ireland's most impressive and atmospheric landscape

DETOUR:
GIANT'S CAUSEWAY TO BALLYCASTLE

Start: ❸ Giant's Causeway

Between the Giant's Causeway and Ballycastle lies the most scenic stretch of the Causeway Coast, with sea cliffs of contrasting black basalt and white chalk, rocky islands, picturesque little harbours and broad sweeps of sandy beach. It's best enjoyed on foot, following the 16.5km of waymarked **Causeway Coast Way** between the Carrick-a-Rede car park and the Giant's Causeway, although the main attractions can also be reached by car or bus.

About 8km east of the Giant's Causeway is the meagre ruin of 16th-century **Dunseverick Castle**, spectacularly sited on a grassy bluff. Another 1.5km on is the tiny seaside hamlet of **Portbradden**, with half a dozen harbourside houses and the tiny, blue-and-white **St Gobban's Church**, said to be the smallest in Ireland. Visible from Portbradden and accessible via the next junction off the A2 is the spectacular **White Park Bay**, with its wide, sweeping sandy beach.

The main attraction on this stretch of coast is the famous (or notorious, depending on your head for heights) **Carrick-a-Rede Rope Bridge** (www.ntni.org.uk; Ballintoy; adult/child £5.60/2.90; ⏰10am-7pm Jun-Aug, to 6pm Mar-May, Sep & Oct). The 20m-long, 1m-wide bridge of wire rope spans the chasm between the sea cliffs and the little island of Carrick-a-Rede, swaying gently 30m above the rock-strewn water.

DETOUR:
HORN HEAD

Start: 4 Dunfanaghy

Horn Head has some of Donegal's most spectacular coastal scenery and plenty of birdlife. Its dramatic quartzite cliffs, covered with bog and heather, rear over 180m high, and the view from their tops is heart-pounding.

The road circles the headland; the best approach by car is in a clockwise direction from the Falcarragh end of Dunfanaghy. On a fine day, you'll encounter tremendous views of Tory, Inishbofin, Inishdooey and tiny Inishbeg islands to the west; Sheep Haven Bay and the Rosguill Peninsula to the east; Malin Head to the northeast; and the coast of Scotland beyond. Take care in bad weather as the route can be perilous.

features, but it is all too often swamped by visitors – around 750,000 each year. If you can, try to visit midweek or out of season to experience it at its most evocative. Sunset in spring and autumn is the best time for photographs.

Visiting the Giant's Causeway itself is free of charge but the overcrowded, council-run car park charges £6 per car. It's an easy 1km walk from the car park down to the causeway.

✗ p66

The Drive >> Follow the A29 and A37 as far as Derry/Londonderry, then cross the invisible border into the Republic and take the N13 to Letterkenny before turning northwest along the N56 to Dunfanaghy. It's a total of 136km.

- - - - - - - - - -

4 Dunfanaghy

Huddled around the waterfront beneath the headland of Horn Head,

Dunfanaghy's small, attractive town centre has a surprisingly wide range of accommodation and some of the finest dining options in the county's northwest. Glistening beaches, dramatic coastal cliffs, mountain trails and forests are all within a few kilometres.

✗ p66

The Drive >> The 145km south to Sligo town will take you back through Letterkenny (this stretch is the most scenic), after which you'll follow the N13 as far as Ballyshannon and then, as you cross into County Sligo, the N13 to Sligo town.

- - - - - - - - - -

5 Sligo Town

Sligo is in no hurry to shed its cultural traditions but it doesn't sell them out either. Pedestrian streets lined with inviting shopfronts, stone bridges spanning the River Garavogue and *céilidh* sessions spilling from pubs contrast

with genre-bending contemporary art and glass towers rising from prominent corners of the compact town.

✗ 🏠 p66

The Drive >> It's 100km to Westport, across the western edge of County Clare – as you follow the N17 (and the N5 once you pass Charlestown), the landscape is flat, the road flanked by fields, hedge rows and clusters of farmhouses. Castlebar, 15km before Westport, is a busy county town.

- - - - - - - - - -

TRIP HIGHLIGHT

6 Westport

There's a lot to be said for town planning, especially if 18th-century architect James Wyatt was the brain behind the job. Westport (Cathair na Mairt), positioned on the River Carrowbeg and the shores of Clew Bay, is easily Mayo's most beautiful town and a major tourist destination for visitors to this part of the country.

Classic Trip

JULIET COOMBE/GETTY IMAGES ©

RIEGER BERTRAND/HEMIS.FR/GETTY IMAGES ©

WHY THIS IS A CLASSIC TRIP
FIONN DAVENPORT, AUTHOR

A trip that explores the edges of the island is an opportunity to drive through its most spectacular landscapes of mountains and jagged coastlines, but also to explore the modern incarnation of the country's earliest settlements, taking you from prehistoric monuments to bustling cities.

Top: Doolin's main street
Left: City Hall, Belfast
Right: Cliffs of Moher

JOHN ELK/GETTY IMAGES ©

It's a Georgian classic, its octagonal square and tidy streets lined with trees and handsome buildings, most of which date from the late 18th century.

The Drive >> Follow the N84 as far as the outskirts of Galway city – a trip of about 100km. Take the N18 south into County Clare. At Kilcolgan, turn onto the N67 and into the heart of The Burren.

----

7 The Burren

The karst landscape of The Burren is not the green Ireland of postcards. But there are wildflowers in spring, giving The Burren brilliant, if ephemeral, colour amid the arid beauty. Soil may be scarce on The Burren, but the small amount that gathers in the cracks is well drained and rich in nutrients. This, together with the mild Atlantic climate, supports an extraordinary mix of Mediterranean, Arctic and alpine plants. Of Ireland's native wildflowers, 75% are found here, including 24 species of beautiful orchids, the creamy-white burnet rose, the little starry flowers of mossy saxifrage and the magenta-coloured bloody cranesbill.

The Drive >> It's 36km southwest to Doolin along the R460 and R476 roads which cut through more familiar Irish

landscapes of green fields. The real pleasures along here are the villages – the likes of Kilfenora and Lisdoonvarna are great for a pit stop and even a session of traditional music.

8 Doolin

Doolin is renowned as a centre of Irish traditional music, but it's also known for its setting – 6km north of the Cliffs of Moher – and down near the ever-unsettled sea, the land is windblown, with huge rocks exposed by the long-vanished topsoil.

Many musicians live in the area, and they have a symbiotic relationship with the tourists: each desires the other and each year things grow a little larger. But given the heavy concentration of visitors, it's inevitable that standards don't always hold up to those in some of the less-trampled villages in Clare.

The Drive » Ferries from Doolin to Inishmór take about 90 minutes to make the crossing; see p296 for details on getting to and from the Aran Islands from Doolin.

TRIP HIGHLIGHT

9 Inishmór

A step (and boat- or plane-ride) beyond

AN ANCIENT FORT

For a look at a well-preserved *caher* (walled fort) of the late Iron Age to early Christian period, stop at **Caherconnell Fort** (www.burrenforts.ie; adult/child €6/4; ⊙10am-6pm Jul & Aug, to 5pm Mar-Jun, Sep & Oct), a privately run heritage attraction that's more serious than sideshow. Exhibits detail how the evolution of these defensive settlements may have reflected territorialism and competition for land among a growing, settling population. The drystone walling of the fort is in excellent condition. The top-notch visitor centre also has information on many other monuments in the area. It's about 1km south of Poulnabrone Dolman on the R480.

the desolate beauty of Connemara are the Aran Islands. Most visitors are satisfied to explore only Inishmór (Árainn) and its main attraction, Dún Aengus, the stunning stone fort perched perilously on the island's towering cliffs.

Powerful swells pound the 60m-high cliff face. A complete lack of rails or other modern additions that would spoil this amazing ancient site means that you can not only go right up to the cliff's edge but also potentially fall to your doom below quite easily. When it's uncrowded, you can't help but feel the extraordinary energy that must have been harnessed to build this vast site.

The arid landscape west of Kilronan (Cill Rónáin), Inishmór's main settlement, is dominated by stone walls, boulders,

scattered buildings and the odd patch of deep-green grass and potato plants.

🛏 p67

The Drive » Once you're back on terra firma at Doolin, it's 223km to Dingle via the N85 through Ennis as far as Limerick City. The N69 will take you into County Kerry as far as Tralee, beyond which it's 50km on the N86 to Dingle.

10 Dingle

Unlike the Ring of Kerry, where the cliffs tend to dominate the ocean, it's the ocean that dominates the smaller Dingle Peninsula. The opal-blue waters surrounding the promontory's multihued landscape of green hills and golden sands give rise to aquatic adventures and to fishing fleets that haul in fresh seafood that appears on the menus of some of the county's finest restaurants.

Centred on charming Dingle town, there's an alternative way of life here, lived by artisans and idiosyncratic characters and found at trad sessions and folkloric festivals across Dingle's tiny settlements.

The classic loop drive around Slea Head from Dingle town is 50km, but allow a day to take it all in – longer if you have time to stay overnight in Dingle town.

✕ ⊨ p67

The Drive » Take the N86 as far as Annascaul and then the coastal R561 as far as Castlemaine. Then head southwest on the N70 to Killorglin and the Ring of Kerry. From Dingle, it's 53km.

- - - - - - - - - - - -

⓫ Ring of Kerry

The Ring of Kerry is the longest and the most diverse of Ireland's big circle drives, combining jaw-dropping coastal scenery with emerald pastures and villages.

The 179km circuit usually begins in Killarney and winds past pristine beaches, the island-dotted Atlantic, medieval ruins, mountains and loughs (lakes). The coastline is at its most rugged between Waterville and Caherdaniel in the southwest of the peninsula. It can get crowded in summer, but even then, the remote Skellig Ring can be uncrowded and serene – and starkly beautiful.

The Ring of Kerry can easily be done as a day trip, but if you want to stretch it out, places to stay are scattered along the route. Killorglin and Kenmare have the best dining options, with some excellent restaurants; elsewhere, basic (sometimes very basic) pub fare is the norm.

The Drive » The Ring's most popular diversion is the Gap of Dunloe, an awe-inspiring mountain pass at the western edge of Killarney National Park. It's signposted off the N72 between Killarney to Killorglin. The incredibly popular 19th-century Kate Kearney's Cottage is a pub where most visitors park their cars before walking up to the gap.

- - - - - - - - - - - -

⓬ Kenmare

If you've done the Ring in an anticlockwise fashion (or cut through the Gap of Dunloe), you'll end up in handsome Kenmare, a largely 18th-century town and the ideal alternative to Killarney as a place to stay overnight.

✕ ⊨ p67

The Drive » Picturesque villages, a fine stone circle and calming coastal scenery mark the less-taken, 143km route from Kenmare to Cork city. When you get to Leap, turn right onto the R597 and go as far as Rosscarbery; or, even better, take twice as long (even though it's only 24km more)

DOOLIN'S MUSIC PUBS

Doolin's three main music pubs (others are recent interlopers) are, in order of importance to the music scene:

» McGann's (Roadford) McGann's has all the classic touches of a full-on Irish music pub; the action often spills out onto the street. The food here is the best of the trio.

» O'Connor's (Fisherstreet) Right on the water, this sprawling favourite packs them in and has a rollicking atmosphere when the music and drinking are in full swing.

» MacDiarmada's (Roadford) Also known as McDermott's, this simple red-and-white old pub can be the rowdy favourite of locals. When the fiddles get going, it can seem like a scene out of a John Ford movie.

Classic Trip

JOHN ELK/GETTY IMAGES ©

Youghal, turn right onto the R671 for Ardmore.

TRIP HIGHLIGHT

⑭ Ardmore

Because it's off the main drag, Ardmore is a sleepy seaside village and one of the southeast's loveliest spots – the ideal destination for those looking for a little waterside R & R.

St Declan reputedly set up shop here sometime between AD 350 and 420, which would make Ardmore the first Christian bastion in Ireland – long before St Patrick landed. The village's 12th-century **round tower**, one of the best examples of these structures in Ireland, is the town's most distinctive architectural feature, but you should also check out the ruins of St Declan's church and well, on a bluff above the village.

and freelance your way along narrow roads near the water the entire way.

⑬ Cork City

Ireland's second city is first in every important respect, at least according to the locals, who cheerfully refer to it as the 'real capital of Ireland'. The compact city centre is surrounded by interesting waterways and is chock full of great restaurants fed by arguably the best foodie scene in the country. See our walking tour (p196) for more.

✗ ⊨ p67

The Drive » It's only 60km to Ardmore, but stop off in Midleton, 24km east of Cork along the N25, and visit the whiskey museum. Just beyond

DUBLIN & EASTERN IRELAND **2** THE LONG WAY ROUND

✓ ## TOP TIP: ## THE HEALY PASS

Instead of going directly into County Cork along the N71 from Kenmare, veer west onto the R571 and drive for 16km along the northern edge of the Beara Peninsula. At Lauragh, turn onto the R574 and take the breathtaking Healy Pass Road, which cuts through the peninsula and brings you from County Kerry into County Cork. At Adrigole, turn left onto the R572 and rejoin the N71 at Glengarriff, 17km east.

Harbour on Ireland's west coast

Eating & Sleeping

Dublin ①

✖ Coppinger Row   Mediterranean €€

(www.coppingerrown.com; Coppinger Row; mains €12-17; ⏰noon-10pm; 🚻) The chefs at this relatively new eatery have combined to create a tasty, unfussy menu of Mediterranean treats, to be enjoyed as main courses or as bar bites. We like the roast guinea fowl with borlotti beans but will settle for the meatball linguini.

🛏 Cliff Townhouse   Guesthouse €€

(☎01-638 3939; www.theclifftownhouse.com; 22 North St Stephen's Green; s/d from €145/155; @🛜) As pied-à-terres go, this is a doozy: the sister property to the much-heralded Cliff House in Ardmore, County Waterford, it has 10 exquisitely appointed bedrooms spread across a wonderful Georgian property whose best views overlook St Stephen's Green. Downstairs is Sean Smith's superb restaurant,.

Belfast ②

✖ Ginger   Bistro £££

(☎028-9024 4421; www.gingerbistro.com; 7-8 Hope St; mains £17-22; ⏰lunch Tue-Sat, dinner Mon-Sat) Ginger is a cosy and informal little bistro with an unassuming exterior, serving food that is anything but ordinary – the flame-haired owner/chef (hence the name) really knows what he's doing, sourcing top-quality Irish produce and turning out exquisite dishes such as scallops with crisp black pudding and chorizo butter.

🛏 Merchant Hotel   Hotel £££

(☎028-9023 4888; www.themerchanthotel.com; 35-39 Waring St; r/ste from £140/200; 🅿@🛜) Belfast's most flamboyant Victorian building (the old Ulster Bank head office) has been converted into the city's most flamboyant boutique hotel, a fabulous fusion of contemporary styling and old-fashioned elegance.

Giant's Causeway ③

✖ 55 Degrees North   International ££

(☎028-7082 2811; www.55-north.com; 1 Causeway St, Portrush; mains £10-18; ⏰dinner) One of the north coast's most stylish restaurants, 55 Degrees North boasts a wall of floor-to-ceiling windows allowing diners to soak up a spectacular panorama of sand and sea. The food is excellent, concentrating on clean, simple flavours and unfussy presentation.

Dunfanaghy ④

✖ Mill Restaurant & Guesthouse   Irish €€€

(☎074-913 6985; www.themillrestaurant.com; Figart, Dunfanaghy; 3-course menu €43.50; ⏰dinner Tue-Sun mid-Mar–mid-Dec; 🅿) An exquisite country setting and perfectly composed meals make dining here a treat. Set in an old flax mill that was for many years the home of renowned watercolour artist Frank Eggington, it also has six high-class guestrooms (single/double €70/100). The mill is just south of the town on the Falcarragh road. Book in advance.

Sligo Town ⑤

✖ Source   Irish €€

(☎071-914 7605; www.sourcesligo.ie; 1 John St; mains €15-20; ⏰9.30am-5pm Mon, to 9.30pm Tue-Sun) Source is all about traceability in the food chain, and it champions local suppliers and foodstuffs. Large, arty photos of its favourite fishermen, farmers and cheese producers grace the walls of the ground-floor restaurant, while there's wine and tapas on offer upstairs in the **wine bar** (dishes €4-9; ⊙3-11pm Tue-Sun).

🛏 Pearse Lodge   B&B €€

(☎071-916 1090; www.pearselodge.com; Pearse Rd; s/d €50/74; 🅿 @ 🛜) Welcoming owners Mary and Kieron not only impeccably maintain the six stylish guestrooms at their cosy B&B but are also up on what's happening in town. Mary's breakfast menu includes smoked salmon, French toast with bananas and homemade muesli (and Illy coffee!). A sunny sitting room opens to a beautifully landscaped garden.

Inishmór 7

🛏 Kilmurvey House   B&B €€

(☎099-61218; www.kilmurveyhouse.com; Kilmurvey; s/d from €65/110; ⊙Apr-Sep) This grand 18th-century stone mansion lies on the path leading to Dún Aengus. It's a beautiful setting, and the 12 rooms are well maintained. Hearty meals (dinner €30) incorporate vegetables from the garden, and local fish and meats. You can swim at a pretty beach that's a short walk from the house.

Dingle Town 10

✕ Doyle's   Seafood €€€

(☎066-915 2674; www.doylesofdingle.ie; 4 John St; mains €25-30; ⊙dinner) Recently reopened, scarlet-fronted Doyle's has reconfirmed its reputation for serving some of the best seafood in the area (which in these parts is really saying something). Starters such as tempura of fish, seafood risotto and seafood pie team up with mains like warm shellfish salad, seafood linguine and lobster.

🛏 Pax House   B&B €€

(☎066-915 1518; www.pax-house.com; Upper John St; s/d from €90/120; 🅿 @ 🛜 🛗) From its highly individual decor (including contemporary paintings) to the outstanding views over the estuary from room balconies and the terrace, Pax House is a treat. Choose from cheaper hill-facing rooms, those that overlook the estuary, and two-room family suites

opening to the terrace. Wi-fi is available in the lounge. It's 1km from the town centre.

Kenmare 12

✕ D'Arcy's Oyster Bar and Grill   Irish €€

(☎064-664 1589; www.darcyskenmare.com; Main St; mains €14.50-25.50; ⊙dinner; 🛜) Local purveyors supply the best in organic produce, cheeses and fresh seafood, all served in modern, low-key surrounds. The raw oysters capture the scent of the bay; the hazelnut-crusted, twice-baked crab and prawn soufflé is divine. Guests staying in its antique-adorned rooms (doubles €50) get discounted evening meals.

🛏 Virginia's Guesthouse   B&B €€

(☎064-664 1021; www.virginias-kenmare. com; Henry St; s/d €60/80; 🛜 🛗) You can't get more central than this award-winning B&B, whose creative breakfasts celebrate organic local produce (rhubarb and blueberries in season, for example, as well as freshly squeezed OJ and porridge with whiskey). Its eight rooms are super comfy without being fussy. Outstanding value.

Cork City 13

✕ Market Lane   International €€

(☎021-427 4710; www.marketlane.ie; 5 Oliver Plunkett St; mains €10-26; ⊙noon-late Mon-Sat, 1-9pm Sun) This bright corner bistro has an open kitchen, and the menu is varied: how about braised ox cheek stew to challenge the palate? Steaks come with awesome aioli.

🛏 Imperial Hotel   Hotel €€

(☎021-427 4040; www.flynnhotels.com; South Mall; r €90-220; 🅿 @ 🛜) The Imperial's 130 rooms are of four-star hotel standard, and include writing desks, restrained decor and modern touches, such as digital music library. A posh Aveda spa is a recent addition – something unheard of when Charles Dickens stayed here.

Howth Yachting and fishing hu[...]
just north of Ireland's capita[...]

A Week Around Dublin

3

You don't have to venture far from the capital in any direction to find distractions, including cosy seaside towns, stunning monastic ruins and palatial 18th-century mansions.

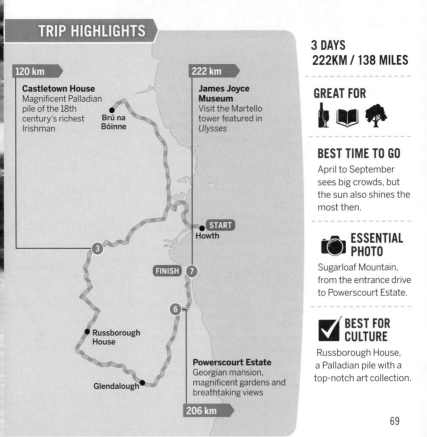

TRIP HIGHLIGHTS

120 km

Castletown House
Magnificent Palladian pile of the 18th century's richest Irishman

Brú na Bóinne

222 km

James Joyce Museum
Visit the Martello tower featured in *Ulysses*

3

START
Howth

FINISH **7**

6

Russborough House

Glendalough

Powerscourt Estate
Georgian mansion, magnificent gardens and breathtaking views

206 km

3 DAYS
222KM / 138 MILES

GREAT FOR

BEST TIME TO GO
April to September sees big crowds, but the sun also shines the most then.

ESSENTIAL PHOTO
Sugarloaf Mountain, from the entrance drive to Powerscourt Estate.

BEST FOR CULTURE
Russborough House, a Palladian pile with a top-notch art collection.

69

A Week Around Dublin

You can plunge into the very depths of Irish history, be awestruck by some of Ireland's most beautiful buildings and lose yourself in stunning countryside without ever being more than 50km from Dublin. This trip explores the very best of what the capital's environs have to offer – from coastal breaks to mountain retreats and a rip-roaring trip through 3500 years of history.

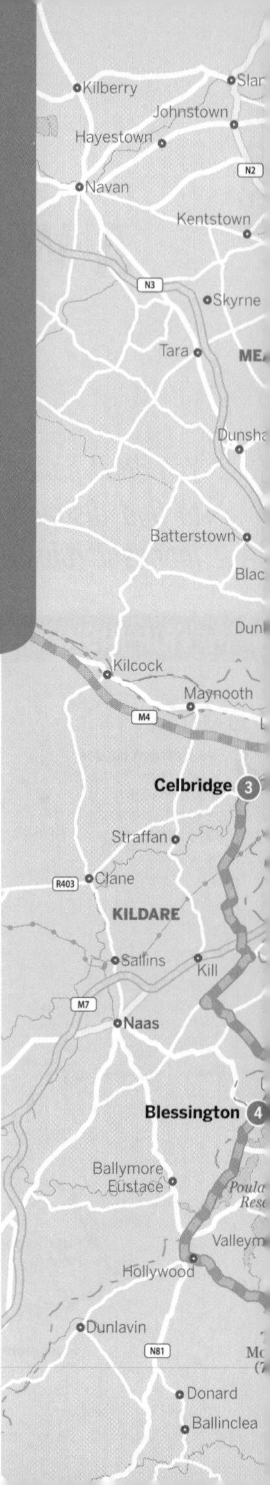

❶ Howth

The pretty little port town of Howth is built on steep streets running down to its small but busy harbour, which has transformed itself from shipping port to yachting and fishing hub. Only 11km north of Dublin's city centre, it has long been a desirable residential suburb.

Howth is essentially a very large hill surrounded by cliffs, and the summit (171m) has excellent views across Dublin Bay right down to Wicklow. From the peak you can walk to the top of the Ben of Howth, which has a cairn said to mark a 2000-year-old Celtic royal grave. The 1814 Baily Lighthouse, at the southeastern corner, is on the site of an old stone fort and can be reached by a dramatic cliff-top walk. There was an earlier hilltop beacon here in 1670.

Besides the views, the other draw is the busy weekend market and the collection of good seafood restaurants huddled around the harbour.

✕ 🛏 p77

The Drive ⟫ Take the right at Sutton onto Harbour Rd (R105) towards Baldoyle; you'll have the Malahide estuary on your right and, on the spit of land beyond it, the famous Portmarnock Golf Links. Turn left onto Moyne Rd and take the M1 north, exiting at Junction 9 for Donore.

Map labels: Kilberry, Slar, Johnstown, Hayestown, N2, Navan, Kentstown, N3, Skyrne, Tara, MEA, Dunsha, Batterstown, Blac, Dun, Kilcock, Maynooth, M4, Celbridge ❸, Straffan, R403, Clane, KILDARE, Salfins, Kill, M7, Naas, Blessington ❹, Ballymore Eustace, Poula Rese, Valleym, Hollywood, Dunlavin, N81, Mo, Donard, Ballinclea

❷ Brú na Bóinne

Pharaoh hadn't even conceived of the pyramids when the neolithic pre-Celts were using mathematical equations unknown to the ancient Greeks to build this vast necropolis on the banks of the River Boyne. Collectively known as Brú na Bóinne (the Boyne Palace), the passage tombs (and superb visitor centre) are one of the most extraordinary sites in Europe and shouldn't be missed. For more information, see Trip 5, The Boyne Valley (p85).

The Drive » Double-back onto the M1 and take the M50 *around* Dublin; take the exit at Junction 7 for the N4 and go west for 7km as far as Junction 5. Follow the R403 as far as Celbridge. The 71km trip should take about an hour.

LINK YOUR TRIP

1 Ireland's Highlights

Dublin is the starting point of this classic trip that delivers the country's five-star attractions.

2 The Long Way Round

From Dublin, take a couple of weeks to explore the country.

TRIP HIGHLIGHT

3 Celbridge

The magnificent **Castletown House** (☎01-628 8252; www.castletownhouse.ie; adult/child €4.50/3.50; ⏰10am-4.45pm Tue-Sun Easter-Oct) simply has no equal. It is Ireland's largest and most imposing Georgian estate, and a testament to the vast wealth enjoyed by the Anglo-Irish gentry during the 18th century.

Built between 1722 and 1732, the house was commissioned by Speaker of the Irish House of Commons William Conolly (1662–1729), who wanted a house suitable to his position as Ireland's richest man.

The original '16th-century Italian palazzo' design of the house was by the Italian architect Alessandro Galilei (1691–1737) in 1718. In 1724 the project was entrusted to Sir Edward Lovett Pearce (1699–1733).

The house is full of Palladian touches, including the terminating pavilions and the superb Long Gallery, full of family portraits and fancy stucco work by the Italian Francini brothers. Thomas Jefferson was such a fan of the style that much of Washington, DC is designed accordingly.

The Drive ≫ The 30km drive will first take you south along the R405, through the western stretch of Dublin suburbia. Take the N82 for 2km. Turn left onto the N81 and travel uphill into the Wicklow Mountains. The huge Poulaphouca Reservoir, which delivers drinking water to the capital, is on your left just before you reach Blessington.

RUSSBOROUGH HOUSE: THE TERRORISTS, THE THIEVES & THE ART LOVERS

In 1974 the IRA decided to get into the art business by stealing 16 paintings from Russborough House. They were eventually all recovered, but 10 years later the notorious Dublin criminal Martin Cahill (aka the General) masterminded another robbery from the Russborough House collection, this time for Loyalist paramilitaries. On this occasion, however, only some of the works were recovered and of those, several were damaged beyond repair – a good thief does not a gentle curator make. In 1988 the owner, Sir Albert Beit, decided to hand over the most valuable of the paintings to the National Gallery; in return, the gallery agreed to lend other paintings to the collection as temporary exhibits. The sorry story didn't conclude there. In 2001 two thieves drove a jeep through the front doors, making off with two paintings worth nearly €4 million, including a Gainsborough that had been stolen, and recovered, twice before. To add abuse to the insult already added to injury, the house was broken into again in 2002, with the thieves taking five more paintings, including two by Rubens. Incredibly, however, both hauls were quickly recovered.

4 Blessington

Dominating the one-street town of Blessington (pubs, shops, a handful of 17th- and 18th-century town houses) is magnificent **Russborough House** (☎045-865 239; www.russborough.ie; adult/child €10/6; ⏰10am-6pm May-Sep, Sun & bank holidays only Apr & Oct), one of Ireland's finest stately homes, built for Joseph Leeson (1705–83), later the first Earl of Milltown and, later still, Lord Russborough. The Palladian pleasure palace was built between 1741 and 1751 to the design of Richard Cassels, who was at the height of his fame as an architect. Richard didn't live to see it finished, but the job was well executed by Francis Bindon.

Enniskerry Powerscourt Estate

The house remained in the Leeson family until 1931. In 1952 it was sold to Sir Alfred Beit, the eponymous nephew of the cofounder of the de Beers diamond-mining company. Uncle Alfred was an obsessive art collector, and when he died, his impressive haul – which includes works by Velázquez, Vermeer, Goya and Rubens – was passed on to his nephew, who brought it to Russborough House.

The admission price includes a 45-minute tour of the house, whic is decorated in typical Georgian style.

🛏 p77

The Drive ›› Follow the N81 south and cut across the Wicklow Mountains on the R756 via the stunning Wicklow Gap. It's a 20km stretch to Laragh; Glendalough is only 3km further on.

- - - - - - - - - - -

⑤ Glendalough

Location, location, location. When St Kevin came to this spectacular glacial valley in the heart of the Wicklow Mountains in 498 to found a small monastic settlement, did he realise that the settlement would grow into one of Ireland's most important centres of learning and, 15 centuries later, one of the country's most popular tourist attractions? Probably not. See p98.

🛏 p77

The Drive ›› Overall distance 28km. Head northeast on the R755 for 16km, skirting the eastern edge of Wicklow Mountains National Park, then follow the road signs for Enniskerry.

DETOUR:
POWERSCOURT WATERFALL

Start: 6 Enniskerry

Signposted from the Powerscourt Estate is the 130m **Powerscourt Waterfall** (admission €5; ⊙9.30am-7pm May-Aug, 10.30am-5.30pm Mar-Apr & Sep-Oct). It's the highest waterfall in Britain and Ireland, and is most impressive after heavy rain. A nature trail has been laid out around the base of the waterfall, taking you past giant redwoods, ancient oaks, beech, birch and rowan trees. There are plenty of birds in the vicinity, including the chaffinch, cuckoo, chiffchaff, raven and willow warbler. It's also a popular 7km walk to the waterfall.

TRIP HIGHLIGHT

6 Enniskerry

Backing onto the pretty village of Enniskerry is the expanse of **Powerscourt Estate** (☎01-204 6000; www.powerscourt.ie; adult/child €8/5; ⊙9.30am-5.30pm Feb-Oct, to 4.30pm Nov-Jan), which gives contemporary observers a true insight into the style of the 18th-century super-rich. The main entrance is 500m south of the village square.

The estate has existed more or less since 1300, when the LePoer (later anglicised to Power) family built themselves a castle here. The property changed Anglo-Norman hands a few times before coming into the possession of Richard Wingfield, newly appointed Marshall of Ireland, in 1603. His descendants were to live here for the next 350 years.

Unfortunately, a fire in 1974 gutted most of the house, which remains largely off-limits, so the biggest draw of the whole pile is the simply magnificent 20-hectare formal **gardens** and the breathtaking views that accompany them.

✕ ⊨ p77

The Drive » Continue onto the M11 north and take the exit for Dun Laoghaire. The Wyatville Rd becomes Church Rd; keep going north and follow the road signs for Sandycove. It's only 19km from Powerscourt to Sandycove.

TRIP HIGHLIGHT

7 Sandycove

The handsome seaside town of Sandycove is now just part of greater Dublin, but it is renowned for its excellent restaurants, pretty beach and a Martello tower – built by British forces to keep an eye out for a Napoleonic invasion – now housing the **James Joyce Museum** (☎01-280 9265; www.visitdublin.com; Joyce Tower; adult/child €6/4; ⊙10am-1pm & 2-5pm Tue-Sat, by appointment only Sep-Mar). This is where the action begins in James Joyce's epic novel *Ulysses*. The museum was opened in 1962 by Sylvia Beach, the Paris-based publisher who first dared to put *Ulysses* into print, and has photographs, letters, documents, various editions of Joyce's work and two death masks of Joyce on display.

✕ p77

Eating & Sleeping

Howth ❶

✕ Aqua   Seafood €€

(☎01-832 0690; www.aqua.ie; 1 West Pier; mains €29-32; ⊙12.30-3.30pm & 5.30-10.30pm Tue-Sat, 4-8.30pm Sun) A contender for best seafood in Howth, Aqua serves top-quality fish dishes in its elegant dining room overlooking the harbour, in a building once home to the Howth Yacht Club.

✕ House   Modern Irish €€

(☎01-839 6388; www.thehouse.ie; 4 Main St; mains €16-22; ⊙9am-3pm Mon-Fri, 11.30am-3pm & 6pm-11pm Sat-Sun) A wonderful spot on the main street leading away from the harbour, where you can feast on dishes like crunchy Bellingham blue cheese polenta or wild Wicklow venison stew as well as a fine selection of fish.

⌂ King Sitric   Boutique Hotel €€

(☎01-832 5235; www.kingsitric.ie; East Pier; r €150-180) One of Howth's best-known restaurants (mains €30 to €45) – always praised for the superb seafood and prize-winning wine list – has eight marvellous rooms to its premises right on the port. Each is named after a lighthouse and is extremely well decorated with wonderful views of the port.

Blessington ❹

⌂ Rathsallagh House & Country Club   Hotel €€€

(☎045-403 112; www.rathsallaghhousehotel.com; Dunlavin; s/d from €135/260) About 20km south of Blessington, this fabulous country manor, converted from Queen Anne stables in 1798, has splendidly appointed rooms, a marvellous golf course and exquisite country-house dining (mains €33 to €42), offering some of the best food you'll eat anywhere in Ireland.

Glendalough ❺

⌂ Glendalough Hotel   Hotel €€

(☎0404-45135; www.glendaloughhotel.com; s/d €110/150; P @ 🛜 ♿) There's no mistaking Glendalough's best hotel, conveniently located next door to the visitor centre. There is no shortage of takers for its 44 fairly luxurious bedrooms.

Enniskerry ❻

✕ Emilia's Ristorante   Italian €€

(☎01-276 1834; Clock Tower, The Square; mains €12-16; ⊙5-10.45pm Mon-Sat, noon-9.30pm Sun) A lovely 1st-floor restaurant to satisfy even the most ardent craving for thin-crust pizzas. Emilia's does everything else just right too, from the organic soups to the perfect steaks down to the gorgeous meringue desserts.

⌂ Summerhill House Hotel   Hotel €€

(☎01-286 7928; www.summerhillhousehotel.com; r from €90; P 🛜 ♿) This truly superb country mansion, about 700m south of town just off the N11, is the best place around to lay your head on soft cotton pillows surrounded by delicate antiques and pastoral views in oils. Everything about the place – including the top-notch breakfast – is memorable.

Sandycove ❼

✕ Caviston's Seafood Restaurant   Seafood €€€

(☎01-280 9245; Glasthule Rd; mains €18-27; ⊙noon-5pm Tue-Thu, to midnight Fri & Sat) All self-respecting crustacean lovers should make the trip to Caviston's for a seafood meal to remember.

Clonmacnoise Ancient monastic ruins at their best

East to West

4

Music, landscape and history are the keys to this trip, which transports you across Ireland's midriff from the bustling capital to the pastoral splendour of the west.

TRIP HIGHLIGHTS

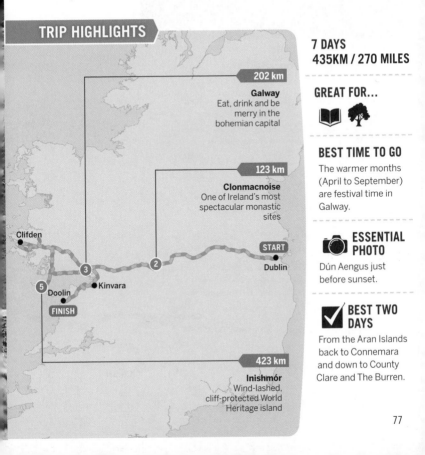

202 km

Galway
Eat, drink and be merry in the bohemian capital

123 km

Clonmacnoise
One of Ireland's most spectacular monastic sites

Clifden

3

2

START

Dublin

5

Doolin

Kinvara

FINISH

423 km

Inishmór
Wind-lashed, cliff-protected World Heritage island

**7 DAYS
435KM / 270 MILES**

GREAT FOR...

BEST TIME TO GO

The warmer months (April to September) are festival time in Galway.

ESSENTIAL PHOTO

Dún Aengus just before sunset.

BEST TWO DAYS

From the Aran Islands back to Connemara and down to County Clare and The Burren.

77

4 East to West

Go West! As you quit Dublin's suburban sprawl the landscape continues to soften and before you know it you're in Galway, gateway to beautiful and brooding Connemara. Explore one of the country's most magnificent spots before looping south into the Burren of County Clare, the spiritual home of Irish traditional music.

1 Dublin

A day in the capital should give you enough time to take a walk around and check out the city's big-ticket items. Culture buffs should definitely take a stroll through the archaeology and history branch of the **National Museum of Ireland** (www. museum.ie; Kildare St; admission free; ⏱10am-5pm Tue-Sat, 2-5pm Sun) – don't miss the Treasury's golden hoard of artefacts from the Bronze and Iron ages.

✕ 🛏 p83

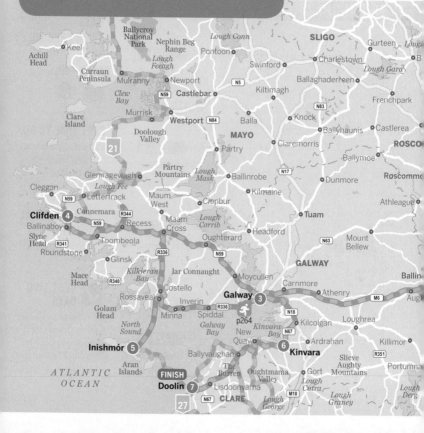

The Drive » The 130km drive to Clonmacnoise is largely uneventful, courtesy of the convenient M4/M6 tolled motorway, from which you see fields and little else. Take exit 7 towards Moate and get on the R444 – Clonmacnoise is signposted as you go.

TRIP HIGHLIGHT

2 Clonmacnoise

Clonmacnoise (www. heritageireland.ie; adult/ child €6/2; ⊙9am-7pm mid-May–mid-Sep, 10am-5.30pm mid-Sep–mid-May; **P**), straddling a hill overlooking a bend in the Shannon, is one of

the main reasons Ireland got the moniker of 'land of saints and scholars.' For greater detail, check out p96.

🛏 p83

LINK YOUR TRIP

21 Best of the West
In Galway you can connect with this trip, which brings you from Sligo south to County Kerry.

27 County Clare
Explore the rest of lyrical County Clare by travelling the 40km from Doolin to Ennis.

The Drive » From Clonmacnoise, take the R357 for 22km towards Ballinasloe, Galway's county town and the first town you'll come to as you enter the county across the River Suck. Here you can rejoin the M6; it's 61km to Galway City.

DETOUR:
THE MAN WHO REALLY
FOUND AMERICA?

Start: ❷ **Clonmacnoise**

About 21km southeast of Ballinasloe along the R355 is the 12th-century **Clonfert Cathedral**, built on the site of a monastery said to have been founded in 563 by St Brendan 'the Navigator', who is believed to be buried here. Although the jury is out on whether St Brendan reached America's shores in a tiny *currach* rowing boat, there are Old Irish Ogham (the earliest form of writing in Ireland) carvings in West Virginia that date from as early as the 6th century, suggesting an Irish presence in America well before Columbus set foot there.

TRIP HIGHLIGHT

❸ Galway City

Galway is the long-established, self-proclaimed and generally accepted capital of bohemian Ireland, with a long-standing tradition of attracting artists, musicians and other creative types to its pub- and cafe-lined streets. For our suggestions for the best pubs in town, check out p41.

🍴 🛏 p83

The Drive » The N59 cuts through the heart of the region – in the distance you'll see Connemara's mountain ranges, the Maumturks and the Twelve Bens. After about 58km, just before Recess, take a 5km detour north along the R344 and take in the majesty of the Lough Inagh Valley before rejoining the road and continuing towards Clifden, 28km further on.

❹ Clifden

Connemara's principal town is a genteel Victorian-era fishing port that makes a good stopover, especially during the summer months, when it casts off its wintry covers and offers visitors a nice taster of what drew 19th-century tourists to it. You can amble about its narrow streets or stare at the sea from the head of the narrow bay into which falls the River Owenglin.

🛏 p83

The Drive » Take the R341 coast road towards Roundstone, but at Ballinaboy cut through the Roundstone Bog, where you might see turf harvested by hand. It's a bad road, but worth the scenery. Rejoin the R341 at Toombeola and go left, taking the N59 for a few kilometres before turning right onto the R340 for either Rossaveal or Minna. You can catch a ferry to Inishmór from Rossaveal or fly from Minna, so it's either a choppy ferry ride or a twin-prop flight. From

CLARINBRIDGE OYSTER FESTIVAL

South of Galway, Clarinbridge (Droichead an Chláirin) and Kilcolgan (Cill Cholgáin) are at their busiest during the **Clarinbridge Oyster Festival** (www.clarenbridge.com), held during the second weekend of September. However, the oysters are actually at their best from May through the summer.

Oysters are celebrated year-round at **Paddy Burke's Oyster Inn** (www.paddyburkesgalway.com; Clarinbridge; mains €10-24; ⏰12.30-10pm), a thatched inn by the bridge dishing up heaped servings in a roadside location on the N18.

Moran's Oyster Cottage (www.moransoystercottage.com; The Weir, Kilcolgan; mains €14-24; ⏰noon-10pm Mon-Sat, 10am-10pm Sun) is a thatched pub and restaurant with a facade as plain as the inside of an oyster shell. Find a seat on the terrace overlooking Dunbulcaun Bay, where the oysters are reared before they arrive on your plate. It's a well-marked 2km west of the noxious N18, in a cove near Kilcolgan.

The Burren Stone walls along the winding coastal road

Clifden, it's 57km to Rossaveal, 64km to Minna. See p296 for more information on getting to and from the Aran Islands.

TRIP HIGHLIGHT

5 Inishmór

Do not doubt that the effort you made to get here isn't worth it, for a visit to the largest of the Aran Islands (indeed, any of the three) is one of the more memorable things you'll do in Ireland. The big draw is the spectacular Stone Age fort of **Dún Aengus** (Dún Aonghasa; www. heritageireland.ie; adult/child €3/1; ☺10am-6pm), but don't forget to explore some of the island's other ruins, scattered about the place like so much historical detritus. There's also a lovely beach at **Kilmurvey** (west of Kilronan), while up to 50 grey seals sun themselves and feed in the shallows of **Port Chorrúch**.

🍴 🛏 p83

The Drive » You'll have to go back to Minna or Rossaveal to pick up your car, but on your way back the R336 to Galway, stop off in Spiddal, in the heart of Connemara's *Gaeltacht*, or Irish-speaking, heartland. Beyond Galway city, turn off the N18 and go 10km along the N67 to Kinvara.

81

THE BURREN

Stretching across northern Clare, from the Atlantic coast to Kinvara in County Galway, The Burren is a unique striated limestone landscape that was shaped beneath ancient seas, then forced high and dry by a great geological cataclysm. In The Burren, land and sea seem to merge into one vast, moody, rocky and at times fearsome space beneath huge skies, accented with ancient burial chambers and medieval ruins.

Visitor Information

The Burren Centre in Kilfenora is an excellent resource.

» **Burren Ecotourism Network** (www.burrenecotourism.com) A vast compilation of all things related to Burren tourism.

» **Burren National Park** (www.burrennationalpark.ie) Portions of The Burren in the southeast have been designated a national park, although it has yet to develop visitor facilities; the website has good info on the natural landscape.

» **Burrenbeo Trust** (www.burrenbeo.com; Main St, Kinvara, Co Galway) A nonprofit dedicated to promoting the natural beauty of The Burren and increasing awareness. Its website is a tremendous source of info.

6 Kinvara

The small stone harbour of Kinvara (sometimes spelt Kinvarra) sits smugly at the southeastern corner of Galway Bay, which accounts for its Irish name, Cinn Mhara (Head of the Sea). It's a posh little village, the kind of place where all the jeans have creases in them. It makes a good pit stop between Galway and Clare.

Dominating one end of the harbour is the chess-piece-style **Dunguaire Castle** (www.shannonheritage.com; adult/child €6/3.40; ⏱10am-5pm Easter-Sep), erected around 1520 by the O'Hynes clan and in excellent condition following extensive restoration. It is widely believed that the castle occupies the former site of the 6th-century royal palace of Guaire Aidhne, the king of Connaught. Dunguaire's owners have included Oliver St John Gogarty (1878–1957) – poet, writer, surgeon and inspiration for James Joyce's fictional Buck Mulligan, one of the cast of *Ulysses*.

The least authentic way to visit the castle is to attend a **medieval banquet** (✆061-360 788; www.shannonheritage.com; banquet adult/child €50/24; ⏱5.30pm & 8.45pm Easter-Sep). Stage shows and shtick provide diversions while you plough through a big group meal.

The Drive » The N67 from Kinvara skirts along the western edge of the Burren; this particularly desolate-looking (but no less beautiful) landscape is in evidence beyond Ballyvaughan, about 20km on. Doolin is a further 23km away; just past Lisdoonvarna, take a right onto the R476.

7 Doolin

Only 6km north of the Cliffs of Moher (see p294), Doolin's rep as a terrific spot to spend a couple of days isn't just down to its proximity to one of the bone fide stars of the Irish tourist trail. It helps, sure, but Doolin's popularity is largely due to its pubs, or, rather, to the musicians that play in them: the area is full of talented players whose exquisite abilities can be enjoyed almost every night. There's lots of pubs to choose from, but if we had to pick one, it'd be **McGann's** (Roadford), complete with turf fires, darts board and great grub.

🛏 p83

Eating & Sleeping

Dublin ❶

🍴 Green Nineteen   Irish €€

(☎01-478 9626; 19 Lower Camden St; mains
€10-12; ⏱10am-11pm Mon-Sat, noon-6pm Sun)
This sleek restaurant specialises in locally
sourced, organic grub and shows that good food
doesn't have to be expensive. We love it, but so
does everybody else. Book ahead.

🛏 Number 31   Guesthouse €€

(☎01-676 5011; www.number31.ie; 31 Leeson
Close; s/d/tr from €100/140/240; 🛜) This
elegant slice of accommodation paradise,
designed for his own use by modernist architect
Sam Stephenson (of Central Bank fame – or
infamy), is unquestionably the most distinctive
of Dublin's hotels. Children under 10 are not
permitted.

Clonmacnoise ❷

🛏 Kajon House   B&B €€

(☎090-967 4191; www.kajonhouse.ie; Creevagh;
d from €70; ⏱Mar-Oct; 🅿) If you want to
stay near the ruins, this is your best option,
just 1.5km away on the road signposted to
Tullamore. It's an incredibly friendly place with
cosy rooms, a spacious yard with a picnic table
and evening meals on offer.

Galway City ❸

🍴 Quays   Irish €€

(Quay St; mains €12-25; ⏱11am-10pm)
This sprawling pub does a roaring business
downstairs in its restaurant, which has hearty
carvery lunches and more ambitious mains at
night. The cold seafood platter is a symphony of
the bounty from Galway Bay.

🛏 House Hotel   Hotel €€€

(☎091-538 900; www.thehousehotel.ie; Spanish
Pde; r €100-200; 🅿🛜) It's a design odyssey

at this boutique hotel. Public spaces contrast
modern art with trad details and bold accents.

Clifden ❹

🛏 Dolphin Beach   B&B €€

(☎095-21204; www.dolphinbeachhouse.com;
Lower Sky Rd; r €80-180; 🅿🛜) It's hard to find
the bones of the 19th-century manor house
that forms the basis for this posh B&B set amid
some of Connemara's best coastal scenery. It's
5km west of Clifden.

Inishmór ❺

🍴 O'Malley's@Bayview   Modern Irish €€

(Kilronan; mains €7-23; ⏱11am-9.30pm Mon-
Fri, from 9am Sat & Sun) The terrace here has
commanding harbour views. The simple menu
belies the talents of the kitchen; choices include
fine fish chowder, good burgers and pizza, plus
fresh fish at night. Even the garlic bread is good.

🛏 Kilmurvey House   B&B €€

(☎099-61218; www.kilmurveyhouse.com;
Kilmurvey; s/d from €65/110; ⏱Apr-Sep) On the
path leading to Dún Aengus is this grand 18th-
century stone mansion. It's a beautiful setting,
and the 12 rooms are well maintained. Hearty
meals (dinner €30) incorporate vegetables
from the garden and local fish and meats.

Doolin ❼

🛏 Cullinan's Guesthouse   Inn €€

(☎065-707 4183; www.cullinansdoolin.com;
Doolin; s €40-60, d €60-90; 🅿🛜) The eight
rooms here are all of a high standard, with
power showers and comfortable fittings. The
restaurant is one of the village's best. The owner
is well-known local musician James Cullinan.

Monasterboice Superb Celtic art and the finest monastic ruins

The Boyne Valley

5

A trip through the cradle of Irish history, from prehistoric tombs to bloody battlefields, with monasteries and old castles thrown in for good measure.

TRIP HIGHLIGHTS

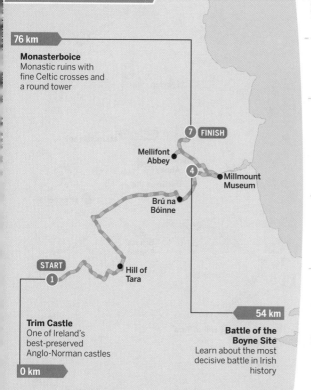

76 km

Monasterboice
Monastic ruins with fine Celtic crosses and a round tower

7 FINISH

Mellifont Abbey

4

Millmount Museum

Brú na Bóinne

START

1

Hill of Tara

54 km

Trim Castle
One of Ireland's best-preserved Anglo-Norman castles

Battle of the Boyne Site
Learn about the most decisive battle in Irish history

0 km

2 DAYS
76KM / 47 MILES

GREAT FOR...

BEST TIME TO GO

The sun doesn't set until after 10pm between June and July, but September often gets the best weather.

 ESSENTIAL PHOTO

The round tower at Monasterboice.

 BEST FOR CULTURE

The magnificent neolithic passage tombs at Brú Na Bóinne.

5 The Boyne Valley

Only 112km long, the River Boyne isn't especially impressive, but its valley can lay claim to being Ireland's most significant historical stage. The breathtaking prehistoric passage tomb complex of Brú na Bóinne is the main highlight, but the remnants of Celtic forts, Norman castles and atmospheric monasteries are but the most obvious clues of the area's rich and longstanding legacy.

TRIP HIGHLIGHT

1 Trim

Remarkably preserved **Trim Castle** (King John's Castle; www.heritageireland.ie; adult/child €4/2; ⊙10am-6pm Easter-Sep, 9.30am-5.30pm Oct, 9.30am-5.50pm Sat & Sun Feb-Easter, 9am-5pm Sat & Sun Nov-Jan) was Ireland's largest Anglo-Norman fortification and is proof of Trim's medieval importance. Hugh de Lacy founded Trim Castle in 1173, but Rory O'Connor, said to have been the last

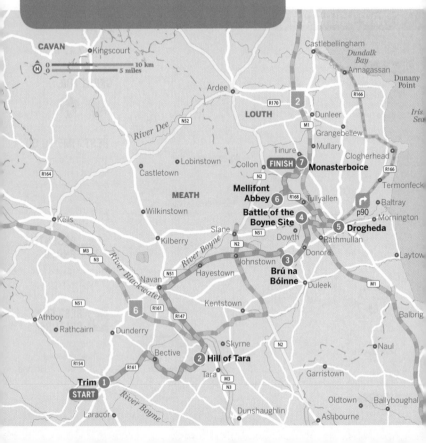

high king of Ireland, destroyed this motte and bailey within a year. The building you see today was begun around 1200 and has hardly been modified since, although it was badly damaged by Cromwellian forces when they took the town in 1649.

✕ ⊨ p91

The Drive ⟫ It's only 15km from Trim to Tara. Eight kilometres northeast of Trim, along the R161, is 12th-century Bective Abbey, built in the lush farmland still in evidence today on both sides of the road as you drive.

- - - - - - - - - - - - -

❷ Hill of Tara

The Hill of Tara is Ireland's most sacred stretch of turf, an entrance to the underworld, occupying a place at the heart of Irish history, legend

LINK YOUR TRIP

6 **Ancient Ireland**
Connect to this trip from Brú na Bóinne and continue time travelling through Ireland's historic past.

2 **The Long Way Round**
From Monasterboice, head north on the M1 to Belfast and this hugely rewarding two-week trip.

and folklore. It was the home of the mystical druids, the priest-rulers of ancient Ireland, who practised their particular form of Celtic paganism under the watchful gaze of the all-powerful goddess Maeve (Medbh). Later it was the ceremonial capital of the high kings – 142 of them in all – who ruled until the arrival of Christianity in the 6th century. It is also one of the most important ancient sites in Europe, with a Stone Age passage tomb and prehistoric burial mounds that date back up to 5000 years. Although little remains other than humps and mounds of earth on the hill, its historic and folkloristic significance is immense.

The **Tara Visitor Centre** (☑046-902 5903; www.heritageireland.ie; adult/child €3/1; ⊙10am-6pm Jun–mid-Sep) is housed within a former Protestant church (with a window by artist Evie Hone) and screens a 20-minute audiovisual presentation about the site.

The Drive ⟫ From Tara, the 29km drive to Brú na Bóinne takes you through the county town of Navan, the crossroads of the busy Dublin road (M3/N3) and the Drogheda–Westmeath road (N51). If you stop here, Trimgate St is lined with restaurants and pubs. Two kilometres south of the centre is the relatively intact 16th-century Athlumney Castle.

- - - - - - - - - - - - -

❸ Brú na Bóinne

The vast neolithic necropolis known as Brú na Bóinne (the Boyne Palace) is one of the most extraordinary sites in Europe and shouldn't be missed. A thousand years older than Stonehenge, it's a powerful and evocative testament to the mind-boggling achievements of prehistoric humans.

The area consists of many different sites; the three principal ones are Newgrange, Knowth and Dowth, but only the first two are open to visitors, and then only as part of an organised tour which departs from the **Brú na Bóinne Visitor Centre** (☑041-988 0300; www.heritageireland.ie; Donore; visitor centre adult/child €3/2, visitor centre, Newgrange & Knowth €11/6; ⊙9am-7pm Jun–mid-Sep, 9am-6.30pm May & mid-end Sep, 9.30am-5.30pm Oct & Feb, 9am-5pm Nov-Jan), from where a bus will take you to the tombs. The centre houses an extraordinary series of interactive exhibits on prehistoric Ireland and its passage tombs, and has an excellent book and souvenir shop.

✕ ⊨ p91

The Drive ⟫ The 7km drive from Brú na Bóinne is along a tiny rural road that takes you through the village of Donore. The battle site is 3km north of Donore, signposted off the N51.

TRIP HIGHLIGHT

4 Battle of the Boyne Site

More than 60,000 soldiers of the armies of King James II and King William III fought on this patch of farmland on the border of Counties Meath and Louth in 1690. In the end, William prevailed and James sailed off to France.

Today, the **battle site** (www.battleofthe boyne.ie; adult/child €4/2; ⏱10am-6pm May-Sep, 9.30am-5.30pm Mar & Apr, 9am-5pm Oct-Feb) is part of the Oldbridge Estate farm. At the visitor centre you can watch a short show about the battle, see original and replica weaponry of the time, and explore a laser battlefield model.

The Drive ≫ It's only 6km to Drogheda; almost immediately you'll find yourself driving from fecund landscape into suburban sprawl as you approach Drogheda's outlying expanse.

5 Drogheda

Across the river from the main town of Drogheda is Millmount, which may have once been a prehistoric burial ground but is now home to a Martello Tower and army barracks.

Part of the barracks is now the **Millmount Museum** (☎041-983 3097; www.millmount.net; museum adult/child €3.50/2.50, museum & tower €5.50/3; ⏱9.30am-5.30pm Mon-Sat, 2-5pm Sun), which has interesting displays about the town and its history. Exhibits include three wonderful late-18th-century guild banners, perhaps the last in the country. There's also a room devoted to Cromwell's brutal siege of Drogheda and the Battle of the Boyne. Across the courtyard, the **Governor's House** opens for temporary exhibitions.

🍴 🛏 p91

The Drive ≫ The rich pastureland that drew the early Irish here has largely disappeared beneath the suburban sprawl, but, after 2km, as you go left off the N1 onto the N51, you'll get a better sense of classic Irish farmland (even though you'll drive under the M1 motorway!). As you get to the Boyne, go right onto the Glen Rd until you get to Mellifont. The whole drive is 11km long.

CROMWELL'S DROGHEDA INVASION

Oliver Cromwell (1599–1658) is lauded as England's first democrat and protector of the people. Cromwell hated the Irish. To him, they were treacherous infidels, a dirty race of papists who had sided with Charles I during the Civil War. So when 'God's own Englishman' landed his 12,000 troops in Dublin in August 1649, he immediately set out for Drogheda, a strategic fort town and bastion of royalist support.

In order to set an example to any other town that might resist his armies, Cromwell taught the defenders a brutal lesson. Over a period of hours, an estimated 3000 people were massacred, mostly royalist soldiers but also priests, women and children. The defenders' leader, Englishman and royalist Sir Arthur Aston, was bludgeoned to death with his own (wooden) leg. Of the survivors, many were captured and sold into slavery in the Caribbean.

Cromwell defended his action as God's righteous punishment of treacherous Catholics, and was quick to point out that he had never ordered the killing of non-combatants: it was the 17th century's version of 'collateral damage'.

Clogherhead Sunset on the shore

DETOUR:
DROGHEDA TO CASTLEBELLINGHAM VIA THE COAST ROAD

Start: ⑤ Drogheda

Most people just zip north along the M1 motorway but if you want to meander along the coast and see a little of rural Ireland, opt for the R166 from Drogheda north along the coast.

The picturesque little village of **Termonfeckin** was, until 1656, the seat and castle of the primate of Armagh. The 15th-century **castle** (admission free; ⊙10am-6pm), or tower house, is tiny and worth a five-minute stop.

About 2km further north is the busy seaside and fishing centre of **Clogherhead**, with a good, shallow Blue Flag beach at Lurganboy. Squint to ignore the caravan parks and take in the lovely views of the Cooley and Mourne Mountains instead.

The 33km route comes to an end in **Castlebellingham**. The village grew up around an 18th-century crenulated mansion, and generations of mud farmers served the landlord within. From here you can come back on the M1; it's only 25km from Castlebellingham to Drogheda.

⑥ Mellifont Abbey

In its Anglo-Norman prime, this **abbey** (☎041-982 6459; www.heritageireland.ie; Tullyallen; adult/child €3/1; ⊙visitor centre 10am-6pm Easter-Sep; Ⓟ) was the Cistercians' first and most magnificent centre in the country. Although the ruins are highly evocative and well worth exploring, they still don't do real justice to the site's former splendour.

Mellifont's most recognisable building, and one of the finest pieces of Cistercian architecture in Ireland, is the lavabo, an octagonal washing house for the monks. It was built in the early 13th century and used lead pipes to bring water from the river. A number of other buildings would have surrounded this main part of the abbey.

The visitor centre describes monastic life in detail. The ruins themselves are always open and there's good picnicking next to the rushing stream. The abbey is about 1.5km off the main Drogheda–Collon road (R168).

The Drive » The easiest way to get to Monasterboice from Mellifont Abbey is to take the Old Mellifont Rd; after 1.5km turn left onto the R168 and then veer right onto The Gables. Three km on, turn left onto the N1 and, almost immediately, right onto the R132. It's only 12km in total.

TRIP HIGHLIGHT

⑦ Monasterboice

Crowing ravens lend an eerie atmosphere to **Monasterboice** (admission free; ⊙sunrise-sunset; Ⓟ), an intriguing monastic site containing a cemetery, two ancient church ruins, one of the finest and tallest round towers in Ireland, and two of the best high crosses.

The high crosses of Monasterboice are superb examples of Celtic art. The crosses had an important didactic use, bringing the gospels alive for the uneducated, and they were probably brightly painted originally, although all traces of colour have long disappeared.

Come early or late in the day to avoid the crowds.

Eating & Sleeping

Trim ①

✖ An Tromán
Cafe €

(http://artisanfoodstoretrim.webs.com; Emmet St; dishes €4.50-7; ☺ breakfast & lunch Mon-Sat) Crammed with gourmet goodies, this fabulous deli is perfect for picking up the makings of a picnic. If it's not picnic weather, you can order daily specials like a bowl of soup and tuna and sweet-corn sandwich, chicken and mushroom pie or a meringue nest with fruit and fresh cream.

⊨ Trim Castle Hotel
Boutique Hotel €€

(☎046-948 3000; www.trimcastlehotel.com; Castle St; d €65-130; P @ ☎ ♿) This stylish hotel is part of a development that's doing its best to spiff up an area close to the castle. The 68 rooms here have a compact but comfortable modern design; facilities include jacuzzis in some rooms, as well as a carvery restaurant.

Brú na Bóinne ③

✖ Brú na Bóinne Visitor Centre Cafe
Cafe €

(dishes €4.50-12; ☺ breakfast & lunch; ♿) On the lower level of the Brú na Bóinne visitor centre, this surprisingly good cafe's extensive vegetarian options include nut and lentil loaf, and eggplant and zucchini cake, plus plenty of other treats like salmon and leek tart and beef lasagne.

⊨ Rossnaree
B&B €€

(☎041-982 0975; www.rossnaree.ie; Newgrange; d €100-120; ☺ Apr-Dec; P ☎) At a sharp corner on the narrow road between Donore and Slane

is this magnificent Italianate country house overlooking the River Boyne and surrounded by a working farm. The four bedrooms are luxuriously furnished. Groups of four or more can arrange dinner in advance. The events related in the tale 'Fionn and the Salmon of Knowledge' are said to have taken place on this very spot.

Drogheda ⑤

✖ Eastern Seaboard Bar & Grill
Irish €€

(☎041-980 2570; www.easternseaboard.ie; 1 Bryanstown Centre, Dublin Rd; mains €10.50-33; ☺ lunch & dinner; ☎ ♿) Build it and they will come... Despite its unpromising location in a business park near the train station, this stylised, contemporary space has been packed since opening, with switched-on staff and quirky details like a backlit decanter collection and metallic fish sculptures. Stunning food like pig's-cheek terrine with apple slaw, smoked mackerel pâté, and coffee jelly and vanilla ice cream is served continuously from lunchtime on. Or you could just drop by for frothy German beers on tap.

⊨ D Hotel
Hotel €€

(☎041-987 7700; www.thed.ie; Scotch Hall, Marsh Rd; d €69-109; P @ ☎ ♿) Slick, hip and unexpected, this is Drogheda's top dog when it comes to accommodation. Minimalist rooms are bathed in light and decked out with designer furniture and cool gadgets. There's a stylish bar and restaurant, a mini gym and fantastic views of the city. The hotel is popular with hen and stag parties, so beware of pounding music on weekends.

Jerpoint Abbey *One of Ireland's finest Cistercian ruins*

Ancient Ireland

6

Go time travelling through middle Ireland's collection of ancient tombs, Celtic sites and monastic cities, and cover 3000 years in four days.

TRIP HIGHLIGHTS

0 km

Brú na Bóinne
One of the world's most important neolithic monuments

Hill of Slane

Loughcrew Cairns

1 **START**

Hill of Tara

219 km

6

Clonmacnoise
Spectacular monastic site on the banks of the Shannon

FINISH

7

Jerpoint Abbey

333 km

Rock of Cashel
Wonderful monastic city crowning a large hill

4 DAYS
529KM / 329 MILES

GREAT FOR...

BEST TIME TO GO
April to September for the long days and best weather.

ESSENTIAL PHOTO
The Rock of Cashel from the ruins of Hore Abbey.

BEST FOR CULTURE
The passage graves at Brú Na Bóinne.

93

6 Ancient Ireland

This trip transports you from the neolithic era to the last days of the first millennium, via the signposts of Ireland's astonishing history: the prehistoric treasure trove of Cruachan Aí; the ancient passage graves of Newgrange and Loughcrew; the Celtic capital at Tara; and the rich monastic settlements of Clonmacnoise, Glendalough and Cashel.

TRIP HIGHLIGHT

❶ Brú na Bóinne

A thousand years older than Stonehenge, the extensive neolithic necropolis known as Brú na Bóinne (the Boyne Palace) is simply breathtaking, even if at first glance it just looks like a handful of raised mounds in the fecund fields of County Meath.

The largest artificial structures in Ireland until the construction of the Anglo-Norman castles 4000 years later,

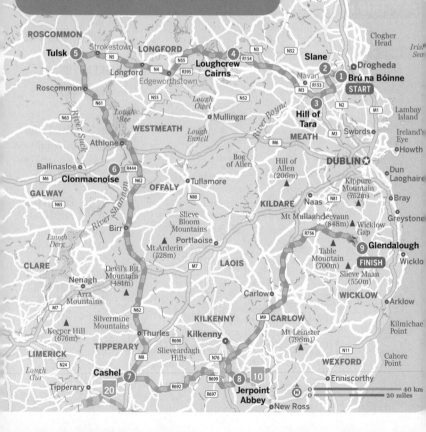

the necropolis was built to house VIP corpses.

Only two of the passage graves are open to visitors (Newgrange and Knowth) and they can only be visited as part of a carefully controlled organised tour departing from the **Brú na Bóinne Visitor Centre** (041-988 0300; www.heritageireland.ie; Donore; visitor centre adult/ child €3/2, visitor centre, Newgrange & Knowth €11/6; 9am-7pm Jun–mid-Sep, 9am-6.30pm May & mid-end Sep, 9.30am-5.30pm Oct & Feb, 9am-5pm Nov-Jan).

📖 p99

The Drive 》 Follow the signposts for Slane and the N2 as you wend your way across the Meath countryside for 8km or so; the Hill of Slane is 1km north of the village.

LINK YOUR TRIP

10 Kilkenny's Treasures

It's 20km from Jerpoint Abbey to Kilkenny, the first stop in the trip dedicated to the county.

20 The Holy Glen

In Cashel you can connect to this trip exploring the very best of County Tipperary.

2 Slane

The fairly plain-looking **Hill of Slane** stands out only for its association with a thick slice of Celto-Christian mythology. According to legend, St Patrick lit a paschal (Easter) fire here in 433 to proclaim Christianity throughout the land.

It was also here that Patrick supposedly plucked a shamrock from the ground, using its three leaves to explain the paradox of the Holy Trinity – the union of the Father, the Son and the Holy Spirit in one.

The Drive 》 Go south on the N2 for 8km and turn right onto the R153. After 2km, take the left fork and keep going for 8km until you hit the R147. After 500m take a right and then, after 250m, the first left until you get to the Hill of Tara.

3 Hill of Tara

The Hill of Tara (Teamhair) has occupied a special place in Irish legend and folklore for millennia, although it's not known exactly when people first settled on this gently sloping hill with its commanding views over the plains of Meath.

Tara's remains are not visually impressive. Only mounds and depressions in the grass mark where the Iron Age hill fort and surrounding ring

forts once stood, but it remains an evocative, somewhat moving place, especially on a warm summer's evening. To make sense of it all, stop by the **Tara Visitor Centre** (046-902 5903; www.heritageireland.ie; adult/ child €3/1; 10am-6pm Jun–mid-Sep).

The Drive 》 Head north and take the M3, which becomes the N3 after 13km. Keep going for 3km and at the roundabout take the first exit onto the R163. Follow it for 8km; it eventually morphs into the R154. The cairns are along here, just west of Oldcastle. The drive is 43km altogether.

4 Loughcrew Cairns

There are 30-odd tombs here but they're hard to reach and relatively few people ever bother, which means you can enjoy this moody and evocative place in peace.

Like Brú na Bóinne, the graves were all built around 3000 BC, but unlike their better-known and better-excavated peers, the Loughcrew tombs were used at least until 750 BC. As at Newgrange, larger stones in some of the graves are decorated with spiral patterns. Some of the graves look like large piles of stones, while others are less obvious, their cairn having been removed.

The Drive 》 The 87km between Loughcrew and Tulsk takes you through the heart of Middle Ireland, past small glacial lakes and low-lying hills. Follow the R395 to Edgeworthstown and take the N4 to Longford. Take the N5 as far as handsome Strokestown, where you should stop for an amble; Tulsk is 10km west along the same road.

---

⑤ Tulsk

Anyone with an interest in Celtic mythology will be enthralled by the area around the village of Tulsk in County Roscommon, which contains 60 ancient national monuments including standing stones, barrows, cairns and fortresses, making it the most important Celtic royal site in Europe.

The **Cruachan Aí Visitor Centre** (www.rathcroghan.ie; adult/child €5/3; ⊙9am-5pm Mon-Sat) has audiovisual displays and informative panels and maps that explain the significance of the sites.

According to the legend of Táin Bó Cúailnge (Cattle Raid of Cooley), Queen Maeve (Medbh) had her palace at Cruachan. The Oweynagat Cave (Cave of the Cats), believed to be the entrance to the Celtic otherworld, is also nearby.

The Drive » As you drive the 75km south to Clonmacnoise along the N61, you'll have Lough Ree on your left for much of the drive. Many of the lake's 50-plus islands were once inhabited by monks and their ecclesiastical treasures. These days, it's mostly anglers, sailors and birdwatchers who frequent it.

TRIP HIGHLIGHT

⑥ Clonmacnoise

Ancient Ireland is sometimes referred to as the 'land of saints and scholars', and one of the reasons why was the monastic city of **Clonmacnoise** (www.heritageireland.ie; adult/child €6/2; ⊙9am-7pm mid-May–mid-Sep, 10am-5.30pm mid-Sep–mid-May, last admission 45min before closing; P), one of Europe's most important centres of study between the 7th and 12th centuries. It was a top university *before* Oxford was a glint in the scholar's eye.

Founded in 548 by St Ciarán, the monastery (whose name in Irish is *Cluain Mhic Nóis,* which means 'Meadow of the Sons of Nós') that became a bustling city is in remarkably good condition: enclosed within a walled field above a bend in the River Shannon are a superb collection of early

JEAN BROOKS/GETTY IMAGES ©

TOP TIP:
THE CASHEL SHOT

Cashel looks good from pretty much every angle, but the most atmospheric photo is from the ruins of **Hore Abbey**, set in flat farmland less than 1km west of Cashel.

Brú na Bóinne Ancient burial mound at Newgrange

churches, high crosses, round towers and graves, including those of the high kings of Ireland.

🛏 p99

The Drive » It's 107km along the N62 to Cashel; overnighting in handsome Birr (which has great accommodation and nightlife) is recommended (p99).

TRIP HIGHLIGHT

❼ Cashel

Straddling a green hill above the town, the **Rock of Cashel** (www.heritageireland.com; adult/child €6/2; ⏱9am-6.15pm Jun-Sep, to 4.45pm Oct-May) is one of Ireland's most important archaeological sites and one of the most evocative of all ancient monuments. An important Celtic power base since the 4th century, most of what you see today dates from when it was gifted to the Church in 1101. Over the next 400 years, various bishops ordered the construction of the 13th-century **cathedral**, a wonderfully complete **round tower**, the finest **Romanesque chapel** in

A NIGHT IN BIRR

Feel-good Birr, County Offaly, is one of the most attractive towns in the Midlands, with elegant pastel Georgian buildings lining its streets, a magnificent old castle, an excellent choice of accommodation and spirited nightlife with great live music. Despite its appeal, Birr remains off the beaten track and you can enjoy its delights without jostling with the crowds. See p99 for one option of where to stay.

the country (1127) and the sturdy walls that surround it all. Although a collection of religious buildings, the rock was heavily fortified; the word 'cashel' is an Anglicisation of the Irish word *caiseal,* which means 'fortress'.

Scattered throughout are monuments, panels from 16th-century altar tombs and coats of arms. If you have binoculars, look for the numerous stone heads on capitals and corbels high above the ground.

✕ 🛏 p99

The Drive >> Tipperary and western Kilkenny are classic examples of good Irish farmland; as you wend your way east along the R692 and R690, you'll pass stud farms and cattle ranches. About 5km north of Cottrellstown, along the R697, is the 29m-high Kilree round tower and, next to it, a 9th-century high cross. The drive to Jerpoint Abbey from Cashel is 65km.

8 Jerpoint Abbey

One of Ireland's finest Cistercian ruins, **Jerpoint Abbey** (📞056-24623; www.heritageireland. ie; Hwy R448; adult/child €3/1; ☺9am-5.30pm Mar-Oct, hours vary Nov-Feb) near Thomastown was established in the 12th century and has been partially restored. The tower and cloister are late 14th or early 15th century. The 45-minute tours are worth it, as the guides flesh out the abbey's fascinating history.

The Drive >> As you come off the M9 and take the R756 east towards Laragh and Glendalough, you'll climb into the wildest parts of the Wicklow Mountains, eastern Ireland's most scenic spectacle. Just before you descend into Laragh you'll drive through the Wicklow Gap, between Mt Tonelagee (816m) to the north and Table Mountain (700m) to the southwest. Total distance to Glendalough: 117km.

9 Glendalough

Of all Ireland's monastic cities, none has the secluded beauty and isolated majesty of Glendalough, whose impressive ruins are more than rivalled by their setting: two dark glacial lakes at the foot of a forested valley that remain, despite the immense popularity of a visit, a profoundly peaceful and spiritual place.

In 498 the solitude-seeking St Kevin went to live in a Bronze Age tomb on the south side of the Upper Lake, but most of what you see dates from the 9th century onwards, when Kevin's settlement rivalled Clonmacnoise as one of Ireland's premier universities: huddled around the eastern end of the Lower Lake are Glendalough's most fascinating buildings, including a roofless cathedral, a couple of churches, a gatehouse and a round tower.

The **Glendalough Visitor Centre** (📞0404-45325; www.heritageireland. ie; adult/child & student €3/2; ☺9.30am-6pm mid-Mar–Oct, to 5pm Nov–mid-Mar) has a 17-minute audiovisual presentation called Ireland of the Monasteries.

Eating & Sleeping

Brú na Bóinne ❶

🛏 Newgrange Lodge   Inn €

(📞041-988 2478; www.newgrangelodge.com; dm €19.50-21, d €70; P @ 🛜) Just east of the Brú na Bóinne visitor centre, you'll find this converted farmhouse with a choice of cosy rooms varying from dorms with four to 10 beds, to hotel-standard rooms. All have private bathrooms. Rates include continental breakfast (with scones!).

Clonmacnoise ❻

🛏 Kajon House   B&B €€

(📞090-967 4191; www.kajonhouse.ie; Creevagh; d from €70; 🕐Mar-Oct; P) If you want to stay near the ruins, this is your best option, just 1.5km away on the road signposted to Tullamore. It's an incredibly friendly place with cosy rooms, a spacious yard with a picnic table and evening meals on offer.

Birr

🛏 Brendan House   B&B €€

(📞057-912 1818; www.tinjugstudio.com; Brendan St; s/d €55/85) Gloriously eccentric and packed to the gills with knick-knacks, books, rugs, art and antiques, this Georgian town house is a bohemian delight. The three rooms share a bathroom, but the four-poster beds, period charm and artistic style of the place more than make up for this. The owners also run an artists' studio and gallery, offer evening meals on request, and can arrange guided mountain walks, castle tours and holistic treatments.

Cashel ❼

✕ Cafe Hans   Cafe €€

(📞062-63660; Dominic St; mains €13-19; 🕐noon-5pm Tue-Sat; 🚹) Competition for the 32 seats is fierce at this gourmet cafe run by the same family as Chez Hans next door. There's a fantastic selection of salads, open sandwiches (including succulent prawns with tangy Marie Rose sauce) and filling fish, shellfish, lamb and vegetarian dishes, with a discerning wine selection and mouth-watering desserts like homemade caramel ice cream with butterscotch sauce. Arrive before or after the lunchtime rush or plan on queuing.

🛏 Cashel Palace Hotel   Hotel €€€

(📞062-62707; www.cashel-palace.ie; Main St; s/d from €95/176; P @ 🛜) Built in 1732 for a Protestant archbishop, this handsome red-brick, late–Queen Anne house is a local landmark. Fully restored, it has 23 antique-furnished rooms in the gracious main building or quaint mews. The **bar** (bar food €10-16; 🕐lunch & dinner) is the place to talk about your upcoming hunt before dining at the vault-ceilinged **Bishops Buttery Restaurant** (2-/3-course menus from €22/25; 🕐lunch & dinner).

Clonmacnoise
Marvellous monastic ruins

Monasteries, Mountains & Mansions

7

From mountains and monastic ruins to stately homes and historic whiskey distilleries, there's nothing fictional about this trip through middle Ireland.

TRIP HIGHLIGHTS

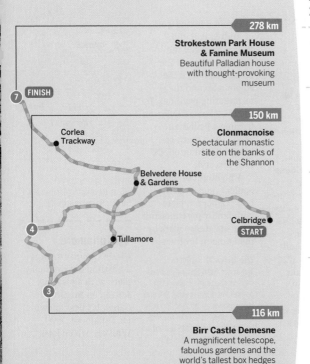

278 km

Strokestown Park House & Famine Museum
Beautiful Palladian house with thought-provoking museum

7 FINISH

150 km

Corlea Trackway

Clonmacnoise
Spectacular monastic site on the banks of the Shannon

Belvedere House & Gardens

Celbridge
START

4

Tullamore

3

116 km

Birr Castle Demesne
A magnificent telescope, fabulous gardens and the world's tallest box hedges

3 DAYS
278KM / 172 MILES

GREAT FOR...

BEST TIME TO GO

Late spring and early autumn are ideal: smaller crowds and good weather.

ESSENTIAL PHOTO

Immortalise the gardens of Birr Castle Demesne.

BEST FOR CULTURE

Explore Ireland's tormented history at Strokestown House & Famine Museum.

101

7

Monasteries, Mountains & Mansions

This is a journey through Irish heritage: handsome towns like Birr and Strokestown may not attract star billing but are all the better for it, while better-known attractions like Clonmacnoise and Castletown House are outstanding examples of monastic splendour and Georgian extravagance, respectively. And did we mention whiskey? How about a visit to the home of the smoothest Irish whiskey of all?

1 Celbridge

Celbridge, County Kildare, is now a satellite town serving Dublin, only 20km to the east, but in the 18th century it was known as the location for Ireland's most magnificent Georgian pile, **Castletown House** (☎01-628 8252; www.castletownhouse.ie; adult/child €4.50/3.50; ⏱10am-4.45pm Tue-Sun Easter-Oct), which simply has no peer.

The house was built between the years 1722 and 1732 for William Conolly (1662–1729), speaker of the Irish House of Commons and, at the time, Ireland's richest man.

Inspired by the work of Andrea Palladio, Pearce enlarged the original design of the house and added the colonnades and the terminating pavilions. In the US, Thomas Jefferson became a Palladian acolyte and much of official Washington, DC is in this style.

A highlight of the opulent interior is the Long Gallery, replete with family portraits and exquisite stucco work by the Francini brothers.

The Drive » It's 74km to Tullamore from Celbridge, and most of the route is along the painless and featureless M4 and M6 motorways; at Junction 11 on the M4, be sure to take the left-hand fork onto the M6 towards Galway and Athlone. Exit the M6 at Junction 5; Tullamore is a further 9km along the N52.

2 Tullamore

Offaly's county town is a bustling but workaday place with a pleasant setting on the Grand Canal. It's best known for Tullamore Dew Whiskey, which hasn't

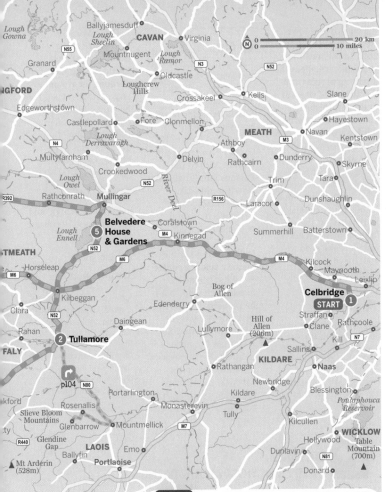

been distilled in the town since 1954, when operations moved to Clonmel, County Tipperary.

But in 2012 it was announced that Tullamore Dew was coming home, when plans were drawn up for a new pot still whiskey and malt distillery for

LINK YOUR TRIP

32 Northwest on Adrenalin

Explore the northwest's heart-racing activities with an easy 61km drive from Strokestown to Sligo.

21 Best of the West

At trip's end, head west to Westport and pick up this western extravaganza.

the outskirts of town, which should open in 2014. In the meantime, you can learn about the distilling process and the history of whiskey in the refurbished **Tullamore Dew Heritage Centre** (www.tullamore-dew. org; Bury Quay; adult/child €6/3.50; ⊙9am-6pm Mon-Sat, noon-5pm Sun May-Sep, 10am-5pm Mon-Sat, noon-5pm Sun Oct-Apr), located in a 19th-century canalside warehouse. At the end of the tour you'll get to sample some produce and, inevitably, be encouraged to buy it for friends and family.

🍴 p107

The Drive » It's only 37km from Tullamore to Birr. As you drive the N52 south towards Birr, you'll skirt the northern edge of the Slieve Bloom Mountains, which rise suddenly from the great plain of middle Ireland.

- - - - - - - - - -

❸ Birr

The main reason to visit handsome Birr is to explore the attractions and gardens of **Birr Castle Demesne** (www. birrcastle.com; adult/child €9/5; ⊙9am-6pm mid-Mar–Oct, 10am-4pm Nov–mid-Mar), built in 1620 by the Parsons family, who still own it to this day.

The Parsons were a remarkable family of pioneering Irish scientists, and their work is documented in the **historic science centre**. Exhibits include the massive telescope built by William Parsons in 1845, for 75 years the largest in the world. It was used to make innumerable discoveries, including the spiral galaxies, and to map the moon's surface. It is currently being restored.

Otherwise, the 50-hectare castle grounds are famous for their magnificent **gardens** set around a large artificial lake. They hold over 1000 species of plants from all over the world; something always seems to be in bloom. Look for one of the world's tallest box hedges, planted in the 1780s and now standing 12m high, and the romantic Hornbeam cloister.

🍴 🛏 p107

The Drive » You'll see mostly fields of cows as you drive the 32km to Clonmacnoise along the N62; at Cloghan, turn left onto the slightly narrower and lonelier R357. You'll have the River Shannon on your left-hand-side when you turn onto the R444 for the last 5km past Shannonbridge, which has a good restaurant (p107).

DETOUR:
SLIEVE BLOOM MOUNTAINS

Start: ❷ Tullamore

Although not as spectacular as some Irish ranges, the Slieve Bloom Mountains' sudden rise from a great plain and the absence of visitors make them highly attractive. You'll get a real sense of being away from it all as you tread the deserted blanket bogs, moorland, pine forests and isolated valleys.

For leisurely walking, **Glenbarrow**, southwest of Rosenallis, has an interesting trail by the cascading River Barrow. Other spots to check out are **Glendine Park**, near the Glendine Gap, and the **Cut mountain pass**.

For something more challenging, you could try the **Slieve Bloom Way**, a 77km signposted trail that does a complete circuit of the mountains, taking in most major points of interest. The recommended starting point is the car park at Glenbarrow, 5km from Rosenallis, from where the trail follows tracks, forest firebreaks and old roads around the mountains. The trail's highest point is at Glendine Gap (460m).

IIC/AXIOM/GETTY IMAGES ©

Birr View of Birr Castle's grounds

TRIP HIGHLIGHT

4 Clonmacnoise

One of the most important monastic sites in Ireland, the marvellous monastic ruins of **Clonmacnoise** (www.heritageireland.ie; adult/child €6/2; ⊙9am-7pm mid-May–mid-Sep, 10am-5.30pm mid-Sep–mid-May, last admission 45min before closing; [P]) are also one of the most popular tourist attractions in the country, so be prepared to share your visit with other awe-struck tourists and busloads of curious schoolkids. For more details on the site, check out p96.

The Drive › About 20km north of Clonmacnoise you'll rejoin the M6 motorway; if you're feeling hungry, head left to Athlone, where there's a good restaurant (p107). At Junction 4, take the N52 north towards Mullingar; on your left, keep an eye out for Lough Ennell, whose claim to fame is having produced the country's largest-ever brown trout – a 11.5kg monster. The far side of the lake is home to Lilliput House, which was frequently used by Jonathan Swift and gave him the name he used in *Gulliver's Travels*. In total, the drive is 64km long.

5 Belvedere House & Gardens

About 5.5km south of Mullingar, overlooking Lough Ennell, is **Belvedere House** (www. belvedere-house.ie; adult/child €8.75/4.75; ⊙house 9.30am-8pm May-Aug, to 4.30pm Sep-Apr), an immense 18th-century hunting lodge set in 65 hectares of gardens. More than a few skeletons have come out of Belvedere's closets: the first earl, Lord Belfield, accused his wife and younger brother Arthur of adultery. She

DETOUR:
SHH... ONE OF IRELAND'S BEST TRADITIONAL PUBS

Start: ⑥ Corlea Trackway

About 10km east of Lanesborough is the tiny hamlet of Killashee, which is home to **Magan's**, a delightful old bar, grocery and hardware store that seems stuck in aspic, completely oblivious to the pull and push of modern life. It's well off the beaten track, and is rarely frequented by anyone other than locals, which makes it an even better destination for a pint.

was placed under house arrest here for 30 years, and Arthur was jailed in London for the rest of his life. Meanwhile, the earl lived a life of decadence and debauchery. On his death, his wife emerged dressed in the fashion of three decades earlier, still protesting her innocence.

The Drive » Head north to Mullingar, where there are a couple of good hotels and restaurants (p107), then drive northwest to cross into County Longford, a quiet place of low hills and pastoral scenes. It has few tourist sights but is a haven for anglers who come for the superb fishing around Lough Ree and Lanesborough. From Belvedere House, the drive to Corlea along the R392 is about 41km.

⑥ Corlea Trackway

Longford's main attraction is the magnificent **Corlea Trackway** (www.heritage ireland.ie; admission free; ⊙10am-6pm mid-Apr–Sep), an Iron Age bog road near Keenagh that was built in 148 BC. An 18m stretch of the historic track has now been preserved in

a humidified hall at the visitor centre, where you can join a 45-minute tour that details the bog's unique flora and fauna, and fills you in on how the track was discovered and methods used to preserve it. Wear a windproof jacket as the bog land can be blowy.

The Drive » Strokestown is 27km northwest of Corlea along the R392 as far as Lanesborough, after which you'll cut through the green, lush countryside along the R371. After 10km, take a left onto the N5, which will take you right into Strokestown, 5km further on.

- - - - - - - - - - - - - -
TRIP HIGHLIGHT

⑦ Strokestown

Roscommon's most handsome town is, for nonresidents, all about **Strokestown Park House & Famine Museum** (www. strokestownpark.ie; house, museum & gardens €12, house or museum or gardens €8; ⊙10.30am-5.30pm), the entrance to which is through the three Gothic arches at the end of Strokestown's main avenue.

Admission to this beautifully preserved Palladian house is by a 45-minute **guided tour**, taking in a galleried kitchen with state-of-the-art clockwork machinery, and a child's bedroom complete with 19th-century toys and fun-house mirrors.

In direct and deliberate contrast to the splendour of the house and its grounds is the harrowing **Strokestown Famine Museum**, which sheds light on the devastating 1840s potato blight. There's a huge amount of information to take in, but you'll emerge with an unblinking insight into the starvation of the poor, and the ignorance, callousness and cruelty of those who were in a position to help. Allow at least half a day to see the house, museum and gardens.

Eating & Sleeping

Tullamore ❷

✕ Sirocco's   Italian €€
(☏057-935 2839; Patrick St; mains €12-25; ⏲lunch Thu, Fri & Sun, dinner Mon-Sat; 🚕)
Serving a good selection of fresh pasta and pizza, as well as meat, chicken and fish dishes, this simple little Italian bistro is a local favourite. Booking is advised.

Birr ❸

✕ Riverbank   Irish €€
(☏057-912 1528; riverbankrest@msn.com; Riverstown; mains €14.50-18.50; ⏲closed Mon) This deep-red place set on the banks of the Little Brosna River is well worth the short trip from town for its superb but honest food and friendly atmosphere. There's always a good choice of fish and seafood as well as steaks, grills and traditional favourites on offer. Riverbank is 1.5km south of Birr on the N52.

🛏 Brendan House   B&B €€
(☏057-912 1818; www.tinjugstudio.com; Brendan St; s/d €55/85) Gloriously eccentric and packed to the gills with knick-knacks, books, rugs, art and antiques, this Georgian town house is a bohemian delight. The three rooms share a bathroom, but the four-poster beds, period charm and artistic style of the place more than make up for this. The owners also run an artists' studio and gallery, offer evening meals on request and can arrange guided mountain walks, castle tours and holistic treatments.

Shannonbridge

✕ Old Fort Restaurant   Irish €€€
(☏090-967 4973; www.theoldfortrestaurant. com; mains €21.50-29.50; ⏲5-9.30pm Wed-Sat, 12.30-2.30pm Sun) In Shannonbridge, about halfway between Birr and Clonmacnoise in County Offaly, is this impressive bridgehead, built as a defence against a possible Napoleonic invasion, and now serving exquisite posh nosh to a discerning local clientele.

Athlone

✕ Kin Khao   Thai €€
(☏090-649 8805; www.kinkhaothai.ie; Abbey Lane; mains €17-19; ⏲12.30-2.30pm Wed-Fri, 5.30-10.30pm Mon-Sat, 1.30-10.30pm Sun) What is possibly the best Thai restaurant in Ireland is tucked away near the Dean Crowe Theatre and is renowned for its extensive menu of authentic dishes. All the chefs and staff are Thai (with the exception of one half of the husband-and-wife team who run the place) and you'd be advised to book ahead if you want to join the band of loyal Kin Khao devotees.

Mullingar

✕ Ilia   Fusion €€
(☏044-934 5947; www.ilia.ie; 37 Dominick St; mains €16-27; ⏲dinner Tue-Sun, lunch Sun) Be sure to book in advance for one of Mullingar's most popular haunts. This cosy but clean-cut restaurant serves up a winning array of gourmet comfort food. Think slow roast pork belly, chicken with Puy lentils and roast peppers, or pumpkin and sage risotto, all cooked with attention and flair. You'll be back for more.

🛏 Annebrook House Hotel   Hotel €€
(☏044-935 3300; www.annebrook.ie; Pearse St; s/d from €55/100; 🅿🛜) Right in the town centre, the hub of this modern hotel is a lovely 19th-century house with strong connections to local author Maria Edgeworth. Accommodation is in a new annexe, where modern rooms in neutral colours are extremely comfortable but lack soul.

Glendalough Home of ancient ruins
nestled in a forest-covered valley

Wicklow Mountains

8

Eastern Ireland's most forbidding mountain range is as magnificent as it is desolate, with narrow roads cutting through the gorse- and bracken-covered hilltops.

TRIP HIGHLIGHTS

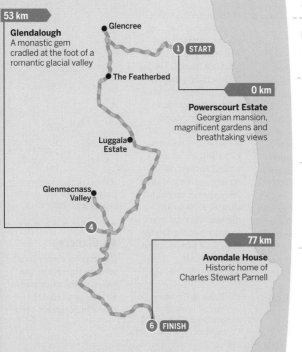

53 km

Glendalough
A monastic gem cradled at the foot of a romantic glacial valley

Glencree

The Featherbed

0 km

1 START

Powerscourt Estate
Georgian mansion, magnificent gardens and breathtaking views

Luggala
Estate

Glenmacnass
Valley

4

77 km

Avondale House
Historic home of Charles Stewart Parnell

6 FINISH

**3 DAYS
77KM / 47 MILES**

GREAT FOR...

BEST TIME TO GO

From late August to September, the crowds thin out and the heather is in bloom.

 ESSENTIAL PHOTO

Looking down on Lough Tay and Luggala from the Sally Gap.

 BEST FOR CULTURE

Glendalough: 1500 years of monastic history beautifully nestled in a glacial valley.

109

8

Wicklow Mountains

This drive takes you down the spine of the Wicklow Mountains, whose dramatic scenery and weather-whipped bleakness make up for what they lack in height. Along the way you'll visit fine Palladian mansions and a beautiful monastic site nestled at the foot of a glacial valley – be prepared to pull over and gawp at the scenery that unfolds.

① Enniskerry

If you're coming from Dublin, Enniskerry is a handsome village at the top of the R117, aka the '21 Bends', but its pretty shops and cafes are merely a prelude to a visit to the superb 64-sq-km **Powerscourt Estate** (☎01-204 6000; www.powerscourt.ie; adult/child €8/5; ⏰9.30am-5.30pm Feb-Oct, to 4.30pm Nov-Jan), whose workers' domestic needs were the very reason Enniskerry was built in the first place.

Due to a fire, you can't visit the Palladian mansion save the ground floor cafe and outlet of the popular Avoca handicrafts store, but it's the gardens that will have you in thrall. Laid out (mostly) in the 19th century, they are a magnificent blend of landscaped gardens, sweeping terraces, statuary, ornamental lakes, secret hollows, rambling walks and walled enclosures replete with more than 200 types of trees and shrubs, all beneath the stunning natural backdrop of the Great Sugarloaf Mountain to the southeast.

✕ ⮕ p115

The Drive » The narrow, twisting L1011 cuts 11km through the northern edge of the mountains, with only a hint of what's to come further on. As you approach Glencree you'll pass through mostly forest.

② Glencree

Glencree is a leafy hamlet set into the side of the valley of the same name which opens east to give a magnificent view

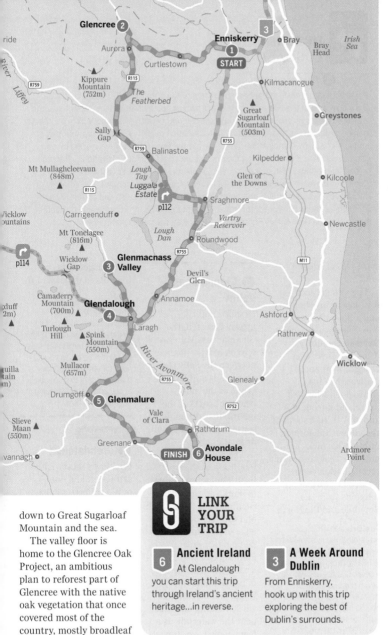

down to Great Sugarloaf Mountain and the sea.

The valley floor is home to the Glencree Oak Project, an ambitious plan to reforest part of Glencree with the native oak vegetation that once covered most of the country, mostly broadleaf trees, but now only

LINK YOUR TRIP

6 **Ancient Ireland**
At Glendalough you can start this trip through Ireland's ancient heritage...in reverse.

3 **A Week Around Dublin**
From Enniskerry, hook up with this trip exploring the best of Dublin's surrounds.

DETOUR: LUGGALA

Start: ➋ **Glencree**

If you turn right (east) at the Sally Gap crossroads onto the R759, you'll be on the Sally Gap, one of the two main east–west passes across the Wicklow Mountains and a stretch of road surrounded by some spectacular countryside. About 5km on, the narrow road passes above the dark and dramatic Lough Tay, whose scree slopes slide into Luggala (Fancy Mountain). This almost fairy-tale estate is owned by one Garech de Brún, member of the Guinness family and founder of Claddagh Records, a leading producer of Irish traditional and folk music. You can't visit the estate itself, but there's a popular looped walk that circles it from a height. The small River Cloghoge links Lough Tay with Lough Dan just to the south. You can continue on the R759 for another 3km or so, turning right onto the R755 for Roundwood, or double-back onto the Old Military Rd and make your way south via Glenmacnass.

covers 1% of Ireland's land mass.

The village, such as it is, has a tiny shop and a hostel but no pub. There's a poignant **German cemetery** (Glencree Deutsche Kriegsgraberstatte) dedicated to 134 servicemen who died in Ireland during WWI and WWII. Just south of the village, the former military barracks are now a retreat house and reconciliation centre for people of different religions from the Republic and the North.

The Drive » At Glencree you'll join Wicklow's loveliest, loneliest road, the Old Military Rd (R115), which cuts through a desolate valley of gorse and brown bog and gets more desolate as you go south. At about 11km you'll reach the Sally Gap crossroads; turn right onto the R759 for the gap itself or continue for another 5km to the Glenmacnass Valley.

➌ Glenmacnass Valley

Desolate and utterly deserted, the Glenmacnass Valley, a stretch of wild bogland between the Sally Gap crossroads and Laragh, is one of the most beautiful parts of the mountains, although the sense of isolation is quite dramatic.

The highest mountain to the west is Mt Mullaghcleevaun (848m), and the River Glenmacnass flows south and tumbles over the edge of the mountain plateau in a great foaming cascade. There's a car park near the top of the **Glenmacnass Waterfall**. Be careful when walking on rocks near the waterfall, as a few people have slipped to their deaths. There are fine walks up Mt Mullaghcleevaun or in the hills to the east of the car park.

The Drive » Beyond the Glenmacnass Valley, the Old Military Rd descends for 13km into Laragh, a busy crossroads village that serves as a supply point for nearby Glendalough. It's a good spot to stop and eat or buy provisions. Glendalough is 3km west of here.

TRIP HIGHLIGHT

➍ Glendalough

Wicklow's most visited attraction and one of the country's most important historic sites is the collection of ruined churches, buildings, shelters and round tower that make up the ancient monastic city of Glendalough, founded in 498 by St Kevin, who came to the (then) desolate valley looking for a spot of contemplative tranquillity. The ruins

Luggala Walkers on track to Lough Dan

are certainly evocative, but it's their setting that makes them special: two dark and mysterious lakes tucked into a deep valley covered in forest.

You could spend a day exploring the ruins and taking in the local scenery, but whatever you do, your exploration should start with a visit to the **Glendalough Visitor Centre** (☎0404-45325; www.heritageireland.ie; adult/child & student €3/2; ☺9.30am-6pm mid-Mar–Oct, to 5pm Nov–mid-Mar), which has a high-quality 17-minute audiovisual presentation called Ireland of the Monasteries.

✕ ⌖ p115

WALKS IN WICKLOW

Glendalough Valley Walks

The Glendalough Valley is all about walking and clambering. There are nine marked ways in the valley, the longest of which is about 10km, or about four hours' walking. Before you set off, drop by the **National Park Information Point** (☎0404-45325; ☺10am-6pm daily May-Sep, to dusk Sat & Sun Oct-Apr) and pick up the relevant leaflet and trail map (all around €0.50). A word of warning: don't be fooled by the relative gentleness of the surrounding countryside or the fact that the Wicklow Mountains are really no taller than big hills. The weather can be merciless here, so be sure to take the usual precautions, have the right equipment and tell someone where you're going and when you should be back. For Mountain Rescue call ☎999.

The Featherbed

One of the best known sections of the Old Military Rd is known as the Featherbed, which is in the shadow of Kippure Mountain (752m; easily recognised due to its TV transmitter) and two glacial lakes, Upper and Lower Lough Bray. You can park your car in a siding by Upper Lough Bray and take a looped 3km walk that skirts the two lakes via a boggy path – you'll need decent boots, waterproofs and a stick.

DETOUR:
THE WICKLOW GAP

Start: ④ Glendalough

Between Mt Tonelagee (816m) to the north and Table Mountain (700m) to the southwest, the Wicklow Gap (R756) is the second major pass over the mountains. The eastern end of the road begins just to the north of Glendalough and climbs through some lovely scenery northwestwards up along the Glendassan Valley. It passes the remains of some old lead and zinc workings before meeting a side road that leads south and up Turlough Hill, the location of Ireland's only pumped-storage power station. You can walk up the hill for a look over the Upper Lake. The western end of the gap meets the N81, from which it's only a few kilometres north to Blessington and Russborough House (see p72).

The Drive 》 As you go deeper into the mountains southwest of Glendalough along the R755, near the southern end of the Military Rd, everything gets a bit wilder and more remote. It's an 11km drive to Glenmalure.

The Drive 》 The tiny rural road to Rathdrum is called Riverside; it takes you down out of the mountains through some lush forest for 12km into Rathdrum for Avondale House.

TRIP HIGHLIGHT

⑤ Glenmalure

Beneath the western slopes of Wicklow's highest peak, Lugnaquilla (924m), is Glenmalure, a dark and sombre blind valley flanked by scree slopes of loose boulders. After coming over the mountains into Glenmalure, you turn northwest at the Drumgoff bridge. From there it's about 6km up the road beside the River Avonbeg to a car park where trails lead off in various directions.

🛏 p115

⑥ Avondale House

The quiet village of Rathdrum at the foot of the Vale of Clara comprises little more than a few old houses and shops, but it's not what's in the town that's of interest to visitors, however, but what's just outside it.

Avondale House
(📞0404-46111; adult/student & child €7/6.50; 🕙11am-6pm May-Aug, Sat & Sun only Apr, by appointment only rest of year) is a fine Palladian mansion surrounded by a marvellous 209-hectare estate, which was the birthplace and Irish home of the 'uncrowned king of Ireland', Charles Stewart Parnell (1846–91), the champion of the struggle for Home Rule and one of the key figures of the Irish independence movement. Designed by James Wyatt in 1779, the house's many highlights include a stunning vermilion-hued library and beautiful dining room.

Surrounding the house, running through the 200 hectares of forest and parkland (all managed by the Irish Forestry Service, Coillte), are many walking trails. You can visit the park during daylight hours year-round.

Eating & Sleeping

Enniskerry ❶

🍴 Emilia's Ristorante
Italian €€

(☎01-276 1834; Clock Tower, The Square; mains €12-16; ⏲5-10.45pm Mon-Sat, noon-9.30pm Sun) A lovely 1st-floor restaurant to satisfy even the most ardent craving for thin-crust pizzas. Emilia's does everything else just right too, from the organic soups to the perfect steaks down to the gorgeous meringue desserts.

🛏 Coolakay House
B&B €€

(☎01-286 2423; www.coolakayhouse.com; Waterfall Rd, Coolakay; r €75; P🖥) A modern working farm about 3km south of Enniskerry (it is signposted along the road), this is a great option for walkers along the Wicklow Way. The four bedrooms are all very comfortable and have terrific views, but the real draw is the restaurant (mains around €11), which does a roaring trade in snacks and full meals.

Glendalough ❹

🍴 Wicklow Heather Restaurant
International €€

(☎0404-45157; www.thewicklowheather.com; Main St, Laragh; mains €16-26; ⏲noon-8.30pm) This is the best place for anything substantial. The menu offers Wicklow lamb, wild venison, Irish beef and fresh fish (the trout is excellent) – most of it sourced locally and all of it traceable from farm to fork.

🛏 Glendalough Hotel
Hotel €€

(☎0404-45135; www.glendaloughhotel.com; s/d €110/150; P@🖥👤) There's no mistaking Glendalough's best hotel, conveniently located next door to the visitor centre. There is no shortage of takers for its 44 fairly luxurious bedrooms.

Glenmalure ❺

🛏 Glenmalure Hostel
Hostel €

(☎01-830 4555; www.anoige.ie; Greenane; dm €15; ⏲Jun-Aug, Sat only Sep-May) No telephone, no electricity (lighting is by gas), just a rustic two-storey cottage with 19 beds and running water. This place has a couple of heavyweight literary links: it was once owned by WB Yeats' femme fatale, Maud Gonne, and was also the setting for JM Synge's play, *Shadow of a Gunman*. It's isolated, but is beautifully situated beneath Lugnaquilla.

🛏 Glenmalure Log Cabin
Self-Catering €€

(☎01-269 6979; www.glenmalure.com; 11 Glenmalure Pines, Greenane; 2 nights €200-290, 3 nights €350-550; 🖥👤) In the heart of Glenmalure, this modern, Scandinavian-style lodge has two rooms with private bathrooms, a fully equipped kitchen and a living room kitted out with all kinds of electronic amusements, including your very own DVD library. Hopefully though, you'll spend much of your time here enjoying the panorama from the sun deck. There's a two-night minimum stay, except for July and August when it's seven days.

County Carlow *Wind through the picturesque villages of Ireland's second-smallest county*

Carlow Back Roads

9

A jaunt through Ireland undisturbed by mass tourism, this trip reveals one of the country's most delightful, unexplored counties.

TRIP HIGHLIGHTS

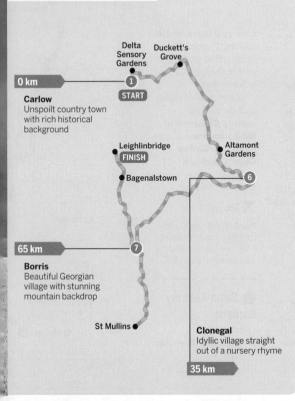

0 km

Carlow
Unspoilt country town with rich historical background

Delta Sensory Gardens

Duckett's Grove

1 START

Leighlinbridge FINISH

Bagenalstown

Altamont Gardens

6

65 km

7

Borris
Beautiful Georgian village with stunning mountain backdrop

St Mullins

Clonegal
Idyllic village straight out of a nursery rhyme

35 km

3 DAYS
118KM / 73 MILES

GREAT FOR...

BEST TIME TO GO
Carlow's flower festivals take place throughout July and September.

 ESSENTIAL PHOTO
Immortalise the Black Castle from the banks of the Barrow.

 BEST FOR GARDENS
The Altamont Gardens are the most spectacular of Carlow's beautiful gardens.

117

9 Carlow Back Roads

Strings of quietly picturesque villages wind through Carlow, Ireland's second-smallest county. The scenic Blackstairs Mountains dominate the southeast, while the region's most dramatic chunk of history is Europe's biggest dolmen, just outside quiet Carlow town. A ruined Gothic mansion and a reputedly haunted castle form the backdrop to two of the county's best flower-filled gardens.

LAOIS · R417

Delta Sensory Gardens 2

Killeshin

Carlow 1 START   Bro
Do

River Barrow

M

10 Leighlinbridge
FINISH

9 Bagenalsto

R705

Goresbridge

7 B

Skeaghvasteen

R729

KILKENNY

Graiguenamanagh · R703

10

Brandon Hill (516m) ▲ · R705   Glynn

St Mullins 8

28 · R700

TRIP HIGHLIGHT

1 Carlow Town

Carlow town's narrow streets and lanes are quiet these days, a far cry from 25 May 1789, when several hundred Irish insurgents were ambushed and executed by British troops during a ferocious battle in the middle of town. The dead were buried in gravel pits on the far side of the River Barrow, at Graiguecullen.

Built by William de Marshall on the site of an earlier Norman motte-and-bailey fort, the 13-century **castle** (Castle Hill) survived Cromwell's attentions but was later converted into a lunatic asylum. The evocative portion that survives is a part of the keep flanked by two towers.

Other notable sights include the 19th-century **Cathedral of the Assumption** (College St) and the **Carlow County Museum** (www.carlowcountymuseum.com; cnr College & Tullow Sts).

✕ 🛏 p123

The Drive » Take the Athy road (R417) north for about 1.5km; the Delta Sensory Gardens are on your left.

---

2 Delta Sensory Gardens

Located in an incongruous industrial

estate on the northern edge of Carlow town are these remarkable **gardens** (www.deltasensorygardens.com; Strawhall Estate, Cannery Rd; adult/child €5/free; ⊙9am-5pm Mon-Fri, from 11am Sat & Sun). Some 16 interconnecting, themed gardens cover 1 hectare and span the five senses – from a sculpture garden to a formal rose garden, water and woodland garden, willow garden and a musical garden with mechanical fountains. Admission proceeds benefit the adjoining Delta Centre, which provides services and respite for adults with learning disabilities.

The Drive » Take the R726 and drive for 3km heading east from Carlow town. You'll have to park the car and walk 300m to the field.

LINK YOUR TRIP

10 Kilkenny's Treasures

From Borris, it's only 10km to Graiguenamanagh, from where you can explore County Kilkenny.

28 Tip to Toe

Travel 14km from St Mullins south to New Ross, where you can join the north-to-south classic trip.

③ Browne's Hill Dolmen

Ireland's largest portal dolmen (tomb chamber) sits in a field and, from the road, doesn't look that impressive. But as you get closer you'll begin to appreciate the enormity of this 5000-year-old monster. The entrance to the chamber is flanked by two large upright stones (known as orthostats or megaliths) topped by a granite capstone that alone weighs well over 100 tonnes.

It's unclear how the stones got here in the first place, but experts have narrowed it down to two possibilities: they were deposited here during the ice age, or Stone Age men ate a hell of a lot of spinach and figured out a way of carrying them to the field.

ARTISANAL GLASS

About 3km east of Kells, in the neighbouring county of Kilkenny, is the small village of Stonyford. The local highlight, the nationally renowned **Jerpoint Glass Studio** (www.jerpointglass.com; ☉shop 10am-6pm Mon-Sat, noon-5pm Sun), is housed in a rural stone-walled farm building 1km south of town, where you can watch workers craft molten glass into exquisite artistic and practical items.

The Drive >> Turn left onto Strawhall Ave (N80) and take the first exit at the Hacketstown Rd roundabout onto the R726. After 2km, take a left at the signpost for Duckett's Grove; the house is 5km on, past the underpass for the M9 motorway.

④ Duckett's Grove

Until the main building burnt in 1933, the Gothic fantasy that was **Duckett's Grove** (www.duckettsgrove.eu; admission free; ☉10am-5.30pm Apr-Oct, to 4pm Nov-Mar) was Carlow's most impressive building, the centrepiece of an estate that once spread across five counties.

The house dates from the late 17th-century, was transformed into a Gothic mansion in 1830 and was used as a training camp for the Irish Republican Army during the War of Independence. The ruins are still impressive, and surrounding them are the original high brick garden walls that frame two sprawling, interconnected formal gardens.

DETOUR:
MT LEINSTER SCENIC DRIVE

Start: ⑦ Borris

The highest peak in the Blackstairs Mountains, Mt Leinster (796m) has magnificent views of counties Waterford, Carlow, Kilkenny and Wicklow from the top.

From Borris, drive south along the R702 and almost immediately take the signposted left for Mt Leinster. Keep going and take the left for Bunclody at the T-junction. Continue around, keeping the mountain on your right; you'll arrive at the car park at Corribut Gap. The ground falls away steeply, offering stunning views of the Coolasnaghta valley to the north.

This is also the spot favoured by those taking advantage of Ireland's best hang-gliding spot – if you fancy taking off from the mountain, contact the **Irish Hang Gliding & Paragliding Association** (www.ihpa.ie) for further information.

The Drive » Start the 18km drive by heading southwest on the R418 to Tullow before continuing south along the N81. After 6km, take a right for the Altamont Estate.

St Mullins Boats on the River Barrow, Graiguenamanagh

5 Altamont Gardens

Generally considered to be the jewel in the Irish gardening crown, the 16-hectare **Altamont Estate** (www.heritageireland. ie; near Ballon; admission free; ⏰10am-7pm summer, to 5pm other times, Mon-Fri only Dec) is made up of informal and formal gardens, including a walled garden with carefully selected plantings arranged in naturalistic, idealised settings.

The estate's main avenue is lined with trees, including imported species like red oak and swamp cypresses, and it leads down to an artificial lake.

The Drive » Take the N80 south for 2km and then the signposted left for Clonegal; the right turn takes you to Ballon, where there are a couple of good restaurants and hotels (p123).

TRIP HIGHLIGHT

6 Clonegal

The idyllic village of Clonegal has a tiny little centre out of a nursery rhyme with an arched stone bridge over a river that boasts swans and water flowers.

Huntington Castle (www.huntingtoncastle.com; castle & gardens tour adult/ child €8/5, gardens only €5/3; ⏰house 2-6pm Jun-Aug, by appointment rest of year, gardens 10am-6pm May-Sep) is a spooky, dusty old keep built in 1625 by the Durdin-Robertson family, who still own it and live here today. The family conduct hour-long tours of the property, which, they claim, is haunted by two ghosts. The gardens combine the formal with rural fantasy.

The Drive » The R724 cuts across southern County Carlow; Borris is 29km away.

TRIP HIGHLIGHT

7 Borris

Handsome Borris is a seemingly untouched Georgian village, strung out like a string bean down the side of a hill, with a dramatic mountain backdrop. That's Mt Leinster, site of an excellent scenic drive.

🛏 p123

The Drive » It's 15km from Borris to St Mullins, mostly along the R729 with the Blackstairs Mountains to your left (east).

8 St Mullins

Tranquil little St Mullins sits 6km downstream from Graiguenamanagh, which is in County Kilkenny. The village is the maternal home of Michael Flatley of Riverdance fame. Sure enough, the river snakes through here in the shadow of Brandon Hill, as does the River Barrow towpath from Borris. From the river, a trail winds uphill to the ruined hulk of an old **monastery** surrounded by the graves of 1798 rebels. A 9th-century Celtic cross, badly worn down over the centuries, still stands beside the monastery. Nearby, **St Moling's Well** is a holy well that seems to attract spare change.

🛏 p123

The Drive » It's 27km from St Mullins to Bagenalstown via Borris. The 12km stretch of the R705 from Borris to Bagenalstown follows the scenic River Barrow Valley, one of the nicest bits of road in all of Carlow.

9 Bagenalstown

About 12km north of Borris is Bagenalstown, which isn't quite as handsome but is home to the **Carlow Brewing Company** (📞059-913 4356; www.carlowbrewing.com; Royal Oak Rd, Bagenalstown; tours by reservation €11) is a microbrewery that offers tours of its O'Hara's-brand beers. Its award-winning Irish stout bursts with flavour and certainly holds its own against that *other* Irish stout.

The Drive » Leighlinbridge is 4km on along the R705.

DETOUR:
KILGRANEY HOUSE HERB GARDENS

Start: 8 **St Mullins**

There are herbs as you've never seen them grow in orderly profusion in **Kilgraney House Herb Gardens** (www.kilgraneyhouse.com; Bagenalstown; admission €5; ⏱2-5pm Thu-Sun May-Sep), which boasts a heady cocktail of medicinal and kitchen plants and also serves as a source of food for the inn and restaurant here. The re-created medieval monastic herb garden is a favourite. It's off the R705 halfway between Borris and Bagenalstown.

---

10 Leighlinbridge

Leighlinbridge would be just another Carlow town if it weren't for the ominous ruins of the **Black Castle** (admission free) on the banks of Barrow. Built in 1181, this was one of the first Norman castles built in Ireland and was bequeathed to John de Claville by Henry II's lieutenant, Hugh de Lacy. The present castle was built by Sir Edward Bellingham in 1547 but was demolished by Cromwell's army in 1650. There's only half of a 14th-century round tower and a chunk of the bawn (defensive wall) left, but it is one of the most photogenic ruins in the whole county. You can access it from the river towpath.

CARLOW IN BLOOM

County Carlow is renowned for its gardens, 16 of which form part of Ireland's first dedicated **garden trail** (www.carlowgardentrail.com). Most tourist offices will have a copy of the invaluable (and free) guide *Carlow Garden Trail*. Flower fans shouldn't miss County Carlow's summertime Garden Festival.

Our top five gardens:

» **Delta Sensory Gardens** A multisensory, fountain-filled oasis.

» **Huntington Castle and Gardens** Rambling, overgrown grounds in the shadow of a haunted castle.

» **Duckett's Grove** Restored walled gardens behind a ruined Gothic mansion.

» **Kilgraney House Herb Gardens** Aromatic gardens filled with medicinal and kitchen plants.

» **Altamont Gardens** Heritage-listed Victorian splendour, hosting a weeklong Snowdrop Festival in February.

Eating & Sleeping

Carlow Town ❶

✗ Lennons   Modern Irish €€

(www.lennons.ie; off College St; mains €8-18; ⏱lunch daily, dinner Thu-Sat) Carlow's best dining is found amid the artsy surrounds of the Visual Centre for Contemporary Arts. It's a sleek and appropriately stylish space, with a wide patio outside where you can see sculpture on the centre's grassy grounds. Lunch features creative sandwiches, salads and hot specials. Dinner is more refined with a seasonal menu that emphasises the organic.

⌂ Red Setter Guest House   B&B €€

(📞059-914 1848; www.redsetterguesthouse. ie; 14 Dublin St; s/d from €40/70; 🅿🛜) Great attention to detail and extra touches like gorgeous bouquets of fresh flowers make this otherwise humble B&B the winning in-town choice. Breakfasts are grand and the owners can't do enough to be helpful.

Ballon ❺

✗ Forge Restaurant   Irish €€

(Kilbride Cross; dishes €5-11; ⏱9.30am-5.30pm Mon-Sat, 11am-6pm Sun) Mary Jordan cooks up steaming soups and hot lunches, as well as baked goods to take away, at this hugely popular roadside inn near Altamont Gardens. Local produce is used, and there's often a wait for a table at weekends. A shop sells local art and crafts.

⌂ Sherwood Park House   Inn €€

(📞059-915 9117; www.sherwoodparkhouse. ie; Kilbride; s/d from €60/100; 🅿) Inside a greystone Georgian manor dating from 1730, the five rooms here are huge and boast such period niceties as satin- and velvet-adorned four-poster beds. You can make arrangements for dinner (€40 per person; BYO wine).

Borris ❼

⌂ Step House Hotel   Hotel €€

(📞059-977 3209; www.stephousehotel.ie; 66 Main St; s/d from €65/130; 🅿🛜) At the top end of town, this Georgian home has undergone a stunning makeover in elegant shades of pistachio. Its 23 rooms boast balconies and have a clever opulence. Views are framed by Mt Leinster. Tables in the Cellar Restaurant are tucked in romantic corners beneath vaulted ceilings.

St Mullins ❽

⌂ Old Grain Store   Cottage €€

(📞051-424 4440; www.oldgrainstorecottages. ie; per week €300-480) Three self-catering cottages sleeping two to four people are set in the coach house, the forge and the stables. The cottages' interiors are stylish yet homey, with shelves of books and wood-burning stoves. A fabulous cafe here serves fresh meals (open 11am to 6pm Tuesday to Sunday in summer, hours vary at other times).

Kilkenny Mesmerising sights and picture-postcard villages

Kilkenny's Treasures

10

Its namesake city is its marvellous centrepiece, but County Kilkenny's rolling hills, dotted with relics of Irish history, will soon have you running out of adjectives for green.

TRIP HIGHLIGHTS

0 km

Kilkenny
A medieval treasure trove amid the alleyways

1
START

● Bennettsbridge

Graiguenamanagh
● FINISH

Thomastown

5

7   **45 km**

35 km

Jerpoint Abbey
Magnificent church ruins in splendid setting

Inistioge
18th-century village with vintage shops and a stone bridge

3 DAYS
58KM / 36 MILES

GREAT FOR...

BEST TIME TO GO

Spring and autumn are ideal: the weather's good but there are fewer visitors.

ESSENTIAL PHOTO

Kells Priory at dusk.

BEST FOR TRADITIONAL CRAFTS

The exquisitely made artisanal crafts at the Nicholas Mosse Irish Country Shop.

125

10 Kilkenny's Treasures

The enduring gift of the Normans, Kilkenny mesmerises visitors with its medieval alleys and castle, ruined abbeys and outstanding modern-day nightlife. Beyond the city limits, tiny roads navigate the beautiful valleys past the mementos of 800 years of Irish history, picture-postcard villages and a dynamic contemporary craft industry whose reputation is admired countrywide.

TRIP HIGHLIGHT

❶ Kilkenny

Kilkenny (Cill Chainnigh) is the Ireland of many visitors' imaginations. Its majestic riverside castle, tangle of 17th-century passageways, rows of colourful, old-fashioned shopfronts and centuries-old pubs with traditional live music all have a timeless appeal, as does its splendid medieval cathedral.

Kilkenny's architectural charm owes a huge debt to the Middle

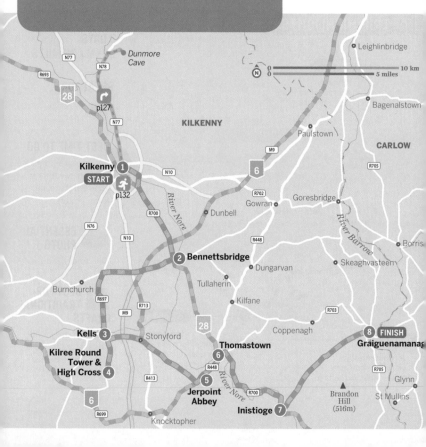

DETOUR: DUNMORE CAVE

Start: ❶ **Kilkenny**

Just 6km north of Kilkenny on the Castlecomer road (N78) are the striking calcite formations of **Dunmore Cave** (📞056-776 7726; www.heritageireland.ie; Ballyfoyle; adult/child €3/1; ⏰9.30am-6.30pm Jun-Sep, to 5pm Mar-May & Sep-Oct, to 5pm Wed-Sun Nov-Mar). In 928 marauding Vikings killed 1000 people at two ring forts near here. When survivors hid in the caverns, the Vikings tried to smoke them out by lighting fires at the entrance. It's thought that they then dragged off the men as slaves and left the women and children to suffocate. Excavations in 1973 uncovered the skeletons of at least 44 people, mostly women and children. They also found coins dating from the 10th century.

Admission to the cave is via a compulsory but highly worthwhile guided tour. Although well lit and spacious, it's damp and cold; bring warm clothes.

Ages, when the city was a seat of political power. It's also sometimes called the 'marble city' because of the local black limestone, used on floors and in decorative trim all over town.

You can cover pretty much everything on foot in half a day (see

LINK YOUR TRIP

 6 **Ancient Ireland**
From Kilree or Jerpoint Abbey you can connect to this trip that visits some of ancient Ireland's most important sites.

28 **Tip to Toe**
Kilkenny is one of the main stops on the classic Tip to Toe trip, which explores Ireland from north to south.

our walking tour, p132), but sampling its many delights will take much longer.

🛏 p131

The Drive » Drive southwest with the castle and the Nore on your immediate left until you reach the R700, aka the Bennettsbridge Rd. It's only a short 7km drive to Bennettsbridge.

❷ Bennettsbridge

Bennettsbridge is an arts-and-crafts treasure chest, although these treasures are scattered throughout the town, rather than within a concentrated area.

In a big mill by the river west of town, the **Nicholas Mosse Irish Country Shop** (www. nicholasmosse.com; ⏰10am-6pm Mon-Sat, 1.30-5pm Sun) specialises in handmade spongeware – creamy-brown pottery decorated with sponged patterns.

It also sells linens and other handmade craft items (although some hail from lands of cheap labour far from Ireland). Its cafe is the best choice locally for lunch, with a creative line-up of soups, sandwiches, hot dishes and its renowned scones.

On a small road above Nicholas Mosse, the **Nore View Folk Museum** (📞056-27749; Danesfort Rd; adult/child €5/2; ⏰10am-6pm) is the labour of love of Seamus Lawlor, a passionate chronicler of Irish life. The museum is full of fascinating facts about his private collection of local items, including farming tools, kitchen utensils and other wonderful old bric-a-brac. Opening hours vary.

The Drive » The 12km drive to Kells takes you across the flat, luscious green plain of central Kilkenny. Follow the Annamult Rd towards the N10, but turn left onto the R697.

❸ Kells

Kells (not to be confused with Kells in County Meath) is a mere hamlet with a fine stone bridge on a tributary of the Nore. However, in **Kells Priory**, the village has one of Ireland's most impressive and romantic monastic sites. This is the best sort of ruin, where visitors can amble about whenever they like, with no tour guides, tours, set hours or fees. At dusk on a vaguely sunny day, the old priory is simply beautiful. Most days you stand a chance of exploring the site alone (apart from bleating and pooping sheep).

The ruins are 500m east of Kells on the Stonyford road.

The Drive » Kilree is only 3km south of Kells along a small country road.

RICHARD CUMMINS/GETTY IMAGES ©

❹ Kilree Round Tower & High Cross

Standing in an overgrown graveyard is a 29m-high round tower that has lost its cap. It was built sometime between the 8th and 11th centuries, and served as a bell tower, although it was also a handy place of refuge for locals looking to escape the unwelcome attention of invaders.

Next to it, standing more than 2m tall, is a simple early high cross that was long believed to be the grave of a 9th-century Irish high king, Niall Caille, who drowned in the nearby river in 847 while attempting the rescue of a servant or soldier, even though experts now reckon the cross is older than that. Still, Niall's resting place lies beyond the church grounds because he wasn't a Christian.

The Drive » The 17km drive will have you doubling back towards Kells, but then taking a right on the Stonyford road, past Kells Priory. You'll pass Mt Juliet on your left. Turn left on the R448, and Jerpoint Abbey is a further 1km on your right.

TRIP HIGHLIGHT

❺ Jerpoint Abbey

Ireland has an abundance of church ruins, but few are quite as magnificent as those of **Jerpoint Abbey** (☏056-24623; www.heritageireland.ie; adult/child €3/1; ⏰9am-5.30pm Mar-Oct, check hours Nov-Feb), a fine exemplar of Cistercian power and church-building. The abbey was first established in the 12th century, with the tower and cloister added sometime in the late 14th or early 15th century. The excellent 45-minute tours happen throughout the day. Set

Kilkenny Flowers in bloom on a Kilkenny street

yourself apart in the remains of the cloisters and see if you can hear the faint echo of a chant.

According to local legend, St Nicholas (or Santa Claus) is buried near the abbey. While retreating in the Crusades, the knights of Jerpoint removed his body from Myra in modern-day Turkey and reburied him in the **Church of St Nicholas** to the west of the abbey. The grave is marked by a broken slab decorated with a carving of a monk.

The Drive » Thomastown is only a quick 2.5km northeast of Jerpoint on the R448.

6 Thomastown

Named after Welsh mercenary Thomas de Cantwell, Thomastown has some fragments of a medieval wall and the partly ruined 13th-century **Church of**

St Mary. Down by the bridge, **Mullin's Castle** is the sole survivor of the 14 castles once here.

Like the rest of Kilkenny, the area has a vibrant craft scene. Look out for **Clay Creations** (Low St; ☺10am-5pm

TEEING OFF IN THOMASTOWN

Just 4km west of Thomastown, high-fliers tee off at the Jack Nicklaus–blessed **Mount Juliet** (www. mountjuliet.ie; green fees from €100). Set over 600 wooded hectares, it also has its own equestrian centre, a gym and spa, two restaurants, wine master-classes, and posh rooms catering to every whim, right down to the pillow menu (accommodation from €120).

TOWN OF BOOKS

Graiguenamanagh's narrow streets spill over in mid-September with booksellers, authors and bibliophiles during the three-day **Town of Books Festival** (www.booktownireland.com). Plans are under way for Graiguenamanagh to become a year-round 'book town' in the same vein as Wales' Hay-on-Wye. Meanwhile, there are a couple of good used and antiquarian bookshops.

Wed-Sat), displaying the quixotic ceramics and sculptures of local artist Brid Lyons.

✗ p131

The Drive ›› The 9km drive south to Inistioge along the R700 is a splendidly scenic one through the valley of the River Nore; keep an eye out for the views of the ruined 13th-century Grennan Castle on your right as you go.

- - - - - - - - - - - -

TRIP HIGHLIGHT

7 Inistioge

The little village of Inistioge (*in*-ish-teeg) is a picture. Its 18th-century, 10-arch **stone bridge** spans the River Nore and vintage shops face its tranquil square.

About 500m south of the village is the heavily forested **Woodstock Gardens** (www.woodstock. ie; ⏱9am-7pm Apr-Sep, 10am-4pm Oct-Mar), a beauty of

a park with expansive 19th-century gardens, picnic areas and trails. The panorama of the valley and village below is spectacular. Coming from town, follow the signs for Woodstock Estate and enter the large gates (despite appearances, it's a public road), then continue along the road for about 1km until you reach the car park (parking €4 in coins).

✗ 🛏 p131

The Drive ›› It's 11km from Inistioge to Graiguenamanagh on the Graigue road, aka the L4209, so narrow that you'll wonder if there's room for oncoming traffic (there is).

- - - - - - - - - - - -

8 Graiguenamanagh

Graiguenamanagh (greg-*na*-muh-na; known locally simply as Graigue)

is the kind of place where you could easily find yourself staying longer than planned. Spanning the Barrow, an ancient six-arch stone bridge is illuminated at night and connects the village with the smaller township of Tinnahinch on the County Carlow side of the river (look for the darker stones on the Carlow side – a legacy from being blown up during the 1798 rebellion).

The big attraction in town is the Cistercian **Duiske Abbey** (⏱8am-6pm), once Ireland's largest and still very much a working parish (thanks to 800 years of changes and additions). To the right of the entrance look for the **Knight of Duiske**, a 14th-century, high-relief carving of a knight in chain mail who's reaching for his sword. On the floor nearby, a glass panel reveals some of the original 13th-century floor tiles, now 2m below the present floor level.

🛏 p131

Eating & Sleeping

Kilkenny ❶

🛏 Butler House   Hotel €€

(☎056-772 2828; www.butler.ie; 16 Patrick St; s €60-120, d €100-180; P @ 🛜) You can't stay in Kilkenny Castle, but this historic mansion is surely the next best thing. Once the home of the earls of Ormonde, who built the castle, these days it houses a boutique hotel with aristocratic trappings including sweeping staircases, marble fireplaces, an art collection and impeccably trimmed gardens. The 13 generously sized rooms are individually decorated. Just to remind you you're staying in history, the floors creak.

🛏 Campagne   Modern Irish €€€

(☎056-777 2858; www.campagne.ie; The Arches, 5 Gashouse Lane; lunch 2-/3-course set menu €24/29, dinner mains €25-30; ⊙lunch Fri-Sun, dinner Tue-Sat) Chef Garrett Byrne, who gained fame and Michelin stars in Dublin, is the genius behind this bold, stylish restaurant in his native Kilkenny. He's passionate about supporting local and artisan producers, and he takes the goods and produces ever-changing, ever-memorable meals. There's a French accent to everything he does.

Thomastown ❻

🍴 Blackberry Cafe   Cafe €

(Market St; dishes €4.50-7.50, ⊙9.30am-5.30pm Mon-Fri, 10am-5.30pm Sat) Superb thick-cut sandwiches and warming soups are served with pumpkin-seed-speckled soda bread here. Much is organic and the tarts and cakes are baked daily. Between noon and 2pm, great-value multicourse hot lunches see the place squeezed to bursting. It's right in town.

Inistioge ❼

🍴 Bassetts at Woodstock   Modern Irish €€€

(☎056-775 8820; www.bassetts.ie; mains €10-28; ⊙lunch Wed-Sun, dinner Wed-Sat) Adjacent to Woodstock Gardens, John Bassett has turned his family home into an inspired dining experience. Saturday nights feature tasting menus (€9.50 per course) paired with wines (from €5 per glass) served at set intervals from 7.30pm. It's a great way to spend an evening with a table of friends. The food is fresh, local and inventive. Future meals graze right outside the door.

🛏 Woodstock Arms   B&B €€

(☎056-775 8440; www.woodstockarms.com; s/d from €45/70) This friendly pub has tables outside overlooking the square and seven simple rooms that are squeaky clean. The triples are particularly spacious. Breakfast is served in a pretty little room out back with wooden tables and blue-and-white china.

Graiguenamanagh ❽

🛏 Waterside   Inn €€

(☎059-972 4246; www.watersideguesthouse. com; The Quay; s/d from €55/80) Down by the boats tied up along the river, this inviting guesthouse and restaurant occupies a converted solid-granite 19th-century corn store. Its 10 renovated rooms have exposed timber beams. The restaurant is well regarded for its interesting modern Irish menu (mains €18 to €26) and its regular 'After Dinner Live' music acts featuring anything from jazz to bluegrass.

STRETCH YOUR LEGS
KILKENNY

Start/Finish Kilkenny Castle

Distance 2.5km

Duration 2 hours

Kilkenny's medieval centre is conveniently compact, with most of the major sights collected between the castle to the south and the cathedral to the north.

Take this walk on Trips

`10` `28`

Kilkenny Castle

Rising above the Nore, **Kilkenny Castle** (www.kilkennycastle.ie; adult/child €6/2.50; ⊕9am-5.30pm Mar-Sep, 9.30am-4.30pm Oct-Feb) is one of Ireland's most visited heritage sites. Regular 40-minute guided tours focus on the **Long Gallery**, in the wing of the castle nearest the river. The gallery, which showcases stuffy portraits of the Butler family members over the centuries, is an impressive hall with high ceilings vividly painted with Celtic and Pre-Raphaelite motifs.

The Walk » Cross Castle Rd; the design centre is adjacent to the castle.

National Craft Gallery & Design Centre

Contemporary Irish crafts are showcased at this imaginative **gallery** (www.ccoi.ie; Castle Yard; ⊕10am-5.30pm Tue-Sat) in the former castle stables that also house the shops of the Kilkenny Design Centre. Ceramics dominate, but exhibits often feature furniture, jewellery and weaving from the members of the Crafts Council of Ireland.

The Walk » Turn left and walk north onto High St until you reach the Tholsel on your right.

Tholsel

The Tholsel (City Hall) on High St was built in 1761 on the spot where Dame Alice Kyteler's maid Petronella was burned at the stake in 1324 for witchcraft (even if it was actually Dame Alice who was most likely the guilty party).

The Walk » The Butter Slip is a narrow alley just right after the Tholsel.

Butter Slip

With its arched entry and stone steps, Butter Slip, a narrow and dark walkway connecting High St with St Kieran's St (previously called Low Lane), is the most picturesque of Kilkenny's many narrow medieval corridors. It was built

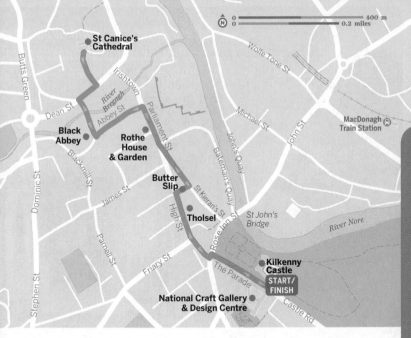

in 1616 and was once lined with the stalls of butter vendors.

The Walk » Turn left on St Kieran's St and rejoin High St; Rothe House is on your left.

Rothe House & Garden

Ireland's best surviving example of a 16th-century merchant's house is the Tudor Rothe House. Built around a series of courtyards, it now houses a **museum** (www.rothehouse.com; Parliament St; adult/child €5/4; ⏰10.30am-5pm Mon-Sat year-round, 2-6pm Sun Apr-Oct) with local artefacts including a well-used Viking sword found nearby and a grinning head sculpted by a Celtic artist. Recent changes include new exhibits about the Rothe family and ongoing restorations of the urban gardens out the back.

The Walk » Turn left on Parliament St and after 200m take a left on Abbey St.

Black Abbey

This Dominican **abbey** (Abbey St; ⏰open daily for Mass) was founded in 1225 by William Marshall and takes its name

from the monks' black habits. In 1543, six years after Henry VIII's dissolution of the monasteries, it was turned into a courthouse. Much of what survives dates from the 18th and 19th centuries, but remnants of more ancient archways are evident within the newer stonework. Look for the 13th-century coffins near the entrance.

The Walk » Walk north through the lane and take a right on Dean St, then a left onto Coach St into the cathedral grounds.

St Canice's Cathedral

Soaring over the north end of the centre is Ireland's second-largest medieval **cathedral** (www.stcanicescathedral.ie; St Canice's Pl; adult/child €4/3; ⏰9am-6pm Mon-Sat, 2-6pm Sun) after St Patrick's in Dublin. Legend has it that the first monastery was built here in the 6th century by St Canice, Kilkenny's patron saint.

The Walk » Go back down Parliament St to the castle, stopping in a pub or two along the way.

Tintern Abbey Secluded amid woode
trails, lakes and idyllic stream

Wexford & Waterford

11

Ireland's favourite beach destinations are dotted along the coastlines of counties Wexford and Waterford, but there's far more to the region than just buckets and spades.

TRIP HIGHLIGHTS

164 km

Dungarvan
Bustling port of pastel-coloured houses and excellent foodie scene

75 km

Tintern Abbey
Moody ruins of a once-powerful Cistercian abbey

START
● Enniscorthy

Arthurstown ● ③

②

⑥

● Ardmore
FINISH

Kilmore Quay
Fishing village straight out of a postcard

43 km

5 DAYS
219KM / 136 MILES

GREAT FOR...

BEST TIME TO GO
April to September for the long days and best weather.

ESSENTIAL PHOTO
Look down on lovely Ardmore from St Declan's Church.

BEST FOR CULTURE
Learn about bloody Irish history at the National 1798 Rebellion Centre.

135

Wexford & Waterford

Collectively labelled the 'sunny southeast', Wexford and Waterford get less rainfall and more sunshine than anywhere else in Ireland, but the southeastern counties are about more than resort towns and pretty beaches. There's history aplenty round here, some stunning inland scenery and a vibrant foodie scene that mightn't be as well known as that in neighbouring Cork but is just as good.

❶ Enniscorthy

Busy Enniscorthy (Inis Coirthaidh) is an attractive hilly town on the banks of the Slaney in the heart of County Wexford, 20km north of Wexford town. For Irishmen, its name is forever linked to some of the fiercest fighting of the 1798 Rising, when rebels captured the town and castle and set up camp nearby at **Vinegar Hill**.

Before climbing the hill (a 2km drive east of town), acquaint

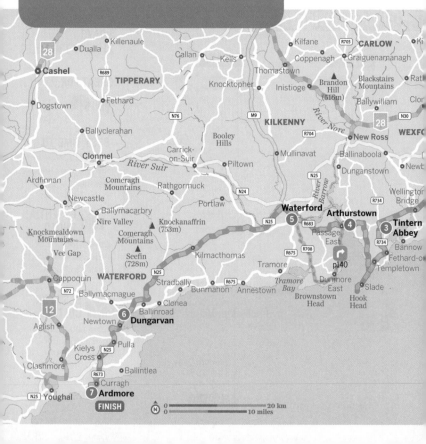

yourself with the story of the rebellion with a visit to the **National 1798 Rebellion Centre** (www.1798centre.ie; Mill Park Rd; adult/child €6/3.50; ⏲9.30am-5pm Mon-Fri, noon-5pm Sat & Sun), which tells the story of Wexford's abortive uprising against British rule in all its gory, fascinating detail. The rebels were inspired by the French and American revolutions, but were beaten back by English troops, who then massacred hundreds of women and children as reprisal for the uprising.

If you want to walk up Vinegar Hill, from Abbey Sq walk out of town along Mill Park Rd or south along the river.

🛏 p141

The Drive » It's 43km to Kilmore Quay. You'll skirt around Wexford Town on your way south along the N11; beyond the town, follow the directions for Rosslare and take the N25. Turn right onto the R739 to Kilmore Quay. The last stretch of road is the most scenic, as the countryside opens up in front of you.

- - - - - - - - - - - - - -

TRIP HIGHLIGHT

② Kilmore Quay

Straight out of a postcard, peaceful Kilmore Quay is a small village on the eastern side of Ballyteige Bay, noted for its lobsters and deep-sea fishing. Lining the attractive main street up from the harbour are a series of pretty whitewashed thatched cottages. The harbour is the jumping-off point for the Saltee Islands, home to Ireland's largest bird sanctuary, clearly visible out to sea.

The four-day **Seafood Festival** (www.kilmorequayseafoodfestival.

com) in the second week of July involves all types of seafood tastings, music and dancing.

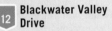 p141

The Drive » It's 29km from Kilmore Quay to the ruins of Tintern Abbey along the narrow R733. The promontory east of the Hook Peninsula, signposted as the Bannow Drive, is littered with Norman ruins, while Bannow Bay is a wildfowl sanctuary. As you cross Wellington Bridge onto the Hook Peninsula, keep an eye out for the remains of medieval Clonmines to the southwest.

- - - - - - - - - - - - - -

TRIP HIGHLIGHT

③ Tintern Abbey

In better structural condition than its Welsh counterpart, from where its first monks hailed, Ireland's moody **Tintern Abbey** (adult/child €3/1; ⏲10am-6pm mid-May–Sep) is secluded amid 40 hectares of woodland. William Marshal, Earl of Pembroke, founded the Cistercian abbey in the early 13th century after he nearly perished at sea and swore to establish a church if he made it ashore.

LINK YOUR TRIP

12 Blackwater Valley Drive

It's only 5km from Ardmore to Youghal and the start of the Blackwater Valley Drive.

28 Tip to Toe

You can hook up to this long country-length trip in Kilmore Quay.

DETOUR: SALTEE ISLANDS

Start: ❷ **Kilmore Quay**

Just 4km offshore and accessible from Kilmore Quay via local boat (depending on the weather), the **Saltee Islands** (www.salteeislands.info; ⏱11.30am-4pm) constitute one of Europe's most important bird sanctuaries, home to over 375 recorded species, principally the gannet, guillemot, cormorant, kittiwake, puffin and the Manx shearwater. It's a noisier but more peaceful existence than its past as the favoured haunt of privateers and smugglers. The islands are also where you'll find some of the oldest rocks in Europe, dating back 2000 million years or more; findings also suggest that the islands were inhabited by the pre-Celts as long ago as 3500 to 2000 BC.

The best time to visit is the spring and early-summer nesting season; once the chicks can fly, the birds leave. By early August it's eerily quiet.

To get here, try **Declan Bates** (☎053-912 9684, 087 252 9736; day trip €30) but be sure to book in advance. You can park the car in the town.

The abbey is 1.5km from the town of Saltmills, amid wooded trails, lakes and idyllic streams. The grounds are always open, and a walk here is worth the trip at any time.

The Drive ≫ The 9km route across the Hook Peninsula along the R753 is the quickest way to Arthurstown, but the most scenic route is the 35km circumference of the peninsula, passing villages like Slade, where the most activity is in the swirl of seagulls above the ruined castle and harbour. Beaches include the wonderfully secluded Dollar Bay and Booley Bay, just beyond Templetown. Don't forget to spot the world's oldest working lighthouse right at Hook Head.

---

❹ Arthurstown

Chef Kevin Dundon is a familiar face on Irish TV, and the author of cookbooks *Full On Irish* and *Great Family Food*.

His spa hotel **Dunbrody Country House** (☎051-389 600; www.dunbrodyhouse.com; s/d €140/225, multicourse meals from €60; P 🛜), in a period-decorated 1830s Georgian manor on 120-hectare grounds, is the stuff of foodies' fantasies, with a gourmet restaurant and cookery school (one-day courses from €175).

Beside the R733, some 6km north of Dundon's pile, the ruined **Dunbrody Abbey** (www.dunbrodyabbey. com; Campile; adult/child €2/1; ⏱11am-5pm May–mid-Sep) is a remarkably intact Cistercian abbey founded by Strongbow in 1170 and completed in 1220. A combined ticket (adult/child €4/2) includes a **museum** with a huge doll's house, minigolf, and a very fun yew-hedge **maze** made up of over 1500 trees.

The Drive ≫ Instead of going the long way around, cut out a long detour around Waterford Harbour and the River Barrow by taking the five-minute car ferry between Ballyhack in County Wexford and Passage East in County Waterford. Then follow the R683 to Waterford City. This way is only 15km long.

---

❺ Waterford City

Inhabited since AD 914, Waterford (Port Láirge) is Ireland's oldest city, and much of the centre's street plan has retained its medieval feel.

Waterford's 1000-year history is told in wonderful fashion in a trio of museums collectively known as the **Waterford Museum of Treasures** (www. waterfordtreasures.com) and include **Reginald's Tower** (The Quay; adult/child €3/1; ⏱10am-5pm), the oldest complete building in

Saltee Islands Home to over 375 recorded bird species including the puffin

DETOUR:
PASSAGE COAST ROAD

Start: ❹ **Arthurstown**

A little-travelled 11km-long coast road wiggles south between Passage East and Dunmore East to the south. At times single-vehicle-width and steep, it offers mesmerising views of the ocean and undulating fields that you won't see from the main thoroughfares. Follow the R708 north to Waterford city.

Ireland; the **Bishop's Palace** (The Mall; adult/child €5/2; ⊙9am-6pm Mon-Sat, from 11am Sun), home to a superb interactive museum; and the brand-new **Chorister's Hall** (Greyfriar's St), which tells the story of Waterford life before 1700.

Since 1783 the city has been famous for its production of high-quality crystal, but the factory closed in 2009 and all that's left is the **House of Waterford Crystal** (www.waterfordvisitorcentre.com; The Mall; adult/child €12/4; ⊙9am-5pm), a flashy showroom where you can see some pieces of crystal being blown, but most of the stuff you buy in the shop is made in Eastern Europe.

❌ 🛏 p141

The Drive » Follow the southern bank of the River Suir and take the N25 to get to Dungarvan, 41km away. Or travel south and take the R675 coastal route along the stunning Copper Coast, where you'll meet cerulean skies, azure waters, impossibly green hills and ebony cliff faces along the way.

TRIP HIGHLIGHT

❻ Dungarvan

It isn't enough that Dungarvan has the looks: pastel-coloured houses huddled around a boat-filled port at the mouth of the River Colligan make it one of the southeast's prettiest towns. It now has the charm, in the form of a foodie reputation that makes it a must-stop destination for anyone looking to get the best of Irish cuisine.

At the heart of the town is the Norman **castle** (www.heritageireland.ie; ⊙10am-6pm Jun-Sep), which is slowly being restored to its once impregnable glory. But the real draws are culinary: Paul Flynn's **Tannery Cookery School** (📞058-45420; www.tannery.ie; 10 Quay St; courses €50-200), adjoining a fruit, veg and herb garden, is one of Ireland's best. The annual **Waterford Festival of Food** (www.waterfordfestivaloffood.com; ⊙mid-Apr) celebrates the area's abundant fresh produce.

❌ 🛏 p141

The Drive » It's an easy 25km drive along the N25 to the turn-off for Ardmore, which then becomes the very rural R673 as you move south to the coast. This is rural Ireland at its most pristine, with farmhouses the only interruption to a stretch of undulating fields and stone walls.

❼ Ardmore

The enticing seaside village of Ardmore may look quiet these days, but it's claimed that St Declan set up shop here between 350 and 420. This brought Christianity to southeast Ireland long before St Patrick arrived from Britain.

In a striking position on a hill above town, the ruins of **St Declan's Church** stand on the site of St Declan's original monastery alongside an impressive cone-roofed, 29m-high, 12th-century **round tower**, one of the best examples of these structures in Ireland.

If you're looking for a bit of beautiful seclusion, you'll find it on **Ballyquin beach**, home to tide pools, fascinating rocks and sheltered sand. It's 1km off the R673, 4km northeast of Ardmore. Look for the small sign.

🛏 p141

Eating & Sleeping

Enniscorthy ❶

🛏 Woodbrook House   Inn €€

(📞053-925 5114; www.woodbrookhouse.
ie; Killanne; s/d from €95/150; ❄ @ 🛜 🏊)
Damaged in the 1798 rebellion, this glorious
country estate is now a three-room guesthouse.
Green practices are used throughout and you
can make arrangements for dinner (organic, of
course). It is 13km west of Enniscorthy.

Kilmore Quay ❷

🍴 Silver Fox
Seafood Restaurant   Seafood €€€

(www.thesilverfox.ie; Kilmore Quay; mains
€18-32; 🕓noon-10pm May-Sep, reduced hours
other times) Just back from the quay, the Silver
Fox's fresh-from-the-ocean offerings include
a creamy fisherman's pie filled with prawns,
monkfish, salmon and cod, plus all manner
of specials depending on what arrives at the
docks.

🛏 Mill Road Farm   B&B €€

(📞053-912 9633; www.millroadfarm.com; R739;
s/d €45/70; 🕓closed late Dec; 🅿 🛜) About
2km northeast of Kilmore Quay on the R739,
this working dairy farm offers simple rooms
and breakfasts featuring homemade bread and
free-range eggs. It closes from Christmas Eve to
New Year's Day.

Waterford City ❺

🍴 L'Atmosphere   French €€

(051-858 426; 19 Henrietta St; mains €12-25;
🕓lunch Mon-Fri, dinner daily; 🛜) Classic
French dishes with modern Irish flair (and
Waterford produce) are served with élan.
Perhaps hard to imagine, but you really will need
to try to save room for dessert – it's superb.

🛏 Waterford Castle   Hotel €€€

(📞051-878 203; www.waterfordcastle.com;
The Island, Ballinakill; s €90-150, d €120-

240; 🅿 @ 🛜) Getting away from it all is an
understatement at this mid-19th-century
turreted castle, which is located on its own
124-hectare island roamed by deer. A free,
private car ferry signposted just east of the
Waterford Regional Hospital provides round-
the-clock access.

Dungarvan ❻

🍴 Tannery   Modern Irish €€€

(📞058-45420; www.tannery.ie; 10 Quay St;
mains €18-29; 🕓12.30-2.30pm Fri & Sun,
6-9.30pm Tue-Sat, also Sun Jul & Aug) An old
leather tannery houses this innovative and
much-lauded restaurant, where Paul Flynn
creates seasonally changing dishes that
focus on just a few flavours and celebrates
them through preparations that are at once
comforting yet surprising. Book so you don't
miss out.

🛏 Powersfield House   B&B €€

(📞058-45594; www.powersfield.com;
Ballinamuck West; s/d from €60/90; 🅿 🛜)
Energetic chef and Tannery cookery instructor
Eunice Power lives in one half of this Georgian
home with her family, and has opened six
beautifully decorated rooms in the other for
guests. It's a five-minute drive north of town on
the road to Clonmel.

Ardmore ❼

🛏 Cliff House Hotel   Hotel €€€

(📞024-87800; www.thecliffhousehotel.com;
r €225-450; 🅿 @ 🛜 🏊) Built into the cliff face,
all guest rooms at this cutting-edge edifice
overlook the bay, and most have balconies or
terraces. Some suites even have two-person
floor-to-ceiling glass showers (strategically
frosted in places) so you don't miss those sea
views. There are also sea views from the indoor
swimming pool, outdoor jacuzzi and spa, the bar
and the much-lauded modern Irish restaurant
(menu from €60). Service is discreet but
anticipatory.

Youghul Explore the River Blackwate_ from the ancient seapo._

Blackwater Valley Drive

12

Great things come in short drives: the Blackwater Valley trip is only 64km long, but packed with history, culture, stunning views and great places to stay – all off the beaten track.

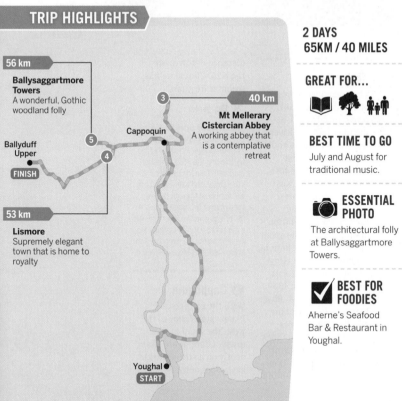
143

Blackwater Valley Drive

This short drive takes you through one of the most scenic and historic stretches of southern Ireland. From the mouth of the River Blackwater in Youghal (where you can take to the river by boat), explore the river valley northwards as far as historic Lismore before turning west with the river to find traditional villages, beautiful mountain passes and one of the country's best centres for traditional music and dancing.

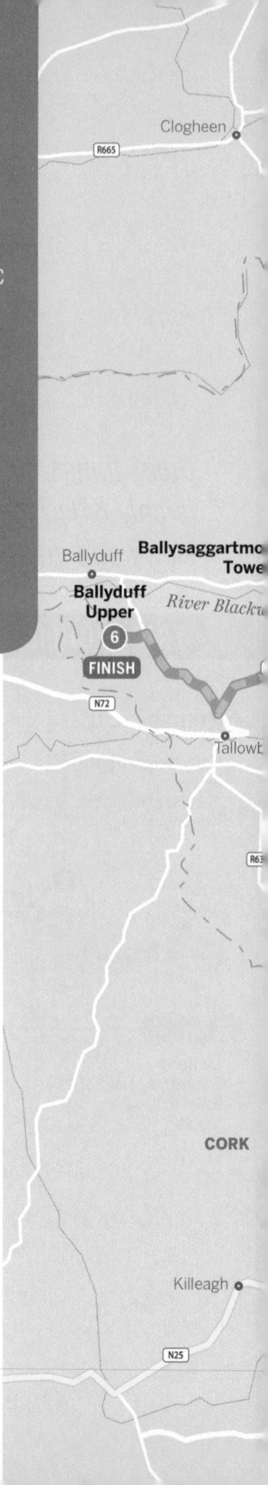

1 Youghal

The ancient seaport of Youghal (Eochaill; pronounced yawl), at the mouth of the River Blackwater, was a hotbed of rebellion against the English in the 16th century. Youghal was granted to Sir Walter Raleigh during the Elizabethan Plantation of Munster, and he spent brief spells living here in his house, Myrtle Grove. Oliver Cromwell spent the winter here in 1649.

Youghal has two Blue Flag beaches, ideal for building sandcastles modelled after the Clock Gate. **Claycastle** (2km) and **Front Strand** (1km) are both within walking distance of town, off the N25. Claycastle has summer lifeguards.

✗ ⌂ p149

The Drive ›› Start the 33km drive by taking the N25 east towards Dungarvan and then go north along the R671 (direction Clonmel). Take the turn for Villierstown and follow the route to Cappoquin through the tree-lined road of Dromana Woods. At the bridge over the River Finisk is a remarkable Hindu-Gothic gate, inspired by the Brighton Pavilion in England and unique to Ireland.

2 Cappoquin

With the picturesque Blackwater Valley to the west, the small market town of Cappoquin sits neatly on a steep hillside at the foot of the rounded,

heathery Knockmealdown Mountains.

Cappoquin House and Gardens (www.cappoquinhouseandgardens.com; house €5, garden €5; ☉9am-1pm Mon-Sat Apr-Jul, by appointment rest of year) is a magnificent 1779-built Georgian mansion and 2 hectares of formal gardens overlooking the River Blackwater. The entrance to the house is just north of the centre of Cappoquin; look for a set of huge black iron gates.

Cappoquin is also a good spot for anglers, as the town is right at the head of the Blackwater estuary, where there's some of the best game and coarse fishing in the country. The fishing season runs from the beginning of February to 30 September; in order to fish for salmon you'll have to purchase a state licence (one day/21 days €20/400) and a day

LINK YOUR TRIP

11 Wexford & Waterford

Ardmore is only 5km from Youghal, from which you can explore the sunny southeast.

20 The Holy Glen

Head 42km north from Lismore to Clonmel and explore some of Ireland's most important monastic sites.

DETOUR:
ARDMORE

Start: ❶ Youghal

Just 5km east of Youghal, and south off the N25 is the beautifully isolated seaside village of Ardmore, whose setting and heritage are unmatched – St Declan brought Christianity here a good century before St Patrick showed up. The ruins of **St Declan's Church** stand on the site of St Declan's original monastery, next to one of Ireland's best examples of a 12th-century round tower.

Ardmore is also home to one of the country's best hotels, the **Cliff House** (☑024-87800; www.thecliffhousehotel.com; r €225-450; P @ 🛜 🎘), which has a Michelin-starred restaurant (menu from €60). From the hotel, there's a lovely, 5km-circular **walk** that takes you past St Declan's Well, Ireland's oldest Christian ruin; the wreck of a crane ship that blew ashore in 1987; and a WWII lookout post.

permit (€20); you can buy both at the **Titelines Tackle & Gift Shop** (☑058-54152; Main St).

✕ 🍴 📋 p149

The Drive » It's only 6.5km to Mt Melleray. Just right off the R669 to Mt Melleray is a signpost for Glenshelane Park, which has lovely forest walks and picnic spots that are popular with locals.

- - - - - - - - - -

TRIP HIGHLIGHT

❸ Mt Melleray Cistercian Abbey

A fully functioning monastery that is home to two dozen Trappist monks, the beautiful 19th-century **Mt Melleray Cistercian Abbey** (www.mountmellerayabbey.org; admission free; ☼7am-7pm) in the Knockmealdown foothills welcomes visitors wishing 'to take time for quiet contemplation'. In 1954 six of the monks departed for New Zealand, where

they founded the Abbey of Our Lady of the Southern Star in a remote location near Takapau, on the North Island. There are tearooms (closed Monday) and a heritage centre.

The Drive » You'll have to double-back to Cappoquin (6.5km) and then take the N72 west for 6km to Lismore. The Blackwater River will be on your left as you go.

- - - - - - - - - -

TRIP HIGHLIGHT

❹ Lismore

Over the centuries, statesmen and luminaries have streamed through quiet, elegant Lismore, the location of a great monastic university founded by St Carthage in the 7th century. King Alfred of Wessex attended the university, Henry II visited the papal legate Bishop Christian O'Conarchy here in 1171, and even Fred Astaire

dropped by when his sister Adele married into the Cavendish family, who own the huge, 19th-century **castle** (www.lismorecastlearts.ie, www.lismorecastle.com; gardens adult/child €8/4; ☼11am-4.45pm mid-Mar–Sep). You can't visit inside (unless you rent it for an event) but you can visit the 3 hectares of ornate and manicured **gardens**. Thought to be the oldest in Ireland, there's a splendid yew walk where Edmund Spenser is said to have written *The Faerie Queen*.

Otherwise, pop into **St Carthage's Cathedral** (1679), deemed by William Thackeray to be 'one of the neatest and prettiest edifices I have seen', and that was *before* the addition of the gorgeous Pre-Raphaelite Edward Burne-Jones stained-glass window.

✕ 🍴 📋 p149

Lismore The 19th-century castle and gardens

DETOUR:
THE VEE GAP

Start: ④ **Lismore**

The R668 north of Lismore cuts through the Knockmealdown Mountains and crosses the border into southern Tipperary. The road rises sharply through lush wooded countryside for about 10km before emerging onto a beautiful upland plateau. A further 6km on, to your left, is Bay Lough, which makes for a nice amble. Beyond it is the Vee Gap, which cuts through the highest point of the mountains and offers superb views over three counties: Tipperary, Waterford and Limerick. Beyond the gap is the village of Clogheen, from where you can keep going to Clonmel.

The Drive >> Take the R666 Lismore to Fermoy road, signposted left over the bridge past Lismore Castle. The scenic drive overlooks the Blackwater; the 'towers' are signposted right about 3km out of Lismore.

TRIP HIGHLIGHT

⑤ Ballysaggartmore Towers

One of the more breathtaking bits of architectural folly in southern Ireland are just off the R666 road to Fermoy, in the heart of a woodland that was once the demesne of Arthur Keily-Ussher, an Anglo-Irish landlord with a reputation for harshness, ordering evictions of famine-stricken tenants for nonpayment of rent.

But he had a soft spot for his wife, who in 1834 demanded that he build her an estate to match that of her sister-in-law, so he ordered the construction of two Gothic-style gate **lodges** (one which serves as a bridge) as a prelude to a huge mansion. But Keily-Ussher ran out of money and the house was never built, a bit of hubris that, given his treatment of his tenants, left locals to delight in his misfortune.

The lodges are free to visit at any time.

The Drive >> Head west on the N72 and after 6km turn right onto the smaller rural road for Ballyduff Upper, which is 3km further on.

⑥ Ballyduff Upper

This rural village (not to be confused with another Ballyduff in County Waterford) is a slice of traditional heaven: beautifully positioned on the Blackwater (the views are stunning), it goes about its business largely unperturbed by the demands of modern tourism.

During the summer, the big draw is the **Booley House** (📞058-60456; www.thebooleyhouse.com; adult/child €15/10; ⊙8.30pm Wed Jul-Aug), which since 1991 has been showcasing traditional Irish music, dancing and storytelling in its weekly show. The **Lismore Heritage Centre** (Main St, Lismore) has details of upcoming shows.

The village's artistic tradition extends to amateur drama: companies from all over the country descend on St Michael's Hall for the annual **West Waterford Drama Festival** (www.adci.ie), which runs for 10 days in March.

BLACKWATER CRUISE

If you want to explore the Blackwater River from the water, the jetty in Youghal is where you'll find the *Maeve*, which does 90-minute **tours** (📞087 988 9076; www.blackwatercruises.com; adult/child €20/10; ⊙May-Sep) of the river north to the remains of Templemichael Castle, about 8km north of Youghal. Captain Tony Gallagher is one of Youghal's best-known characters, as is his first mate, a dog called Pharaoh.

Eating & Sleeping

Youghal ❶

✕ Aherne's Seafood Bar & Restaurant
Seafood €€

(☎024-92424; 163 North Main St; bar food €10-18, dinner €24-40; ☺bar food noon-10pm, dinner 6.30-9.30pm; @ 🛜) Three generations of the same family have run Aherne's, an award-winning restaurant, justifiably famous for its terrific menu. Besides the restaurant there is a stylish, cosy bar and a much larger one popular with locals. The pub food is excellent. Singles/doubles here are €130/150.

🛏 Avonmore House
B&B €€

(☎024-92617; www.avonmoreyoughal. com; South Abbey; s/d €55/100) This grand Georgian house near the clock tower was built in 1752 on the site of a Franciscan abbey destroyed by Cromwellian troops. Avonmore belonged to the earls of Cork before passing into private hands in 1826. Rooms are basic and multicoloured.

Cappoquin ❷

✕ Barron's Bakery
Bakery €

(The Square; dishes €3-8, ☺8.30am-5.30pm Mon-Sat) Barron's has used the same Scotch brick ovens since 1887. Sandwiches, light meals and a mouth-watering selection of cakes and buns baked on the premises are available in its spearmint-green-painted cafe, while its breads are also sold throughout the area.

🛏 Richmond House
Boutique Hotel €€

(☎058-54278; www.richmondhouse.net; N72; s/d from €70/120; P 🛜) Dating to 1704, Richmond House was built by the Earl of Cork, and is set on 5.5 hectares of woodlands. All

the same, its 10 guest rooms – furnished with countrified plaids, prints and mahogany – are cosy rather than imposing, and service is genuinely friendly. Nonguests are welcome at its modern Irish restaurant (open for dinner nightly April and May, Tuesday to Saturday October to March), where local produce includes West Waterford lamb and Helvick monkfish (five-course menu €55).

Lismore ❹

✕ Lismore Farmers Market
Market €

(Castle Ave; ☺10am-4pm Sun) The upscale surrounds attract a fab collection of vendors including Dungarvan's Naked Lunch, whose tasty sandwiches you can enjoy in the park or at tables set up on the gravel path.

✕ O'Brien Chophouse
Modern Irish €€

(☎058-53810; www.obrienchophouse.ie; Main St; mains €14-28; ☺lunch & dinner Wed-Sun; 🛜) Up here in Waterford's hills the sea seems distant, which makes the menu of steaks and chops all the more appropriate at this bastion of traditional cooking. But there's modern flair in the kitchen and always a surprise or two on the specials board. The Victorian decor of this old pub has been beautifully restored.

🛏 Glencairn Inn & Pastis Bistro
B&B €€

(☎058-56232; www.glencairninn.com; Glencairn; s/d from €60/95; ☺closed mid-Nov–mid-Jan; P 🛜) Painted the colour of churned butter, this south-of-France-style country inn has four rooms with brass beds, classic French cuisine (mains €20 to €30, open for dinner Thursday to Saturday and for lunch on Sunday), and a quintessentially Provençal pétanque pitch. Follow the signposts 4km west of town.

Trim Home of the impressive medieval Trim Castle

Family Fun

13

Want to keep everybody in the car happy, distracted and entertained? From pet farms to adventure centres, this trip is one for the whole family.

TRIP HIGHLIGHTS

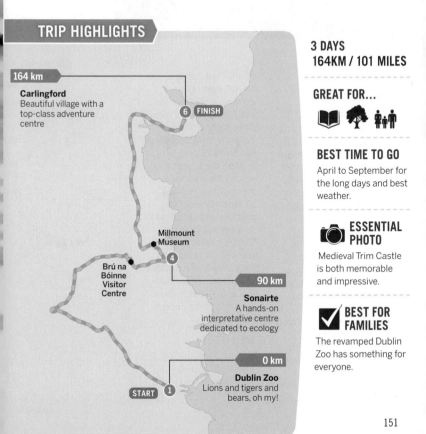

164 km

Carlingford
Beautiful village with a top-class adventure centre

6 FINISH

Millmount Museum

4

Brú na Bóinne Visitor Centre

90 km

Sonairte
A hands-on interpretative centre dedicated to ecology

0 km

Dublin Zoo
Lions and tigers and bears, oh my!

START 1

**3 DAYS
164KM / 101 MILES**

GREAT FOR...

BEST TIME TO GO
April to September for the long days and best weather.

ESSENTIAL PHOTO
Medieval Trim Castle is both memorable and impressive.

BEST FOR FAMILIES
The revamped Dublin Zoo has something for everyone.

13 Family Fun

Within an hour's drive of Dublin is a wealth of child-friendly activities and distractions. The big draws are the interactive exhibits of Brú na Bóinne and the superb adventure centre in Carlingford, but there's plenty more in between, including a popular pet farm where kids get to play with the animals and an ecological centre where they can learn about bee-keeping.

TRIP HIGHLIGHT

❶ Dublin

A bit of useless, interesting trivia: the original lion that roars at the beginning of all MGM films was Slats, born in the 12-hectare **Dublin Zoo** (www.dublinzoo.ie; Phoenix Park; adult/child/family €14/9.50/40; ⏱9.30am-6pm Mar-Sep, to dusk Oct-Feb) in 1919. The zoo's other claim to fame is that it's one of the world's oldest, established in 1844. The lion-breeding program, established in 1857, is another highlight, and you can see these tough cats – from a distance – on the recently established 'African Plains', part of an expansion that saw the zoo double in size; other areas include 'World of Primates' and 'Fringes of the Arctic'.

Meet the Keeper is a big hit with kids, especially as they get a chance to feed the animals and participate in other activities. The City Farm is also excellent: it brings you within touching distance of chickens, cows, goats and pigs. There's also a zoo train and a nursery for infants.

🛏 p157

The Drive » The 44km to Trim will take you through the 337-hectare Phoenix Park on your way north towards the

M1 motorway, passing Áras an Uachtaráin (the residence of the President) and the American Ambassador's residence along the way. Stay on the M3 and get off at the first exit after the toll: Trim is 15km further on along the R154.

- - - - - - - - - - - - -

② Trim

If you've watched *Braveheart,* Mel Gibson's 1996 epic about Scots rebel William Wallace, then you may recognise the remarkably preserved **Trim Castle** (King John's Castle; www.heritageireland.ie; adult/child €4/2; ⏱10am-6pm Easter-Sep, 9.30am-5.30pm Oct, 9.30am-5.50pm Sat & Sun Feb-Easter, 9am-5pm Sat & Sun Nov-Jan), which made a very acceptable stand-in for the castle at York.

Founded in 1173 by Hugh de Lacy, this was Ireland's largest Anglo-Norman fortification, but the original was destroyed by Rory O'Connor, Ireland's

LINK YOUR TRIP

29 **The North in a Nutshell**

From Carlingford, it's only 80km along the A1 to Belfast and the beginning of this trip.

6 **Ancient Ireland**

You can connect to this trip through time at Brú na Bóinne.

last high king, within a year of its construction: what you see here is the reconstruction, dating from 1200, and it's hardly changed since (even though it was given one hell of a shellacking by Cromwellian forces in 1649).

✗ p157

The Drive » Halfway along the 33km drive to Brú na Bóinne you'll hit the county town of Navan, which is pretty unremarkable except for the traffic – expect delays. Past Navan, the R147 is a classic rural road, with nothing but fields on either side and private houses.

- - - - - - - - - - - -

③ Brú na Bóinne Visitor Centre

Bringing the neolithic period to life and putting the extraordinary accomplishments of Brú na Bóinne's constructors in remarkable and fascinating context is this excellent **visitor centre** ([☎]041-988 0300; www.heritageireland.ie; visitor centre adult/child €3/2, visitor centre,

Newgrange & Knowth €11/6; [⊙]9am-7pm Jun–mid-Sep, 9am-6.30pm May & mid-end Sep, 9.30am-5.30pm Oct & Feb, 9am-5pm Nov-Jan). It explains in brilliant, interactive detail exactly how people lived 3500 years ago and how they managed to garner the mathematical genius to construct a passage tomb that allows for the precise alignment of the sun during the winter solstice.

A bus will bring you from the visitor centre to the passage tomb itself, where a guide explains how it all came about. The tour finishes with a re-creation of the winter solstice illumination: even with artificial light it's a pretty cool moment.

The Drive » The quickest way to go is the 16km via the small village of Donore, passing the site of the Battle of the Boyne (1690). Take the R152 for 3km and then turn left onto the R150. After 6km, take a left then the first right (still the R150) and keep going until you reach Sonairte, on your right about 1km shy of Laytown.

DESIGN PICS/THE IRISH IMAGE COLLECTION/GETTY IMAGES ©

TRIP HIGHLIGHT

④ Sonairte

Just outside the seaside village of Laytown, on the road to Julianstown, is **Sonairte** ([☎]041-982 7572; http://sonairte.ie; adult/child €3/1; [⊙]10.30am-5pm Wed-Sun), the National Ecology Centre. Dedicated to promoting ecological awareness, the centre is a wonderful place for kids to learn about sustainable living and organic horticulture. You can take a guided tour of the organic gardens and 200-year-old orchard, follow the

---

NEWGRANGE WINTER SOLSTICE

From the Brú na Bóinne Visitor Centre take the bus to Newgrange where there lies the finest Stone Age passage tomb in Ireland. From here, at 8.20am on the winter solstice (between 18 and 23 December), the rising sun's rays shine through the roof box above the entrance, creep slowly down the long passage and illuminate the tomb chamber for 17 minutes. There is little doubt that this is one of the country's most memorable, even mystical, experiences. There's a simulated winter sunrise for every group taken into the mound.

Dublin A cartload of chimpanzees at the zoo

nature trail or river walk, or take a course in anything from bee-keeping to foraging for wild food and organic gardening. There's a shop and organic cafe on-site, and a **farmers market** from 10.30am to 4pm.

Laytown itself is best known for the **Laytown Races** (www.meath.ie), the only official beach-run horse race in Europe, which has been run here in late August or early September since 1876.

The Drive » Head west on the R150 for 2km and turn right (north) onto the R132

NEWGRANGE FARM

One for the kids. A few hundred metres down the hill to the west of Newgrange tomb is a 135-hectare **working farm** (☎041-982 4119, www.newgrangefarm.com; Newgrange; adult/child €9/9; ◷10am-5.30pm Mon-Fri, 2-5.30pm Sun Easter-Sep, also 2-5.30pm Sat Jul & Aug). The truly hands-on, family-run farm allows visitors to feed the ducks and lambs, and tour the exotic bird aviaries. Charming Farmer Bill keeps things interesting, and demonstrations of threshing, sheepdog work and shoeing a horse are absorbing. Sunday at 3pm is a very special time when the 'sheep derby' is run. Finding jockeys small enough wasn't easy, so teddy bears are tied to the animals' backs. Visiting children are made owners of their own sheep for the race. There are good family rates (two people €15, four €28, six €42).

DETOUR: FLAGSTAFF VIEWPOINT

Start: 6 Carlingford

Travelling along the Cooley Peninsula from Carlingford to Newry in Northern Ireland, a quick 3km detour rewards you with sweeping views of Carlingford Lough, framed by rugged, forested mountains, green fields and glittering blue Irish Sea beyond.

Flagstaff Viewpoint lies *just* over the border in County Armagh. Heading northwest along the coast road (the R173), follow the signs to your left onto Ferryhill Rd, then turn right up to the viewpoint's car park. The quickest way to reach Newry from here is to retrace your steps and rejoin the R173.

for Drogheda, 6km further on. Keep left so as not to cross the river: Millmount will be on your left as you proceed down John St.

5 Drogheda

If the younger kids can stomach a little more history, the **Millmount Museum** (☎041-983 3097; www.millmount.net; museum adult/child €3.50/2.50, museum & tower €5.50/3; ⏰9.30am-5.30pm Mon-Sat, 2-5pm Sun), across the river from the main town of Drogheda, has 9000 years of it to tell. But it does so in an engaging, interactive way: the various collections touch on all aspects of the area's past, from geology to Cromwell's brutal siege of the town.

The cobbled basement is full of gadgets and utensils from bygone times, including a cast-

iron pressure cooker and an early model of a sofa bed. A series of craft studios allow you to see the work of craftspeople working in a variety of mediums, from ceramics to silk.

✕ 🛏 p157

The Drive » Carlingford is 60km north of Drogheda along the M1 and, for the last 14km, the R173. Alternatively, you can take the longer, but much more scenic, coastal R166, which wends its way through the lovely villages of Termonfeckin and Clogherhead before rejoining the main road at Castlebellingham.

TRIP HIGHLIGHT

6 Carlingford

Amid the medieval ruins and whitewashed houses, this vibrant little village buzzes with great pubs, chic restaurants and upmarket boutiques, spirited festivals and

gorgeous views of the mountains and across Carlingford Lough to Northern Ireland.

Besides the medieval ruins, attractions include a pretty interesting **heritage centre** (☎042-937 3454; www.carlingfordheritagecentre.com; Churchyard Lane; adult/concession €3/1.50; ⏰10am-12.30pm & 2-4pm Mon-Fri) on the town's history, and the beginning of the 40km **Táin Trail**, which makes a circuit of the Cooley Peninsula through the Cooley Mountains. The route is a mixture of surfaced roads, forest tracks and green paths.

We strongly recommend you check out the **Carlingford Adventure Centre** (☎042-937 3100; www.carlingfordadventure.com; Tholsel St), which runs a wide range of activities including sailing, kayaking, windsurfing, rock climbing and archery.

If you're here in mid-August, the **Carlingford Oyster Festival** (www.carlingford.ie) celebrates Carlingford's famous oysters with an oyster treasure hunt, fishing competition, music, food markets and a regatta on Carlingford Lough.

🛏 p157

Eating & Sleeping

Dublin ❶

🛏 Trinity Lodge · Guesthouse €€

(🖉01-617 0900; www.trinitylodge.com; 12
S Frederick St; s/d from €130/170; 🛜👪)
Martin Sheen's grin greets you on entering this
cosy, award-winning guesthouse. Not that he's
ditched movies for hospitality: he just enjoyed
his stay (and full Irish breakfast, presumably)
at this classically refurbished Georgian pad so
much that he let them take a mugshot. Room 2
has a lovely bay window. There are a number of
comfortable family rooms and triples.

Trim ❷

🍴 An Tromán · Cafe €

(http://artisanfoodstoretrim.webs.com;
Market St; dishes €4.50-7; ⏱breakfast & lunch
Mon-Sat) Crammed with gourmet goodies,
this fabulous deli is perfect for picking up the
makings of a picnic. If it's not picnic weather,
you can order daily specials like a bowl of soup
and tuna and sweetcorn sandwich, or chicken
and mushroom pie and a meringue nest with
fruit and fresh cream.

Drogheda ❺

🍴 Eastern Seaboard
Bar & Grill · Irish €€

(🖉041-980 2570; www.easternseaboard.ie; 1
Bryans Town Centre, Dublin Rd; mains €10.50-33;
⏱lunch & dinner; 🛜👪) Build it and they
will come... Despite its unpromising location
in a business park near the train station, this
stylised, contemporary space has been packed
since opening, with switched-on staff and quirky
details like a backlit decanter collection and
metallic fish sculptures. Stunning food like
pig's-cheek terrine with apple slaw, smoked
mackerel pâté, and coffee jelly and vanilla ice
cream is served continuously from lunchtime
on. The kids' menu is terrific – the smaller
portions are reasonably priced (€7) – and the
crudités are free. Parents will also appreciate
the distracting crayons and colouring sheets.

Salthouse · B&B €€

(🖉041-983 4426; 46 John St; d from €40) This
Aussie-owned guesthouse is a good bet, with
simple but clean rooms with pine furniture
and white linen. It's above its namesake
restaurant (mains €15-26; ⏱breakfast,
lunch & dinner), which has a popular bar (with
regular live music) and an underutilised terrace
overlooking the river.

Carlingford ❻

Belvedere House · B&B €€

(🖉042-938 3828; www.belvederehouse.ie;
Newry St; d €90; 🛜) An excellent deal, rooms
at this lovely B&B are modern but cosy with
antique pine furniture, subtle lighting and pretty
colour schemes. Guests have access to leisure
facilities at the local Four Seasons hotel and
breakfast is served in the downstairs Bay Tree
restaurant.

Cork & Southwest Ireland

THE SOUTHWEST CONTAINS SOME OF IRELAND'S MOST ICONIC SCENERY: crenulated coastlines, green fields criss-crossed by tumbledown stone walls, and mist-shrouded mountain peaks and bogs.

This idyllic area claims the country's top three peninsula drives – the Ring of Kerry, Dingle Peninsula and Ring of Beara – as well as a shoal of charming fishing towns and villages that have helped establish the southwest as a gourmet heartland, fanning out from the country's spirited second-largest city, Cork.

The region's exquisite beauty makes it one of Ireland's most popular tourist destinations, but there's always an isolated cove or untrodden trail to discover along its roads.

Cobh St Colman's Cathedral overlooking the town's coloured houses (Trip 16)
CONNIE COLEMAN/GETTY IMAGES ©

Cork & Southwest Ireland

MAYO
Lough Mask
Ballymoe
Dunmore
Roscommon
Athleague
Bally
Lough Ree
N61
Cong
Maam Cross
Tuam
N17
Mount Bellew
ROSCOMMON
Ath
M6
N6
Lough Corrib
GALWAY
M6
Ballinasloe
Aughrim
Shannonbr
Galway
Galway Bay
N18
Laurencetown
Killimor
Banagher
OI
New Quay
Inishmór
Inishmaan
Inisheer
Aran Islands
Gort
Portumna
Bi
Carron
Lough Derg
Borrisokane
Roscrea
Liscannor
Corofin
Whitegate
N52
Inagh
M18
CLARE
Nenagh
Ennis
Ballina
M7
Templemore
Doonbeg
N68
Shannon
Bunratty
19
TIPPERARY
Kilkee
Kilrush
Labasheeda
Limerick
Thurles
Carrigaholt
R487
R473
Tarbert
Foynes
N69
Kilbaha
Mouth of the Shannon
Ballybunion
Glin
Rathkeale
Adare
N21
LIMERICK
N24
Listowel
Kilmallock
20
Bansha
R563
Banna
Abbeyfeale
N20
Newtown
Tralee Bay
KERRY
N21
Charleville
Cahir
Maharees Islands
Cloghane
Castleisland
Newmarket
Buttevant
Castletownroche
M8
C
Dunquin
15
Dingle Peninsula
Castlemaine
Farranfore
Kanturk
N73
Fermoy
WATERF
Tralee
N72
Mallow
N72
Great Blasket
Dingle
Killorglin
R563
N72
Tallow
Kells
N70
Killarney
Millstreet
M8
Rathcormack
Cahirciveen
Moll's Gap
Killarney National Park
R582
N20
CORK
Yo
Valentia Island
Kenmare
N22
Macroom
Cork
Midleton
N25
Waterville
Sneem
N70
N71
N22
Cobh
Cloyne
N70
14
Lauragh
16
Dunmanway
Bandon
Kinsale
Caherdaniel
Scariff
Glengarriff
R585
N71
Eyeries
R754
Bantry
Drimoleague
Timoleague
Allihies
R572
Adrigole
Durrus
18
Dursey Island
Beara Peninsula
Sheep's Head Peninsula
N71
Ballydehob
17
Clonakilty
Rosscarbery
Goleen
Skibbereen
Baltimore
Mizen Head Peninsula
Clear Island

ATLANTIC OCEAN

N   0 ————— 50 km
    0 ————— 25 miles

Garinish (Ilnacullin) Island The view from the exotic gardens on the island (Trip 18)

 Classic Trip
14 Ring of Kerry 4 Days
Weave your way past jaw-dropping scenery as you circumnavigate the Iveragh Peninsula. (p163)

15 Dingle Peninsula 3–4 Days
Dingle's ancient landscape is ringed by quaint fishing villages and spectacular beaches. (p175)

 Classic Trip
16 Southwest Blitz 4 Days
Blitz the best of southwest Ireland's coast, countryside and cosmopolitan city life. (p185)

17 Southwestern Pantry 5 Days
Sample some of the country's finest seafood, artisan produce and sociable markets. (p199)

18 West Cork Villages 7 Days
Colourful villages burst with life in West Cork, including its picturesque peninsulas. (p207)

19 Shannon River Route 4 Days
Meander alongside Ireland's mightiest river and get out on the water too. (p215)

20 The Holy Glen 2–3 Days
Awe-inspiring mountain vistas and sacred sites including the extraordinary Rock of Cashel. (p223)

DON'T MISS

Hunt Museum
Limerick's true treasure hunt – open drawers and poke around its collections on Trip 19

Garinish (Ilnacullin) Island
Sail from Glengarriff past islands and seal colonies to Garinish's subtropical gardens on Trip 18

Killarney Jaunting Cars
Clip-clop in a traditional horse-drawn jaunting car on Trips 14 15 16

Cork City Gaol
Models of suffering prisoners bring home the harshness of the 19th-century penal system on Trip 16

Rough Point Diving
Dive crystal-clear waters and spot whales and dolphins on Trip 15

Durrus Farmhouse Cheese
Taste Durrus' famous cheese at its farm on Trip 17

Waterville *Rugged coastlines, plunging cliffs and soaring mountains*

Ring of Kerry

14

Circumnavigating the Iveragh Peninsula, the Ring of Kerry is the longest and most diverse of Ireland's prized peninsula drives, combining jaw-dropping cliffs with soaring mountains.

TRIP HIGHLIGHTS

62 km

Muckross Estate
Magnificent garden-set mansion, deer parks, waterfall and abbey

Rossbeigh Strand

START/ FINISH
● Killarney

⑩ ⑪

● Kenmare

Caherdaniel
Aquatic activities galore and horse rides along the beach

⑦

90 km

148 km

Gap of Dunloe
Rocky bridges cross crystal-clear streams and lakes

4 DAYS
179KM / 111 MILES

- - -

GREAT FOR...

📖 🌳

- - -

BEST TIME TO GO

Late spring and early autumn for temperate weather free of summer crowds.

- - -

 ESSENTIAL PHOTO

Ross Castle from a boat while crossing to Inisfallen Island.

- - -

 BEST FOR WILDLIFE

Killarney National Park, home to Ireland's only wild herd of native red deer.

163

14 Ring of Kerry

You *can* drive the Ring of Kerry in a day, but the longer you spend, the more you'll enjoy it. The circuit winds past pristine beaches, the island-dotted Atlantic, medieval ruins, mountains and loughs (lakes), with the coastline at its most rugged between Waterville and Caherdaniel in the peninsula's southwest. And you'll find plenty of opportunities for serene, starkly beautiful detours, such as the Skellig Ring and the Cromane Peninsula.

❶ Killarney

A town that's been practising the tourism game for over 250 years, Killarney is a well-oiled machine driven by the sublime scenery of its namesake national park, and competition keeps standards high. Killarney nights are lively and most pubs put on live music.

Killarney and its surrounds have been inhabited probably since the Neolithic period and were certainly important

Bronze Age settlements, based on the copper ore mined on Ross Island. Killarney changed hands between warring tribes, the most notable of which were the Fir Bolg ('bag men'), expert stonemasons who built forts and devised Ogham script. It wasn't until much later, in the 17th century, that Viscount Kenmare developed the town as an Irish version of England's Lake District. Among its notable 19th-century tourists were Queen Victoria and Romantic

poet Percy Bysshe Shelley, who began *Queen Mab* here.

The town itself can easily be explored on foot in an hour or two; to get around by horse-drawn jaunting car, see p176, and for more dining and accommodation options, see p183.

p173

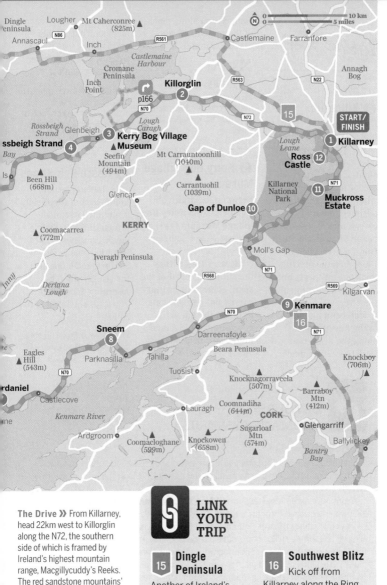

The Drive » From Killarney, head 22km west to Killorglin along the N72, the southern side of which is framed by Ireland's highest mountain range, Macgillycuddy's Reeks. The red sandstone mountains' elegant forms were carved by minor glaciers, with summits buttressed by ridges of purplish rock. The name derives from the ancient Mac Gilla Muchudas clan; reek means 'pointed hill'. In Irish, they're known as Na Crucha Dubha (the black tops).

LINK YOUR TRIP

15 Dingle Peninsula

Another of Ireland's iconic peninsula drives, the picturesque Dingle Peninsula is on Killarney's doorstep.

16 Southwest Blitz

Kick off from Killarney along the Ring of Kerry's coastline and continue into captivating County Cork.

competition along much of the route until you reach Kenmare).

 p173

The Drive » Killorglin sits at the crossroads of the N72 and the N70; continue 35km along the N70 to the Kerry Bog Village Museum.

❷ Killorglin

Killorglin (Cill Orglan) is quieter than the waters of the River Laune that lap against its 1885-built eight-arched bridge – except in mid-August, when there's an explosion of time-honoured ceremonies at the famous pagan festival, the **Puck Fair**, first recorded in 1603. A statue of King Puck (a goat) peers out from the Killarney side of the river.

Killorglin has some of the finest eateries along the Ring (that said, there's not much

❸ Kerry Bog Village Museum

Between Killorglin and Glenbeigh, the **Kerry Bog Village Museum** (www. kerrybogvillage.ie; admission €5; ⊗8.30am-6pm) recreates a 19th-century bog village, typical of the small communities that carved out a precarious living in the harsh environment of Ireland's ubiquitous peat bogs. You'll see the thatched

homes of the turfcutter, blacksmith, thatcher and labourer, as well as a dairy, and meet rare Kerry Bog ponies.

The Drive » It's less than 1km from the museum to the village of Glenbeigh; turn off here and drive 2km northwest to unique Rossbeigh Strand.

❹ Rossbeigh Strand

This unusual beach, 1.6km west of Glenbeigh, is a tendril of sand protruding into Dingle Bay, with views of Inch Point and the Dingle Peninsula. On one side, the sea is ruffled by Atlantic winds; on the other, it's sheltered and calm.

The Drive » Rejoin the N70 and continue 25km south to Caherciveen.

DETOUR: CROMANE PENINSULA

Start: ❷ Killorglin

Open fields give way to spectacular water vistas and multihued sunsets on the Cromane Peninsula, the tiny namesake village of which sits at the base of a narrow shingle spit.

Cromane's exceptional restaurant, **Jack's Coastguard Restaurant** (☎066-976 9102; www.jackscromane.com; mains €16.50-27; ⊗dinner Thu-Sat, lunch & dinner Sun), is a local secret and justifies the trip. Entering this 1866-built coastguard station feels like arriving at a low-key village pub, but a narrow doorway at the back of the bar leads to a striking, whitewashed contemporary space with lights glittering from midnight blue ceiling panels, stained glass and metallic fish sculptures, a pianist, and huge picture windows overlooking the water. In addition to seafood, menu standouts include chicken liver and aged pork pâté on homemade bread.

For more info on the area, visit www.cromane.net.

Cromane is 9km from Killorglin. Heading southwest from Killorglin along the N70, take the second right and continue straight ahead until you get to the crossroads. Turn right; Jack's Coastguard Restaurant is on your left.

DETOUR:
VALENTIA ISLAND & THE SKELLIG RING

Start: ❺ Caherciveen

If you're here between April and September, and you're detouring via Valentia Island and the Skellig Ring, a **ferry service** (☎087 241 8973) from Reenard Point, 5km southwest of Caherciveen, provides a handy shortcut to Knightstown. The five-minute crossing costs €5 one way for a car, and departs every 10 minutes between 7.45am (9am Sunday) and 9.30pm (10pm in July and August). Alternatively, there's a bridge from Portmagee onto Valentia Island.

Crowned by Geokaun Mountain, 11km-long Valentia Island (Oileán Dairbhre) makes an ideal driving loop, with some lonely ruins that are worth exploring. Knightstown, the only town, has pubs, food and walks.

The **Skellig Experience** (☎066-947 6306; www.skelligexperience.com; adult/child €5/3; ⏰10am-7pm Jul & Aug, to 6pm May, Jun & Sep) heritage centre, in a distinctive building with turf-covered barrel roofs, has informative exhibits on the Skellig Islands offshore. From April to September, it also runs two-hour cruises (adult/child €27.50/14.50, including Skellig Experience entry) around the Skelligs. If the weather's bad, there's often the option of a 90-minute minicruise (€22/11 including entry) in the harbour and channel.

Immediately across the bridge on the mainland, Portmagee's single street is a rainbow of colourful houses. On summer mornings, the small pier comes to life with boats embarking on the choppy crossing to the Skellig Islands.

Portmagee holds **set-dancing workshops** (www.moorings.ie) over the May bank holiday weekend, with plenty of stomping practice sessions in the town's **Bridge Bar** (bar food €10-22), a friendly local gathering point that's also good for impromptu music by locals year-round and more formal sessions in summer.

The wild and beautiful 18km-long Skellig Ring road links Portmagee and Waterville via a Gaeltacht (Irish-speaking) area centred on Ballinskelligs (Baile an Sceilg), with the ragged outline of Skellig Michael never far from view.

- - - - - - - - - -

❺ Caherciveen

Caherciveen's population, over 30,000 in 1841, was decimated by the Great Famine and emigration to the New World. A sleepy outpost remains, overshadowed by the 688m peak of **Knocknadobar**. It looks rather dour compared with the peninsula's other settlements, but the atmospheric remains of 16th-century **Ballycarbery Castle**, 2.4km along the road to White Strand Beach from the centre, are well worth a visit.

Along the same road are two stone ring forts. The larger, **Cahergall**, dates from the 10th century and has stairways on the inside walls, a *clochán* (circular stone building shaped like an old-fashioned beehive) and the remains of a house. The smaller, 9th-century **Leacanabuile** has the entrance to an underground passage. Their inner walls and chambers give a strong sense of what life was like in a ring fort. Leave your car in the parking area next to a stone wall and walk up the footpaths.

The Drive ≫ From Caherciveen you can continue 17km along the classic Ring of Kerry on the N70 to Waterville, or take the ultrascenic route via Valentia Island and the Skellig Ring, and rejoin the N70 at Waterville.

Classic Trip

LOCAL KNOWLEDGE
ALOYSIUS 'WEESHIE'
FOGARTY, RADIO PRESENTER
AND EX-KERRY FOOTBALLER

Each season in Killarney is
special. There's the green haze of
summer, the rich bloom of spring and the bare frost
of winter, when the whole place might be enveloped
in snow. But my favourite is the brown of the
autumn, when the Deenagh River ripples through
the park into the lakes. Killarney is the doorway to
the Ring of Kerry – you haven't seen Ireland until
you've seen the Ring.

Left: Ross Castle, Killarney.
Right: Killarney National Park.

6 Waterville

A line of colourful
houses on the N70
between Lough Currane
and Ballinskelligs Bay,
Waterville is charm-
challenged in the way of
many mass-consumption
beach resorts. A statue
of its most famous guest,
Charlie Chaplin, beams
from the seafront. The
Charlie Chaplin Comedy

CS / THE IRISH IMAGE COLLECTION/GETTY IMAGES ©

JORG GREUEL/GETTY IMAGES ©

Film Festival (charliechap lincomedyfilmfestival.com) is held in August.

Sights in the town itself are few, but at the north end of Lough Currane, **Church Island** has the ruins of a medieval church and beehive cell reputedly founded as a monastic settlement by St Finian in the 6th century.

🛏 p173

The Drive » Squiggle your way for 12km along the Ring's most tortuous stretch past plunging cliffs and soaring mountains to Caherdaniel.

- - - - - - - - - -

TRIP HIGHLIGHT

❼ Caherdaniel

The scattered hamlet of Caherdaniel counts two of the Ring of Kerry's highlights: Derrynane National Historic Park (p188), surrounded by subtropical gardens, and bar-restaurant Scarriff Inn (p188), with picture windows framing what it plausibly claims is 'Ireland's finest view' over rugged cliffs and islands.

Most activity here centres on the Blue Flag beach. **Derrynane Sea Sports** (📞087 908 1208; www.derrynaneseasports. com) organises sailing,

Classic Trip

canoeing, windsurfing and water-skiing for all levels; **Eagle Rock Equestrian Centre** (☎066-947 5145; www.eaglerockcentre.com) offers beach, mountain and woodland horse treks for all levels from €30 per hour.

The Drive » Wind your way east along the N70 for 21km to Sneem.

----

8 Sneem

Sneem's Irish name, An tSnaidhm, translates as 'the knot', which is thought to refer to the River Sneem that swirls, knotlike, into nearby Kenmare Bay.

Take a gander at the town's two cute squares, then pop into the **Blue Bull** (South Sq; mains €12-22; ☺lunch & dinner), a perfect little old stone pub, for a pint.

🛏 p173

The Drive » Along the 27km drive to Kenmare, the N70 drifts away from the water and coasts along under a canopy of trees.

----

9 Kenmare

The copper-covered limestone spire of Holy Cross Church, drawing the eye to the wooded hills above town, may make you forget for a split second that Kenmare is a seaside town. But with rivers named Finnihy, Roughty and Sheen emptying into Kenmare Bay, you couldn't be anywhere other than southwest Ireland.

In the 18th century Kenmare was laid out on an X-shaped plan, with a triangular market square in the centre. Today the inverted V to the south is the focus. Kenmare Bay stretches out to the southwest, and there are glorious views of the mountains. For more see p189.

Signposted southwest of the square is an early Bronze Age **stone circle**, one of the biggest in southwest Ireland. Fifteen stones ring a boulder dolmen, a burial monument rarely found outside this part of the country.

🍴 🛏 p173

The Drive » The coastal scenery might be finished but if anything the trip gets more stunning as you head north from Kenmare on the vista-crazy N71, winding between rock and lake, with plenty of lay-bys to stop and admire the views (and recover from the switchback bends) to the Gap of Dunloe.

TRIP HIGHLIGHT

10 Gap of Dunloe

Just west of Killarney National Park, the Gap of Dunloe is ruggedly beautiful. In the winter it's an awe-inspiring mountain pass, overshadowed by Purple Mountain and Macgillycuddy's Reeks. In high summer, though, it's a bottleneck for the tourist trade, with buses ferrying countless visitors for horse-and-trap rides through the Gap.

On the southern side, surrounded by lush, green pastures, is **Brandon's Cottage** (dishes €3-6; ☺breakfast & lunch Apr-Oct), accessed by turning left at Moll's Gap on the R568, then taking your

**TOP TIP:
AROUND (AND ACROSS) THE RING**

Tour buses travel the Ring in an anticlockwise direction, and authorities generally encourage visitors to drive in the same direction to avoid traffic congestion and accidents. If you travel clockwise at any point on your trip, be sure to watch out on blind corners. There's little traffic on the Ballaghbeama Gap, which cuts across the peninsula's central highlands, with some spectacular views.

KILLARNEY NATIONAL PARK

Designated a Unesco Biosphere Reserve in 1982, **Killarney National Park** (www.killarneynationalpark.ie) is among the finest of Ireland's national parks. And while its proximity to one of the southwest's largest and liveliest urban centres (including pedestrian entrances right in Killarney's town centre) is an ongoing risk due to the high visitor numbers, it's an important conservation area for many rare species. Among its 102.36 sq km are Ireland's only wild herd of native red deer, which has lived here continuously for 12,000 years, as well as the country's largest area of ancient oak woods and views of most of its major mountains.

The glacial Lough Leane (the Lower Lake or 'Lake of Learning'), Muckross Lake and the Upper Lake make up about a quarter of the park. Their peaty waters are as rich in wildlife as the surrounding soil: cormorants skim across the surface, deer swim out to graze on the islands, and salmon, trout and perch prosper in a pike-free environment. Lough Leane has vistas of reeds and swans.

With a bit of luck, you might see white tailed sea eagles, with their 2.5m wingspan, soaring overhead. The eagles were reintroduced here in 2007 after more than 100 years of extinction. There are now over 50 in the park and they're starting to settle in Ireland's rivers, lakes and coastal regions. And like Killarney itself, the park is also home to plenty of summer visitors, including migratory cuckoos, swallows and swifts.

Keep your eyes peeled too for the park's smallest residents, its insects, including the northern emerald dragonfly, which isn't normally found this far south in Europe and is believed to have been marooned here after the last ice age.

first right, another right at the bottom of the hill, then right again at the crossroads (about 8km from the N71 all up). A simple old 19th-century hunting lodge, it has an open-air cafe and a dock for boats crossing Killarney National Park's Upper Lake. From here a (very) narrow road weaves up the hill to the Gap – theoretically you can drive this 6km route to the 19th-century pub **Kate Kearney's Cottage** (☎064-664 4146; www.katekearneyscottage.com; mains €8.50-19.50; ⊙lunch & dinner) and back *but* only outside summer and even then walkers and cyclists have right of way, and

the precipitous hairpin bends are nerve-testing. It's worth walking or taking a jaunting car (or, if you're carrying two wheels, cycling) through the Gap, however: the scenery is a fantasy of rocky bridges over clear mountain streams and lakes. Alternatively, there are various options for exploring the Gap from Killarney.

The Drive ≫ Continue on the N71 north through Killarney National Park to Muckross Estate.

- - - - - - - - - - -

TRIP HIGHLIGHT

⑪ Muckross Estate

The core of Killarney National Park is the Muckross Estate,

donated to the state by Arthur Bourn Vincent in 1932. **Muckross House** (☎064-667 0144; www.muckross-house.ie; adult/child €7/3, combined ticket with farms €12/6; ⊙9am-7pm Jul & Aug, to 5.30pm Sep-Jun) is a 19th-century mansion, restored to its former glory and packed with contemporaneous fittings. Entrance is by guided tour.

The beautiful **gardens** slope down, and a block behind the house contains a restaurant, craft shop and studios where you can see potters, weavers and bookbinders at work. Jaunting cars wait to run you through deer parks

Classic Trip

and woodland to **Torc Waterfall** and **Muckross Abbey** (about €20 each return; haggling can reap discounts). The visitor centre has an excellent cafe.

Adjacent to Muckross House are the **Muckross Traditional Farms** (☎064-663 1440; adult/child €7.50/4, combined ticket with Muckross House €12/6; ⏱10am-6pm Jun-Aug, 1-6pm May & Sep, 1-6pm Sat, Sun & public holidays Apr & Oct). These reproductions of 1930s Kerry farms, complete with chickens, pigs, cattle and horses, re-create farming and living conditions when people had to live off the land.

The Drive » Continuing a further 2km north through the national park brings you to riveting Ross Castle.

⑫ Ross Castle

Restored by Dúchas, **Ross Castle** (☎064-663 5851; www.heritageireland. ie; Ross Rd; adult/child €6/2; ⏱9am-5.45pm Apr-Sep, 9.30am-5.45pm Oct & mid-late Mar) dates back to the 15th century, when it was a residence of the O'Donoghues. It was the last place in Munster to succumb to Cromwell's forces, thanks partly to its cunning spiral staircase, every step of which is a different height in order to break an attacker's stride. Access is by guided tour only.

You can hire boats (around €5) from Ross Castle to row to **Inisfallen Island**, the largest of Killarney National Park's 26 islands. The first monastery on Inisfallen is said to have been founded by St Finian

the Leper in the 7th century. The island's fame dates from the early 13th century when the Annals of Inisfallen were written here. Now in the Bodleian Library at Oxford, they remain a vital source of information on early Munster history. Inisfallen shelters the ruins of a 12th-century oratory with a carved Romanesque doorway and a monastery on the site of St Finian's original.

The Drive » It's just 3km north from Ross Castle back to Killarney.

Eating & Sleeping

Killarney ❶

🛏 Aghadoe Heights Hotel — Hotel €€€

(☎064-31766; www.aghadoeheights.com; Aghadoe; d/ste €200/300; 🅿@🛜🏊) A huge, glassed-in swimming pool overlooking the lakes is the centrepiece of this stunning contemporary hotel, but you can also soak up the views from the **bar** (mains €12-23; 🕑lunch & dinner) and **Lake Room Restaurant** (mains €18-38; 🕑dinner), both of which are open to nonguests, as is the decadent spa.

Killorglin ❷

🍴 Bianconi — Irish €€

(☎066-976 1146; www.bianconi.ie; Bridge St; mains €12.50-25; 🕑lunch & dinner Mon-Sat) Bang in the centre of town, this low-lit inn has a classy ambience and cooked-to-perfection modern Irish fare like sage-stuffed roast chicken with cranberry sauce and spectacular meal-size salads.

🛏 Coffey's River's Edge — B&B €€

(☎066-976 1750; www.coffeysriversedge.com; the Bridge; s/d €50/70; 🅿🛜) Next to the bridge footsteps from the town centre, you can sit out on the balcony overlooking the river at this contemporary B&B, with spotless spring-toned rooms and hardwood floors.

Waterville ❻

🛏 Brookhaven House — B&B €€

(☎066-947 4431; www.brookhavenhouse. com; New Line; d €90-110; 🅿🛜📶) The pick of Waterville's B&Bs is this stylish contemporary house run by a friendly family, with spick-and-span rooms and comfy beds. Piping-hot breakfasts are dished up with sea views in the sunny dining room.

Sneem ❽

🛏 Parknasilla Resort & Spa — Hotel €€€

(☎064-667 5600; www.parknasillahotel.ie; d from €180; 🅿@🛜🏊) Set over 200 hectares with incomparable views of the Kenmare River and Beara Peninsula, this castle hotel has been wowing guests since 1895. From the top-grade spa to the elegant restaurant, this is Irish hospitality at its very best.

Kenmare ❾

🍴 D'Arcy's Oyster Bar & Grill — Irish €€

(☎064-664 1589; www.darcyskenmare.com; Main St; mains €14.50-25.50; 🕑dinner; 🛜) Local purveyors supply the best in organic produce, cheeses and fresh seafood, all served in modern, low-key surrounds. The raw oysters capture the scent of the bay; the hazelnut-crusted, twice-baked crab and prawn soufflé is divine. Guests staying in its antique-adorned rooms (doubles €50) get discounted meals.

🍴 Horseshoe — Pub €€

(☎064-664 1553; www.thehorseshoekenmare. com; 3 Main St; mains €14.50-26.50; 🕑lunch & dinner) Ivy frames the entrance to this gastropub, which has a short but excellent menu that runs from Kenmare Bay mussels in creamy apple cider sauce to local lamb on mustard mash and Kerry's best burgers.

🛏 Virginia's Guesthouse — B&B €€

(☎064-664 1021; www.virginias-kenmare.com; Henry St; s/d €60/80; 🛜📶) You can't get more central than this award-winning B&B, the creative breakfasts of which celebrate organic local produce, such as rhubarb and blueberries in season. Its eight rooms are supercomfy without being fussy. Outstanding value.

Dunquin *Take off for the Blasket Islands from Dunquin harbour*

Dingle Peninsula

15

Driving around this history-steeped peninsula, you'll encounter churches, castles, neolithic monuments, captivating scenery and artistic little Dingle town, the peninsula's delightful 'capital'.

TRIP HIGHLIGHTS

90 km

Gallarus Castle & Gallarus Oratory
Two exceptional centuries-old edifices

152 km

Glanteenassig Forest Recreation Area
Oasis of woodlands, mountains and lakes

● Tralee
FINISH

Riasc Monastic Settlement ⑦

● Connor Pass

③

④

⑩

Killarney ●
START

64 km

Dingle
Sprinkled with studios, galleries and wonderful music-filled pubs

Slea Head
Beehive huts, forts, inscribed stones and church sites

73 km

**3–4 DAYS
185KM / 115 MILES**

GREAT FOR...

BEST TIME TO GO
June to August offer the best beach weather.

ESSENTIAL PHOTO
Snap a perfect peninsula panorama from the Connor Pass summit.

BEST FOR HISTORY
Slea Head's astonishing concentration of ancient sites.

175

Dingle Peninsula

As you twist and turn along this figure-eight drive, the coast is the star of the show. The opal blue waters surrounding the Dingle Peninsula provide a wealth of aquatic adventures and impossibly fresh seafood, and you'll find it's where the promontory meets the ocean — at whitewater-pounded rocks, secluded coves and wide, gold-sand beaches — that Dingle's beauty is at its most unforgettable.

① Killarney

The lively tourist town of Killarney is an ideal place to kick off your trip, with a plethora of places to eat, drink and, when you need a break, sleep. If you have time, the 10.236-sq-km Killarney National Park (p171), immediately to its south, and the Gap of Dunloe (p170), with its rocky terrain, babbling brooks and alpine lakes, are well worth exploring. On a tight schedule, however, you can still get a good overview of the

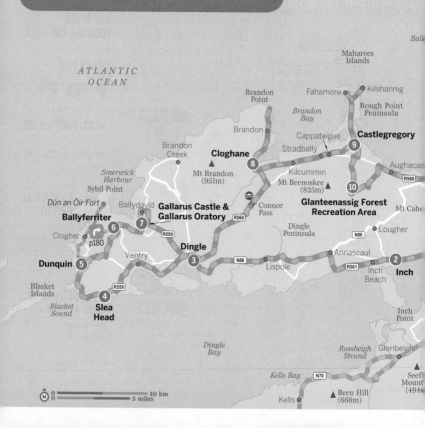

area – and entertaining commentary too – aboard a horse-drawn **jaunting car** (☎064-663 3358; www.killarneyjauntingcars.com), also known as a trap, which comes with a driver called a jarvey. The pick-up point, nicknamed 'the Ha Ha' or 'the Block', is on Kenmare Pl. Trips cost €30 to €70, depending on distance; traps officially carry four people.

🍴 🛏 p183

The Drive ≫ The quickest route from Killarney to the peninsula passes through Castlemaine. Turn west onto the R561; you'll soon meet the coast before coming to the seaside town of Inch (41km all up).

----

② Inch

Inch's 5km-long sand spit was a location for both *Ryan's Daughter* and *Playboy of the Western World*. Sarah Miles, love interest in the former film, described her stay here as 'brief but bonny'.

The dunes are certainly bonny, scattered with the remains of shipwrecks and Stone Age and Iron Age settlements. The west-facing beach is also a hot surfing spot; waves average 1m to 3m. You can learn to ride them with **Westcoast Surf School** (☎086 836 0271; www.westcoastsurfschool.ie; lessons per adult/child from €30/20).

Cars are allowed on the beach, but don't end up providing others with nonstop laughs by getting stuck.

Sammy's (☎066-915 8118; mains €12.50-19; ☺lunch & dinner; @ 🛜 👫), at the entrance to the beach, is the nerve centre of the village: in addition to its beach-facing bar-restaurant, there's a shop, tourist information and trad sessions during the summer.

The Drive ≫ Shadowing the coast, about 7km west of Inch, Annascaul (Abhainn an Scáil; also spelled Anascaul) is

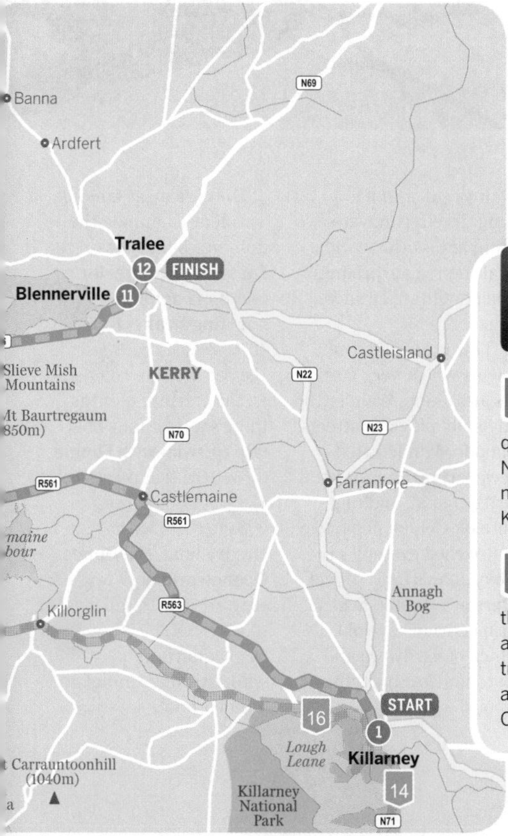

LINK YOUR TRIP

14 Ring of Kerry
From Tralee, it's a quick 22km zip along the N22 to pick up Ireland's most famous driving loop in Killarney.

16 Southwest Blitz
Killarney is also the jumping-off point for another classic Irish road trip along the Ring of Kerry and a stunning swath of County Cork.

ROBERT HARDING PRODUCTIONS/GETTY IMAGES ©

home to the cracking pub the South Pole Inn run by Antarctic explorer Tom Crean in his retirement and now something of a Crean museum. Continuing 18km west of Annascaul brings you into Dingle town.

TRIP HIGHLIGHT

❸ Dingle Town

Framed by its fishing port, the peninsula's charming little 'capital' is quaint without even trying. Dingle is one of Ireland's largest Gaeltacht (Irish-speaking) towns (although locals have voted to retain the name Dingle rather than go by the officially sanctioned – and dictated – An Daingean), and has long drawn runaways from across the world, making it a surprisingly cosmopolitan, creative place.

This is one of those towns whose very fabric is its attraction. Wander the higgledy-piggledy streets, shop for handcrafted jewellery, arts, crafts and artisan food, and pop into old-school pubs; two untouched examples are **Foxy John's** (Main St) and **Curran's** (Main St), which respectively have old stock of hardware and outdoor clothing lying about.

Dingle's most famous 'resident' is Fungie the dolphin. Boats leave Dingle's pier daily for one-hour **dolphin-spotting trips** (☎066-915 2626; www.dingledolphin.com; The Pier; adult/child €16/8). In the warmer months there's a two-hour boat trip to **swim with Fungie** (☎066-915 1146; per person €25, plus wetsuit hire €20; ⏰8am or 9am Apr–mid-Sep). On dry land, the **Dingle Oceanworld** (www.dingle-oceanworld.ie; Dingle Harbour; adult/child/€13/7.50; ⏰10am-5pm) aquarium has a walk-through tunnel and a touch pool.

Dingle Peninsula Fort on the waters of the peninsula

Don't leave Dingle without catching traditional live music at pubs such as the **Small Bridge Bar** (An Droichead Beag; Lower Main St; ☺ music from 9.30pm) and standout seafood at its restaurants.

✕ ⊨ p183

The Drive » West of Dingle along the R559, the Slea Head drive runs around the tip of Dingle Peninsula. This clockwise direction offers the best views and although it's a mere 50km in length, doing this stretch justice requires a full day, at least.

TRIP HIGHLIGHT

❹ Slea Head

Overlooking the mouth of Dingle Bay, Mt Eagle and the Blasket Islands, Slea Head has fine beaches and superbly preserved structures from Dingle's ancient past, including beehive huts, forts, inscribed stones and church sites. The village of **Ventry** (Ceann Trá), 6km west of Dingle town, is idyllically set next to a wide sandy bay. The **Celtic & Prehistoric Museum** (www.celticmuseum. com; Kilvicadownig, Ventry; admission €5; ☺10am-5.30pm mid-Mar–Oct), 3km west of the village, squeezes in an incredible collection of Celtic and prehistoric artefacts.

About 4km further west, the Iron Age **Dunbeg Fort** is a dramatic example of a promontory fortification, perched atop a sheer sea cliff. Inside the fort's four outer stone walls are the remains of a house and a beehive hut, as well as an underground passage. The **Fahan beehive huts**, including two fully intact huts, are 500m west of Dunbeg Fort on the inland side of the road. When the kiosks are open in summer, expect to be charged €2 to €3 for entrance to the sights.

The Drive » Continuing northwest from Slea Head for just over 2km brings you to Dunmore Head, the westernmost point on the Irish mainland and the site of the wreckage in 1588 of two Spanish Armada ships. From here it's around 3km to Dunquin.

❺ Dunquin

Yet another pause on a road of scenic pauses, Dunquin is a scattered village beneath Mt Eagle and Croaghmarhin. The local website (www.dunchaoin.com) notes that it is the next parish to America. Dunquin is a hub for the Blasket Islands, 5km out into the Atlantic, which are the most westerly in Europe. **Blasket Island Ferries** (📞066-915 1344, 066-915 6422; www.blasketisland.com; adult/child €20/10) depart from Dunquin Harbour and take 20 minutes; add €15 for an ecotour of the island. Call for seasonal sailing times.

Even if you can't make it out to the islands, Dunquin's **Blasket Centre** (Ionad an Bhlascaoid Mhóir; 📞066-915 6444; www.heritageireland.ie; adult/child €4/2; ☺10am-6pm Apr-Oct) is a wonderful interpretive centre with a floor-to-ceiling window overlooking the islands. Great Blasket Island's rich community of storytellers and

DETOUR:
DÚN AN ÓIR FORT

Start: ❺ Dunquin

En route between Dunquin and Ballyferriter, turn north 1km east of Clogher, from where narrow roads run to the east of the Dingle Golf Links course to **Dún an Óir Fort** (Fort of Gold), the scene of a hideous massacre during the 1580 Irish rebellion against English rule. All that remains is a network of grassy ridges, but it's a pretty spot overlooking sheltered Smerwick Harbour.

The fort is about 6km from Clogher; return on the same road to just south of the golf course and turn east to rejoin the R559 and continue to Ballyferriter.

musicians is profiled along with its literary visitors like John Millington Synge, writer of *Playboy of the Western World*. Prosaic practicalities of island life are covered by exhibits on shipbuilding and fishing. There's a cafe with Blasket views and a bookshop.

The Drive » North from Dunquin is Clogher Head (a short walk takes you out to the head with views down to a perfect little beach at Clogher – a prime resting spot for seals). Follow the road another 500m around to the crossroads where a narrow paved track leads to the beach. Back on the loop road, head inland towards Ballyferriter (about 9km in all).

❻ Ballyferriter

Housed in the 19th-century schoolhouse in the tiny village of Ballyferriter (Baile an Fheirtearaigh), the **Dingle Peninsula**

Museum (Músaem Chorca Dhuibhne; 📞066-915 6100; www.westkerrymuseum.com; admission €3.50; ☺10am-5pm Jun-Sep, by appointment rest of year) has displays on the peninsula's archaeology and ecology. Across the street there's a lonely, lichen-covered church.

The remains of the 5th- or 6th-century **Riasc Monastic Settlement** are an impressive, haunting sight, particularly the pillar with beautiful Celtic designs. Excavations have also revealed the foundations of an oratory first built with wood and later stone, a kiln for drying corn and a cemetery. The ruins are signposted as 'Mainistir Riaisc' along a narrow lane off the R559, about 2km east of Ballyferriter.

The Drive » The landscape around Ballyferriter is a rocky patchwork of varying shades of green, stitched by miles and miles of ancient stone walls. Wind your way along the R559 some 2km east of the Riasc Monastic Settlement turn-off to reach one of the peninsula's few surviving castles and an amazing dry-stone oratory.

- - - - - - - - - -

TRIP HIGHLIGHT

7 Gallarus Castle & Gallarus Oratory

None of its battlements remain but you can now access the superbly restored interior of **Gallarus Castle** (www.heritageireland.ie; adult/child €3/free; ☺10am-6pm Jun-Aug), built by the FitzGeralds around the 15th century.

A few hundred metres to the southeast, the dry-stone **Gallarus Oratory** (www.heritageireland.ie; admission free; ☺10am-6pm Jun-Aug) is quite a sight, standing in its lonely spot beneath the brown hills as it has done for some 1200 years. It has withstood the elements perfectly, apart from a slight sagging in the roof. Traces of mortar suggest that the interior and exterior walls may have been plastered. Shaped like an upturned boat, it has a doorway on the western side and a round-headed window on the east. Inside the doorway are two projecting stones with holes that once supported the door.

There's no parking next to the castle and parking by the oratory is extremely limited, but there is a nearby private parking area at the **visitor centre** (adult/child €3/free; ☺9am-9pm Jun-Aug, 10am-6pm Feb-May & Sep-10 Nov).

The Drive » Pass back through Dingle town before cutting across the Connor Pass to reach the northern side of the peninsula. About 6km before you reach Kilcummin, a narrow road leads north to the quiet villages of Cloghane (23km) and Brandon, and finally to Brandon Point overlooking Brandon Bay.

- - - - - - - - - -

8 Cloghane

Cloghane (An Clochán) is another little piece of peninsula beauty. The village's friendly pubs nestle between Mt Brandon and Brandon Bay, with views across the water to the Stradbally Mountains.

For many, the main goal is scaling 951m-high **Mt Brandon** (Cnoc Bhréannain), Ireland's eighth-highest peak. If that sounds too energetic, there are plenty of coastal strolls.

The 5km drive from Cloghane out to **Brandon Point** follows ever-narrower single-track roads wandered by sheep, culminating in cliffs with fantastic views north and east.

On the last weekend in July, Cloghane celebrates the ancient Celtic harvest festival **Lughnasa** with events – especially bonfires – both in the village and atop Mt Brandon. The **Brandon Regatta**, a traditional *currach* (rowing boat race), takes place in late August.

The Drive » Retrace your route to Cloghane and head east to Kilcummin (7km) and continue a further 7km east to Castlegregory, the Dingle Peninsula's water-sports playground.

CONNOR PASS

At 456m, the Connor (or Conor) Pass is Ireland's highest mountain pass. On a foggy day you'll see nothing but the road just in front of you, but in fine weather it offers phenomenal views of Dingle Harbour to the south and Mt Brandon to the north. The road is in good shape, despite being very narrow and *very* steep (large signs portend doom for buses and trucks).

The summit car park yields views down to two lakes in the rock-strewn valley below, plus the remains of walls and huts where people once lived impossibly hard lives. When visibility is good, the 10-minute climb to the summit is well worthwhile for the kind of vistas that inspire mountain climbers.

⑨ Castlegregory

A highlight of the quiet village of Castlegregory (Caislean an Ghriare) is the vista back to the often snowy hills to the south (a lowlight is the sprawl of philistine holiday homes).

However, things change when you drive up the sand-strewn road along the **Rough Point Peninsula**, the broad spit of land between Tralee Bay and Brandon Bay. Great underwater visibility makes this one of Ireland's best diving areas, where you can glimpse pilot whales, orcas, sunfish and dolphins. Professional dive shop **Waterworld** (☏066-713 9292; www. waterworld.ie; single-tank dive incl gear €45) is based at Harbour House (p183). **Jamie Knox Watersports** (☏066-713 9411; www. jamieknox.com; Brandon Bay) offers surf, windsurf, kitesurf, canoe and pedalo hire and lessons.

✗ p183

The Drive ≫ Follow the road signs 7km south of Castlegregory to one of the Dingle Peninsula's least-known gems, the Glanteenassig Forest Recreation Area.

TRIP HIGHLIGHT

⑩ Glanteenassig Forest Recreation Area

Encompassing 450 hectares of woodland, mountain, lake and bog, **Glanteenassig Forest Recreation Area** (www. coillte.ie; ⊙7am-10pm May-Aug, 9am-6pm Sep-Apr) is a magical, little-visited treasure. There are two **lakes**; you can drive right up to the higher lake, which is encircled by a plank boardwalk, though it's too narrow for wheelchairs or prams.

The Drive ≫ From Glanteenassig Forest Recreation Area, follow the signs for 7km to the village of Aughacasla – home to the wonderful Seven Hogs inn – on the northern coast road (the R560), which links up with the N86.

⑪ Blennerville

Blennerville, just over 1km southwest of central Tralee on the N86, used to be the city's chief port, though the harbour has long since silted in. A 19th-century flour **windmill** here has been restored and is the largest working mill in Ireland and Britain. Its modern **visitor centre** (adult/child €5/3; ⊙9am-6pm Jun-Aug, 9.30am-5.30pm Apr-May & Sep-Oct) houses an exhibition on grain-milling, and on the thousands of emigrants who boarded 'coffin ships' from what was then Kerry's largest embarkation point. Admission includes a 30-minute guided windmill tour.

The Drive ≫ Staying on the N86 brings you into the heart of Tralee.

⑫ Tralee

Although Tralee is Kerry's county town, it's more engaged with the business of everyday life than the tourist trade. Elegant Denny St and Day Pl are the oldest parts of town, with 18th-century buildings, while the Square, just south of the Mall, is a pleasant, open contemporary space hosting **farmers markets** (liveliest on Saturdays).

In Ireland and beyond, Tralee is synonymous with the **Rose of Tralee** (http://roseoftralee.ie) beauty pageant, open to Irish women and women of Irish descent from around the world (the 'roses'), which takes place amid five days of celebrations in August.

An absolute treat is the **Kerry County Museum** (Denny St; adult/child €5/free; ⊙9.30am-5.30pm), with excellent interpretive displays on Irish historical events and trends. The Medieval Experience re-creates life (smells and all) in Tralee in 1450.

Ingeniously converted from a terrace house, **Roundy's** (5 Broguemakers Lane; ⊙from 5pm) is Tralee's hippest little bar, spinning old-school funk; **Baily's Corner** (Lower Castle St) is deservedly popular for its traditional sessions.

🛏 p183

Eating & Sleeping

Killarney ❶

✗ Vanilla Pod
Irish €€

(📞064-662 6559; www.thevanillapodrestaurants.com; Old Market Lane; mains €18-27; ⏲breakfast, lunch & dinner) By day, Gavin Gleeson's gem of a cafe serves dishes like beer-battered salmon and salads such as almond-crusted goat's cheese with raspberry dressing. Dinner, offering mains like maple-glazed pork, is a more upmarket affair.

🛏 Fairview
Inn €€

(📞064-663 4164; www.fairviewkillarney.com; College St; d from €110; P 🛜) Done out in beautiful timbers, the individually decorated rooms at this boutique guesthouse offer better bang for your buck than bigger, less personal places around town. The elegant on-site restaurant is a winner come evening.

Dingle Town ❸

✗ John Benny's
Pub €€

(www.johnbennyspub.com; Strand St; mains €10-19; ⏲lunch & dinner) A toasty cast-iron wood stove, stone slab floor, memorabilia on the walls and the best bar menu in town (including scrumptious seafood chowder) make this one of Dingle's most enjoyable traditional pubs. Local musos pour in most nights for rockin' trad sessions.

✗ Out of the Blue
Seafood €€€

(📞066-915 0811; The Wood; lunch €10-20, mains €15-30; ⏲dinner daily, lunch Sun) This rustic blue-and-yellow, fishing-shack-style restaurant is, somewhat incongruously, Dingle's best restaurant, with an intense devotion to fresh local seafood (if they don't like the catch, they don't open). Creative dishes like pan-seared scallops flambéed in Calvados change nightly.

🛏 Harbour Nights
B&B €€

(📞066-915 2499; www.dinglebandb.com; The Wood; d €70-80; P @ 🛜 ♿) Right on the waterfront, away from the hustle and bustle, yet less than five minutes' walk from town, all 14 rooms at this roomy B&B have stunning views of Dingle's harbour.

🛏 Pax House
B&B €€

(📞066-915 1518; www.pax-house.com; Upper John St; s/d from €90/120; P @ 🛜 ♿) From its highly individual decor (including contemporary paintings) to the outstanding views over the estuary from room balconies and the terrace, Pax House is a treat.

Castlegregory ❾

✗ Harbour House
Seafood €€

(📞066-713 9292; www.maharees.ie; Scraggane Pier; mains €6-15; ⏲dinner; P 🛜 ♿) The family who run this hotel with leisure centre/restaurant/dive school overlooking the Maharees Islands have their own fishing boat, bringing catches 'from the tide to the table', with vegetables grown in the garden out the back. Its 15 rooms (single/double from €40/80) are comfortable and contemporary.

Tralee ⓬

🛏 Meadowlands
Hotel €€

(📞066-718 0444; www.meadowlandshotel.com; Oakpark; d €90-110; P @ 🛜 ♿) Strolling distance from town but far enough away to be quiet, Meadowlands is an unexpectedly romantic four-star hotel. Rooms are done out in autumnal hues; its upmarket dinner-only restaurant (three-course menu €32) and its bar (bar food €12 to €21.50) are as popular with locals as they are with visitors.

Bantry An idyllic inlet famed for its oysters and mussels

Southwest Blitz

16

Catch the very best of Ireland's southwest along this classic route as it curls from Killarney along the Ring of Kerry coast and across County Cork's lush countryside through to Youghal.

TRIP HIGHLIGHTS

128 km

Kenmare
Board a seal-spotting cruise accompanied by sea shanties

236 km

Cork
Thriving, cultured metropolis made glorious by its location

Killorglin **START**
Killarney

Youghal
7
Cobh **FINISH**

5

4

6

155 km

Bantry
Visit Bantry House gardens' enormous 'stairway to the sky'

Caherdaniel
Subtropical gardens at Derrynane's historic park

84 km

4 DAYS
290KM / 180 MILES

GREAT FOR...

BEST TIME TO GO

Late spring and early autumn for the best weather and manageable crowds.

ESSENTIAL PHOTO

The Scarriff Inn's view across rocky coastline and scattered islands.

BEST FOR FAMILIES

Ride the train or stroll around animal-filled Fota Wildlife Park.

Classic Trip

16 Southwest Blitz

On this drive around the country's stunning southwest you'll encounter soaring stone castles, dizzying sea cliffs, wide, sandy beaches, crystal-clear lakes, dense woodlands and boat-filled harbours. Villages spill over with brightly painted buildings, vibrant markets and cosy pubs with toe-tapping live music, perfectly poured pints and fantastic craic. It all conjures up iconic impressions of Ireland.

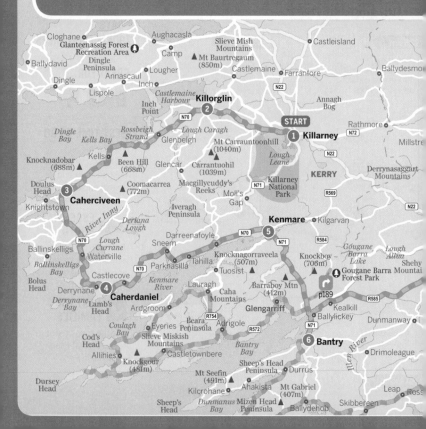

❶ Killarney

Killarney's biggest attraction, in every sense, is Killarney National Park (p171), with magnificent Muckross Estate at its heart. If you're not doing the classic Ring of Kerry route that brings you through the park, you should definitely consider a detour here. Right in town, there are pedestrian entrances to the park opposite **St Mary's Cathedral** (Cathedral Pl), a superb example of neo-Gothic revival architecture, built between 1842 and 1855.

Also worth a visit in the town centre is the 1860s **Franciscan Friary** (Fair Hill), with an ornate Flemish-style altarpiece, some impressive tilework and, most notably, stained-glass windows by Harry Clarke. The Dublin artist's organic style was influenced by art nouveau, art deco and symbolism.

Plunkett and College Sts are lined with pubs; behind leaded glass

LINK YOUR TRIP

12 Blackwater Valley Drive

Youghal is the starting point for a glorious drive through the Blackwater Valley.

18 West Cork Villages

Head 76km southwest of Youghal to Kinsale to wind your way around West Cork's picturesque peninsulas.

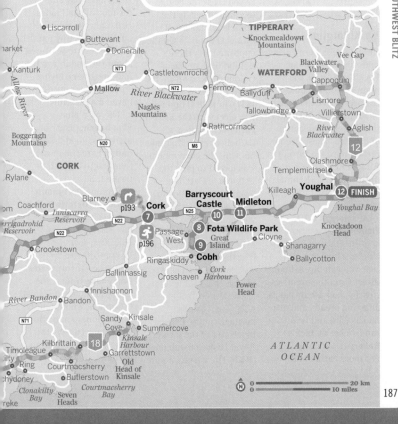

Classic Trip

doors, tiny traditional pub **O'Connor's** (High St) is one of Killarney's most popular haunts, with live music every night.

p183

The Drive » It's 22km west to Killorglin on the N72. To visit the too-gorgeous-for-words Gap of Dunloe (p170) en route, after 5km turn south onto Gap Rd and follow it for 3km to Kate Kearney's Cottage, where many drivers park in order to walk up to the Gap. You can also hire ponies and jaunting cars here (bring cash).

❷ Killorglin

Unless you're here during mid-August's ancient Puck Fair (p166), the main reason to pause at the pretty riverside town of Killorglin (Cill Orglan) is its excellent selection of eateries. These become rather more scarce on the Ring of Kerry coast road until you get to Kenmare, so considering picking up picnic fare here too.

At smokery **KRD Fisheries** (www.krdfisheries .com; The Bridge; ⊙9am-5pm Mon-Fri, to 1pm Sat, to 11am Sun), you can buy salmon direct from the premises. Nearby, Jack Healy bakes amazing breads and also makes pâté and beautiful sandwiches at **Jack's Bakery** (Lower Bridge St). For more eating and

sleeping options, see also p173.

p195

The Drive » It's 40km from Killorglin to Caherciveen. En route, you'll pass the turn-off to the little-known Cromane Peninsula, with a truly exceptional restaurant; the quaint, insightful Kerry Bog Village Museum; and the turn-off to Rossbeigh Strand, with dazzling views north to the Dingle Peninsula (see our Ring of Kerry trip, p163, for these highlights).

❸ Caherciveen

The ruined cottage on the eastern bank of the Carhan River, on the left as you cross the bridge to Caherciveen, is the humble birthplace of Daniel O'Connell. On the opposite bank there's a stolid bust statue of O'Connell. Known as 'the Great Liberator' (1775–1847), in 1828 O'Connell was elected to the British Parliament, but as a Catholic, he couldn't take his seat; the government was forced to pass the 1829 Act of Catholic Emancipation, allowing some well-off Catholics voting rights and the right to be elected as MPs. Learn more about it at the **Barracks** (www .theoldbarracks.com; off Main St; adult/child €4/2; ⊙10am-4.30pm Mon-Fri, 11.30am-4.30pm Sat, 1-5pm Sun) heritage centre, housed in a tower of the former Royal Irish Constabulary (RIC). The barracks were

burnt down in 1922 by anti-Treaty forces.

Ballycarbery Castle and ring forts (p167) are located here; Caherciveen is also a jumping-off point for exploring Valentia Island and the Skellig Ring (p167).

The Drive » Continue from Caherciveen for 17km along the N70 to Waterville. From Waterville, the rugged, rocky coastline is at its most dramatic as the road twists, turns and twists again along the 12km-long stretch to Caherdaniel.

TRIP HIGHLIGHT

❹ Caherdaniel

Hiding between Derrynane Bay and the foothills of Eagles Hill, Caherdaniel barely qualifies as a tiny hamlet. Businesses are scattered about the undergrowth like smugglers, fitting since this was once a haven for the same.

There's a Blue Flag **beach**, plenty of activities, good hikes and pubs where you may be tempted to break into pirate talk.

Sublime **Derrynane National Historic Park** (www.heritageireland.ie; Derrynane; adult/child €3/1; ⊙10.30am-6pm Apr-Sep, 10.30am-5pm Wed-Sun Oct-late Nov) incorporates **Derrynane House**, the ancestral home of Daniel O'Connell, whose family made money smuggling from their base by the dunes; and astonishing **gardens**, warmed by the Gulf Stream, with palms, 4m-high tree ferns, gunnera ('giant rhubarb') and other South American species. A **walking track** through the gardens leads to wetlands, beaches and cliff tops.

Wall-to-wall windows frame what the owners plausibly claim is 'Ireland's finest view' across the rocky coastline and scattered islands to Kenmare Bay and Bantry Bay at the **Scarriff Inn** (📞066-947 5132; http://scarriffinn.com; Caherdaniel; mains €16-24; ⏱restaurant lunch & dinner; 🅿). Drink it in over a snack, steak or seafood (call ahead to confirm seasonal kitchen hours) or just a pint. Or

wake up to them from one of its six airy rooms with private bathrooms at its neighbouring B&B (d €70), which can also organise dive trips and fishing gear.

The Drive ❯❯ The N70 zigzags for 21km east to the quaint, colourful little village of Sneem. This area is home to one of the finest castle hotels in the country, the Parknasilla Resort & Spa (p173). It's a further 27km drive along the N70 to Kenmare.

- - - - - - - - - - - -

TRIP HIGHLIGHT

❺ Kenmare

Set around its triangular market square, the sophisticated town of Kenmare is stunningly sited by Kenmare Bay.

Reached through the tourist office, the

Kenmare Heritage Centre (📞064-664 1233; kenmaretio@eircom.net; The Square; ⏱vary) tells the history of the town from its founding as Neidín by the swashbuckling Sir William Petty in 1670. The centre also relates the story of the Poor Clare Convent, founded in 1861, which is still standing behind Holy Cross Church.

Local women were taught needlepoint lace-making at the convent and their lacework catapulted Kenmare to international fame. Upstairs from the Heritage Centre, the **Kenmare Lace and Design Centre** (www.kenmarelace.ie; ⏱vary)

DETOUR:
GOUGANE BARRA FOREST PARK

Start: ❻ Bantry

Almost alpine in feel, **Gougane Barra** (www.gouganebarra.com) is a truly magical part of inland County Cork, with spectacular vistas of craggy mountains, silver streams and pine forests sweeping down to a mountain lake, the source of the River Lee. St Finbarre, the founder of Cork, established a monastery here in the 6th century. He had a hermitage on the island in Gougane Barra Lake (Lough an Ghugain), which is now approached by a short causeway. The small chapel on the island has fine stained-glass representations of obscure Celtic saints. A road runs through the park in a loop, with plenty of opportunities to walk the well-marked network of paths and nature trails through the forest.

The only place to air your hiking boots is the **Gougane Barra Hotel** (📞026-47069; www.gouganebarrahotel.com; r from €99). There's an on-site restaurant (serving a hearty dinner for €42), a cafe and a pub next door. The hotel runs a summer theatre festival.

About 6km north of Bantry, turn off the N71 onto the R584 and follow it north for 23km to Gougane Barra. Retrace your route to the N71 to continue back to Bantry and on to Cork City.

Classic Trip

WHY THIS IS A CLASSIC TRIP
CATHERINE LE NEVEZ, AUTHOR

Cresting from Killarney around to Youghal, this trip not only incorporates all of Ireland's definitive elements but plenty of unexpected ones too, from the *Titanic*'s fateful final port to exotic animals roaming free in an island-set zoo, and a spine-tingling former prison – as well as countless opportunities for serendipitous detours (because, of course, serendipity is what makes a road trip a true classic).

Top: View of St Fin Barre's Cathedral across the rooftops of Cork city
Left: Bantry House gardens
Right: Cork's English Market

ROBERT MCGRATH/GETTY IMAGES ©

190

has displays including designs for 'the most important piece of lace ever made in Ireland' (in a 19th-century critic's opinion).

Star Sailing (☎064-664 1222; www.staroutdoors.ie; R571, Dauros) offers activities including sailing (from €65 per hour for up to six people; you'll need some prior experience), sea kayaking (single/double per hour €18/32) and hill walking for all levels.

Warm yourself on tea, coffee, rum and the captain's sea shanties on an entertaining two-hour voyage with **Seafari** (☎064-664 2059; www.seafariireland.com; Kenmare Pier; adult/child €20/12.50; ⏱Apr-Oct) to spot Ireland's biggest seal colony and other marine life. Binoculars (and lollipops!) are provided.

🛏 p195

The Drive » Leave the Ring of Kerry at Kenmare and take the N71 south for 33km to Bantry. For a scenic alternative, consider driving via the Ring of Beara, encircling the Beara Peninsula (p212). If you don't have time to do the entire Ring, a shorter option is to cut across the Beara's spectacular Healy Pass Rd (R574).

TRIP HIGHLIGHT

6 Bantry

Framed by the craggy Caha Mountains, sweeping Bantry Bay is an idyllic inlet famed for its oysters and mussels.

Classic Trip

On approach, 1km southwest of the town centre on the N71 is **Bantry House** (☎027-50047; www.bantryhouse.com; Bantry Bay; adult/child €10/3; ☺10am-6pm mid-Mar–Oct), the former home of Richard White, who earned his place in history when in 1798 he warned authorities of the imminent landing of patriot Wolfe Tone and his French fleet to join the countrywide rebellion of the United Irishmen. Storms prevented the fleet from landing, altering the course of Irish history. The house's **gardens** are its great glory, and it hosts the weeklong **West Cork Chamber Music Festival** (www.westcorkmusic.ie) in June/July, when it closes to the public (the garden, craft shop and tearoom remain open).

✗ ⊨ p213

The Drive » Head north on the N71 to the crossroads at Ballylickey and take the R585 then the N22 through rugged terrain softening to patchwork farmland along the 86km journey to Cork city.

- - - - - - - - - - - -

TRIP HIGHLIGHT

❼ Cork City

Ireland's second city is first in every important respect, at least according to the locals, who cheerfully refer to it as the 'real capital of Ireland'.

A flurry of urban renewal has resulted in new buildings, bars and arts centres and tidied up thoroughfares. The best of the city is still happily traditional, though – snug pubs with regular live-music sessions, excellent local produce in an ever-expanding list of restaurants and a genuinely proud welcome from the locals.

Cork swings during the **Guinness Jazz Festival** (www.corkjazzfestival.com), with an all-star line-up in venues across town in October. An eclectic weeklong program of international films screens in October/November during the **Cork Film Festival** (www.corkfilmfest.org).

About 2km west of the city centre, faint-hearted souls may find the imposing former prison **Cork City Gaol** (www.corkcitygaol.com; Convent Ave, Sunday's Well; adult/child €7/4; ☺9.30am-5pm) grim, but it's actually very moving, bringing home the harshness of the 19th-century penal system. An audio tour guides you around the restored cells, with models of suffering prisoners and sadistic-looking guards. The most common crime was simply poverty; many of the inmates were sentenced to hard labour for stealing loaves of bread. The prison closed in 1923, and reopened in 1927 as a radio station; the Governor's House has been converted into the Radio Museum Experience.

See also our Cork City walking tour, p196; foodies should check out the Southwestern Pantry trip, p202.

✗ ⊨ p195

The Drive » Head east of central Cork via the N8 and N25, and take the turn-off to Cobh to reach Fota Wildlife Park (18km).

- - - - - - - - - - - -

❽ Fota Wildlife Park

Kangaroos bound, monkeys and gibbons leap and scream on wooded islands, and cheetahs run without a cage or fence in sight at the huge outdoor **Fota Wildlife Park** (☎021-481 2678; www.fotawildlife.ie; Carrigtwohill; adult/child €14/9; ☺10am-6pm Mon-Sat, 11am-6pm Sun, last admission 1hr before closing).

A **tour train** (1 way/return €1/2) runs a circuit round the park every 15 minutes in high season, but the 2km **circular walk** offers a more close-up experience.

From the wildlife park, you can stroll to the Regency-style **Fota House** (☎021-481 5543; www.fotahouse.com; Carrigtwohill; adult/child €6/3; ☺10am-5pm Mon-Sat, from 11am

DETOUR:
BLARNEY CASTLE

Start: **7** **Cork City**

If you need proof of the power of a good yarn, then join the queue to get into the 15th-century **Blarney Castle** (☎021-438 5252; www.blarneycastle.ie; Blarney; adult/child/student €10/3.50/8; ☻9am-7pm Mon-Sat, 9am-5.30pm Sun Jun-Aug, 9am-6.30pm Mon-Sat, 9.30am-5.30pm Sun May & Sep, 9am-sundown Sun Oct-Apr), one of Ireland's most inexplicably popular tourist attractions.

The clichéd **Blarney Stone** is perched at the top of a steep climb up slippery spiral staircases. On the battlements, you bend backwards over a long, long drop (with safety grill and attendant to prevent tragedy) to kiss the stone. Once you're upright, don't forget to admire the stunning views before descending.

Queen Elizabeth I is said to have invented the term 'to talk blarney' out of exasperation with Lord Blarney's ability to talk endlessly without ever actually agreeing to her demands.

If the throngs get too much, vanish into the Rock Close, part of the beautiful and often ignored gardens.

Head out of central Cork via Merchant's Quay and the N20; Blarney is about 10km northwest of the city.

Sun Apr-Oct). The mostly barren interior contains a fine kitchen and ornate plasterwork ceilings; interactive displays bring the rooms to life.

Attached to the house is the 150-year-old **arboretum**, which has a Victorian fernery, a magnolia walk and some beautiful trees, including giant redwoods and a Chinese ghost tree.

The Drive ≫ From Fota Wildlife Park, head south for 5km to Cobh.

- - - - - - - - - - - -

9 Cobh

For many years Cobh (pronounced 'cove') was the port of Cork, and it has always had a strong connection with Atlantic crossings,

including many fateful ones. During the Famine, some 2.5 million people left Ireland from the port of Cobh through the glistening estuary. In 1838 the *Sirius,* the first steamship to cross the Atlantic, sailed from Cobh, and the *Titanic* made its final stop here in 1912.

Standing dramatically above Cobh on a hillside terrace, the massive French Gothic **St Colman's Cathedral** (Cathedral Pl; admission by donation) is out of all proportion to the unassuming town. Its most exceptional feature is the 47-bell carillon, the largest in Ireland, weighing a stonking 3440kg.

In 1849 Cobh was renamed Queenstown after Queen Victoria paid a visit; the name lasted until Irish independence in 1921. Housed in the old train station, **Cobh, The Queenstown Story** (☎021-481 3591; www.cobhheritage.com; adult/child €8/4; ☻10am-6pm, last admission 1hr before closing) has interactive exhibits evoking the Famine tragedy, a genealogy centre and cafe.

🛏 p195

The Drive ≫ Return from Cobh to the N25; 2km east of the turn-off to Cobh near Carrigtwohill, less than 1km south of the N25, is Barryscourt Castle.

Classic Trip

⑩ Barryscourt Castle

Immigrants from Wales in the 12th century, the Barry family quickly began intermarrying with important Irish families of the time. Soon they had huge tracts of land and real wealth. In order to protect their fortune, the clan began building a vast fortification in the 15th century.

More impressive and much less crowded than Blarney Castle, **Barryscourt Castle** (www .heritageireland.ie; admission free; ⏱10am-6pm Jun-Sep) survives in remarkably good condition (albeit with a lot of restoration). An authentic 16th-century kitchen and decorative gardens have been re-created.

The Drive » Once you're back on the N25, it's an easy 6km run east into Midleton.

⑪ Midleton

The number-one attraction in Midleton (p204) is the former whiskey distillery now housing the Jameson Experience. Attractive cafes and a great farmers market make it worth stopping for a while.

The Drive » Continue on the N25 for the final 28km leg to Youghal.

⑫ Youghal

The ancient seaport of Youghal (Eochaill; pronounced 'yawl'), at the mouth of the River Blackwater, was a hotbed of rebellion against the English in the 16th century, and Oliver Cromwell wintered here in 1649 as he sought to drum up support for his war in England and quell insurgence from the Irish. Youghal was granted to Sir Walter Raleigh during the Elizabethan Plantation of Munster.

The curious **Clock Gate** was built in 1777, and served as a clock tower and jail concurrently; several prisoners taken in the 1798 Rising were hanged from its windows.

Main St has an interesting curve that follows the original shore; many of the shopfronts are from the 19th century. Further up the street are six almshouses built by Englishman Richard Boyle, who bought Raleigh's Irish estates and became the first earl of Cork in 1616 in recognition of his work in creating 'a very excellent colony'. Across the road is the 15th-century tower house **Tynte's Castle** (www.tyntescastle.com), which originally had a defensive riverfront position before the River Blackwater silted up and changed course.

Built in 1220, **St Mary's Collegiate Church** incorporates elements of an earlier Danish church dating back to the 11th century. The churchyard is bounded by a fine stretch of the 13th-century town wall and one of the remaining turrets.

Beside the church, **Myrtle Grove** is the former home of Sir Walter Raleigh. His **gardens**, on the other side of St Mary's, are open to the public.

Eating & Sleeping

Killorglin ②

✕ Giovannelli   Italian €€
(📞087 123 1353; Lower Bridge St; mains €15-30; 🕐lunch & dinner Tue-Sat) **Northern Italian native Daniele Giovannelli** makes all of his pasta by hand at this simple but intimate little restaurant. Highlights of the blackboard menu might include seafood linguine with mussels in shells, and beef ravioli.

✕ Sol Y Sombra   Tapas €€
(📞066-976 2347; www.solysombra.ie; Lower Bridge St; tapas €6.50-12, mains €15-20; 🕐dinner Wed-Sun) Set in a beautifully renovated 1816 church, Sol Y Sombra transports you to Mediterranean soil with its tapas and larger *raciones* dishes for sharing, such as grilled squid, marinated anchovy fillets and an array of tostadas. Bands often play.

Kenmare ⑤

🛏 Sheen Falls Lodge   Boutique Hotel €€€
(📞064-664 1600; www.sheenfallslodge.ie; d €115-230; 🕐Feb-Dec; 🅿@🛜) The marquis of Landsdowne's former summer residence still feels like an aristocrats' playground, with a spa and 66 rooms with Italian marble bathrooms, and views of the falls and across Kenmare Bay. Amenities are many (clay-pigeon shooting, anyone?).

Cork City ⑦

✕ Jacques Restaurant   Modern Irish €€€
(📞021-427 7387; www.jacquesrestaurant.ie; 9 Phoenix St; mains €22-27; 🕐6-10pm Mon-Sat) Jacqueline and Eithne Barry have built up a terrific network of local suppliers to help them realise their culinary ambitions – the freshest Cork food cooked simply. The menu, served in an elegant dining room, changes daily.

✕ Market Lane   International €€
(📞021-427 4710; www.marketlane.ie; 5 Oliver Plunkett St; mains €10-26; 🕐noon-late Mon-Sat, 1-9pm Sun) It's always hopping at this bright corner bistro with an open kitchen. Service is quick and attentive, but you may want to pause at the long wooden bar anyway. The menu is broad, and changes often to reflect what's fresh; there are lots of wines by the glass.

🛏 Auburn House   B&B €€
(📞021-450 8555; www.auburnguesthouse.com; 3 Garfield Tce, Wellington Rd; s/d €58/80; 🅿🛜) There's a warm family welcome at this neat B&B near the fun of MacCurtain St. It has smallish but well-kept rooms brightened by window boxes. Back rooms have sweeping views over the city.

🛏 Imperial Hotel   Hotel €€
(📞021-427 4040; www.flynnhotels.com; South Mall; r €90-220; 🅿@🛜) Fast approaching her bicentenary, the 130-room Imperial knows how to age gracefully. Public spaces resonate with opulent period detail such as marble floors, elaborate floral bouquets and more; modern touches include a digital music library and Aveda spa.

Cobh ⑨

🛏 Commodore Hotel   Hotel €€
(📞021-481 1277; www.commodorehotel.ie; Westbourne Pl; s/d €60/100; @🛜🏊) A classic seaside hotel with soaring chandeliered hallways and 42 well-appointed rooms (it's worth paying extra for one with a sea view). The pool is indoors and a roof garden offers yet more views.

STRETCH YOUR LEGS
CORK CITY

Start/Finish Lewis Glucksman Gallery

Distance 4.7km

Duration 3 hours

The River Lee flows around Cork's central island of grand Georgian parades, 17th-century alleys and modern masterpieces. As you crisscross it between galleries and architectural attractions, you'll discover that the single-best sight is the city itself.

Take this walk on Trips

2 16 17

Lewis Glucksman Gallery

Situated on the leafy campus of prestigious University College Cork (UCC), the award-winning limestone, steel and timber **Lewis Glucksman Gallery** (www.glucksman.org; University College Cork; suggested donation €5; ☻10am-5pm Tue-Sat, noon-5pm Sun) displays the best in national and international contemporary art and installation.

The Walk » From UCC, you can take a short cut through the car park en route to St Fin Barre's Cathedral.

St Fin Barre's Cathedral

Spires, gargoyles and sculpture adorn Cork's Protestant **St Fin Barre's Cathedral** (www.cathedral.cork.anglican.org; Bishop St; adult/child €4/2; ☻9.30am-5.30pm Mon-Sat, 12.30-5pm Sun). Local legend says the golden angel on the eastern side will blow its horn when the Apocalypse is due to start... The grandeur continues inside, with marble floor mosaics, a huge pulpit and a bishop's throne.

The Walk » Turn east on Bishop St and follow the riverside quays; cross the bridge north at Mary St to reach the English Market.

English Market

Cork's ornate **English Market** (Princes St; ☻9am-5.30pm Mon-Sat) is a must-see but you're also spoiled for dining options; see also p202.

The Walk » Princes St meets St Patrick's St, the main shopping and commercial area. Turn left onto Academy St and right on Emmet Pl to the city's premier gallery.

Crawford Municipal Art Gallery

Highlights of the excellent permanent collection at Cork's public gallery, **Crawford Municipal Art Gallery** (www.crawfordartgallery.ie; Emmet Pl; ☻10am-5pm Mon-Sat, to 8pm Thu), covering the 17th century to today, include works by Sir John Lavery, Jack B Yeats, Nathaniel Hone and a room devoted to Irish women artists including Mainie Jellet

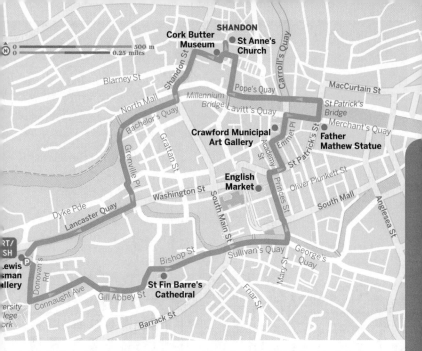

and Evie Hone. The Sculpture Galleries contain plaster casts of Roman and Greek statues, given to King George IV by the pope in 1822.

The Walk » Continue on Emmet Pl, passing Cork Opera House before turning right on Lavitt's Quay and rejoining St Patrick's St.

Father Mathew Statue

The imposing **statue** on St Patrick's St, just south of the River Lee North Channel, is of Father Theobald Mathew, who crusaded against the ills of alcohol in the 1830s and 1840s with such success that a quarter of a million people took the 'pledge' and whiskey production was cut in half.

The Walk » Head north over St Patrick's Bridge and turn west to the hillside neighbourhood of Shandon, with galleries, antique shops and cafes along its old lanes and squares lined with tiny old row houses.

St Anne's Church

Shandon is dominated by the 1722 **St Anne's Church** (www.shandonbells.org;

John Redmond St; ⏰10am-5pm Mon-Sat), aka the 'Four-Faced Liar', so called as each of the tower's four clocks used to tell a different time. Ring the **bells** (adult/child €6/5) on the 1st floor and continue the 132 steps to the top for 360-degree views of the city.

The Walk » It's a short walk south on Exchange St and right on John Redmond St to the Cork Butter Museum.

Cork Butter Museum

Cork's long tradition of butter manufacturing is related through displays and dioramas in the **Cork Butter Museum** (www.corkbutter.museum; O'Connell Sq; adult/child €4/3; ⏰10am-5pm Mar-Jun & Sep-Oct, to 6pm Jul & Aug). The square in front is dominated by the round **Firkin Crane** building, central to the old butter market and now housing a dance centre.

The Walk » Head across the island along the 1.5km walk back to UCC and the Lewis Glucksman Gallery.

Cork Go beyond the city's port and explore Cork's serious food scene

Southwestern Pantry

17

County Cork has earned itself a justifiable reputation as the gourmet capital of Ireland. Graze your way around the county on this foodie's fantasy and feast on its sumptuous scenery too.

TRIP HIGHLIGHTS

139 km

Belvelly
Sublime smoked salmon at Ireland's oldest smokehouse

120 km

Cork City
Cork's 1788-established English Market showcases the county's fare

START
Durrus

FINISH
Midleton

58 km

Clonakilty
Home to the country's most famous black pudding

Kinsale
Sensational seafood, food festivals and gourmet purveyors galore

97 km

5 DAYS
154KM / 96 MILES

GREAT FOR...

BEST TIME TO GO
Produce is at its most abundant from spring onwards.

ESSENTIAL PHOTO
Kinsale's boat-filled harbour is a picture.

BEST FOR FOOD
The English Market in Cork City showcases the county's tantalising bounty.

199

17 Southwestern Pantry

Farmers markets, farmhouse cheeses, fishing fleets hauling in fresh-as-it-gets seafood, the country's oldest smokehouse and its most famous black pudding, as well as icons like Cork's mouth-watering English Market, Jameson's old whiskey distillery, the wonderful Ballymaloe House and prestigious cookery school and some of the nation's finest eateries are among the treats awaiting in Ireland's Southwestern Pantry. *Bain taitneamh as do bhéil* (bon appétit)!

❶ Durrus

This little crossroads at the head of Dunmanus Bay has become something of a gourmet hot spot in recent years and earned an international reputation for its cheese, thanks to the likes of **Durrus Farmhouse** (📞027-61100; Coomkeen; 🕙10.30am-noon Thu & Fri), the produce of which is sold here and as far afield as America. You can't visit the production area but Jeffa Gill gives informal 10-minute presentations. To reach

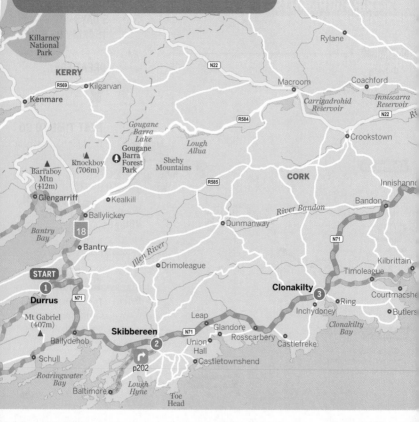

the farm, drive 900m out of Durrus along the Ahakista road, turn right at St James' Church and continue for 3km until you see the sign for the farm.

Popular cooking courses at **Good Things Café** (☎027-61426; www.thegoodthingscafe.com; Ahakista Rd; lunch mains €10-20, dinner mains €21-38; ☺12.30-3pm & 7-9pm Thu-Mon mid-Jun–Dec) include a two-day Kitchen Miracle program (€375).

The Drive >> From Durrus, zigzag 30km southeast via the N71 to Skibbereen.

2 Skibbereen

Try to time your journey through the busy market town of Skibbereen (Sciobairín) to catch the **county market** (☺12.30-2.30pm Fri) and/or the **farmers market** (☺10am-1.30pm Sat) on Old Market Sq. If you're in town in mid-September, don't miss the **Taste of West Cork Food Festival** (www.atasteofwestcork.com), with a lively market and events at local restaurants.

The Drive >> It's 33km along the N71 from Skibbereen to Clonakilty; there are slower but more scenic alternatives along the coast; see p210.

TRIP HIGHLIGHT

3 Clonakilty

Clonakilty is legendary as the birthplace of Michael Collins (see p209), commander-in-chief of the army of the Irish Free State that won independence from Britain in 1922. It's also home to the most famous black pudding in the country. The best place to buy the town's renowned blood sausage is **Edward Twomey** (☎023-883 3733; www.clonakiltyblackpudding.ie; 16 Pearse St; from €2.75), with different varieties based on the original 1880s recipe. Look out for it too at Clonakilty's twice-weekly **farmers market** (McCurtain Hill; ☺10am-2pm Thu & Sat).

✗ ⛔ p205

LINK YOUR TRIP

18 West Cork Villages

Return to Kinsale to discover Cork's picturesque peninsulas.

12 Blackwater Valley Drive

Head 26km east along the N25 for more glorious food over the border in County Waterford.

The Drive » Continue 50km east via the N71 through farming country interspersed with towns and villages to Kinsale (alternatively you can take the narrow R600 for 35km – see p208).

TRIP HIGHLIGHT

4 Kinsale

Harbour-set Kinsale (Cionn tSáile) is revered for its foodie scene, thanks in large part to its busy fishing fleet.

The **Quay Food Co** (www.quayfood.com; Market Quay; sandwiches €4-6; ⏲9am-6pm) is good for local produce, as is **Market Garden** (The Glen; ⏲9am-7pm Mon-Sat), a low-ceilinged warren of organic and local fruit and veg. Window displays at **Tom's Artisan Bakery** (46 Main St; ⏲8am-5pm Mon-Sat) are suitably artful.

There's a weekly **farmers market** (⏲9.30am-1.30pm Tue) in front of Jim Edwards' restaurant on Market Quay.

Kinsale's roots with the old wine trade are on display at the early-16th-century **Desmond Castle** (☎021-477 4855; www. heritageireland.ie; Cork St; adult/child €3/1; ⏲10am-6pm Tue-Sun Easter-Sep), which houses a small **wine museum** (www.winegeese.ie).

Tastings, meals and harbour cruises take place during Kinsale's **Gourmet Festival** (www. kinsalerestaurants.com) in early October.

 p205

The Drive » Head north for 27km on the R600 through patchwork farmland to Ireland's second-largest city.

TRIP HIGHLIGHT

5 Cork City

Cork city's food scene is reason enough to visit. To stretch your legs on a walking tour (and work off all that fine food), as well as visit its Butter Museum, see p196.

Cork's **English Market** (Princes St; ⏲9am-5.30pm Mon-Sat) is a local – no, make that national – treasure. It could just as easily be called the Victorian Market for its ornate vaulted ceilings and columns. Scores of vendors sell some of the very best local produce, meats, cheeses and takeaway food in the region. Favourites include **On the Pig's Back**, serving house-made sausages and incredible cheeses.

DETOUR: BALTIMORE

Start: 2 **Skibbereen**

Not only does Baltimore (p210), 13km south of Skibbereen on the R595, have aquatic activities galore, its seafood is sublime.

Over the last full weekend of May, Baltimore's **Seafood Festival** (www.baltimore.ie) sees jazz bands perform, wooden boats parade, and pubs bring out the mussels and prawns.

The Breton-inspired **Chez Youen** (☎028-20136; The Quay; dinner from €30; ⏲6-10pm, closed Nov & Feb) was the town's gourmet pioneer and it's still as good as ever, especially for its luscious shellfish platter (€50) of lobster, prawns, brown crab, velvet crab, shrimps and oysters at their unadorned best.

At **Casey's of Baltimore** (☎028-20197; lunches €4-10, mains €14-28; ⏲12.30-3pm & 6.30-9pm) your food comes with fantastic views. Seafood includes mussels fresh from Casey's own shellfish farm in Roaringwater Bay, and the house speciality, crab claws in garlic butter. Bar food is served all day.

Cork Olives at the English Market

On a mezzanine overlooking part of the market is one of Cork's best eateries. **Farmgate Café** (☎021-427 8134; English Market; lunch €4-13, dinner €18-30; ☺8.30am-10pm Mon-Sat) is an unmissable experience. Everything from rock oysters to ingredients for Irish stew and raspberry crumble is sourced from the market below. The best seats are at the balcony counter overlooking the passing parade of shoppers. On fine days, picnic in nearby **Bishop Lucey Park**.

The narrow, pedestrianised streets in Cork's **Huguenot Quarter** north of St Patrick's St throng with cafes and restaurants with outside tables; many serve till late.

Don't leave Cork without sampling the heavenly Chocolatier's Hot Chocolate (€4) at **O'Connaill** (☎021-437 3407; 16B French Church St) confectioners.

✕ ⛺ p205

The Drive » Some 20km east of Cork via the N25 is the feted Belvelly smokehouse.

203

DETOUR:
BALLYMALOE HOUSE & COOKERY SCHOOL

Start: **7** **Midleton**

Drawing up at wisteria-clad **Ballymaloe House** (☎021-465 2531; www.ballymaloe.ie; Shanagarry; s/d from €130/260; 🛜🐾), 12km southeast of Midleton on the R629, you know you've arrived somewhere special. Rooms are period furnished and the beautiful grounds include a tennis court, swimming pool and shop. The menu at its celebrated restaurant is drawn up daily according to the produce from Ballymaloe's extensive farms and other local sources. It also runs wine and gardening weekends.

Just over 3km further east (go through the village of Shanagarry and turn left opposite the church), TV personality Darina Allen runs the famous **Ballymaloe Cookery School** (☎021-464 6785; www.cookingisfun.ie). Book lessons, starting from half-day sessions (€75 to €115), well in advance. There are pretty cottages amid the 40-hectare organic farm for overnight students.

---

6 Belvelly

No trip to County Cork is complete without a visit to an artisan food producer, and the effervescent Frank Hederman is more than happy to show you around **Belvelly** (☎021-481 1089; www.frankhederman. com), the oldest natural smokehouse in Ireland. Seafood and cheese are smoked here, but the speciality is fish – in particular, salmon. In a traditional process that takes 24 hours from start to finish, the fish is filleted and cured before being hung in the tiny smokehouse over beech woodchips. Phone or email Frank to arrange your visit.

The Drive » It's just 2km from Belvelly to Midleton.

7 Midleton

Aficionados of fine Irish whiskey will know the main reason to linger in this bustling market town is to visit the restored 200-year-old building housing the **Jameson Experience** (☎021-461 3594; www. jamesonwhiskey.com; Old Distillery Walk; tours adult/ child/student €13.50/8/11; ⏰shop 9am-6.30pm, tour times vary) and purchase bottles, of course. Exhibits and tours explain the process of taking barley and creating whiskey (Jameson is today made in a modern factory in Cork).

Midleton's **farmers market** (Main St ⏰Sat morning), behind the courthouse, is one of Cork's best markets,

with bushels of local produce and producers who are happy to chat.

The original and sister establishment to Cork's Farmgate Café, **Farmgate Restaurant** (☎021-463 2771; www. farmgate.ie; The Coolbawn; restaurant mains around €18; ☕coffee & snacks 9am-5.30pm, lunch noon-3.30pm Mon-Sat, dinner 6.30-9.30pm Thu-Sat) also has a shop selling amazing baked goods and local, often organic, produce, cheeses and preserves.

Eating & Sleeping

Clonakilty ❸

✗ Malt House Granary   Modern Irish €€€
(☎023-883 4355; 30 Ashe St; mains €18-25; ⏱5-10pm Mon-Sat) You'll be able to check out the Clonakilty black pudding, Boilie goat's cheese, Gubbeen chorizo and Bantry Bay mussels, among other ingredients, as everything on your plate originates from West Cork.

🛏 Emmet Hotel   Hotel €€
(☎023-883 3394; www.emmethotel.com; Emmet Sq; r €65-120; 🛜) This lovely Georgian accommodation option on the elegant square has 20 large, plush rooms; O'Keeffe's restaurant on-site serves up tasty Irish food made from organic and local ingredients.

Kinsale ❹

✗ Bulman Bar & Toddies   Seafood €€
(☎021-477 2131; Summercove; mains €16-21; ⏱12.30-9.30pm) Salty informality is a style in its own right at this gastropub. Seafood excels here, whether swimming in chowder or laid out seductively on a platter. Herbs are right from the kitchen garden. The more formal restaurant **Toddies** (⏱dinner Wed-Sat) serves beautifully prepared seafood – the lobster risotto is recommended.

✗ Fishy Fishy Cafe   Seafood €€
(☎021-470 0415; www.fishyfishy.ie; Crowley's Quay; mains €13-34; ⏱noon-4pm Mon-Fri, to 4.30pm Sat & Sun) Arguably the best seafood restaurant in the country, Fishy Fishy Cafe has a wonderful setting and a terrific decked terrace out front. All the fish is caught locally; it also runs the superb **Fishy Fishy Shop & Chippie** (Guardwell; meals €8-15; ⏱noon-9pm Apr-Oct) with tables inside and out.

✗ Jim Edwards   Seafood €€
(☎021-477 2541; www.jimedwardskinsale.com; Market Quay; bar meals €7-20, restaurant meals €15-30; ⏱bar 12.30-10pm, restaurant 6-10pm) If Fishy Fishy has a serious rival, it's this unassuming pub, where the bar food is way above standard and the restaurant exceptional.

🛏 Pier House   B&B €€
(☎021-477 4475; www.pierhousekinsale.com; Pier Rd; r €80-140; P🛜) Set in a sheltered garden, this superb guesthouse has pristine rooms with shell-and-driftwood sculptures and black granite bathrooms with power showers and underfloor heating.

Cork City ❺

✗ Cafe Paradiso   Vegetarian €€€
(☎021-427 7939; www.cafeparadiso.ie; 16 Lancaster Quay; mains €23-25; ⏱noon-3pm & 6-10.30pm Tue-Sat) How about sweet chilli-glazed pan-fried tofu with Asian greens in a coconut and lemongrass broth, soba noodles and a gingered aduki bean wonton; or spring cabbage dolma of roast squash, caramelised onion and hazelnut with cardamom yoghurt, harissa sauce, broad beans and saffron-crushed potatoes? Reservations at this contender for Cork's best eatery are essential.

🛏 Garnish House   B&B €€
(☎021-427 5111; www.garnish.ie; Western Rd; s/d €75/80; P🛜) Every attention is lavished upon guests at this award-winning 14-room B&B. The legendary breakfast menu (30 choices!) includes fresh fish, French toast, omelettes and freshly cooked porridge with creamed honey and your choice of whiskey or Baileys. Enjoy it out on the garden terrace. Reception is open 24 hours.

Beara Peninsula *One of Ireland's podium peninsula drives*

West Cork Villages

18

West Cork claims some of Ireland's most scenic driving country, with three spectacular peninsulas, and a cache of maritime villages filled with colourful shops and pubs alive with music.

TRIP HIGHLIGHTS

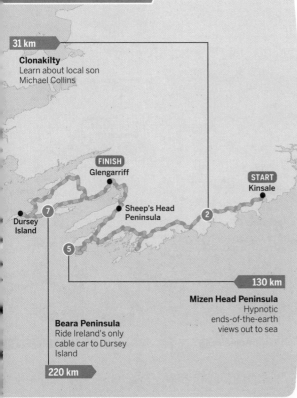

31 km

Clonakilty
Learn about local son Michael Collins

FINISH
Glengarriff

START
Kinsale

Sheep's Head Peninsula

7
Dursey Island

5

2

130 km

Mizen Head Peninsula
Hypnotic ends-of-the-earth views out to sea

Beara Peninsula
Ride Ireland's only cable car to Dursey Island

220 km

7 DAYS
354KM / 220 MILES

GREAT FOR...

BEST TIME TO GO
West Cork's villages are liveliest between April and October.

 ESSENTIAL PHOTO

Plumes of white water at the far-flung Mizen Head Signal Station.

✔ **BEST FOR AERIAL VIEWS**

Take the cable car from the Beara Peninsula to tiny Dursey Island.

207

West Cork Villages

This trip contains one of Ireland's trinity of top peninsula drives, the spellbinding Beara Peninsula, straddling Counties Cork and Kerry. Beara's southern side along Bantry Bay harbours working fishing villages, while on the rugged northern side craggy roads cut in and out of its nooks and crannies and tiny coves are like pearls in a sea of rocks.

1 Kinsale

Narrow winding streets lined with artsy shops and a harbour full of bobbing fishing boats and pleasure yachts make Kinsale (Cionn tSáile) one of Ireland's favourite midsized towns; its superb foodie reputation is a bonus.

The peninsula of Scilly is barely a 10-minute walk southeast, from where a lovely walking path continues 3km east to Summercove and the vast 17th-century star-shaped **Charles Fort** (☎021-477

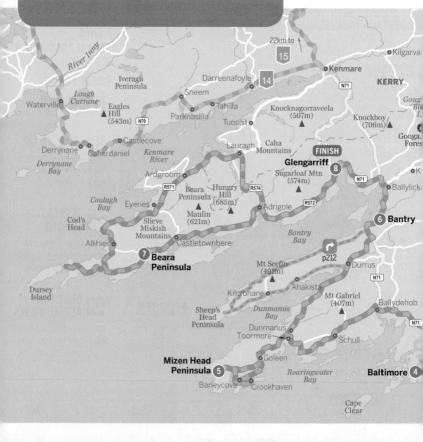

2263; www.heritageireland.ie; adult/child €4/2; ☺10am-6pm mid-Mar–Oct).

✕ ⏜ p205

The Drive » At times you'll meet the coast as you wind 35km west along the R600 to Clonakilty.

- - - - - - - - - - - -

TRIP HIGHLIGHT

② Clonakilty

Cheerful Clonakilty is a bustling market town coursed by little waterways. It serves as a hub for the scores of beguiling little coastal towns that surround it.

Reconstructed on its original site, the **Lisnagun** (Lios na gCon; ☎023-883 2565; www.liosnagcon.com; adult/child €5/3; ☺tours noon-4pm summer) ring fort, complete with souterrain and central thatched hut, gives a vivid impression of 10th-century farmstead life.

A visit to the **Michael Collins Centre** (☎023-884 6107; www.michaelcollinscentre.com; adult/child €6/3; ☺10.30am-5pm Mon-Fri, 11am-2pm Sat mid-Jun–Sep), signposted off the R600 between Timoleague and Clonakilty, is an excellent

§ **LINK YOUR TRIP**

14 Ring of Kerry
Head 27km north from Glengarriff to pick up the Ring of Kerry in Kenmare.

15 Dingle Peninsula
Killarney is the gateway to the charming Dingle Peninsula.

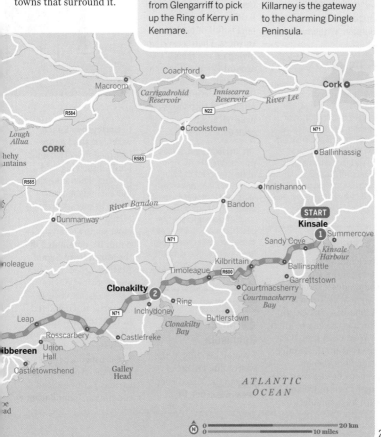

way to make sense of the life of Clonakilty's most famous son, Irish Free State commander-in-chief Michael Collins. The main negotiator of the 1921 Anglo-Irish Treaty, Collins was forced to make major concessions, including the partition of the country, famously declaring that he was signing his own death warrant. He was tragically correct, as Civil War broke out in the treaty's aftermath. A tour reveals photos, letters and a reconstruction of the 1920s country lane where Collins was killed, complete with armoured vehicle.

✕ 🛏 p205

The Drive » It's 33km along the N71 from Clonakilty to Skibbereen but it's possible to freelance along the coast the entire way. As a taster, at Rosscarbery, you can turn left onto the R597, which takes you past the pretty villages of Glandore (Cuan Dor) and Union Hall, and the turn-off to the Drombeg Stone Circle, and rejoin the N71 at Leap.

3 Skibbereen

Weekending swells and yachties from Dublin descend on the busy market town of Skibbereen (Sciobairín), which is as close to glitzy as West Cork gets. It's a far cry from the Famine, when Skib was hit perhaps harder than any other town in Ireland, with huge numbers of the local population emigrating or dying of starvation or disease. The **Skibbereen Heritage Centre** (☎028-40900; www.skibbheritage.com; Old Gasworks Bldg, Upper Bridge St; adult/child €6/3; ☉10am-6pm) puts its history into harrowing perspective.

🛏 p213

The Drive » Islands are dotted offshore to the west as you drive 13km south on the R595 to Baltimore.

4 Baltimore

Crusty old seadog Baltimore's busy little port is full of fishing trawlers. There's excellent **diving** on the reefs around Fastnet Rock (the waters are warmed by the Gulf Stream and a number of shipwrecks lie nearby), and a variety of **cruises**.

The Drive » Retrace your route north to the N71 from where it rolls west through Ballydehob, the gateway to the Mizen, and then on to the pretty village of Schull (pronounced 'skull'). Travelling on into the undulating countryside along the coastal road takes you through ever-smaller settlements to the village of Goleen. Baltimore to Goleen is 48km.

TRIP HIGHLIGHT

5 Mizen Head Peninsula

Even on arriving at the welcoming village of **Goleen** the Mizen isn't done. Continue first

STEPHEN SAKS/GETTY IMAGES ©

to **Barleycove Beach**, with vast sand dunes hemmed in by two long bluffs dissolving into the surf. Then take the increasingly narrow roads to spectacular Mizen Head, Ireland's most southwesterly point. It's dominated by the **Mizen Head Signal Station** (☎028-35225/115; www.mizenhead.ie; Mizen Head; adult/child €6/3.50; ☉10am-6pm), completed in 1909 to warn ships off rocks that appear in the water around here like crushed ice in cola. From the visitors centre, various pathways lead to the station, culminating

Kinsale Cafes and shops line a Kinsale street

in the crossing of a spectacular **arched bridge** that spans a vast gulf in the cliffs.

Pints in the sunshine are the reward for venturing on the crooked road to the outpost of **Crookhaven** (if it's raining, make that 'pints by the fireplace...'). In its heyday Crookhaven's natural harbour was an important anchorage, and mail from America was collected here.

Leaving Crookhaven, you'll spot the turn-off to the left, marked **Brow Head** – the Irish mainland's southernmost

point. Park at the bottom of the hill – the track is very narrow and there's nowhere to pull over should you meet a tractor coming the other way. After 1km the road ends and a path continues to the head.

🛏 p213

The Drive ⟩⟩ Bear north to join the scenic coast road that follows the edge of Dunmanus Bay for most of the way to Durrus and continue north to Bantry, some 60km north of Goleen.

- - - - - - - - - - - -

⑥ Bantry

Don't miss a visit to Bantry House (p191) and its glorious gardens 1km southwest of the town centre on the N71.

✕ 🛏 p213

The Drive ⟩⟩ Continue north on the N71 to Glengarriff and the Beara Peninsula. The striations of the peninsula's underlying bedrock become evident as you drive west on the R572 towards Castletownbere, 50km from Bantry. On the highest hills, Sugarloaf Mountain and Hungry Hill, rock walls known as 'benches' snake backwards and forwards across the slopes.

DETOUR:
SHEEP'S HEAD PENINSULA

Start: 5 Mizen Head Peninsula

At Durrus, one road heads for Bantry; take the other, which turns west to Sheep's Head Peninsula, to circumnavigate it and rejoin the N71 at Bantry.

The least visited of Cork's three peninsulas, Sheep's Head has a charm all its own – and plenty of sheep. There are good seascapes from along most of the loop road. The Goat's Path Rd has terrific views and runs between Gortnakilly and Kilcrohane (on the north and south coast respectively) over the western flank of Mt Seefin.

Ahakista (Atha an Chiste) consists of a couple of pubs and a few houses stretched out along the R591. An ancient **stone circle** is signposted at the southern end of Ahakista; access is via a short pathway. The peninsula's other village is **Kilcrohane**, 6km to the southwest, beside a fine beach. You can get pub food in both villages.
For more information about the area, visit www.thesheepshead.com.

TRIP HIGHLIGHT

7 Beara Peninsula

Encircling the Beara Peninsula, the Ring of Beara is – along with the Ring of Kerry and Dingle – one of Ireland's podium peninsula drives.

In the fishing town of **Castletownbere** (Baile Chais Bhéara), you'll recognise the front-cover photo of the late Pete McCarthy's bestseller, *McCarthy's Bar,* in three dimensions on Main St.

Tiny **Dursey Island**, at the end of the peninsula, is reached by Ireland's only **cable car** (adult/child return €4/1; ☉9-11am, 2.30-5pm & 7-8pm Mon-Sat, 9-10am, 1-2.30pm & 7-7.30pm Sun year-round, plus 4-5pm Sun Jun-Aug), which sways 30m above Dursey Sound; livestock take precedence over humans in the queue.

From **Allihies** (Na hAilichí), the beautiful R575 coast road, with hedges of fuchsias and rhododendrons, twists and turns for about 12km to **Eyeries**, a cluster of brightly coloured houses overlooking Coulagh Bay. From Eyeries, you can forsake the R571 for the even smaller coast roads (lanes really) to the north and east with views north to the Ring of Kerry.

At the crossroads of **Ardgroom** (Ard Dhór) heading east towards Lauragh, look for signs pointing to the Bronze Age **stone circle**.

✕ ⌐ p213

The Drive » Cut across the spectacular Healy Pass Rd (R574) to Adrigole and return on the R572 to Glengarriff (32km). Alternatively, leaving Lauragh, you can skip Glengarriff a second time and take the R573, which hugs the coast, rejoining the more no-nonsense R571 at

Tuosist for the 16km run east to Kenmare in County Kerry.

---

8 Glengarriff

Offshore from the village of Glengarriff, subtropical plants flourish in the rich soil and warm climate in the magical Italianate garden on **Garinish (Ilnacullin) Island** (☎027-63040; www.heritageireland.ie; adult/senior & child €4/3; ☉10am-6.30pm, from 11am Sun Jun-Sep, to 4pm Oct, last admission 1hr before closing). Ferry companies including **Blue Pool Ferry** (☎027-63333; adult/child return €12/6) leave every 20 to 30 minutes for the 10-minute boat trip past islands and seal colonies when the garden is open; fares exclude garden entry.

⌐ p213

The Drive » Heading north from Glengarriff, you can pick up the circular Ring of Kerry early in Kenmare, 27km to the north.

Eating & Sleeping

Skibbereen ③

🛏 Bridge House   B&B €€

(📞028-21273; www.bridgehouseskibbereen.
com; Bridge St; s/d €40/70; 📶) Mona Best has
turned her entire house into a work of art, filling
the rooms with fabulous Victorian tableaux and
period memorabilia, fragrant fresh flowers and
black satin sheets on request.

Mizen Head Peninsula ⑤

🛏 Heron's Cove   B&B €€

(📞028-35225; www.heronscove.com; Goleen;
s/d €40/80) In a delightful location, on the
shores of the tidal inlet of Goleen Harbour,
rooms have been refurbished in a restful style
and several have balconies overlooking the
inlet. The small **restaurant** (mains €16-25;
🕐dinner Apr-Oct, year-round for guests) here
has an excellent menu of organic and local food.

Bantry ⑥

✗ Fish Kitchen   Modern Irish €€

(📞027-56651; New St; mains €8-20; 🕐noon-
9pm Tue-Sat) This outstanding little restaurant
above a fish shop does seafood to perfection,
including the local oysters (served with lemon
and tabasco sauce), and pan-seared and juicy
steak too. Friendly, unfussy and absolutely
delicious.

✗ Stuffed Olive   Bakery €

(📞027-55883; New St; meals €4-7; 🕐8am-
5pm Mon-Sat) This exquisite bakery and deli
has a fine coffee bar and stools along a narrow
counter in the sunny front window. Pick up
luscious baked goods and one of the excellent
bottles of wine for a perfect picnic.

🛏 Ballylickey House   B&B €€

(📞027-50071; www.ballylickeymanorhouse.
com; Ballylickey; r €90-180; 🕐Mar-Nov; 📶🏊)

Choose from rooms in the manor house or cute
cottages set round a swimming pool. All are
spacious and comfortably furnished.

🛏 Bantry House   Manor House €€€

(📞027-50047; www.bantryhouse.com; Bantry
Bay; r €180-250; 🕐Mar-Oct; 📶) Bantry House's
pale-hued guest rooms have a mixture of
antiques and contemporary furnishings; play
croquet, lawn tennis or billiards and lounge in
the house's library once the doors shut to the
public.

Beara Peninsula ⑦

✗ Olde Bakery   Modern Irish €€

(📞027-70869; www.oldebakery.com;
Castletown House, Castletownbere; mains €13-
21; 🕐5.30-9.30pm daily, plus noon-4.30pm Sun)
One of the best restaurants in Castletownbere,
the Olde Bakery serves hearty portions of top
regional seafood.

🛏 Rodeen B&B   B&B €€

(📞027-70158; www.rodeencountryhouse.com;
Castletownbere; s/d €40/76; 🕐Mar-Oct) A
delightful six-room haven, tucked away above
the eastern approach to Castletownbere. The
musical-instrument-filled house has stunning
sea views and is surrounded by gardens full of
crumbling Delphic columns. Flowers from the
garden grace the breakfast table, and there are
home-baked scones with honey from landlady
Ellen's bees.

Glengarriff ⑧

🛏 Eccles Hotel   Hotel €€

(📞027-63003; www.eccleshotel.com;
Glengarriff Harbour; r €100-140; @) Just
east of the centre, the Eccles has a long and
distinguished history dating from 1745, and 66
big, bright rooms – ask for a bayside room on
the 4th floor.

Bunratty *Visit the popular centuries-old castle*

Shannon River Route

19

Follow the majestic River Shannon as it wends from Lough Derg to the broad estuary opening out at vibrant Limerick city, and take in the stupendous views at Loop Head.

TRIP HIGHLIGHTS

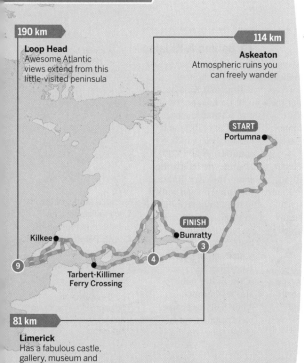

190 km

Loop Head
Awesome Atlantic views extend from this little-visited peninsula

114 km

Askeaton
Atmospheric ruins you can freely wander

START
Portumna

FINISH
Bunratty
3

Kilkee

9

Tarbert-Killimer
Ferry Crossing

4

81 km

Limerick
Has a fabulous castle, gallery, museum and cathedral

4 DAYS
296KM / 184 MILES

GREAT FOR...

BEST TIME TO GO
Even in high summer there are plenty of crowd-free escapes.

ESSENTIAL PHOTO
The soaring cliffs on the aptly named 'Scenic Loop' road west of Kilkee.

BEST FOR DOLPHIN-SPOTTING
Estuary-set Kilrush has a nature centre, dolphin trail and cruises.

215

19 Shannon River Route

Ireland's longest river provides a stunning backdrop to this route, but you'll also get out on the water. The car-ferry crossing from Tarbert in County Kerry to Killimer in County Clare takes just 20 minutes and, because the estuary is sheltered, you can usually look forward to smooth sailing.

Lettermullen

Kilronan

Aran Islands

ATLANTIC OCEAN

Kilkee **8**

Loop Head **9**   R487 Carriga

Kilbaha

Mouth of the Shannon   Bally

Ballyduff

1 Portumna

In the far southeastern corner of County Galway, the lakeside town of Portumna is popular for boating and fishing.

Impressive **Portumna Castle & Gardens** (www.heritageireland.ie; Castle Ave; adult/child €3/1; ☺9.30am-6pm Apr-Oct) was built in the early 1600s by Richard de Burgo and boasts an elaborate, geometrically laid-out organic garden.

The Drive » From Portumna, cross the River Shannon – also the county border – into County Tipperary. Take the N65 south for 7km, then turn west onto the R493, winding through farmland. At Hogan's Pass, turn west on the R494, and follow it to Ballina (52km in all).

2 Ballina & Killaloe

Facing each other across a narrow channel, Ballina and Killaloe (Cill Da Lúa) are really one destination, even if they have different personalities (and counties). A fine 1770 13-arch one-lane **bridge** spans the river, linking the pair. You can walk it in five minutes or drive it in about 20 (a Byzantine system of lights controls traffic).

Ballina, in County Tipperary, has some of the better pubs and restaurants, while Killaloe typifies picturesque County Clare. It lies on the western banks of lower Loch Deirgeirt (the southern extension of Lough Derg), where it narrows at one of the principal crossings of the Shannon.

The Drive » Continue following the R494 as it swings south to Limerick City (about 24km in total).

TRIP HIGHLIGHT

❸ Limerick City

Limerick city straddles the Shannon's broadening tidal stream, where the river runs west to meet the Shannon Estuary. Despite some unexpected glitz and gloss, it doesn't shy away from its tough

LINK YOUR TRIP

23 Mountains & Moors

Head 70km northwest of Portumna to discover County Galway's romantic landscapes.

27 County Clare

It's just 25km north from Bunratty to Ennis for a tour of County Clare's cliff-framed coast, the otherworldly Burren and music-filled pubs.

past, as portrayed in Frank McCourt's *Angela's Ashes*.

Limerick has an intriguing **castle** (King John's Castle; www.shannonheritage.com; Nicholas St; adult/child €9/5.50; 🕙10am-5pm Mon-Fri, to 5.30pm Sat & Sun), built by King John of England between 1200 and 1212 on King's Island; the dynamic **Limerick City Gallery of Art** (www.limerickcitygallery.ie; Carnegie Bldg, Pery Sq; admission free; 🕙10am-5.30pm Mon, Wed & Fri, 11am-5.30pm Tue, 10am-8.30pm Thu, 10am-5pm Sat, noon-5pm Sun) in the city's Georgian area; the fabulous **Hunt Museum** (www.huntmuseum.com; Palladian Custom House,

Rutland St; adult/child €8/4.25; 🕙10am-5pm Mon-Sat, 2-5pm Sun) with the finest collection of Bronze Age, Iron Age and medieval treasures outside Dublin; and a contemporary cafe culture (especially along its revitalised riverbanks) to go with its uncompromising pubs – as well as locals who go out of their way to welcome you.

Limerick's ancient **St Mary's Cathedral** (www.cathedral.limerick.anglican.org; Bridge St; admission donation €2; 🕙vary) was founded in 1168 by Donal Mór O'Brien, king of Munster.

The city centre is renowned for its nightlife, and, unfortunate nickname 'Stab City' aside, is not any less safe than other urban Irish areas. The free *Limerick Event Guide* (LEG; www.eightball.ie) can be found in pubs, eateries and hotels all over town.

🍴 🛏 p221

The Drive » The narrow, peaceful N69 road follows the Shannon Estuary west from Limerick; 27km along you come to Askeaton.

- - - - - - - - - -
TRIP HIGHLIGHT

❹ Askeaton

Hidden just off the N69, evocative ruins in the pint-sized village of Askeaton include the mid-1300s **Desmond Castle**, a 1389-built

DETOUR: ADARE

Start: ❸ Limerick City

Frequently dubbed 'Ireland's prettiest village', Adare centres on its clutch of perfectly preserved thatched cottages built by the 19th-century English landlord, the earl of Dunraven, for workers constructing Adare Manor (now a palatial hotel; see p221). Today, the cottages house craft shops and some of the region's finest restaurants.

In the middle of the village, Adare's **heritage centre** (📞061-396 666; www.adareheritagecentre.ie; Main St; admission free; 🕙9am-6pm summer, 9.30am-5pm winter) has entertaining exhibits on the history and the medieval context of the village's buildings and can point you to a number of fascinating religious sites. It also books tours of **Adare Castle** (tours adult/family €6/15; 🕙tours hourly 10am-5pm Jun-Sep). Dating back to around 1200, this picturesque feudal ruin was wrecked by Cromwell's troops in 1657. Restoration work is ongoing; look for the ruined great hall with its early-13th-century windows. You can view the castle from the main road, or the riverside footpath or the grounds of the Augustinian priory.

From Limerick city, the fastest way to reach Adare is to take the M20 and N21 16km southwest to the village on the banks of the River Maigue. From Adare, it's 9km northwest to rejoin the N69 at Kilcornan. Alternatively, you can take the less-travelled N69 from Limerick to Kilcornan and slip down to Adare.

Loop Head View of the Loop Head lighthouse

Franciscan friary, and **St Mary's Church of Ireland** and **Knights Templar Tower**, built around 1829, as well as the 1740-built **Hellfire** gentlemen's club. Restoration of the ruins started in 2007 and is expected to continue until 2017. The town's **tourist office** (☎061-392 149; askeatontouristoffice@gmail. com; The Square; ⊙9am-5pm Mon-Sat) has details of ruins that you can freely wander (depending on restoration works) and can arrange free **guided tours** lasting about one hour led by passionate local historians.

The Drive » Stunning vistas of the wide Shannon Estuary come into view as you drive 12km to Foynes.

5 Foynes

Foynes is an essential stop along the route to visit the fascinating **Foynes Flying Boat Museum** (www. flyingboatmuseum.com; adult/child €9/5; ⊙9am-5pm Apr-Oct). From 1939 to 1945 this was the landing place for the flying boats that linked North America with the

219

British Isles. Big Pan Am clippers – there's a replica here – would set down in the estuary and refuel.

The Drive » The most scenic stretch of the N69 is the 24km from Foynes to Tarbert in northern County Kerry, which hugs the estuary's edge.

⑥ Tarbert

The lively little harbour town of Tarbert, County Kerry, is where you'll hop on the car ferry to Killimer, County Clare, saving yourself 137km of driving.

Before you do so, though, it's worth visiting the renovated **Tarbert Bridewell Jail & Courthouse** (http://tarbertbridewell.com/museum.html; adult/child €5/2.50; ◷10am-6pm Apr-Oct), which has exhibits on the rough social and political conditions of the 19th century. From the jail, the 6.1km **John F Leslie Woodland Walk** runs along Tarbert Bay towards the river mouth.

The ferry dock is clearly signposted 2.2km west of Tarbert. Services are operated by **Shannon Ferry Limited** (☎068-905 3124; www.shannonferries.com; 1 way/return bicycle & foot passengers €5/7, motorcycles €9/14, cars €18/28; ◷7.30am-9.30pm Jun-Aug, to 7.30pm Sep-May, from 9.30am Sun year-round). Ferries depart hourly (every half-hour in high summer).

The Drive » The crossing takes 20 minutes from Tarbert to Killimer, from where it's an 8km drive west to Kilrush.

⑦ Kilrush

Opportunities for up-close encounters with the bottlenose dolphins living in the Shannon abound in the atmospheric town of Kilrush (Cill Rois), which also harbours the remarkable 'lost' Vandeleur Walled Garden; see p###.

✘ p297

The Drive » Continue 14km west along the N67 to the beach haven of Kilkee.

⑧ Kilkee

The centrepiece of Kilkee (Cill Chaoi) is its wide, sheltered, powdery white-sand beach. The sweeping semicircular bay has high cliffs on the north end and weathered rocks to the south. The waters are very tidal, with wide open sandy expanses replaced by pounding waves in just a few hours.

Kilkee has plenty of guesthouses and B&Bs, though during high season rates can soar and vacancies are scarce.

✘ p221

The Drive » The 26.5km drive from Kilkee south to Loop Head ends in cliffs plunging into the Atlantic.

TRIP HIGHLIGHT

⑨ Loop Head

Capped by a working lighthouse, Loop Head (Ceann Léime) is County Clare's southernmost point, with breathtaking views as well as cycling, fishing and snorkelling opportunities (including hire). See also p295.

The Drive » On the R487, follow the 'Scenic Loop' (an understatement): you'll be struck by one stunning vista of soaring coastal cliffs after another. From Killimer continue north on the R473 to Kilbreckan, where you can hop on the M18 south to Bunratty (102km all up).

⑩ Bunratty

Bunratty (Bun Raite) draws more tourists than any other place in the region. The namesake **castle** has stood over the area for centuries. In recent decades it's been spiffed up and swamped by attractions and gift shops. A **theme park** (Bunratty Castle & Folk Park; www.shannonheritage.com; joint-entry ticket to castle & folk park adult/child €16/9; ◷castle 9am-4pm year-round, folk park 9am-6pm Jun-Aug, to 5.30pm Sep-May) re-creates a clichéd – and sanitised – Irish village of old.

With all the hoopla, it's easy to overlook the actual village, at the back of the theme park, which has numerous leafy spots to eat and sleep.

Eating & Sleeping

Limerick City ③

✕ Market Square Brasserie   Irish €€€

(✆061-448 700; www.savoylimerick.com; Henry St; 6-course menu €35; ⊙dinner Tue-Sat) Now at home inside the five-star Savoy Hotel, chef Liam Murrell ingeniously prepares and artfully presents local produce. The likes of game terrine with foie gras, almond- and caper-crusted halibut, and caramelised popcorn parfait appear on the ever-changing menu. Service is smooth, the wine list long and the cheese selection inspired.

✕ Sage Cafe   Cafe €€

(www.thesagecafe.com; 67-68 Catherine St; dishes €5.50-12; ⊙breakfast & lunch Mon-Sat; ⊕) Breakfast treats and baked goods give way to a line-up of lunch sandwiches, salads such as tiger prawn and cashew nut, and hot plates like lambs liver with apricot stuffing and black pudding potato cake.

🛏 Boutique Hotel   Hotel €€

(✆061-315 320; www.theboutique.ie; Denmark St; s €49-65; d €59-69; @ 🖥 ⊕) Rotating works of original art by Limerick artist Claire De Lacy, a fish tank in the lobby, a glassed-in breakfast room on the 1st-floor balcony and red-and-white-striped decor set this groovy little hotel apart from the pack. There's a popular pub downstairs.

🛏 George Boutique Hotel   Hotel €€

(✆061-460 400; www.thegeorgeboutiquehotel.com; O'Connell St; s/d from €74/128; P @ 🖥 ⊕) Designed like something out of a Sunday supplement – all warm and luxurious with gadgets like iPod docks – this sleek place has an atrium lobby and small terrace above the busy city centre.

Adare

✕ Wild Geese   Irish €€

(✆061-396 451; www.thewild-geese.com; Main St; mains €21-24.50; ⊙lunch Sun, dinner Tue-Sat) This inviting cottage restaurant keeps the standard consistently high. The ever-changing menu celebrates the best of southwest Ireland's produce – from scallops to sumptuous racks of lamb – and the bread basket is divine.

🛏 Adare Manor   Hotel €€€

(✆061-605 200; www.adaremanor.com; Main St; d €290-390; P @ 🖥 ⊛ ⊕) The Earl of Dunraven's magnificent estate is an intimate castle hotel. Individually decorated rooms have autumnal tones and antique furniture; dining options, also open to nonguests, include its superb **Oak Room Restaurant** (mains €21-34.50; ⊙dinner) and **high tea** (veg/nonveg €18/26.50; ⊙2-5pm) served on tiered plates in the stately drawing room. Guests get reduced rates at the Adare Manor Golf Club.

🛏 Dunraven Arms   Inn €€€

(✆061-396 633; www.dunravenhotel.com; Main St; s/d from €135/155; @ 🖥 ⊛ ⊕) This jewel of an inn, built in 1792, sits discreetly behind hedged gardens. All 86 rooms have a high standard of traditional luxury. Its **restaurant** (mains €16.50-25; ⊙dinner) has an ambitious menu (pan-seared duck with lavender risotto, warm white chocolate cake), but its **bar menu** (mains €13-14.50; ⊙lunch & dinner) is a worthy, more affordable alternative.

Kilkee ⑧

✕ Pantry Cafe   Bakery, Cafe €

(O'Curry St; meals €6-12; ⊙8am-6pm Apr-Oct) With a Euro-sleek look, this bakery/deli/cafe is filled with surprises and fresh treasures. The scones are plainly the best in Clare and pretty much everything else you order from the seemingly simple menu will have you saying, 'That's the best...I've ever had'.

Cahir Castle One of the country's largest, most intact medieval castles

The Holy Glen 20

This hallowed patch of County Tipperary shelters the Glen of Aherlow and the Rock of Cashel, crowned by historic buildings that seem like an ethereal extension of the landscape itself.

TRIP HIGHLIGHTS

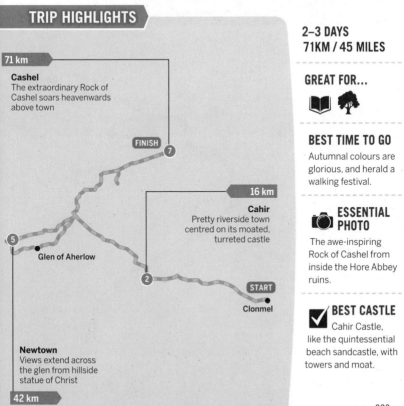

71 km

Cashel
The extraordinary Rock of Cashel soars heavenwards above town

FINISH 7

5

Glen of Aherlow

16 km

Cahir
Pretty riverside town centred on its moated, turreted castle

2

START
Clonmel

Newtown
Views extend across the glen from hillside statue of Christ

42 km

2–3 DAYS
71KM / 45 MILES

GREAT FOR...

BEST TIME TO GO
Autumnal colours are glorious, and herald a walking festival.

ESSENTIAL PHOTO

The awe-inspiring Rock of Cashel from inside the Hore Abbey ruins.

BEST CASTLE
Cahir Castle, like the quintessential beach sandcastle, with towers and moat.

20 The Holy Glen

The landscapes are sublime viewed from your car windows, and it's easy to get out and about among them too. The Glen of Aherlow is renowned for its walking. You will encounter varying terrain, from lush riverbanks on the Aherlow to pine forests in the hills and windswept, rocky grasslands that seem to stretch on forever.

1 Clonmel

County Tipperary's largest and busiest town, Clonmel (Cluain Meala; 'Meadows of Honey') sits on the northern bank of the River Suir, where historic buildings include the beautifully restored **Main Guard** (www.heritageireland.ie; Sarsfield St; ⊘9.30am-6pm Easter-Sep, hours can vary), a Butler courthouse dating from 1675; the 1802-built **County Courthouse** (Nelson St), where the Young Irelanders of 1848 were tried and sentenced

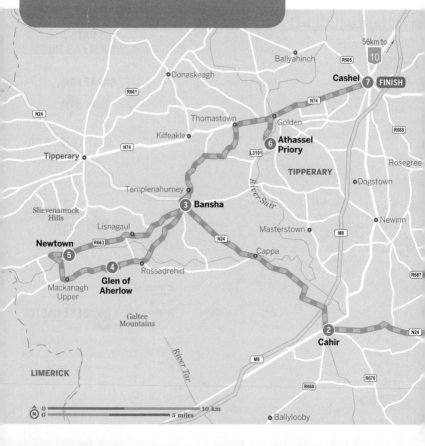

to transportation to Australia; and the **Franciscan Friary** (Mitchell St) – inside, near the door, a 1533 Butler tomb depicts a knight and his lady. There's some fine modern stained glass, especially in St Anthony's Chapel.

Informative displays on County Tipperary's history from Neolithic times to the present are covered at the well-put-together **South Tipperary County Museum** (www .southtippcoco.ie; Mick Delahunty Sq; ◷10am-5pm Tue-Sat), which also hosts changing exhibitions.

✕ ⊨ p229

The Drive » It's a quick 17km trip along the N24 west to Cahir.

- - - - - - - - - - - - -

TRIP HIGHLIGHT

② Cahir

At the eastern tip of the Galtee Mountains, the compact town of Cahir (An Cathair; pronounced 'care') encircles the moated **Cahir Castle** (www.heritageireland.ie; Castle St; adult/child €3/1; ◷9am-6.30pm mid-Jun–Aug, 9.30am-5.30pm mid-Mar–mid-Jun & Sep–mid-Oct, 9.30am-4.30pm mid-Oct–mid-Mar), a feudal fantasy of rocky foundations, massive walls, turrets and towers, defences and dungeons. Founded by Conor O'Brien in 1142, it passed to the Butler family in 1375. In 1599 the earl of Essex used cannons to shatter its walls, and it was surrendered to Cromwell in 1650. Its future usefulness may have discouraged the typical Cromwellian 'deconstruction' and it remains one of Ireland's largest and most intact medieval castles.

Walking paths follow the banks of the **River Suir** – a pretty path from behind the town car park meanders 2km south to the thatched **Swiss Cottage** (www .heritageireland.ie; Cahir Park; adult/child €3/1; ◷10am-6pm Apr-late Oct), surrounded by roses, lavender and honeysuckle. A lavish example of Regency Picturesque, it's more a sizeable house. The compulsory 30-minute guided tours are thoroughly enjoyable.

The Drive » Drive northwest for 14km through farmland along the N24 (which, despite being a National Road, is narrow and twisting) to the village of Bansha, the jumping-off point for the Glen of Aherlow.

- - - - - - - - - - - - -

③ Bansha

The tiny village of Bansha (An Bháinseach, meaning 'a grassy place') sits at the eastern end of the Glen of Aherlow.

R692 R689

Fethard ○

○ Ballyclerahan

R689

43km to 12

N24

Clonmel
START

ourmilewater

WATERFORD

§ LINK YOUR TRIP

12 Blackwater Valley Drive

Travel 87km south from Cashel to Youghal (County Cork), via Lismore, for the beautiful Blackwater Valley.

10 Kilkenny's Treasures

Head 60km northeast of Cashel via the M8 and R693 to discover the medieval treasures of County Kilkenny.

Although Bansha itself has just a handful of facilities, it makes a good pit stop before embarking on the prettiest stretch of this trip.

The Drive » From Bansha the drive west takes in the best of County Tipperary's verdant, mountainous landscapes. Leave Bansha on the R663 and, after 500m, follow the left fork (repeat: *left* fork) in the road. Keep your eyes peeled for walkers and cyclists as you drive.

GARETH MCCORMACK/GETTY IMAGES ©

④ Glen of Aherlow

Cradled by the Slievenamuck Hills and the Galtee Mountains, this gorgeous valley is a scenic drive within a scenic drive. From Bansha you'll travel through a scattering of hamlets including Booleen, Rossadrehid and Mackanagh Upper, with majestic mountain views.

The Drive » At Mackanagh Upper, turn north to connect with R663 then follow the R663 east to reach the glen's tourism hub, Newtown.

TRIP HIGHLIGHT

⑤ Newtown

The R663 from Bansha and the R664 south from Tipperary town both converge at Newtown at the **Coach Road Inn**, a fine old pub that's popular with walkers who've worked up a thirst.

Hidden around the back of the pub, the enthusiastically staffed Glen of Aherlow **tourist office** (☏062-56331; www .aherlow.com; ◷9.30am-5pm Mon-Fri year-round, plus 10am-4pm Sat Jun-Aug) is an excellent source of local information, including **walking festivals**.

For views of biblical proportions, head 1.6km north of Newtown on the R664 to its lofty **viewing point** and **statue of Christ**, *Christ the King,* on the side of the Slievenamuck Hills facing the Galtee Mountains. The statue's raised hand is believed to bless those who pass by it and live beneath it. Initially erected in 1950, the original statue was damaged in 1975, but replaced soon after with an identical sculpture.

Glen of Aherlow Cows grazing with the Galtee Mountains in the background

There's a good range of rural accommodation including some bucolic campgrounds.

 p229

The Drive » Continue along the scenic R663 to Bansha and head northeast on Barrack St (the N24) towards Thomastown to connect with N74 east to the village of Golden. From Golden, head 2km south along the narrow road signposted Athassel Priory (23.5km all up).

6 Athassel Priory

The atmospheric – and, at dusk, delightfully creepy – ruins of Athassel Priory sit in the shallow and verdant River Suir Valley. The original buildings date from 1205, and Athassel was once one of the richest and most important monasteries in Ireland. What survives is substantial: the gatehouse and portcullis gateway, the cloister and stretches of walled enclosure, as well as some medieval tomb effigies.

Roadside parking is limited and very tight. The priory is reached across often-muddy fields.

The Drive » Return to Golden and continue east along the N74

THE GALTEE MOUNTAINS

Extending west from Cahir for 23km, the Galtees stand slightly aloof from the other mountain groups in Ireland's south; they rise comparatively gradually from the sprawling 'Tipperary Plain' and much more steeply from beautiful Glen of Aherlow to the north. The range's highest peak is Galtymore Mountain (919m), which towers over at least 12 other distinct summits. A prominent landmark far and wide, it stands proud of the rest of the range by almost 100m and is one of Ireland's 12 munros (peaks or summits over 3000 feet). Valleys bite deep into the main ridge, composed of old red sandstone, so that the Galtees (pronounced with a short 'a' as in 'fact') are characterised by long spurs reaching out from the relatively narrow main ridge. Tors, created by frost-shattering during the last Ice Age, are scattered along the ridge, and notably form a heap of conglomerate boulders known as O'Loughnan's Castle. The north face of the range is punctuated by corries, relics of the Ice Age that hide Lough Muskry and Bohreen Lough, impounded by massed moraine. A third small lake, Lough Curra, is a hollow predating glaciation and later blocked off by moraine. The uplands of the range are largely covered with blanket bog, and conifer plantations are widespread across the lower slopes. The Glen of Aherlow tourist office (p226) in Newtown has walking information.

for 7km to the grand finale of the trip, Cashel, resplendently crowned by the Rock of Cashel.

- - - - - - - - - - - - - -

TRIP HIGHLIGHT

7 Cashel

Rising from a grassy plain on the edge of the town, the **Rock of Cashel** (www .heritageireland.com; adult/child €6/2; 9am-6.15pm Jun-Sep, to 4.45pm Oct-May) is one of Ireland's most spectacular archaeological sites. The 'Rock' is a prominent green hill, banded with limestone outcrops, which bristles with ancient fortifications – the word 'cashel' is an Anglicised version of the Irish word *caiseal,* meaning 'fortress'. Sturdy walls circle an enclosure that contains a complete round tower, a 13th-century Gothic cathedral and the finest

12th-century Romanesque chapel in Ireland. For more than 1000 years the Rock of Cashel was a symbol of power and the seat of kings and churchmen who ruled over the region. It's a five-minute stroll from the town centre to the Rock; pretty paths include the **Bishop's Walk**. There are a couple of parking spaces for visitors with disabilities at the top of the approach road to the ticket office.

Just under 1km from the Rock in flat farmland is the formidable ruin of 13th-century **Hore Abbey**. Originally Benedictine and settled by monks from Glastonbury in England at the end of the 12th century, it later became a Cistercian house.

Next to the car park below the Rock, heritage centre **Brú Ború** (062-61122; www.comhaltas.ie/locations/detail/bru_boru; admission €3; 9am-5pm, hours can vary) offers an absorbing insight into Irish traditional music, dance and song.

Town museums include the engaging **Cashel Folk Village** (062-62525; www .cashelfolkvillage.ie; Dominic St; adult/child €5/2; 9.30am-5.30pm, hours can vary) exhibiting old buildings, shopfronts and memorabilia from around Cashel.

✗ ⌂ p229

Eating & Sleeping

Clonmel ❶

🍴 Befani's   Mediterranean €€
(📞052-617 7893; www.befani.com; 6 Sarsfield
St; s/d €40/70, mains €15-28.50; 🕑restaurant
breakfast, lunch & dinner; @ 📶) Between the
Main Guard and the Suir, Befani's brings the
Mediterranean to Clonmel. Throughout the day
there's a tapas menu – be sure to try the Tunisian
crab parcels. Its guest rooms aren't huge, but
they're attractively fitted out in the sunny colours
of the Med.

🛏 Hotel Minella   Hotel €€€
(📞052-612 2388; www.hotelminella.ie; Coleville
Rd; d €120-180, ste €250-300; P @ 📶 🏊 🐾)
Refined yet unpretentious, this family-run
luxury hotel sits amid extensive grounds 2km
east of the centre. The 90 rooms span an 1863
mansion, and a new wing with almost every
kind of convenience including two suites with
their own hot outdoor tubs on private terraces
overlooking the river.

Newtown ❺

🛏 Aherlow House Hotel   Hotel €€€
(📞062-56153; www.aherlowhouse.ie; Newtown;
s/d/self-catering lodge from €99/120/175,
bar food €11-16, restaurant mains €20-30;
P @ 📶 🐾) Up a pine-forested track from the
R663, a 1928 hunting lodge has been turned
into a luxurious woodland retreat with a flowing
bar, a fine dinner-only restaurant, and glorious
mountain views from the terrace.

🛏 Ballinacourty House Camping
Park & B&B   Campground, B&B €€
(📞062-56559; www.ballinacourtyhse.com;
Glen of Aherlow; campsites €23, s/d €51.50/70,
4-course menu €20-30; P 🐾) Against a great

backdrop of the Galtees, excellent facilities
include a beautiful garden, a much-loved local
restaurant serving Sunday lunch and dinner
Wednesday to Saturday, a tennis court and
minigolf.

🛏 Homeleigh Farmhouse   B&B €€
(📞062-56228; www.homeleighfarmhouse
.com; Newtown; s/d €54/80, dinner €28; P 📶)
The friendly owners of this working farm just
west of Newtown and the Coach Road Inn are
founts of local info. The modern house has five
comfortable rooms with private bathrooms;
book ahead to enjoy a three-course home-
cooked meal.

Cashel ❼

🍴 Cafe Hans   Cafe €€
(📞062-63660; Dominic St; mains €13-19;
🕑noon-5pm Tue-Sat; 🐾) Competition for the
32 seats is fierce at this gourmet cafe run by
the same family as the esteemed **Chez Hans**
(📞062-61177; www.chezhans.net; Dominic St;
mains €26-39; 🕑dinner Tue-Sat) next door.
There's a fantastic selection of salads, open
sandwiches and filling fish, shellfish, lamb
and vegetarian dishes, with a discerning wine
selection and mouthwatering desserts like
homemade caramel ice cream. Arrive before or
after the lunchtime rush.

🛏 Cashel Palace Hotel   Hotel €€€
(📞062-62707; www.cashel-palace.ie; Main
St; s/d from €95/176; P @ 📶) Built in 1732
for a Protestant archbishop, this handsome
red-brick, late-Queen Anne house is a local
landmark, with 23 antique-furnished rooms
in the gracious main building or quaint mews.
There's a stately **bar** (bar food €10-16; 🕑lunch
& dinner) and vaulted-ceilinged **Bishops
Buttery Restaurant** (2-/3-course menus
from €22/25; 🕑lunch & dinner).

Galway & the West of Ireland

LITTLE WONDER THE WEST OF IRELAND is top of most must-see lists – apart from the weather, it has it all. Mayo offers wild, romantic beauty, but without the crowds. Timeless Connemara, with its bogs, lonely valleys, white beaches and intriguing villages, is one of Europe's most stunning corners.

For fun and frolic, Westport and Galway deliver, though you may never leave the cosy bars of County Clare or the mesmerising landscapes of The Burren and Aran Islands.

Counties Kerry and Cork feature Ireland's iconic scenery: crenulated coastlines, green fields criss-crossed by stone walls, ancient sites and mist-shrouded peaks. A plethora of fine eateries, pubs and entertainment add to the rewards.

Galway The banks of the River Corrib (Trips 1, 4, 21, 22, 23, 24)
JOHN ELK/GETTY IMAGES ©

Galway &
the West of
Ireland

ATLANTIC
OCEAN

Bun-
Mullaghmore
Grange
Rosses N15
Point
Sli
Strandhill
Belderrig
Ballycastle
Easkey
Ballinaboy
R314
Killala
Bay
Enniscrone
Ballysadare
Bangor
Erris
Killala
N59
Ballinacarrow
26
Ballycroy
National
Park
Ballina
Ballymote
Achill
Island
Dugort
Crossmolina
Lough Conn
Kesh
Ballycroy
SLIGO
Keel
R319
Mulranny
Foxford
N17
Charlestown
Curraun
Peninsula
N59
Newport
Swinford
N5
Fren
Clew
Bay
Castlebar
Kilkelly
ROSCOM
Clare
Island
Louisburgh
N5
N60
Knock
Westport
Ballymoe
Inishturk
N59
Tourmakeady
MAYO
Roscom
Inishbofin
R335
Ballinrobe
Delphi
Leenane
N17
Dunmore
Athleag
Letterfrack
Lough
Mask
Ballinrobe
Omey
Island
Cong
Tuam
Mou
Clifden
R344
Maam Cross
24
Bell
Recess
R341
N59
N17
GALWAY
Ball
Roundstone
23
Oughterard
Lough
Corrib
Cloonboo
Moycullen
N84
Athenry
Carraroe
R336
Galway
M6
Au
Spiddal
Galway
Bay
Kilcolgan
N18
K
Inishmór
Ballyvaughan
New
Quay
Inishmaan
R477
Gort
Portu
Inisheer
Carron
Whitegate
Aran
Islands
Kilfenora
M18
Lough
Derg
Ner
Liscannor
Corofin
CLARE
Inagh
R476
Ballina
Doonbeg
22
Ennis
N67
M18
Kilkee
N68
Shannon
27
Bunratty
Limeric
R487
Carrigaholt
Kilrush
R473
N69
Adare
Kilbaha
Foynes
N21
Mouth of
the Shannon
Tarbert
Rathkeale
N.
Ballybunion
Listowel
LIMERICK
N
21
Banna
KERRY
N20
Kilmallo
Maharees
Islands
Tralee
Bay
N69
Abbeyfeale
Charleville
Cloghane
Tralee
N21
Castleisland
Newmarket
Buttevant
Dingle
Peninsula
Castlemaine
N73
N72
Dunquin
N86
Farranfore
N72
Kanturk
Mallow
Dingle
N70
Killorglin
Rathcormac
Great
Blasket
Kells
Killarney
Millstreet
N20
Caherciveen
Moll's
Gap
R582
Iveragh
Peninsula
Killarney
National
Park
N22
Macroom
Cork
M
Valentia
Island
Sneem
N70
Kenmare
N22
Co
Waterville
N70
Lauragh
N71
CORK
Caherdaniel
Beara
Peninsula
R572
Glengarriff
Dunmanway
Bandon
Kinsal
Allihies
Adrigole
Bantry
N71
Durrus
Drimoleague
Timoleague
Sheep's Head
Peninsula
Ballydehob
Clonakilty
N
0
50 km
Goleen
Skibbereen
Rosscarbery
0
25 miles
Mizen Head
Peninsula
Baltimore
Clear
Island

Connor Pass View of Mt Brandon

 DON'T MISS

Céide Fields
One of the world's major prehistoric sites still feels as undiscovered as it really was 50 years ago. Unearth it on Trip **21**

Inisheer
A trip to the smallest of the Aran Islands will take you far from 21st-century living. Sail there on Trips **22** **27**

Ennistymon
This authentic market town in County Clare gives a genuine taste of country living. Savour its fine bars on Trips **22** **27**

Dingle Town
A colourful fishing village at the end of the earth (well, the Connor Pass) provides delightful eateries, dolphin- and people-watching. Dive in on Trip **21**

Galway
You may find it hard to leave the City of Tribes. Go for its culture, conviviality and craic on Trips **21** **22** **23** **24**

233

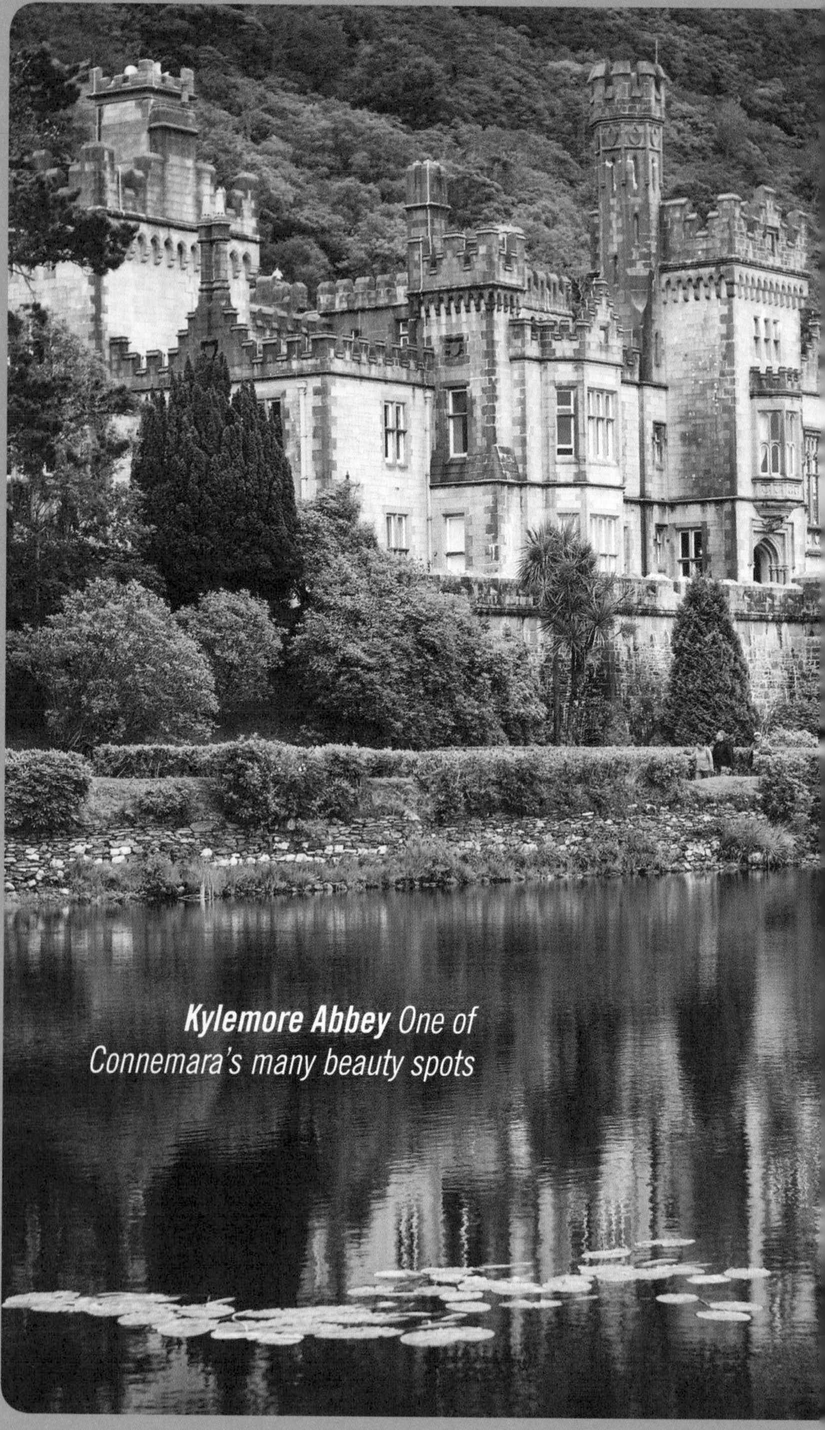

Kylemore Abbey One of Connemara's many beauty spots

Classic Trip

Best of the West

21

This is a rewarding foray through the west's ultimate stops, taking in mysterious megalithic remains, historic national parks and lively market towns, all in an epic coastal landscape.

TRIP HIGHLIGHTS

260 km

Galway
Bohemian swirl of pubs, cafes and culture galore by the sea

30 km

Dingle
Quaint village crammed with grocer-pubs and secondhand bookshops

10 km

Castletownshend
Grand houses and higgledy-piggledy 17th-century stone cottages

**6 DAYS
890KM / 553 MILES**

GREAT FOR...

BEST TIME TO GO
July for the best selection of summer festivals.

ESSENTIAL PHOTO
Clew Bay's many islands from the foot of Croagh Patrick.

BEST FOR DOLPHIN-WATCHING
Fungie the dolphin in Dingle Bay delivers thrills to young and old.

21 Best of the West

The most westerly fringe of Europe is the wild, rugged and incredibly beautiful west of Ireland; and this is one drive that really delivers. Here you'll discover the best beaches in Europe, the epic landscapes of Connemara, culture-packed Galway and Clare, and the kingdom of Kerry right round to West Cork's wonderful fishing villages.

ATLANTIC OCEAN

1 Céide Fields

A famous wit once described archaeology as being all about 'a series of small walls'. But it's not often said walls have experts hopping up and down with such excitement as at Céide Fields, 8km northwest of Ballycastle (see also p319). During the 1930s, local man Patrick Caulfield was digging in the bog when he noticed piled-up stones buried beneath it. About 40 years later, his son Seamus, who had become an archaeologist on the basis of his father's discovery, uncovered the world's most extensive Stone Age monument, consisting of stone-walled fields, houses and megalithic tombs – as early as five millennia ago a thriving farming community had lived here. The award-winning **Interpretive Centre** (☑096-43325; www.heritageireland.ie; R314; adult/child €4/2; ☉10am-6pm Jun-Sep, last tour 1hr prior to closing) gives a fascinating

Dingle 8
Ann
Dingle Bay
Caherciveen
Waterville
Derryna
Dursey Island

Ⓝ 0 ————— 40
0 ————— 20 miles

glimpse into these times. However, it's a good idea to take a guided tour of the site itself, or it may seem nothing more than, well, a series of small walls.

The Drive › Wind your way round the coast, stopping at some of Ireland's wildest beaches, heading south through the hillside village of Mulranny, and overlooking a wide Blue Flag beach and a prime vantage point for counting the 365 or so saucer-sized islands that grace Clew Bay. En route to the picturesque 11th-century village of Newport look for signs for 15th-century Rockfleet Castle. A wiggling 12km drive south you'll reach the atmospheric pub-packed heritage town of Westport.

❷ Westport

Bright and vibrant even in the depths of winter, Westport is a photogenic Georgian town with tree-lined streets, a riverside mall and a great vibe. A couple of kilometres west

LINK YOUR TRIP

26 **Sligo Surrounds**
From Céide Fields continue northeast for a glimpse of Sligo's wild side.

11 **Wexford & Waterford**
When you hit Cork, keep going east through Ardmore to experience Ireland's sunny southeast.

on Clew Bay, the town's harbour, Westport Quay is a picturesque spot for a sundowner. Matt Malloy, the fife player from the Chieftains, opened **Matt Molloy's** (Bridge St), an old-school pub, years ago and the good times haven't let up. Head to the back room around 9pm and you'll catch live *céilidh* (traditional music and dancing). Or perhaps an old man will simply slide into a chair and croon a few classics. Westport House (p276) is a charming Georgian mansion, gardens and adventure playground that makes a terrific day's outing for all ages.

p244

The Drive » Just 8km southwest of town is Croagh Patrick, one of Ireland's most famous pilgrimage sites.

GALWAY HOOKERS

Obvious jokes aside, Galway hookers are the iconic small sailing boats that were the basis of local seafaring during the 19th century and part of the 20th century. Small, tough and highly manoeuvrable, these wooden boats are undergoing a resurgence thanks to weekend sailors and hobbyists. The hulls are jet black, due to the pitch used for waterproofing, while the sails flying from the single mast are a distinctive rust colour. Expect to see them all along the Galway coast.

③ Croagh Patrick

St Patrick couldn't have picked a better spot for a pilgrimage than this conical mountain (also known as 'the Reek'). On a clear day the tough two-hour climb rewards with stunning views over Clew Bay and its sandy islets. It was on Croagh Patrick that Ireland's patron saint fasted for 40 days and nights, and where he reputedly banished venomous snakes. Climbing the 765m holy mountain is an act of penance for thousands of pilgrims on the last Sunday of July (Reek Sunday). The truly contrite take the original 40km route from Ballintubber Abbey, Tóchar Phádraig (Patrick's Causeway), and ascend the mountain barefoot. The trail taken by the less repentant begins in the village of Murrisk.

The Drive » This beautiful scenic route along Dooagh Valley on the R335 to Leenane is the site of a tragic Famine walk of 1849, when in icy weather 400 people died as they walked from Louisburgh to Delphi and back, in vain search of aid from a landlord. The side roads to the north and west of the valley lead to glorious, often-deserted beaches.

④ Leenane

The small village of Leenane (also spelled Leenaun) rests on the shore of dramatic **Killary Harbour**. Dotted with mussel rafts, the long, narrow harbour is Ireland's only fjord – maybe. Slicing 16km inland and more than 45m deep in the centre, it certainly looks like a fjord, although some scientific studies suggest it may not actually have been glaciated. **Mt Mweelrea** (819m) towers to its north.

Leenane boasts both stage and screen connections. It was the location for *The Field* (1989), a movie with Richard Harris based on John B Keane's play about a tenant farmer's ill-fated plans to pass on a rented piece of land to his son.

p244

The Drive » From Leenane, an ultrascenic loop of Connemara via the N59 crosses the beauty spots of Kylemore Abbey (p262) and Connemara National Park (p272) and then on through the lively town of Clifden (p80), where you continue

FESTIVALS OF FUN

Galway's packed calendar of festivals turns the city and surrounding communities into what feels like one nonstop party – streets overflow with revellers, and pubs and restaurants often extend their opening hours. The following are highlights:

Cúirt International Festival of Literature (www.galwayartscentre.ie/cuirt) Top-name authors converge on Galway in April for one of Ireland's premier literary festivals.

Galway Arts Festival (www.galwayartsfestival.ie) A two-week extravaganza of theatre, music and comedy in mid-July.

Galway Film Fleadh (www.galwayfilmfleadh.com) One of Ireland's biggest film festivals, held in July.

Galway Race Week (www.galwayraces.com) Horse races in Ballybrit, 3km east of the city, are the centrepiece each August of Galway's biggest, most boisterous festival of all.

Galway International Oyster Festival (www.galwayoysterfest.com) Oysters are washed down with plenty of pints in the last week in September.

east through Maam Cross into Galway City in under two hours.

TRIP HIGHLIGHT

⑤ Galway City

Galway city (see also p248 and p258) is a swirl of enticing old pubs that hum with trad music sessions throughout the year. More importantly, it has an overlaying vibe of fun and frolic that's addictive. Galway is often referred to as the 'most Irish' of Ireland's cities (and it's the only one where you're likely to hear Irish spoken in the streets, shops and pubs). **Séhán Ua Neáchtain** (17 Upper Cross St), a 19th-century pub, known simply as Neáchtain's (*nock*-tans) or Naughtons and painted a bright cornflower blue, has a

wraparound string of tables outside, many shaded by a large tree. It's a must-stop place where a polyglot mix of locals plop down and let the world pass them by. The long-established and award-winning **Druid Theatre** (☎091-568 617; www.druidtheatre.com; Chapel Lane) is famed for staging experimental works by young Irish playwrights, as well as new adaptations of classics.

🍴 🛏 p244

The Drive » Take time to smell the oysters on the busy seaside route between Galway city and County Clare. If you're a sucker for oysters, you're in for a welcome pit stop at Clarinbridge and Kilcolgan.

⑥ Clarinbridge & Kilcolgan

Some 16km south of Galway, Clarinbridge (Droichead an Chláirin) and Kilcolgan (Cill Cholgáin) are at their busiest during the **Clarinbridge Oyster Festival** (www.clarinbridge.com), held during the second weekend of September. However, the oysters are actually at their best from May through the summer. Oysters are celebrated year-round at **Paddy Burke's Oyster Inn** (www.paddyburkesgalway.com; Clarinbridge; mains €14-24; ⊙12.30-10pm), a thatched inn by the bridge dishing up heaped servings in a roadside location on the N18. **Moran's**

Classic Trip

WHY THIS IS A CLASSIC TRIP
ODA O'CARROLL, AUTHOR

Coming from near the west of Ireland I may be biased, but if you do one trip in Ireland this should be it. The Atlantic scenery from Donegal to Cork's Beara Peninsula is some of Europe's best. Grab a picnic in foodie town Westport and climb Croagh Patrick for glorious views over Clew Bay. A sandwich will never have tasted so good.

Top: Traditional Irish dancing
Left: Sea stack in the ocean, The Burren
Right: Waterfall at Connor Pass

Oyster Cottage (www
.moransoystercottage.com;
The Weir, Kilcolgan; mains
€15-38; ⊘ noon-9.30pm
Sun-Thu, to 10pm Fri & Sat)
is a thatched pub and
restaurant with a facade
as plain as the inside
of an oyster shell. Find
a seat on the terrace
overlooking Dunbulcaun
Bay, where the oysters
are reared before they
arrive on your plate, and
you'll think the world's
your... It's a well-marked
2km west of the busy
N18, in a quiet cove near
Kilcolgan.

The Drive » From the N67, it's
just a short jaunt down to the
sleepy but atmospheric stone
harbour village of Kinvara, a
quaint place with a couple of
nice bars. From Ballyvaughan
(p293) the scenery along the
R480 as it passes through the
region is inspiring, highlighting
the barren Burren at its best.
Amazing prehistoric stone
structures can be found
throughout this area. Pass
through Corofin and Ennis
(p248) to the impossibly quaint
Adare. Just over two hours
driving in all.

- - - - - - - - - - -

7 Adare

Often dubbed 'Ireland's
prettiest village', Adare
centres on its clutch
of perfectly preserved
thatched cottages built
by the 19th-century
English landlord, the
earl of Dunraven, for
workers constructing
Adare Manor. Today,
the cottages house
craft shops and some
of the county's finest

restaurants, with prestigious golf courses nearby. Unsurprisingly, tourists are drawn to the postcard-perfect village, on the River Maigue, by the busload. Dating back to around 1200, **Adare Castle** (tours adult/family €6/15; ☉ tours hourly 10am-5pm Jun-Sep), a picturesque feudal ruin, saw rough usage until it was finally wrecked for good by Cromwell's troops in 1657.

✖ ⌖ p244

The Drive » It's about two hours' drive southwest to Dingle (128km). The scenery ramps up several notches as you head from Tralee onto the peninsula – where the roads are pretty twisty – and over the famously picturesque Connor Pass.

TRIP HIGHLIGHT

8 Dingle Town

If you've arrived via the dramatic mountain-top Connor Pass, the fishing town of Dingle can feel like an oasis at the end of the earth...and maybe that's just what it is. Chocolate-box quaint, though grounded by a typical Kerry earthiness, its streets are crammed with brightly painted grocer-pubs and great restaurants, secondhand bookshops and, in

summer, coachloads of visitors. Announced by stars in the pavement bearing the names of its celebrity customers, **Dick Mack's** (http://dickmacks .homestead.com; Green St) has an irrepressible sense of self. Ancient wood and ancient snugs dominate the interior, which is lit like the inside of a whiskey bottle.

✖ ⌖ p245

The Drive » Dragging yourself away from Dingle, take the peninsula's lower road (N86) back, passing the windswept 5km stretch of dune-backed Inch Beach and veer south at Castlemaine round the jewel of the southwest, the Ring of Kerry (p163) through Kenmare to the magnificent Killarney National Park (p171). The scenery becomes a lot wilder at Glengarriff on the awe-inspiring Beara Peninsula.

9 Glengarriff

Hidden deep in the Bantry Bay area, Glengarriff (Gleann Garbh) is an attractive village that snares plenty of passers-by. In the second half of the 19th century, Glengarriff became a popular retreat for prosperous Victorians, who sailed from England. The tropical Italianate garden on **Garinish Island** (p212) is the top sight in Glengarriff. Subtropical plants flourish in the rich soil and warm climate. The camellias, magnolias and rhododendrons

especially provide a seasonal blaze of colour. This little miracle of a place was created in the early 20th century, when the island's owner commissioned the English architect Harold Peto to design him a garden on the then-barren outcrop.

⌖ p245

The Drive » Wend your way down the N71 through Ballydehob to Castletownshend. Glengarriff to Castletownshend is 57km.

TRIP HIGHLIGHT

10 Castletownshend

With its grand houses and higgledy-piggledy stone cottages dating back to the 17th and 18th centuries tumbling down the precipitously steep main street, Castletownshend is one of Ireland's most intriguing villages. At the bottom of the hill is a small quayside and the castle (really a crenellated mansion), after which the village is named, and en route a chapel with fine stained-glass windows designed by renowned Irish artist Harry Clarke. The **castle** (☎028-36100; www.castle -townshend.com; r €60-90), sitting imposingly on the waterfront, is a rocky fantasy. Huge mullioned windows obviate any authenticity of the decorative defensive touches. The seven guest

TOP TIP: THAT'S A GAS

A word of caution for visitors driving the wilds of Connemara: they're not called wilds for nothin'. There are long distances between filling stations on those gorgeous swaths of uninhabited valley and sheep-dotted mountainside. What's more, the few stations there are often closed by early evening, so make sure you have enough fuel to keep you going for at least 80km. Find stations at Recess, Clifden and Kylemore.

rooms range from one with an old four-poster, where you can play 'royal and consort' games, to small but bright rooms.

The Drive » From the main road it's less than 10km to the dual villages of Union Hall and Glandore at Glandore Harbour.

⑪ Union Hall & Glandore

The pretty waterside villages of Union Hall and Glandore (Cuan Dor) burst into life in summer when fleets of yachts tack into the shelter of the Glandore Harbour inlet. A tangle of back roads meander across the area; you should, too. Accessible from Glandore via a long, narrow causeway over the estuary, Union Hall was named after the 1800 Act of Union, which abolished the separate Irish parliament. The 1994 film *War of the Buttons,* about two battling gangs of youngsters, was filmed here.

The Drive » From here you'll glide into Cork city, 70km away, in about 1½ hours.

⑫ Cork City

Competing fiercely with Dublin for recognition, the south's largest city has arguably every bit as much to offer as the capital, yet on a smaller and even friendlier scale. The River Lee flows around the centre, an island packed with grand Georgian parades, cramped 17th-century alleys and modern masterpieces such as the opera house. Dotted around the compact centre are a host of historic buildings, cosmopolitan restaurants, local markets and cosy traditional bars. The award-winning **Lewis Glucksman Gallery** (📞021-490 2760; www .glucksman.org; University College Cork; suggested donation €5; ⏱10am-5pm Tue-Sat, 2-5pm Sun) in the grounds of University College Cork (UCC) is a startling limestone, steel and timber construction that displays the best in both national and international contemporary art and installation. It's always buzzing with people coming to attend lectures, view the artwork or procrastinate in the cafe.

See also our walking tour (p196).

🍴 🛏 p245

Classic Trip

Eating & Sleeping

Westport ②

✗ Quay Cottage   Seafood €€

(☎098-26412; Harbour; mains €18-25; ⊗ dinner mid-Feb–mid-Jan) Serving seafood straight off the boats and steeped in salty-dog charm (including lobster pots hanging from the roof beams), this is the pick of the places to eat on Westport's lively harbourfront.

🛏 St Anthony's   B&B €€

(☎098-28887; www.st-anthonys.com; Distillery Rd; s/d €45/80; P) This genteel B&B sits under cover of a large hedge and thick, twisted vines inhabited by birds' nests. The interior shelters six simple but elegant rooms; two have jacuzzi-style baths. Call ahead to arrange your arrival time.

Leenane ④

🛏 Delphi Lodge   Inn €€€

(☎095-42222; www.delphilodge.ie; s/d from €130/200; P @ 🛜) You'll wish the dreamy views at this gorgeous country estate could follow you into your dreams. Set among truly stunning mountain and lake vistas, this isolated country house has 12 posh bedrooms and a bevy of common areas including a library and billiards room. The cooking is modern Irish, sourced locally. Meals are taken at a vast communal table. Walks, fishing and much more await outside.

Galway City ⑤

✗ Ard Bia at Nimmo's   Irish €€

(www.ardbia.com; Spanish Arch; cafe dishes €6-12, lunch mains €10-14, dinner mains €17-24; ⊗ cafe noon-3pm, restaurant 6-10pm) In Irish, Ard Bia means 'High Food', and that's somewhat apt, given its location in the 18th-century customs house near the Spanish Arch. Local seafood and organic produce feature on the seasonal menu in a setting that defines funky chic. The cafe is a perfect place for a coffee and carrot cake.

🛏 St Martins B&B   B&B €€

(☎091-568 286; 2 Nun's Island Rd; s/d from €50/80; @ 🛜) This beautifully kept, renovated older house right on the canal has a flower-filled garden overlooking the William O'Brien Bridge and the River Corrib. The four rooms have all the comforts and the breakfast comes with freshly squeezed orange juice.

Adare ⑦

✗ Wild Geese   Irish €€

(☎061-396 451; www.thewild-geese.com; Main St; mains €21-24.50; ⊗ lunch Sun, dinner Tue-Sat) In a town where upmarket competition is downright fierce, this inviting cottage restaurant keeps the standard consistently high. The ever-changing menu celebrates the best of southwest Ireland's produce, from scallops to sumptuous racks of lamb. The service is genial, preparations are imaginative and the bread basket divine.

🛏 Adare Manor   Hotel €€€

(☎061-605 200; www.adaremanor.com; Main St; d €290-390; P @ 🛜 ⛳ 🐾) The Earl of Dunraven's magnificent estate is now an imposing yet wonderfully intimate castle hotel. Individually decorated rooms have autumnal tones and antique furniture; dining options, also open to nonguests, include its superb **Oak Room Restaurant** (mains €21-34.50; ⊗ dinner) and **high tea** (veg/nonveg €18/26.50; ⊗ 2-5pm) served on tiered plates in the stately drawing room. Guests get reduced rates at the Adare Manor Golf Club.

Dingle Town ⑧

✕ Out of the Blue   Seafood €€€

(☎066-915 0811; The Wood; lunch €10-20, mains €15-30; ⊙dinner daily, lunch Sun) 'No chips', reads the menu of this funky blue-and-yellow, fishing-shack-style restaurant on the waterfront. Despite its rustic surrounds, this is Dingle's best restaurant, with an intense devotion to fresh local seafood; if they don't like the catch, they don't open. Creative dishes change nightly, but might include steamed crab claws in garlic butter or pan-seared scallops flambéed in Calvados. Who needs chips?

⇤ Dingle Benner's Hotel   Hotel €€€

(☎066-915 1638; www.dinglebenners.com; Main St; s €97-127, d €144-204; ℗ 🔊) A Dingle institution, melding old-world elegance, local touches and modern comforts in the quiet rooms, lounge, library and refurbished, very popular Mrs Benners Bar. Rooms in the 300-year-old wing have the most character; those in the new parts are quieter.

Glengarriff ⑨

⇤ Eccles Hotel   Hotel €€

(☎027-63003; www.eccleshotel.com; Glengarriff Harbour; r €110-140; @) Just east of the centre, the Eccles has a long and distinguished history (since 1745), counting the British War Office, Thackeray, George Bernard Shaw and WB Yeats as former occupants. The decor is an attempt to combine 19th-century grandeur with early 1990s style, but the 66 rooms are big and bright. Ask for a bayside room on the 4th floor.

Cork City ⑪

✕ Cafe Paradiso   Vegetarian €€€

(☎021-427 7939; www.cafeparadiso.ie; 16 Lancaster Quay; mains €23-25; ⊙noon-3pm & 6-10.30pm Fri & Sat) A contender for best eatery in town, this down-to-earth vegetarian restaurant serves a superb range of dishes, including vegan fare: how about sweet chilli-glazed pan-fried tofu with Asian greens in a coconut and lemongrass broth, soba noodles and a gingered aduki bean wonton; or spring cabbage dolma of roast squash, caramelised onion and hazelnut with cardamom yoghurt, harissa sauce, broad beans and saffron-crushed potatoes? Reservations are essential.

✕ Fresco   International €

(☎021-490 1848; www.glucksman.org; Lewis Glucksman Gallery, University College Cork; dishes €4-8; ⊙10am-4pm Tue-Sat, noon-4pm Sun) This above-par museum cafe has sweeping views of the university grounds and a broad range of dishes on its menu – from burgers to burritos, salads, pastas and a pretty tasty club sandwich, it's all freshly made and served with style.

⇤ Hayfield Manor   Hotel €€€

(☎021-484 9500; www.hayfieldmanor.ie; Perrott Ave, College Rd; r €160-590; ℗ @ 🔊) Roll out the red carpet and pour yourself a sherry for *you have arrived*. Just 1.5km from the city centre, but with all the ambience of a country house, Hayfield combines the luxury and facilities of a big hotel with the informality and welcome of a small one. The 88 beautiful bedrooms (choose from traditional or contemporary styling) enjoy 24-hour room service, although you may want to idle the hours away in the library.

Doolin The hub of traditional Irish music

Musical Landscapes

22

From the busker-packed streets of Galway city, this rip-roaring ride takes you around County Clare and the Aran Islands to discover fine traditional music pubs, venues and festivals.

TRIP HIGHLIGHTS

155 km

Inisheer
End-of-the-earth landscape and traditional drumming festival

START
Galway

shmór

⑨
FINISH

Doolin ● Lisdoonvarna
Kilfenora ●

④

Miltown Malbay ●

②

65 km

Ennistymon
Country village with roaring Cascades and music at every turn

110 km

Ennis
Medieval town simply bursting with fine pubs featuring trad music

5 DAYS
155KM / 96 MILES

GREAT FOR...

BEST TIME TO GO
The summer months for outdoor *céilidh* (traditional dancing) and music festivals.

📷 ESSENTIAL PHOTO
Nightly set-dancing at the crossroads, in Vaughan's of Kilfenora.

✔ BEST FOR SONG
Ennis, on summer nights, where local musicians ply their wares.

22 Musical Landscapes

Pick the big bawdy get-togethers of Galway's always-on music scene, the atmospheric small pub sessions in crossroad villages like Kilfenora or Kilronan on the Aran Islands, where nonplaying patrons are a minority, or the rollicking urban boozers in Ennis. Whatever way you like it, this region is undeniably one of Ireland's hottest for traditional music.

1 Galway City

Galway (Gaillimh; see also p258) has a young student population and largely creative community that give a palpable energy to the place. Colourful medieval streets packed with heritage shops, sidewalk cafes and pubs ensure there's never a dull moment. Galway's pub selection is second to none and some swing to tunes every night of the week. **Crane Bar** (2 Sea Rd), an

atmospheric old pub west of the Corrib, is the best spot in Galway to catch an informal *céilidh* most nights. Or for something more contemporary, **Róisín Dubh** (www.roisindubh.net; Upper Dominick St) is *the* place to hear emerging international rock and singer-songwriters.

See also our walking tour, p264.

 p254

The Drive » From Galway city centre, follow either the coast road (R338) east out of town, or the inner R446, signposted Dublin or Limerick, as far as the N18 and then cruise south to Ennis where your great musical tour of Clare begins.

TRIP HIGHLIGHT

2 Ennis

Ennis (Inis), a medieval town in origin (see also p292), simply bursts with pubs featuring trad music. **Brogan's** (24

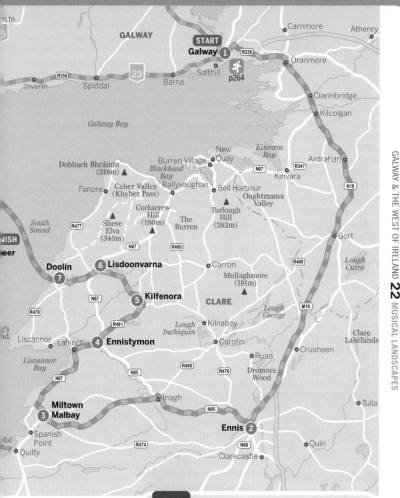

O'Connell St), on the corner of Cooke's Lane, sees a fine bunch of musicians rattling even the stone floors almost every night in summer, and the plain-tile-fronted **John O'Dea** (66 O'Connell St) is a hideout for local musicians serious about their trad sessions. **Cois na hAbhna**

LINK YOUR TRIP

23 Mountains & Moors

From Galway take in some of Connemara's loveliest points.

25 North Mayo & Sligo

Cruise up to Westport to join this wondrous trail around the hidden gems of north Connaught.

(☎065-682 0996; www.coisnahabhna.ie; Gort Rd), a pilgrimage point for traditional music and culture, has frequent performances and a full range of classes in dance and music, an archive and library of Irish traditional music, song, dance and folklore. Traditional music aficionados might like to time a visit with **Fleadh Nua** (www.fleadhnua.com), a lively festival held in late May.

✕ ⇙ p254

The Drive » From the N85 that runs south of The Burren, you'll meet the smaller R460 at the blink-and-you'll-miss-it village of Inagh. Here you'll find the Biddy Early Brewery, which sells a draught ale, Red Biddy, made using local Burren plants and seaweeds for flavouring. Refuelled, it's a straight run into Miltown Malbay.

❸ Miltown Malbay

Like Kilkee, Miltown Malbay was a resort favoured by well-to-do Victorians, though the beach itself is 2km south at **Spanish Point**. To the north of the Point, there are beautiful **walks** amid the low cliffs, coves and isolated beaches. A classically friendly place in the chatty Irish way, Miltown Malbay hosts the annual Willie Clancy

Irish Music Festival, one of Ireland's great trad music events. **O'Friel's Bar** (Lynch's; ☎065-708 4275; The Square) is one of a couple of genuine old-style places with occasional trad sessions. The other is the dapper **Hillery's** (Main St).

⇙ p255

The Drive » Hugging the coast, continue north until you come to the small seaside resort of Lahinch, more or less a single street backing a wide beach renowned for its surfing. From here, it's only 4km up the road to the charming heritage town of Ennistymon.

TRIP HIGHLIGHT

❹ Ennistymon

Ennistymon (Inis Díomáin; see also p295) is a timeless country village where people go about their business barely noticing the characterful buildings lining Main St. And behind this facade there's a surprise: the roaring **Cascades**, the stepped falls of the River Inagh. After heavy rain they surge, beer-brown and foaming, and you risk getting drenched on windy days in the flying drizzle. Not to be missed, **Eugene's** (Main St) is intimate, cosy and has a trademark collection of visiting cards covering its walls, alongside photographs of famous writers and musicians. The inspiring collection of whiskey

(Irish) and whisky (Scottish) will have you smoothly debating their relative merits. Another great old pub is **Cooley's House** (☎065-707 1712; Main St), with music most nights in summer and on Wednesday (trad night) in winter.

⇙ p255

The Drive » Heading north through a patchwork of green fields and stony walls on the R481, you'll land at the tiny village of Kilfenora, some 9km later. Despite its diminutive size, the pulse of Clare's music scene beats strongly in this area.

❺ Kilfenora

Underappreciated Kilfenora (Cill Fhionnúrach) lies on the southern fringe of The Burren. It's a small place, with a diminutive 12th-century cathedral and is best known for its **high crosses**. The town has a strong music tradition that rivals that of Doolin but without the crowds. The **Kilfenora Céilí Band** (www.kilfenoraceiliband.com) is a celebrated community that's been playing for 100 years, its traditional music featuring fiddles, banjos, squeeze boxes and more. **Vaughan's Pub** (www.vaughanspub.ie; Main St) has music in the bar every night during the summer and terrific set-dancing sessions in its barn on Thursday and Sunday nights.

THE PIED PIPER

Half the population of Miltown Malbay seems to be part of the annual **Willie Clancy Irish Summer School** (☎065-708 4281; www.oac.ie), a tribute to a native son and one of Ireland's greatest pipers. The eight-day **festival**, now in its fourth decade, begins on the first Saturday in July, when impromptu sessions occur day and night, the pubs are packed and Guinness is consumed by the barrel – up to 10,000 enthusiasts from around the globe turn up for the event. Specialist workshops and classes underpin the event; don't be surprised to attend a recital with 40 noted fiddlers.

The Drive >> From Kilfenora the road meanders northwest 8km to Lisdoonvarna, home of the international matchmaking festival.

6 Lisdoonvarna

Lisdoonvarna (Lios Dún Bhearna), often just called 'Lisdoon', is well known for its mineral springs. For centuries people have been visiting the local spa to swallow its waters. Down by the river at **Roadside Tavern** (Kincora Rd), third-generation owner Peter Curtin knows every story worth telling. There are trad sessions daily in summer. Look for a trail beside the pub that runs 400m down to two **wells** by the river. One is high in sulphur, the other iron. Mix and match for a cocktail of minerals. Next door, **Burren Smokehouse** (☎065-707 4432; www.burrensmokehouse.ie; Kincora Rd; ⊙9am-6pm Mon-Sat, 10am-6pm Sun May-Oct) is where you can learn about the ancient Irish art of oak-smoking salmon.

The Drive >> Just under 10 minutes' drive west of here, you'll reach the epicentre of Clare's trad music scene, at Doolin. Also known for its setting – 6km north of the Cliffs of Moher – what's called Doolin is really three small neighbouring villages. Fisherstreet, right on the water, Doolin itself, about 1km east on the little River Aille and Roadford, another 1km east.

7 Doolin

Doolin gets plenty of press as a centre of Irish traditional music, owing to a trio of pubs that have sessions through the year. **McGann's** (Roadford) has all the classic touches of a full-on Irish music pub; the action often spills out onto the street. Right on the water, **O'Connor's** (Fisherstreet), a sprawling favourite, has a rollicking atmosphere. It easily gets the most crowded and has the highest tourist quotient. **MacDiarmada's** (Roadford), also known as McDermott's, a simple red-and-white old pub, can be the rowdy favourite of locals. When the fiddles get going, it can seem like a scene out of a John Ford movie.

🛏 p255

The Drive >> You'll need to leave your car at one of Doolin's many car parks. For ferries to the Aran Islands, see p296.

8 Inishmór

The Aran Islands sing their own siren song to thousands of travellers each year who find their desolate beauty beguiling. The largest and most accessible Aran, Inishmór, is home to ancient fort **Dún Aengus**, one of the oldest archaeological remains in Ireland, as well as some lively pubs and restaurants, particularly in the only town, Kilronan. Irish remains the local tongue, but most locals speak English with visitors. **Joe Watty's Bar** (Kilronan) is the best pub in Kilronan, with traditional sessions most nights. Turf fires warm the air on the 50 weeks a year when this is needed. Informal music sessions, turf fires and a broad terrace with harbour views make **Tí Joe Mac's** (Kilronan) a local favourite while jovial **Tigh Fitz** (Killeany), near the airport, has

Classic Trip

LOCAL KNOWLEDGE
STEVE WALL, SINGER WITH THE WALLS

For a great session in my home town Ennistymon I'd go to Cooley's House (p250) or in Ennis to Brogan's (p248). Vaughan's (p250) in Kilfenora is another great spot or for serious immersion in trad; the Willie Clancy Irish Summer School (p251) really is unmissable.

Top: Abandoned stone cottage on Inishmór
Left: Eugene's in Ennistymon
Right: Street musician playing the banjo

traditional sessions and set dancing every weekend. It's 1.6km from Kilronan (about a 25-minute walk).

🛏 p255

The Drive 》 Ferries can be picked up between Aran islands but tickets must be prebooked. For timetables and prices, visit the websites listed on p296.

TRIP HIGHLIGHT

9 Inisheer

On Inisheer (Inis Oírr), the smallest of the Aran Islands, the breathtakingly beautiful end-of-the-earth landscape adds to the island's distinctly mystical aura. Steeped in mythology, traditional rituals are still very much respected here. Locals still carry out a pilgrimage with potential healing powers known as the *Turas* to the Well of Enda, an ever-burbling spring in the southwest. For a week in late June the island reverberates to the thunder of traditional drums during **Craiceann Inis Oírr International Bodhrán Summer School** (www.craiceann .com). Bodhrán master classes, workshops and pub sessions are held as well as Irish dancing. Rory Conneely's atmospheric inn **Tigh Ruaírí** (Strand House; ☎099-75020) hosts live music sessions and, here since 1897, **Tigh Ned** is a welcoming, unpretentious place, with harbour views and lively traditional music.

🛏 p255

253

Eating & Sleeping

Galway City ❶

✖ Ard Bia at Nimmo's   Irish €€

(www.ardbia.com; Spanish Arch; cafe dishes €6-12, lunch mains €10-14, dinner mains €16-24; ⏰ cafe 10am-3.30pm, restaurant 6-10pm) In Irish, Ard Bia means 'High Food', and that's somewhat apt, given its location in the 18th-century customs house near the Spanish Arch. Local seafood and organic produce feature on the seasonal menu in a setting that defines funky chic. The cafe is a perfect place for coffee and carrot cake.

✖ Cava   Spanish €€

(www.cavarestaurant.ie; 51 Lower Dominick St; meals €10-25; ⏰ noon-10pm, later Fri & Sat) Now that no one can afford a trip to Iberia the next best thing is a meal at this superb West Side storefront. From typical fare like roasted potatoes with aioli to more fanciful dishes such as free-range quail with dried figs, the kitchen's efforts never fail to astound.

🛏 Salmon Weir Hostel   Hostel €

(📞091-561 133; www.salmonweirhostel.com; 3 St Vincent's Ave; dm/d from €15/36; @ 📶) Galway's hippie vibe finds its spiritual home in the Salmon Weir's guitar-strewn lounge room, where informal jam sessions take place most nights. The hostel has a share-house feel, including shared bathrooms for all rooms. There's no breakfast, although coffee and tea are free. The train and bus stations are a five-minute walk.

🛏 St Martins B&B   B&B €€

(📞091-568 286; 2 Nun's Island Rd; s/d from €50/80; @ 📶) This beautifully kept, renovated older house right on the canal has a flower-filled garden overlooking the William O'Brien Bridge and the River Corrib. The four rooms have all the comforts and the breakfast is a few cuts above the norm (fresh-squeezed OJ!).

Ennis ❷

✖ Food Heaven   Cafe €

(21 Market St; meals €7-10; ⏰ 8.30am-6.30pm Mon-Sat) One of several fine choices in the Market St area, this small cafe-deli lives up to its ethereal name with creative and fresh fare. Sandwiches come on renowned brown bread, while soups and salads change daily. Hot specials are just that. Be ready to queue at lunch.

✖ Zest   Bakery, Cafe €

(Market Pl; meals €5-10; ⏰ 8am-6pm Mon-Sat) A much-welcomed addition to Ennis' fresh food scene, Zest combines a deli, bakery, shop and cafe. Excellent prepared foods from the region are offered along with salads, soups and much more. It's ideal for a coffee or lunch.

🛏 Newpark House   Inn €€

(📞065-682 1233; www.newparkhouse.com; s/d from €60/100; ⏰ Apr-Oct; P @) A vine-covered country house dating from 1650, Newpark is 2km north of Ennis. The six rooms have a mix of furnishings old and new; garden views are a fine thing first thing in the morning. To get here, go along Tulla Rd to the Scarriff road (R352) and turn right at the Roselevan Arms.

🛏 Old Ground Hotel   Hotel €€

(📞065-682 8127; www.flynnhotels.com; O'Connell St; s/d from €100/140; P @ 📶) The lobby at this local institution is always a scene: old friends sprawl on the sofas, deals are cut at the tables and ladies from the neighbouring church's altar society exchange gossip over tea. Parts of this rambling landmark date back to the 1800s. The 83 rooms vary greatly in size and decor – don't hesitate to inspect a few.

Miltown Malbay ③

🛏 An Gleann B&B
B&B €€

(📞065-708 4281; www.angleann.net; Ennis Rd; s/d from €25/60; P 📶) Possibly the friendliest welcome in town is at this B&B off the R474 about 1km from the centre. The five rooms are basic and comfy and owner Mary Hughes is a delight. Cyclists are catered for.

Ennistymon ④

🛏 Byrne's
Inn €€

(📞065-707 1080; www.byrnes-ennistymon .ie; Main St; r from €70; P) The Cascades are just out back at this historic guesthouse and restaurant. When the air is not heavy with mist, you can enjoy a drink at a back-terrace table. The menu is substantial, with plenty of seafood specials (mains €16 to €28). Six large and comfortable rooms await up the creaky heritage stairs.

🛏 Falls Hotel
Hotel €€

(📞065-707 1004; www.fallshotel.ie; s/d from €59/100; P @ 🏊) This handsome and sprawling Georgian house, built on the ruins of an O'Brien castle, has 140 modern rooms and a large, enclosed pool. Fittings throughout are heavy and traditional. The view of the Cascades from the entrance steps is breathtaking, and there are walks around the 20 hectares of wooded gardens. Welsh poet Dylan Thomas' wife Caitlin once lived here and there's a bar named after him.

Doolin ⑦

🛏 Cullinan's Guesthouse
Inn €€

(📞065-707 4183; www.cullinansdoolin.com; Doolin; s €40-70, d €60-96; P 📶) The eight rooms here are all of a high standard, with power showers, and it has a lovely back terrace for enjoying the views. The **restaurant** (mains €21-27; 🕑6-9pm Thu-Sat, Mon & Tue Apr-Oct), serving creative seafood and local specialities, is one of the village's best. The owner is well-known local musician James Cullinan.

Inishmór ⑧

🛏 Man of Aran Cottage
B&B €€

(📞099-61301; www.manofarancottage.com; Kilmurvey; s/d from €55/80; 🕑Mar-Oct) Built for the 1930s film of the same name, this thatched B&B doesn't trade on past glories – its authentic stone-and-wood interiors define charming. The owners are avid organic gardeners (the tomatoes are famous) and their bounty can become your meal (€35).

Inisheer ⑨

🛏 Fisherman's Cottage & South Aran House
B&B €€

(📞099-75073; www.southaran.com; s/d €48/76; 🕑Apr-Oct; 📶) Slow-food enthusiasts run this sprightly B&B and cafe that's a mere five-minute walk from the pier. Lavender grows in profusion at the entrance; follow your nose. Meals (lunch and dinner, mains €13 to €20) are also open to nonguests and celebrate local seafood and organic produce. Rooms are simple yet stylish. Kayaking and fishing are among the activities on offer.

Connemara National Park *Take in the wild surrounds of Connemara*

Mountains & Moors

23

A whirl around Connemara's end-of-the-earth landscape of valleys, fjords and secret strands will leave you pining for more. So we've added cottages, abbeys and a quaint gastro village.

TRIP HIGHLIGHTS

175 km

Kylemore Abbey
Crenulated neo-Gothic fantasy with Victorian walled gardens

Glassilaun

Clifden

Oughterard

START/ FINISH
Galway

Spiddal

115 km

Roundstone
Terraces and pubs overlooking the dark recess of Bertraghboy Bay

120 km

Gurteen Bay & Dog's Bay
A dog-bone-shaped peninsula lined with idyllic beaches

6 DAYS
206KM / 128 MILES

GREAT FOR...

BEST TIME TO GO
Winter when the sea and landscape are at their wildest.

ESSENTIAL PHOTO
Create your own historic movie still at the Quiet Man Bridge.

BEST FOR DIVING
The turquoise water of Glassilaun Bay offers superb diving.

257

23 Mountains & Moors

West of Galway the scenery becomes increasingly wilder and more rugged. Crossing the Gaeltacht beyond Spiddal, take in revolutionary writer Padraig Pearse's cottage, and sophisticated Roundstone for exceptional food and the impossibly blue waters of its adjoining bays. A spin through Connemara's heartland to gothic Kylemore Abbey takes you to pretty Oughterard and back on to Galway.

1 Galway City

County Galway's namesake city (see also p248) is such a charmer you might not tear yourself away to the countryside. Arty, bohemian Galway city (Gaillimh) is renowned for its pleasures. Brightly painted pubs heave with live music, while cafes offer front-row seats for observing street performers, weekend hen parties run amok, lovers entwined and more.

Steeped in history, the city nonetheless

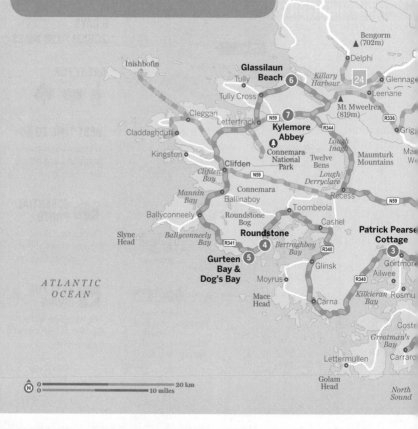

has a contemporary vibe. Remnants of the medieval town walls lie between shops selling Aran sweaters, handcrafted Claddagh rings, and stacks of secondhand and new books. Framing the river east of Wolfe Tone Bridge, the **Spanish Arch & Medieval Walls** (1584) is thought to be an extension of Galway's medieval walls. Today it reverberates to the beat of bongo drums, and the lawns and riverside form a gathering place for locals and visitors on any sunny day. See also our walking tour, p264.

🍴 🛏 p263

The Drive » The slow coastal route between Galway and Connemara takes you past pretty seascapes and villages. Opposite the popular Blue Flag beach Silver Strand, 4.8km west of Galway on the R336, are the Barna Woods, a dense, deep-green natural oak forest perfect for rambling and picnicking before hitting Spiddal.

---

② Spiddal

Spiddal (An Spidéal) is a refreshingly untouched little village, and the start of the Gaeltacht (Gaelic-speaking territory) region. On your right as you approach the village are the **Spiddal Craft & Design Studios** (www.ceardlann.com; ⏱ hours vary), where you can watch woodworkers, leatherworkers, sculptors and weavers plying their crafts. Exceptional traditional music sessions take place at **Tigh Hughes** – it's not uncommon for major musicians to turn up unannounced and join in the craic (fun).

🛏 p263

The Drive » West of Spiddal, the scenery becomes more dramatic, with parched fields criss-crossed by low stone walls rolling to a ragged shore. Carraroe (An Cheathrú Rua) has fine beaches, including the Coral Strand. It's worth wandering the small roads on all sides of Greatman's Bay to discover tiny inlets and coves, often watched

🔗 LINK YOUR TRIP

22 Musical Landscapes

This rip-roaring ride takes you from Galway's music bars to the best trad sessions of Clare.

24 Loughs of the West

Cruise Galway's gorgeous inland waterways on this tour of its lakes and rivers. Pick it up at Delphi, near Leenane.

over by the local donkeys – the perfect scenic muse for a nationalist writer such as Pádraig Pearse.

❸ Patrick Pearse's Cottage

Near Gortmore, along the R340, is **Patrick Pearse's Cottage** (Teach an Phiarsaigh; www .heritageireland.ie; adult/child €3/1; ☺10am-6pm Easter & Jun–mid-Sep). Pádraig Pearse (1879–1916) led the Easter Rising with James Connolly in 1916; after the revolt he was executed by the British. Pearse wrote some of his short stories and plays in this small thatched cottage in a wonderfully picturesque location. Although the interior was burned out during the War of Independence, it has been restored and contains an interesting exhibition about Pearse's life.

The Drive » The scenic R340 swings south along Kilkieran Bay, an intricate system of tidal marshes, basins and bogs containing an amazing diversity of wildlife. Sticking to the R340 the road meanders past Cashel, skirting Cloonisle Bay on towards Clifden, but a short trip takes you south on the R341 at Toombeola to the picture-postcard village of Roundstone.

TRIP HIGHLIGHT

❹ Roundstone

Clustered around a boat-filled harbour, Roundstone (Cloch na Rón) is one of Connemara's gems. Colourful terrace houses and inviting pubs overlook the dark recess of Bertraghboy Bay, which is home to lobster trawlers and traditional *currachs* (rowing boats with tarred canvas bottoms stretched over wicker frames). Wander the short **promenade** for views over the water

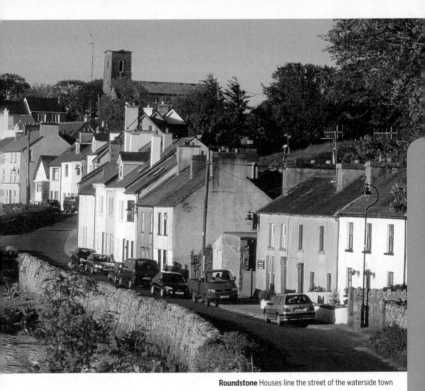

Roundstone Houses line the street of the waterside town

to ribbons of eroded land. Malachy Kearns' **Roundstone Musical Instruments** (www.bodhran.com; Michael Killeen Park; ⏱9am-7pm Jul-Sep, 9.30am-6pm Mon-Sat Oct-Jun) is just south of the village in the remains of an old Franciscan monastery. Kearns is Ireland's only full-time maker of traditional bodhráns (hand-held goatskin drums). Watch him work and buy a tin whistle, harp or booklet filled with Irish ballads; there's also a small free folk museum and a cafe.

✗ ⇨ p263

The Drive ›› The R341 shadows the coast from Roundstone to Clifden. Beaches along here have such beautiful white sand and turquoise water that, if you added 10°C to the temperature, you could be in Antigua. Don't believe us? Feast your eyes on the azure waters of Gurteen Bay and Dog's Bay ahead.

TRIP HIGHLIGHT

5 Gurteen Bay & Dog's Bay

About 2.5km from Roundstone, look for the turn to Gurteen Bay (sometimes spelt Gorteen Bay). After a further 800m there is a turn for Dog's Bay. Together, the pair form the two sides of a dog-bone-shaped peninsula lined with idyllic **beaches**. Park and enjoy a day strolling the grassy heads and frolicking on the hard-packed sand.

The Drive ›› Dusting the sand off, continue north to the village of Ballyconneely, renowned as a breeding ground for the famous Connemara pony. Although Connemara is a pearl necklace of sights, the north coast is diamond encrusted. Gorgeous beaches compete for your attention with stark, raw mountain vistas and views out to the moody sea. Heading from Clifden north, the nearby coast is a magnet for outdoors adventure seekers.

BRIDGING THE QUIET MAN

Whenever an American cable TV station needs a ratings boost, they invariably trot out the iconic 1952 *The Quiet Man*. Starring John Wayne and filmed in lavish colour to capture the crimson locks of his co-star Maureen O'Hara, the film regularly makes the top-10 lists of aging romantic-comedy lovers for its portrayal of rural Irish life, replete with drinking and fighting, fighting and drinking etc. Director John Ford returned to his Irish roots and filmed the movie almost entirely on location in Connemara and the little village of Cong, just over the border in County Mayo. One of the most photogenic spots from the film, the eponymous **Quiet Man Bridge**, is just 3km west of Oughterard off the N59. Looking much as it did in the film, the picture-perfect arched span (whose original name was Leam Bridge) is a lovely spot. Purists will note, however, that the scene based here had close-ups done on a cheesy set back in Hollywood. That's showbiz. Hard-core fans will want to buy the superb *The Complete Guide to The Quiet Man* by Des MacHale. It's sold in most tourist offices in the area.

⑥ Glassilaun Beach

Look for a turn to **Rosroe Quay**, where a truly magnificent crescent of sand awaits at Glassilaun Beach, arguably one of Connemara's best beaches. If you're drawn to the beauty of the underwater world, **Scuba Dive West** (☎095-43922; www.scubadivewest.com), based at Glassilaun Beach, runs highly recommended courses and dives. Beginners are welcome.

The Drive » Continue southeast along the final 5km stretch of road that runs along Lough Fee. In spring when the gorse explodes in yellow bloom, the views here are, again, simply breathtaking. When you hit the N59 head south to the unmistakable imposing beauty of Kylemore Abbey.

TRIP HIGHLIGHT

⑦ Kylemore Abbey

Magnificently situated on the shores of a lake, the crenulated 19th-century neo-Gothic fantasy **Kylemore Abbey** (www.kylemoreabbey.com; adult/child €12.50/free; ⏰9am-7pm summer, 11am-4.30pm winter). was built for a wealthy English businessman, Mitchell Henry, who spent his honeymoon in Connemara. His wife died tragically young. Admission also covers the abbey's tranquil **Victorian walled gardens**. You can stroll around the lake and surrounding woods for free. Prepare for large volumes of visitors in high summer when it's best to arrive in the early morning for uncluttered views.

The Drive » Heading back towards Galway, you'll cruise through a kaleidoscopic tapestry of typical Connemara valley scenery. It feels like the end of the earth with large swaths of land – colours changing from lime green, to mustard to purple on the mountain side – only interrupted by dry-stone walls, the odd derelict cottage or oblivious sheep crossing your path.

⑧ Oughterard

The writer William Makepeace Thackeray sang the praises of the small town of Oughterard (Uachtar Árd), saying, 'A more beautiful village can scarcely be seen'. Even if those charms have faded over the years, shadows of its former Georgian glory remain. And it is one of Ireland's principal angling centres. If you see tourists wandering around, talking with a drawl and calling people 'pilgrim', it's probably because they are here to relive the iconic film *The Quiet Man*.

The Drive » Heading east again, stop close by for a great photo op at 16th-century Aughnanure Castle, 3km east of Oughterard, off the N59. From here it's a quick run into Galway city for a well-deserved pint at Galway's finest, Tigh Neachtain.

Eating & Sleeping

Galway City ➊

✗ Ard Bia at Nimmo's   Irish €€

(www.ardbia.com; Spanish Arch; cafe dishes
€6-12, lunch mains €10-14, dinner mains €16-24;
⊙ cafe 10am-3.30pm, restaurant 6-10pm) In the
18th-century customs house near the Spanish
Arch, this is one of Galway's best eateries. Local
seafood and organic produce feature on the
seasonal menu in a setting that defines funky
chic. The cafe is a perfect place for a coffee and
carrot cake.

✗ Bar No 8   Pub €€

(3 Dock Rd; mains €12-22; ⊙ 11am-11pm)
Bentwood chairs and overstuffed sofas provide
comfort in this at once funky and stylish bar
overlooking the harbour. Art by patrons is on
display. The emphasis on creative pub food
places this firmly in the eating category. The fish
in the fish and chips is even battered with local
Hooker beer.

✗ Sheridans Cheesemongers   Deli €€

(14 Churchyard St; ⊙ 9.30am-6pm Mon-Fri,
9am-6pm Sat) Sheridans Cheesemongers is
redolent with the superb local and international
cheeses and other deli items within, many with
a Med bent. Its real secret, however, is up a
narrow flight of stairs. Sample from a huge wine
list in an airy and woodsy room while enjoying
many of the best items from below (open 2pm to
10pm Tuesday to Friday, noon to 8pm Saturday).

⌂ House Hotel   Hotel €€€

(☎ 091-538 900; www.thehousehotel.ie; Spanish
Pde; r €79-340; P 🛜) It's a design odyssey
at this boutique hotel. Public spaces contrast
modern art with trad details and bold accents.
The 40 rooms are plush, with beds having
elaborately padded headboards and a range of
colour schemes. Bathrooms are commodious
and ooze comfort.

⌂ Spanish Arch Hotel   Hotel €€

(☎ 091-569 600; www.spanisharchhotel.ie; Quay
St; r from €59; P @) In a sensational spot on
the main drag, this 20-room boutique hotel
is housed in a 16th-century former Carmelite
convent. Its solid-timber bar has a great line-up
of live music, so the rooms at the back, while
smaller, are best for a quiet night's sleep.
Rooms have a coffee-bar palette of creams and
browns.

Spiddal ➋

⌂ Cloch na Scíth   Inn €€

(☎ 091-553 364; www.thatchcottage.com;
Kellough; d €72-76; P) Set in a story-book
garden roamed by ducks and chickens, this
century-old thatched cottage has a warm,
friendly host, Nancy, who cooks bread in an
iron pot over the peat fire (as her grandmother
taught her and as she'll teach you).

Roundstone ➍

✗ O'Dowd's   Seafood €€

(☎ 091-35809; Main St; mains €15-22;
⊙ restaurant noon-10pm Apr-Sep, noon-3pm &
6-9.30pm Oct-Mar) This well-worn, comfortable
old pub hasn't lost any of its authenticity
since it starred in the 1997 Hollywood flick
The Matchmaker. Specialities at its adjoining
restaurant include seafood sourced off the old
stone dock right across the street.

⌂ Cashel House Hotel   Hotel €€

(☎ 095-31001; www.cashel-house-hotel.com;
Cashel; s/d from €95/290; P 🛜) At the head of
Cashel Bay less than 10km west of Roundstone,
this flowered fantasy of a country mansion has
32 period rooms surrounded by 17 hectares of
woodland and gardens. It also has a stable of
Connemara ponies (riding lessons available),
a superb dining room and even a small private
beach. Potentates who have graced its sheets
include Charles de Gaulle.

STRETCH YOUR LEGS
GALWAY

Start/Finish Spanish Arch

Distance 1.8km

Duration 2 hours

The best way to soak up Galway's convivial atmosphere is to wander its cobblestoned streets. This walk takes you from the city's medieval roots, through its cafe- and bar-lined heart to some of its finest historic buildings.

Take this walk on Trips

1 4 21 22 23 24

Spanish Arch & Medieval Walls

Framing the river east of Wolfe Tone Bridge, the Spanish Arch (1584) is thought to be an extension of Galway's medieval walls. The arch appears to have been designed as a passageway through which ships entered the city to unload goods, such as wine and brandy from Spain. Today, the lawns and riverside form a gathering place for locals and visitors on any sunny day.

The Walk >> A mere step from the Spanish Arch, you can't miss the modernist Galway City Museum. For cake and coffee before you go, Ard Bia, right opposite, will hit the spot beautifully.

Galway City Museum

The **Galway City Museum** (Spanish Pde; admission free; ⊘10am-5pm Apr-Oct) is in a glossy, glassy building that reflects the old walls. Exhibits trace aspects of daily life through Galway's history; especially good are the areas dealing with life – smelly and otherwise – during medieval times. Look for the photos of President John F Kennedy's 1963 visit to Galway, including one with dewy-eyed nuns looking on adoringly.

The Walk >> A few minutes' walk from here, crossing the plaza and heading up bustling Quay St, take the first right at the Quays Pub onto Druid Lane, also home to the acclaimed Druid Theatre (see p239).

Hall of the Red Earl

Back in the 13th century when the de Burgo family ran the show in Galway, Richard – the Red Earl – had a large **hall** (www.galwaycivictrust.ie; Druid Lane; admission free; ⊘9.30am-4.45pm Mon-Fri) built as a seat of power. The hall fell into ruin and was lost until 1997 when expansion of the city's Custom House uncovered its foundations. It now gives a fascinating sense of Galway life some 900 years ago.

The Walk >> Back on Quay St walk up as far as Neáchtain's pub (see p239), and left onto Cross

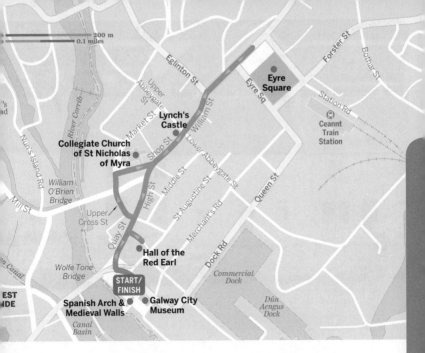

St where you continue for 50m. You'll spot the Church of St Nicholas on your right.

Collegiate Church of St Nicholas of Myra

Crowned by a pyramidal spire, the **Collegiate Church of St Nicholas of Myra** (Market St; admission by donation; ⏲9am-5.45pm Mon-Sat, 1-5pm Sun Apr-Sep) is Ireland's largest medieval parish church still in use. Dating from 1320, the church has been rebuilt and enlarged over the centuries. St Nicholas is the patron saint of sailors – Christopher Columbus reputedly worshipped here in 1477.

The Walk » Outside on Market St continue to Shop St and straight up to Eyre Sq, 600m from the church.

Eyre Square

Galway's central public square is an open space with sculptures and pathways. The eastern side is taken up almost entirely by the Hotel Meyrick, an elegant grey limestone pile.

Guarding the upper side of the square, **Browne's Doorway** (1627), a classy, if forlorn, fragment is from the home of one of the city's merchant rulers.

The Walk » From north of the square, make your way back down Shop St. Not far down on the right-hand side you'll spot the stone facade of Lynch's Castle, now a bank.

Lynch's Castle

Considered the finest town castle in Ireland, the old stone house **Lynch's Castle** (cnr Shop & Upper Abbeygate Sts) was built in the 14th century. The Lynch family was the most powerful of the 14 ruling Galway 'tribes'. Stonework on the castle's facade includes ghoulish gargoyles and many coats of arms.

The Walk » It may take you a while to navigate the pleasant bustle of Shop St with its many buskers and shoppers. Return to the Spanish Arch via High St, stopping at Murphy's pub for a sup.

Galway Experience the west's colourful and cosmopolitan city

Loughs of the West

24

This trip takes you around beautiful, less-visited backwaters to see lakeside scenery at its most untarnished, visiting epic castles and intriguing islands en route.

TRIP HIGHLIGHTS

243 km

Inishbofin
Deserted lanes, green pastures and sandy beaches grace this sleepy island

128 km

Delphi
Striking mountain perfect for hiking or relaxing

Tourmakeady

(10) FINISH

(7)

Leenane

Ballinrobe

(3)

58 km

Cong
Timeless Irish village immortalised by classic film *The Quiet Man*

Galway
START

3–4 DAYS
243KM / 151 MILES

GREAT FOR...

BEST TIME TO GO

May for ultimate fishing and the Inishbofin Arts Festival.

📷 ESSENTIAL PHOTO

Cong with spectacular vista of Ashford Castle and the lake as backdrop.

✓ BEST FOR FISHING

Loughs Corrib and Mask are world-renowned for their brown trout.

267

Loughs of the West

Following the lay of the lakes, this panoramic waterside drive takes in the very best of Loughs Corrib and Mask. Pass the picture-postcard villages of Cong and Tourmakeady before crossing the barren beauty of Connemara to dramatic mountain-backed Delphi. Cruising Connemara's filigreed northern coast, you'll discover pretty strands and ancient remains both on shore and at the striking island of Inishbofin.

Mt Knock

Inishturk

FINISH
10 Inishbofin

Inishshark

Cle

Omey 9 Cladd
Strand
Kingston

Cli

Ballina

Ballyconneely

Slyne   *Ballyc*
Head   *B*

*ATLANTIC
OCEAN*

1 Galway City

Galway's Irish name, Gaillimh (see also p258), originates from the Irish word *gaill,* meaning 'outsiders' or 'foreigners', and the term resonates throughout the city's history. This small city is colourful and cosmopolitan – many dark-haired, olive-skinned Galwegians consider themselves descended from the Spanish Armada. Bridges arc the salmon-filled River Corrib, and a long promenade leads to the seaside suburb of **Salthill**, on Galway Bay, the source of the area's famous oysters. A favourite pastime for Galwegians and visitors alike is walking along the seaside **Prom**, running from the edge of the city along Salthill. Local tradition dictates 'kicking the wall' across from the diving boards before turning around. In and around Salthill are plenty of cosy pubs from where you can watch storms roll over the bay.

See also our walking tour, p264.

✗ 🛏 p254 and p263

The Drive ≫ From Galway take the inspiringly named Headford Rd north onto the N84 into, well, Headford, skirting Lough Corrib, the Republic's biggest lake, which virtually cuts off western Galway from the rest of the country.

2 Lough Corrib

Just under 7km west of Headford you can reach Lough Corrib at the pretty Greenfields pier. Over 48km long and covering some 200 sq km, it encompasses more than 360 islands, including **Inchagoill**, home to some 5th-

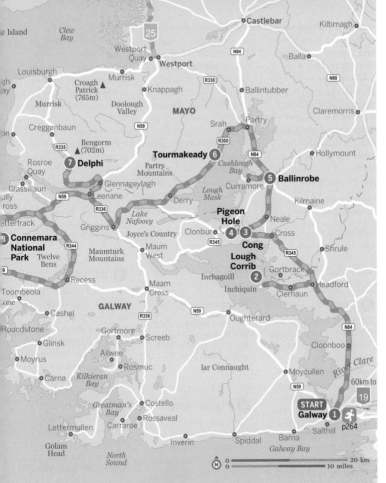

century monastic remains, a simple graveyard and Ogham stone. **Inchiquin** island, associated with St Brendan, can be accessed by road from the pier. It's world-famous for its salmon, sea trout and brown trout, with the highlight of the fishing calendar being mayfly

LINK YOUR TRIP

19 Shannon River Route

From the waters to the wild, continue on the west's inland waterways at Portumna.

25 North Mayo & Sligo

Continue exploring the northwest's incredible coastline, joining the route at Westport.

269

season, when zillions of the small bugs hatch over a few days (usually in May) and drive the fish – and anglers – into a frenzy. Salmon begin running around June. Upstream is the curiosity **Ballycurrin Lighthouse**, built in 1772 when the lake may have seen more traffic – it's Europe's only inland lighthouse.

The Drive ›› From Headford, take the R334 north out of town as far as Cross, where you'll join the R346, which takes you into the outstanding village of Cong, some 16km later.

TRIP HIGHLIGHT

❸ Cong

Sitting on a sliver-thin isthmus between Lough Corrib and Lough Mask, Cong complies with romantic notions of a traditional Irish village. Time appears to have stood still ever since the evergreen classic *The Quiet Man* was filmed here in 1951 (see also p262). Though popular on the tour-bus circuit, the

wooded trails between the lovely 12th-century Augustinian abbey and stately **Ashford Castle** (☎094-954 6003; www.ashford.ie; grounds admission €5; ⊙9am-dusk), with its wooded grounds, offer genuine quietude. First built in 1228 as the seat of the de Burgo family, one-time owner Arthur Guinness (of stout fame) turned the castle into a regal hunting and fishing lodge, which it remains today. A range of **cruises** (www.corribcruises.com; adult/child €20/10) on Lough Corrib depart from the Ashford Castle pier.

🍴 🛏 p273

The Drive ›› From Cong take the R345 west out of town and after 2km or so in the woods you'll come to the famous sink hole, Pigeon Hole.

❹ Pigeon Hole

The Cong area is honeycombed with 10 limestone caves, each with a colourful legend or story to its credit.

Keep an eye out for the white trout of Cong, a mythical woman who turned into a fish to be with her drowned lover at **Pigeon Hole**, one of the best caves. Steep, slippery stone steps lead down into the cave, where subterranean water flows in winter. Pigeon Hole can be reached by road or by the walking track from across the river.

The Drive ›› It's a 15-minute drive on the R345 north, veering left into Ballinrobe.

❺ Ballinrobe

The small market town of Ballinrobe (Baile an Roba), on the River Robe, is a good base for exploring trout-filled Lough Mask, the largest lake in the county. **St Mary's Church** has an impressive collection of stained-glass windows by Ireland's renowned 20th-century artist, Harry Clarke. One depicts St Brendan 'the Navigator', with oar in

BOYCOTT BEGINNINGS

It was near the unassuming little village of Neale, near Cong, that the term 'boycott' came into use. In 1880 the Irish Land League, in an effort to press for fair rents and improve the lot of workers, withdrew field hands from the estate of Lord Erne, who owned much of the land in the area. When Lord Erne's land agent, Captain Charles Cunningham Boycott, evicted the striking labourers, the surrounding community began a campaign to ostracise the agent. Not only did farmers refuse to work his land, people in the town refused to talk to him, provide services or sit next to him in church. The incident attracted attention from the London papers, and soon Boycott's name was synonymous with such organised, nonviolent protests. Within a few months, Boycott gave up and left Ireland.

JOHN ELK/GETTY IMAGES ©

Connemara The road to the Twelve Bens

hand, who reputedly sailed to America long before Columbus. You can access Lough Mask at **Cushlough Bay**, just 5km west of town. Take the Castlebar road north and immediately on the left you'll see signs for Cushlough. For boat hire try **Halls Angling Centre** (☎094-954 1389; www. lakeshoreholidays.com).

The Drive » Take the N84 north from Ballinrobe veering west at Partry. The landscape is made up of mostly small farm holdings, rusty bogland and tumbledown dry-stone walls. Follow the serene lakeside route (R300) through Srah to a great waterside pit stop to take in the lake at Tourmakeady.

6 Tourmakeady

With the backdrop of the Partry Mountains acting as a picturesque backdrop to its west, the small village of Tourmakeady, on the shore of Lough Mask, is part of an Irish-speaking community. Once a flax-growing area, its name is derived from Tuar Mhic Éadaigh, meaning 'Keady's field', referring to the field where the flax was once laid out to dry before spinning. Tourmakeady Woods, with a spectacular 58m-high **waterfall** at its centre, makes a

wonderful spot for a picnic. Alternatively, you could water the horses at the cosy Paddy's Thatched Bar, overlooking the water.

The Drive » Follow the lakeside road, pulling in at stunning Lake Nafooey, at the foot of Maumtrasna, to take in the view. Head north at the R336 through Leenane and around the harbour, passing Assleagh Falls to Delphi, a scenic 45km in all.

TRIP HIGHLIGHT

7 Delphi

Geographically just inside County Mayo, but administratively in County Galway, this

271

swath of mountainous moorland is miles from any significant population, allowing you to set about the serious business of relaxing. At the southern extent of the Doolough Valley, the area was named by its most famous resident, the second marquis of Sligo, who was convinced that it resembled the land around Delphi, Greece. If you can spot the resemblance, you've a better imagination than most, but in many ways it's even more striking than its Mediterranean namesake. At the beautiful **Delphi Mountain Resort** (📞095-42208; www. delphimountainresort.com; d from €128; 🅿 @) opt for a day's surfing, kayaking or rock climbing, followed by a stay and some pampering spa treatments using hand-harvested local seaweed.

🛏 p273

The Drive >> Follow the N59 the short way to Letterfrack, 300m south of the crossroads, then make a worthwhile stop at the Connemara National Park.

- - - - - - - - - - - -

8 Connemara National Park

Spanning 2000 dramatic hectares of bog, mountain and heath, **Connemara National Park** (📞095-41054; www. npws.ie, www.heritageireland. ie; admission free; ☉visitor centre & facilities 9am-5.30pm)

encloses a number of the Twelve Bens, including Bencullagh, Benbrack and Benbaun. The heart of the park is **Gleann Mór** (Big Glen), through which the River Polladirk flows. There's fine walking up the glen and over the surrounding mountains. There are also short, self-guided walks and, if the Bens look too daunting, you can hike up **Diamond Hill** nearby. Various types of flora and fauna native to the area are explained, including the huge elephant hawkmoth, in the excellent visitor centre.

🛏 p273

The Drive >> Join the R344 down through Lough Inagh Valley, on the western side of the brooding Twelve Bens. Following the jagged coastline north of Clifden brings you to the tiny village of Claddaghduff (An Cladach Dubh), which is signposted off the road to Cleggan. If you turn west here down by the Catholic church, you will come out on Omey Strand.

- - - - - - - - - - - -

9 Omey Strand

At low tide you can drive or walk across the sand at Omey Strand to **Omey Island** (population 20), a low islet of rock, grass, sand and a handful of houses. During summer, horse races are held on Omey Strand.

The Drive >> Double back a five-minute drive to Cleggan to park up and take the 30 minute ferry to glorious Inishbofin.

- - - - - - - - - - - -

TRIP HIGHLIGHT

10 Inishbofin

By day sleepy Inishbofin is a haven of tranquillity. You can walk or bike its narrow, deserted lanes, green pastures and sandy beaches, with farm animals and seals for company. But with no *gardaí* (Irish Republic police) on the island to enforce closing times at the pub, by night – you guessed it – Inishbofin has wild craic (good times). Situated 9km offshore, Inishbofin is only 6km long by 3km wide and its highest point is a mere 86m above sea level. Inishbofin's pristine waters offer superb scuba diving, sandy beaches and alluring trails that encourage exploring. The island well and truly wakes up during the **Inishbofin Arts Festival** (www.inishbofin.com) in May, which includes accordion workshops, archaeological walks, art exhibitions and concerts by such high-profile Irish bands as De Dannan and The Stunning. Ferries from Cleggan to Inishbofin are run by **Island Discovery** (📞095-45894; www.inishbofinislanddiscovery. com; adult/child return €20/10). In summer there are three ferries a day. Dolphins often swim alongside the boats.

🛏 p273

Eating & Sleeping

Cong 3

✕ Hungry Monk   Cafe €

(Abbey St; mains €7-16; ☺10am-6pm Mon-Sat, 11am-5pm Sun Apr-Aug; @) This cheery little cafe with its bright colours and artfully mismatched furniture is the best lunch spot in town. Locally sourced ingredients make up the fab sandwiches (such as home-baked ham served with mango chutney), soups and salads, the luscious cakes are all homemade and it brews the best coffee in town.

🛏 Lisloughrey Lodge   Hotel €€€

(☎094-954 5400; www.lisloughreylodgehotel. ie; The Quay; r from €160; P @ 🛜) The lodge, built in the 1820s by Ashford Castle's owners, has been stunningly renovated in bold, contemporary cranberry and blueberry tones, with 50 guest rooms named for wine regions and champagne houses. Kick back in the bar, billiards room or beanbag-strewn Wii room. Nab a room in the original house for old-world character.

Delphi 7

🛏 Delphi Lodge   Inn €€€

(☎095-42222; www.delphilodge.ie; s/d from €130/200, cottages per week from €700; P @) A wonderful Georgian mansion built by the marquis of Sligo, and dwarfed by its mountain backdrop. Blurring the boundaries between private house and country hotel, this place will immediately put you at ease. Boasts beautiful interiors, vast grounds, incredible food (dinner €45), delightful staff and a serious lack of pretension.

Connemara National Park 8

🛏 Lough Inagh Lodge   Inn €€€

(☎091-34706; www.loughinaghlodgehotel.ie; r from €130-200, dinner €40; P 🛜) Steeped in Victorian grandeur, the atmospheric Lough Inagh is midway up the gorgeous Lough Inagh Valley off the R344. Set against a hill, it has a plum position on the water. Turf fires lend the cosy public spaces a scent that says 'country'. You start breathing deeply from the time you enter one of the 13 rooms.

Inishbofin 10

🛏 Doonmore Hotel   Hotel €€

(☎095-45804; www.doonmorehotel.com; r from €50-80; ☺Apr-Sep; 🛜) Close to the harbour, Doonmore has comfortable, unpretentious rooms. Lunch (€15) and dinner (€35) in the dining room take advantage of the abundance of locally caught seafood, and the hotel can pack lunches for you to take while exploring the island.

🛏 Dolphin Hotel & Restaurant   Inn €€

(☎095-45991; www.dolphinhotel.ie; r €50-800; ☺Apr-Sep; @) A panoply of beiges dominates the guest rooms at this stylish study in modern minimalism. Solar panels on the roof and an organic kitchen garden lend green cred. Local seafood and vegetarian dishes dominate the menu (mains €15 to €25). There is usually a two-night minimum stay.

Achill Island For a far-flung island feeling

North Mayo & Sligo

25

Travel from country-cosmopolitan Westport to nature at its most visceral on windswept Achill Island. Then, carry on through superb surfscapes to Sligo, Yeats' beloved adopted home town.

TRIP HIGHLIGHTS

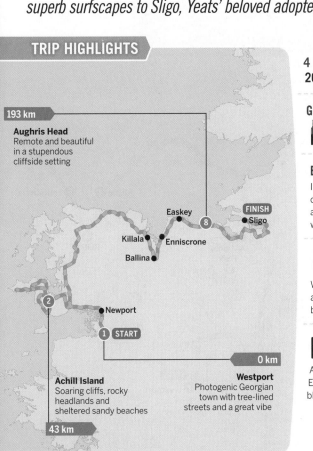

193 km

Aughris Head
Remote and beautiful in a stupendous cliffside setting

Easkey

Killala
Enniscrone

Ballina

FINISH
Sligo

8

2

Newport

1 START

0 km

Achill Island
Soaring cliffs, rocky headlands and sheltered sandy beaches

Westport
Photogenic Georgian town with tree-lined streets and a great vibe

43 km

**4 DAYS
266KM / 165 MILES**

GREAT FOR...

BEST TIME TO GO

In early autumn crowds have abated and the sea is warmest.

ESSENTIAL PHOTO

Wild Atlantic rollers at sunset on Easkey beach.

BEST FOR OUTDOORS

Achill Island and Easkey offer surf and blustery beach walks.

25 North Mayo & Sligo

This area has something quietly special – the rugged and remote Atlantic scenery of the west, but with fewer crowds. Grab a board and face off an invigorating roller at Achill, take a restorative seaweed bath at Enniscrone, walk in WB Yeats' footsteps round the 'Lake Isle of Innisfree' at the foot of Benbulben and enjoy the unpretentious company of lively Westport.

TRIP HIGHLIGHT

1 Westport

Bright and vibrant even in the depths of winter, Westport (see also p237) is a photogenic Georgian town with tree-lined streets, a riverside mall and a great vibe. With an excellent choice of accommodation, restaurants and pubs renowned for their music, it's an extremely popular spot yet has never sold its soul to tourism. A couple of kilometres west on Clew Bay, the town's

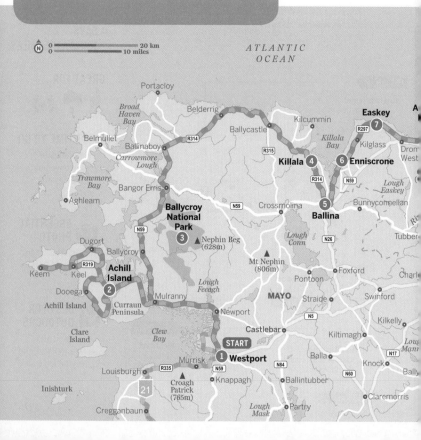

harbour, Westport Quay is a picturesque spot for a sundowner.

Westport House
(☎098-27766; www. westporthouse.ie; Quay Rd; house & gardens adult/child €12/6.50; ⊙house & gardens 10am-6pm mid-Apr–Aug), built in 1730 on the ruins of Grace O'Malley's 16th-century castle, is a charming Georgian mansion that retains much of its original contents and has some stunning period-styled rooms. The house is set in glorious gardens. Children will love the

Pirate Adventure Park, complete with a swinging pirate ship, a 'pirate's playground' and a roller-coaster-style flume ride through a water channel.

✗ p281

The Drive ⟩⟩ A wiggling 12km drive north of Westport is the picturesque 18th-century village of Newport. Skip its main road to Achill Island in favour of the longer, narrower and infinitely more scenic Atlantic Dr, looking out for signs to Burrishoole Abbey and Rockfleet Castle, a 15th-century tower associated with 'pirate queen' Grace O'Malley.

- - - - - - - - - - - - - - -

TRIP HIGHLIGHT

2 Achill Island
Ireland's largest offshore island, Achill (An Caol), is connected to the mainland by a short bridge. Despite its accessibility, it has plenty of that far-flung-island feeling: soaring cliffs, rocky headlands, sheltered sandy beaches, broad expanses of blanket bog and rolling mountains. **Slievemore Deserted Village** at the foot of Slievemore

Mountain is a poignant reminder of the island's past hardships. In the mid-19th century, as the Potato Famine took hold, starvation forced the villagers to emigrate, or die. Except in the height of the holiday season, the Blue Flag beaches at **Dooega**, **Keem**, **Dugort** and **Golden Strand** are often deserted.

✗ 🛏 p281

The Drive ⟩⟩ As you leave Achill (if you can), you'll pass the village of Mulranny on a narrow isthmus overlooking a wide Blue Flag beach and 365 or so islands that grace Clew Bay. From here north the countryside throws out beautifully bleak boglands dotted with dry-stone walls and wandering sheep. About 18km along the road, you might want to stop for a picnic lunch with a very fine backdrop, at Ballycroy National Park.

- - - - - - - - - - - - - - -

3 Ballycroy National Park
Covering one of Europe's largest expanses of blanket bog, **Ballycroy National Park** (www. ballycroynationalpark.ie; admission free; ⊙visitor centre

Cliffony
LEITRIM
N15   Dartry/
Grange   Mountains
26   Benbulben
    ▲(525m)
rumcliff
FINISH   N16
Sligo 10
Lough Gill 9
    Dromahair
    Ballysadare
olloney
IGO   N4
Drumfin   Riverstown
N17
lymote
    Castlebaldwin
Bricklieve
Mountains   Ballinafad
urteen   Curlew Mountains
    Lough   Boyle
    Gara
N61
haderreen
    Frenchpark
ROSCOMMON
gh
m   Castlerea   Tulsk
    60
GALWAY

LINK YOUR TRIP

26 **Sligo Surrounds**
Continue from Sligo to explore the county's rich megalithic remains, blustery beaches and Yeats' old stomping ground.

21 **Best of the West**
The crème de la crème of Ireland's west coast; pick up this route in Westport for a scenic and cultural feast.

THE PIRATE QUEEN

The life of Grace O'Malley (Gráinne Ní Mháille or Granuaile; 1530–1603) reads like an unlikely work of adventure fiction. Twice widowed and twice imprisoned for acts of piracy, she was a fearsome presence in the troubled landscape of 16th-century Ireland, when traditional chieftains were locked in battle with the English for control of the country. Grace was ordered to London in 1593, whereupon Queen Elizabeth I granted her a pardon and offered her a title: she declined, saying she was already Queen of Connaught. Westport House now resides on the ruins of Grace's 16-century castle.

10am-5.30pm late Mar-Oct) is a gorgeously scenic region, where the River Owenduff wends its way through intact bogs.

The park is home to a diverse range of flora and fauna including peregrine falcons, corncrakes and whooper swans. A nature trail with interpretation panels leads from the visitor centre across the bog with great views to the surrounding mountains. If you wish to explore further, the **Bangor Trail** crosses the park and leads to some of its most spectacular viewpoints.

The Drive » Ballycroy is 18km south of Bangor on the N59. Continuing north from here on the R314 through Ballycastle and passing the magnificent Stone Age monument at Céide Fields (p236) you'll come to the historic town of Killala.

❹ Killala

The town itself is pretty enough, but Killala is more famous for its namesake **bay** nearby, and for its role in the French invasion, when in 1798 more than 1000 French troops landed at Kilcummin in Killala Bay. It was hoped that their arrival would inspire the Irish peasantry to revolt against the English.

Lackan Bay **beach** is a stunning expanse of golden sand. There's good surf here, but you'll need to bring your own equipment.

The Drive » Back on the R314, it's only 12km or so down to the authentic provincial hub of Ballina.

❺ Ballina

Mayo's second-largest town, Ballina, is synonymous with salmon. If you're here during fishing season, you'll see droves of green-garbed waders, poles in hand, heading for the River Moy – one of the most prolific rivers in Europe for catching the scaly critters – which pumps right through the heart of town. You'll also spot salmon jumping in the Ridge (salmon pool), with otters and grey seals in pursuit.

One of the best outdoor parties in the country, the weeklong **Ballina Salmon Festival** (www.ballinasalmonfestival.ie) takes place in mid-July.

The Drive » Taking the N59 east out of town towards Enniscrone, head back up to the coast on the small R297, which you'll meet just over 4km from Ballina.

❻ Enniscrone

Enniscrone is famous for its traditional seaweed baths (see p280), which are some of the best and most atmospheric in the country. A stunning beach known as the **Hollow** stretches for 5km. Surf lessons and board hire are available from Enniscrone-based **Seventh Wave Surf School** (☎087 971 6389; www.surfsligo.com).

The Drive » Some 14km north you'll come to the little village of Easkey.

❼ Easkey

Easkey seems blissfully unaware that it's one of Europe's best year-round surfing destinations. Pub conversations revolve around hurling and

Achill Island

Gaelic football, and the road to the beach isn't even signposted (turn off next to the childcare centre). Facilities are few; most surfers camp (free) around the castle ruins by the sea. If you're planning on hitting the waves, information and advice are available from **Easkey Surfing & Information Centre** (Irish Surfing Association; ☎096-49428; www.isasurf.ie).

The Drive ≫ From Easkey, you'll hug the winding coast road (R297) until you see signs for Aughris Head.

TRIP HIGHLIGHT

8 Aughris Head

An invigorating 5km walk traces the cliffs around remote Aughris Head, where dolphins and seals can often be seen swimming into the bay. Birdwatchers should look out for kittiwakes, fulmars, guillemots, shags, storm petrels and curlews along the way. In a stupendous setting on the lovely beach by the cliff walk, the **Beach Bar** (www.thebeachbarsligo.com; mains €10-19; ⊙food served 1-8pm daily summer) is tucked inside a

IRELAND'S SEAWEED BATHS

Ireland's only native spa therapy is the stuff of mermaid (or merman) fantasies. Part of Irish homeopathy for centuries, steaming your pores open then submerging yourself in a seaweed bath is said to help rheumatism and arthritis, thyroid imbalances, even hangovers. Certainly it leaves your skin feeling baby-soft: seaweed's silky oils contain a massive concentration of iodine, a key presence in most moisturising creams.

Seaweed baths are prevalent along the west coast but two places stand out. **Kilcullen's Seaweed Baths** (☎091-36238; www.kilcullenseaweedbaths.com; Enniscrone; s/tw bath €25/40; ⏰10am-8pm Jun-Sep, noon-8pm Mon-Fri, 10am-8pm Sat & Sun Oct-May), in Enniscrone, is the most traditional and has buckets of character. Set within a grand Edwardian structure, it seems perfectly fitting to sit with your head exposed and your body ensconced in an individual cedar steam cabinet before plunging into one of the original gigantic porcelain baths filled with amber water and seaweed.

For an altogether more modern setting, try **Voya Seaweed Baths** (☎071-916 8686; www.celticseaweedbaths.com; Shore Rd, Strandhill; s/tw bath €25/50; ⏰noon-8pm Mon & Tue, 11am-8pm Wed-Fri, 10am-8pm Sat & Sun), which has a beachfront location.

If too much relaxation is barely enough, both establishments also offer the chance to indulge in various other seaweed treatments, including body wraps and massages.

17th-century thatched cottage, with cracking traditional music sessions and superb seafood.

📖 p281

The Drive » From Aughris follow the N59 southeast and onto the N4 towards Sligo until you see a sign for Dromahair (R287). Take this small, leafy road east, skirting the south of Lough Gill and on through Dromahair, making sure to stop at Cheese Etc for some excellent picnic supplies.

- - - - - - - - - - - - - -

⑨ Lough Gill

The mirrorlike 'Lake of Brightness', Lough Gill is home to as many legends as fish. One that can be tested easily is the story that a silver bell from the abbey in Sligo was thrown into the lough and only those free from sin can hear it peeling. (We didn't hear it...)

Two magical swaths of woodland – **Hazelwood** and **Slish Wood** – have loop trails; from the latter, there are good views of Innisfree Island, subject of WB Yeats' poem 'The Lake Isle of Innisfree'. You can take a cruise on the lake from **Parke's Castle**.

The Drive » Having soaked up the atmosphere of Yeats' back yard, make your way a few kilometres north to the hub of Yeats country, Sligo town.

- - - - - - - - - - - - - -

⑩ Sligo Town

Sligo town is in no hurry to shed its cultural traditions but it doesn't sell them out, either. Pedestrian streets lined with inviting shop fronts, stone bridges spanning the River Garavogue, and *céilidh* (sessions of traditonal music and dancing) spilling from pubs contrast with contemporary art and glass towers rising from prominent corners of the compact town. A major draw of Sligo's **County Museum** (Stephen St; ⏰9.30am-12.30pm & 2-4.50pm Tue-Sat May-Sep) is the Yeats room, which features photographs, letters and newspaper cuttings connected with the poet WB Yeats, as well as drawings by his brother Jack B Yeats, one of Ireland's most important modern artists.

🍴📖 p281

Eating & Sleeping

Westport ❶

✗ Quay Cottage   Seafood €€
(☎098-26412; Harbour; mains €18-25; ☺dinner mid-Feb–mid-Jan) Serving seafood straight off the boats and steeped in salty-dog charm (including lobster pots hanging from the roof beams), this is the pick of the places to eat on Westport's lively harbourfront.

Achill Island ❷

✗ Calvey's Restaurant   Irish €€
(☎098-43158; www.calveysofachill.com; Keel; lunch mains €8-14, dinner mains €16-28; ☺lunch & dinner Easter–mid-Sep) As it's attached to its own organic butchery, it's no surprise that the speciality at this award-winning restaurant is meat. Don't miss the rack of organic Achill lamb with its distinct island flavour. There's also a good choice of fish and seafood cooked with seasonal local ingredients.

⌂ Bervie   B&B €€
(☎098-43114; Keel; s/d €75/110; P 🐾) Once a coastguard station, this delightful B&B is a wonderfully friendly place with views over the ocean and direct access onto the beach from the well-tended garden. The 14 rooms are bright but cosy, with white bedspreads and wooden furniture. There's a great welcome for families and a playroom with a pool table for wet days. Evening meals are available on request (€45).

Aughris Head ❽

⌂ Aughris House   B&B, Campground €
(☎071-917 6465; tent/van sites €10/20, s/d €30/60; P 🛜) This cosy place next door to the Beach Bar has seven comfy rooms and an adjacent campsite.

Sligo Town ❿

✗ Hargadons   Pub €
(www.hargadons.com; 4 O'Connell St; mains €7-10, tapas dishes €7-10; ☺Mon-Sat) A winning blend of old-world fittings and gastropub style, this pub dating from 1864 has uneven stone floors, turf fire, antique signage and snug corners, all adding up to a wonderful charm. You'll also enjoy some excellent food (think oysters in a hot chorizo and tabasco sauce or confit of duck leg) and the smoothest of pints.

✗ Source   Irish €€
(☎071-914 7605; www.sourcesligo.ie; 1 John St; mains €15-20; ☺9.30am-5pm Mon, to 9.30pm Tue-Sun) Source champions local suppliers and produce in its ground-floor restaurant with open kitchen and buzzy atmosphere, while upstairs in the **wine bar** (dishes €4-9; ☺3-11pm Tue-Sun) things are more sedate with wine from the owners' vineyard in France and plates of Irish-style tapas on offer.

⌂ Pearse Lodge   B&B €€
(☎071-916 1090; www.pearselodge.com; Pearse Rd; s/d €50/74; P @ 🛜) Welcoming owners Mary and Kieron not only impeccably maintain the six stylish guest rooms at their cosy B&B but are also up on what's happening in town. Mary's breakfast menu includes smoked salmon, French toast with bananas and homemade muesli (and Illy coffee!). A sunny sitting room opens to a beautifully landscaped garden.

County Sligo Look out for a bounty of sites and villages among the wild and well-known coast

Sligo Surrounds 26

Sligo is as varied as a county this size gets. On top of its exceptional beaches, there's a wealth of prehistoric sites and Yeats literary heritage, along with fine traditional bars.

TRIP HIGHLIGHTS

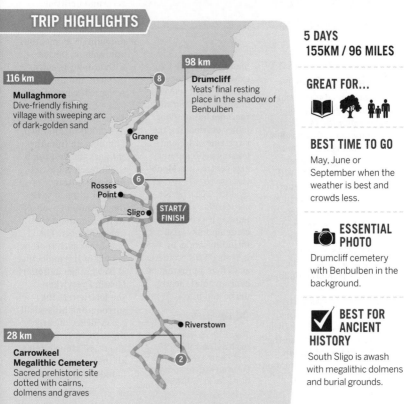

98 km

116 km ⑧

Mullaghmore
Dive-friendly fishing village with sweeping arc of dark-golden sand

Drumcliff
Yeats' final resting place in the shadow of Benbulben

Grange

Rosses Point

⑥

START/ FINISH

Sligo ●

● Riverstown

28 km

Carrowkeel Megalithic Cemetery
Sacred prehistoric site dotted with cairns, dolmens and graves

②

5 DAYS
155KM / 96 MILES

GREAT FOR...

BEST TIME TO GO
May, June or September when the weather is best and crowds less.

ESSENTIAL PHOTO
Drumcliff cemetery with Benbulben in the background.

BEST FOR ANCIENT HISTORY
South Sligo is awash with megalithic dolmens and burial grounds.

Sligo offers wild beauty, but with quietude too. Lush fields, lakes and flat-topped mountains provided inspiration for William Butler Yeats. And among the stretches of golden sands and legendary breaks that lure the surfing cognoscenti, you'll find a bounty of prehistoric sites, elegant Georgian towns, little fishing villages and good old-fashioned country hospitality.

1 Sligo Town

For a small provincial hub, Sligo (see also p280), with its galleries, museum and atmospheric old-man pubs, is quite the cultural magnet. Thanks largely to WB Yeats' childhood affection for, and his association with, the area, Sligo attracts visitors keen to learn more about the poet's formative environment. In the **Yeats Memorial Building** (www.yeats-sligo.com; ◷10am-5pm Mon-Fri, tearoom 10am-6pm Mon-Sat), in a pretty setting near Hyde Bridge, you can visit the **WB Yeats Exhibition**, with a video presentation and valuable draft manuscripts; the €2 exhibition catalogue makes a good souvenir of Sligo. The charming **tearoom** has outdoor tables overlooking the river. One of Ireland's leading contemporary-arts centres, the **Model** (www.themodel.ie; The Mall; ◷10am-5.30pm Tue-Sat, noon-5pm Sun) houses an impressive collection of contemporary Irish art, including works by Jack B Yeats (WB's brother), as well as a program of experimental theatre, music and film.

✕ ⌷ p289

The Drive ≫ Heading south and west off the N4 road, Carrowkeel Megalithic Cemetery is closer to Boyle than Sligo Town. There's another Carrowkeel 6km south of Sligo, but this isn't the one you're looking for. From the N4, turn right in Castlebaldwin at Tower Hill guesthouse, then left at the fork; the cemetery is 2km uphill from the gateway.

TRIP HIGHLIGHT

2 Carrowkeel Megalithic Cemetery

With a God's-eye view of the county from high in the Bricklieve Mountains, it's little wonder this hilltop site was sacred in prehistoric times. The windswept location is simultaneously eerie and uplifting, its undeveloped, spectacular setting providing a momentous atmosphere. Dotted with around 14 cairns, dolmens and the scattered remnants of other graves, Carrowkeel dates from the late Stone Age (3000 to 2000 BC). Climbing up from the car park the first tomb you'll reach is Cairn G. Above its entrance is a **roofbox** aligned with the midsummer sunset which illuminates the inner chamber. The only other such roofbox known in Ireland is that at Newgrange in County Meath. Everywhere you look across the surrounding hills you'll see evidence of early life here, including about 140 **stone circles**, all that remain of the foundations of a large

village thought to have been inhabited by the builders of the tombs.

The Drive >> Head south from Carrowkeel and into Kesh (sometimes spelt Keash), around 6km south of Ballymote. The Caves of Kesh are rich with mythology and are believed to extend for miles. From here continue till you meet the R295 and turn right for Ballymote and across the N4 to Riverstown.

3 Riverstown

The endearing **Sligo Folk Park** (☑071-916 5001; www.sligofolkpark.com; Millview House, Riverstown; adult/child €6/4; ☺10am-5pm Mon-Sat Jun-Oct) revolves around a lovingly restored 19th-century cottage. Humble thatched structures complement this centrepiece, along with scattered farm tools and an exhibit that honours the old country life.

LINK YOUR TRIP

32 Northwest on Adrenalin

There's plenty more surf to be found on Donegal's beach beauties. From Grange stick north on the N15.

24 Loughs of the West

From the northwest's wild coast, turn it down a little for a tour of the west's serene lakelands, from Sligo on the N17.

Another fine reason to come here is to attend a course on permaculture, bee-keeping or even solar-panel building at the green-roofed **Gyreum** (☎071-916 5994; www. gyreum.com; Corlisheen, Riverstown; dm €15-20, d €40-50; P), a pudding-shaped building hidden by the surrounding hills. You can also give your own sermon on a Sunday morning, volunteer to help out or stay in the simple rooms.

The Drive » Returning to the N4, follow the Sligo road for some 15km till you veer off in the direction of Ballina (R292). The seaside resort of Strandhill is signposted shortly after.

4 Strandhill

The great Atlantic rollers that sweep the shorefront of Strandhill make this long, red-gold **beach** unsafe for swimming. They have, however, made it a surfing mecca. Gear hire and lessons can be arranged through **Perfect Day Surf Shop** (www.perfectdaysurfing.com; Shore Rd). Alternatively, take a gentler, warmer dip in the Voya Seaweed Baths (see p280). A few kilometres towards Sligo, you can walk – at low tide only! – to **Coney Island**. Its New York namesake was supposedly named by a man from Rosses Point. The island's wishing well is reputed to have been

dug by St Patrick (who, if all these tales are to be trusted, led a *very* busy life). Check tide times to avoid getting stranded.

🍴 🛏 p289

The Drive » From here follow the R291 out of town and along the coast to Rosses Point, 8km northwest of Sligo. This road can get busy with holidaymakers in summer.

5 Rosses Point

Rosses Point is a picturesque seaside resort with grassy dunes rolling down to the golden strand. Benbulben, Sligo's most recognisable landmark, arches skywards in the distance. Offshore, the odd **Metal Man** beacon dates from 1821. Rosses Point has two wonderful beaches. Drop into **Harry's Bar** (on your right as you come into Rosses Point) for a pint and a peek at its historic well, aquarium and maritime bric-a-brac.

🛏 p289

The Drive » Returning to the R291 you'll pick up the busy N15, where you head north to the quaint town of Drumcliff, at the foot of Benbulben, Yeats' final resting place.

TRIP HIGHLIGHT

6 Drumcliff

Visible right along Sligo's northern coast, **Benbulben** (525m) resembles a table covered by a pleated

cloth: its limestone plateau is uncommonly flat, and its near-vertical sides are scored by earthen ribs. Benbulben's beauty was not lost on WB Yeats. Before the poet died in Menton, France in 1939, he had requested: 'If I die here, bury me up there on the mountain, and then after a year or so, dig me up and

286

DEB SNELSON/GETTY IMAGES ©

Benbulben The Sligo mountain with an uncommonly flat top

bring me privately to Sligo'. **Yeats' grave** is next to the doorway of the Protestant church in Drumcliff, and his youthful bride Georgie Hyde-Lee is buried alongside. Historic **Lissadell House**, west of Drumcliff off the N15 just past Yeats Tavern, was recently restored to its former glory by its

private owners but is not open to visitors.

The Drive ≫ The light on Benbulben looming in the distance inland often changes it from dark blue, to purple or a mossy shade of green. Continue on the N15 less than 9km into the small village of Grange.

- - - - - - - - - - -

7 Grange

From the village of Grange, signs point towards **Streedagh Beach**, a grand crescent of sand that saw some 1100 sailors perish when three ships from the Spanish Armada were wrecked nearby. Views extend from the beach to the cliffs at Slieve League

287

MICHAEL QUIRKE: WOODCARVER OF WINE STREET

The inconspicuous studio of Michael Quirke, woodcarver, raconteur and local character, is filled with the scents of locally felled timbers and offcuts of beech stumps. A converted butcher shop on Wine St in Sligo town, it retains some of the implements of the butcher's trade, including an electric bone saw. Quirke, himself formerly a butcher, began to use his tools for cutting and carving wood in 1968. He divided his time between his twin callings for 20 years, after which he gave up meat, so to speak. Quirke's art is inspired by Irish mythology, a subject about which he is passionate and knowledgable, and as he carves he readily chats with the customers and the curious who enter his shop and end up staying for hours. 'Irish mythology, unlike Greek mythology, is alive and constantly changing', he says. 'It's not set in stone, and that's why it's interesting.' He draws unforced connections between Irish myths, music, history, flora, fauna and contemporary events, as well as comparisons in the wider world, such as Australian Aboriginal and Native North American lore. As he talks and carves, Quirke frequently pulls out a county map, pointing to places that spring from the conversation, leading you on your own magical, mystical tour of the county.

in Donegal. Locals regularly swim here, even in winter. Don't leave Grange without stopping into **Langs Pub** (☏071-916 3105; www.langs. ie) for a bite or to water the horses in the well-preserved front bar, with its bottles of Guinness among the old washing powder and cereal boxes. It's one of the county's finest old grocery-draper-bars.

The Drive ≫ Keep heading north on the N15 till you reach the sleepy crossroads of Cliffony. Take a left at the church, onto the R279 to Mullaghmore.

- - - - - - - - - - - -

TRIP HIGHLIGHT

8 Mullaghmore

The sweeping arc of dark-golden sand and the safe shallow waters make the pretty fishing village of Mullaghmore a popular family destination. It was a favoured holiday spot of Lord Mountbatten, who was killed here when the IRA rigged his boat with explosives in 1979. Take time to drive the scenic road looping around Mullaghmore Head, where wide shafts of rock slice into the Atlantic surf. En route you'll pass **Classiebawn Castle** (closed to the public), a neo-Gothic turreted pile built for Lord Palmerston in 1856 and later home to the ill-fated Lord Mountbatten. Mullaghmore Head is becoming known as one of Ireland's premier big wave surf spots, with swells of up to 17m allowing for Hawaiian-style adventure. Mullaghmore's clear waters, rocky outcrops and coves are also ideal for diving.

🛏 p289

The Drive ≫ It's a straight run back on the N15 some 27km back to Sligo, where you can enjoy a creamy pint in a snug at one of the region's finest traditional pubs, Connolly's on Holborn St.

Eating & Sleeping

Sligo Town ❶

✕ Ósta   Cafe €

(www.osta.ie; Hyde Bridge, Left Bank; light meals
€6-13; ⏰8am-7.30pm Mon-Sat, 9am-6pm
Sun) Ósta is a cafe and a wine bar, and it's well
suited to both callings. An array of preserved
meats, seafood and Irish farmhouse cheeses
accompany its well-chosen wines. It's intimate
and well lit, and has a prime quayside location
for gazing at the river charging beneath Hyde
Bridge.

✕ Tobergal Lane   Irish €€

(☎071-914 6599; Tobergal Lane; lunch dishes
€6-9, dinner mains €9-20; ⏰10am-10pm
Mon-Sat, 11am-10pm Sun) There's a wonderfully
warm, relaxed vibe at this arty cafe hidden
down a curving laneway. The menu is simple but
creatively prepared, with specials such as duck
confit with puy lentils or baked sea trout with
lime and ginger sauce. There's live jazz on Friday
nights and Sunday afternoons.

🛏 Pearse Lodge   B&B €€

(☎071-916 1090; www.pearselodge.com;
Pearse Rd; s/d €50/74; 🅿@🛜) Welcoming
owners Mary and Kieron not only impeccably
maintain the six stylish guest rooms at their
cosy B&B but are also up on what's happening
in town. Mary's breakfast menu includes
smoked salmon, French toast with bananas and
homemade muesli (and Illy coffee!). A sunny
sitting room opens to a beautifully landscaped
garden.

🛏 Sligo Park Hotel   Hotel €€

(☎071-919 0400; www.sligoparkhotel.com;
Pearse Rd; s/d from €89/95; 🅿🛜🏊) Set on
the edge of town in landscaped gardens with
mature trees, this large but tranquil hotel is a
local favourite. The pretty, tastefully decorated
rooms are bright and modern, there's a pool and
spa and excellent service.

Strandhill ❹

✕ Trá Bán   Seafood €€

(☎071-912 8402; www.trabansligo.ie; Shore Rd;
mains €17-24; ⏰closed Mon) This justifiably
popular spot serves a menu strong on seafood,
but with a good selection of steak and pasta
dishes thrown in. It has a lovely relaxed
atmosphere and chic decor. You're advised to
book in advance.

🛏 Strandhill Lodge & Hostel   Hostel €

(☎071-916 8313; www.strandhillaccommodation
.com; Shore Rd; dm/s/d from €10/40/50;
🅿@🛜) Surfer dudes and dudettes thaw out
by the open fire in the common room of this
well-run, 34-bed hostel a few paces from the
strand. The owners also operate a rather frilly
B&B next door and a surf school.

Rosses Point ❺

🛏 Rosses Point Guesthouse   Inn €

(☎086 805 1390; www.rossesspointguesthouse.
com; dm/d from €20/50; 🛜) A sparkly clean
place in the centre of the village with simple
but pristine rooms, a good kitchen and lively
atmosphere. The team behind it also run **LSD
Kiteboarding** (www.lsdkiteboarding.com) and
offer a two-night accommodation and boarding
package for €410.

Mullaghmore ❽

🛏 Pier Head Hotel   Hotel €

(☎071-916 6171; www.pierheadhotel.ie;
Mullaghmore; s/d €50/60; ⏰closed late Dec;
🅿🛜🏊) Location, location, location. If you're
lucky you'll get magnificent views from a
room at this pristine hotel by the harbour. The
rooms are clean and crisp, there's a tiny gym,
a panoramic rooftop terrace with hot tub, and
decent food in the bar (mains €10-20).

Cliffs of Moher *The limestone cliffs never cease to amaze*

County Clare **27**

Experience scenic coastline including the breathtaking Cliffs of Moher, the Aran Islands, market towns with cracking pubs and Clare's jewel, the geological wonder of The Burren.

TRIP HIGHLIGHTS

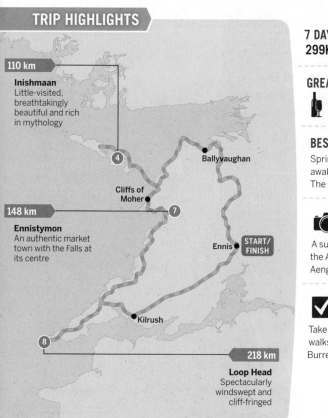

110 km

Inishmaan
Little-visited, breathtakingly beautiful and rich in mythology

Ballyvaughan

Cliffs of Moher

148 km

Ennistymon
An authentic market town with the Falls at its centre

Ennis • START/ FINISH

Kilrush

218 km

Loop Head
Spectacularly windswept and cliff-fringed

**7 DAYS
299KM / 185 MILES**

GREAT FOR...

BEST TIME TO GO

Spring for the awakening of nature in The Burren.

ESSENTIAL PHOTO

A sunset shot over the Atlantic from Dún Aengus.

BEST FOR RAMBLING

Take blustery cliff walks, or cross The Burren on foot.

27 | County Clare

From friendly market towns Ennis and Ennistymon down the cliff-fringed coast of Clare to its southernmost tip, the raggedly beautiful Loop Head, you'll encounter sandy strands and quiet coves just begging for company. Cruise out to the Aran Islands for their historic relics and a taste of a simpler life before returning to the mainland's homely resorts of Kilrush and Kilkee.

1 Ennis

Ennis (Inis) is the busy commercial centre of Clare (see also p248). It lies on the banks of the smallish River Fergus, which runs east, then south into the Shannon Estuary. It's the place to stay if you want a bit of urban flair; short on sights, the town's strengths are its food, lodging and traditional entertainment. The town's medieval origins are indicated by its irregular, narrow streets. Its most important historical site is **Ennis Friary**, founded

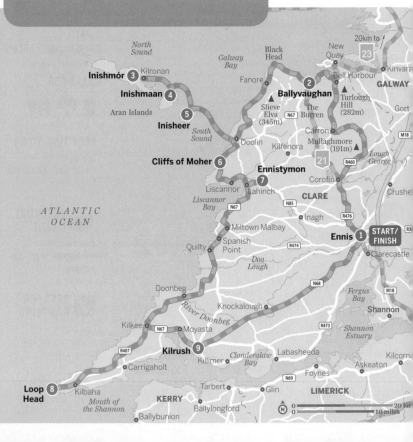

in the 13th century by the O'Briens, kings of Thomond, who also built a castle here.

✕ p297

The Drive ›› A jaunt north on the R476 through Corofin finds you in wondrous karst limestone Burren heartland. Make sure you stop and take in primroses and other flora dotted in the crevices in spring. Skirting the Burren National Park, you'll turn left onto the N67 all the way into Ballyvaughan. It's 55km from Ennis to Ballyvaughan taking this route.

2 Ballyvaughan

Something of a hub for the otherwise dispersed charms of The Burren, Ballyvaughan (Baile Uí Bheacháin) sits between the hard land of the hills and a quiet leafy corner of Galway Bay. Just west of the village's junction is the **quay**, built in 1829 at

LINK YOUR TRIP

21 **Best of the West**
Having sampled the delicious Clare coast take a wild southerly bite of Kerry and West Cork from Limerick down.

23 **Mountains & Moors**
If you like The Burren, you'll love Connemara. Join this trip at Ballyvaughan and wander west at Galway.

a time when boats traded with the Aran Islands and Galway, exporting grain and bacon and bringing in turf – a scarce commodity in the windswept rocks of Burren.

✕ 🛏 p297

The Drive ›› From Ballyvaughan it's a leisurely 40-minute coastal route (R749) down to Doolin (p251), with splendid views over to the Aran Islands on your right. From here, park up and catch the ferry (see p296) to Inishmór, the first of the three splendid Aran Islands.

3 Inishmór

Most visitors who venture out to the islands don't make it beyond 14.5km long Inishmór (Árainn; see also p251) and its main attraction, **Dún Aengus** (Dún Aonghasa; www.heritageireland.ie; adult/child €3/1; ☉9.45am-6pm), the stunning stone fort perched perilously on the island's towering cliffs. The arid landscape west of Kilronan (Cill Rónáin), Inishmór's main settlement, is dominated by stone walls, boulders, scattered buildings and the odd patch of deep-green grass and potato plants. It gets pretty crowded in summer but on foot or on bike (for hire at the pier), you can happily set your own pace. There's an EU Blue Flag white-sand beach (awarded for cleanliness) at **Kilmurvey**, peacefully

situated west of bustling Kilronan.

🛏 p297

The Drive ›› It's easy to travel between the Aran Islands, but you'll need to prebook your ticket with one of the ferry companies and check their timetables for crossing times (see p296).

TRIP HIGHLIGHT

4 Inishmaan

The least-visited of the islands, with the smallest population, Inishmaan (Inis Meáin) is a rocky respite. Early Christian monks seeking solitude were drawn to Inishmaan, as was the author JM Synge, who spent five summers here over a century ago. The island they knew largely survives today: stoic cows and placid sheep, impressive old forts and warm-hearted locals, who may tell you with a glint in their eye that they had a hard night on the whiskey the previous evening. Inishmaan's scenery is breathtaking, with a jagged coastline of startling cliffs, empty beaches, and fields where the main crop seems to be stone. **Teach Synge** (☎099-73036; admission €3; ☉by appointment), a thatched cottage on the road just before you head up to the fort, is where JM Synge spent his summers.

🛏 p297

WAYNE WALTON/GETTY IMAGES ©

5 Inisheer

Inisheer (Inis Oírr), the smallest of the Aran Islands with a population of only 200, has a palpable sense of enchantment, enhanced by the island's deep-rooted mythology, its devotion to traditional culture and ethereal landscapes. Wandering the lanes with their ivy-covered stone walls and making discoveries here and there is the best way to experience the island. At **O'Brien's Castle**, a 100m climb to the island's highest point yields dramatic views over clover-covered fields to the beach and harbour. Dating from 1960, an iconic island sight is a freighter, **Plassy**, that was thrown up on the rocks in bad weather. An aerial shot of the wreck was used in the opening sequence of the seminal TV series *Father Ted*.

🛏 p297

The Drive 》 From Doolin, it's a pleasurable 10-minute cruise on the coastal R478 to the famed, unmistakable Cliffs of Moher.

6 Cliffs of Moher

Star of a million tourist brochures, the Cliffs of Moher (Aillte an Mothair, or Ailltreacha Mothair) are one of the most popular sights in Ireland. But like many an ageing star, you have to look beyond the famous facade to appreciate the inherent attributes behind the postcard image. The entirely vertical cliffs rise to a height of 203m, their edge falling away abruptly into the constantly churning sea. A series of heads, the dark limestone seems to march in a rigid

Aran Islands Black Fort wall and clochan remains

formation that amazes, no matter how many times you look. Such appeal comes at a price: mobs. But, if you're willing to walk for 10 minutes past the end of the 'Moher Wall' south, there's still a **trail** along the cliffs to Hag's Head – few venture this far. For uncommon views of the cliffs and wildlife you might consider a **cruise**. The boat operators in Doolin (see the boxed text p296) offer popular tours of the cliffs.

The Drive » A short drive takes you to the small seaside resort of Lahinch and from there up the proverbial hill (in this case the N67) to a more traditional, authentic rural experience, at the market town of Ennistymon.

- - - - - - - - - -

TRIP HIGHLIGHT

7 Ennistymon

Ennistymon (Inis Díomáin) is a genuinely charming market town (see also p250). On the first Monday of each month **Ennistymon Horse Market** is one of Clare's great spectacles: the horse market literally takes over the town's streets as people from around the region come to buy and sell donkeys, mares, thoroughbreds and old nags.

🛏 p297

The Drive » It's about a 74km scenic trip down the coastal N67. The land from the old-fashioned resort of Kilkee south to Loop Head has subtle undulations that suddenly end in dramatic cliffs falling off into the Atlantic. It's a windswept place with timeless striations of old stone walls.

- - - - - - - - - -

TRIP HIGHLIGHT

8 Loop Head

While others are dodging sweater vendors at the Cliffs of Moher, discriminating travellers are coming here for coastal views

GETTING TO & FROM THE ARAN ISLANDS

Doolin (p251) is one of two ferry departure points to the Aran Islands (from April to October); the other is at Rossaveal in County Galway, from where there are year-round crossings. Various ferry companies offer departures in season from Doolin. It takes around half an hour to cover the 8km to Inisheer; a boat to Inishmór takes at least 1½ hours with an Inisheer stop. Ferries to Inishmaan are infrequent. Rates vary but Inisheer should cost about €20 to €25 return. Each boat has an office at Doolin Pier at the harbour or you can book online. Most of the boats also offer various Cliffs of Moher tours, which are best done late in the afternoon when the light is from the west.

Cliffs of Moher Cruises (☎065-707 5949; www.mohercruises.com; Doolin Pier; ⏱Apr-Oct) Offers combined Aran Islands trips with Cliffs of Moher cruises on the *Jack B*.

Doolin Ferries (☎065-707 4466; www.doolinferries.com; Doolin Pier) Offers sailings to the islands and the cliffs on the *Happy Hooker*.

O'Brien Line (☎065-707 5555; www.obrienline.com) Usually has the most sailings; also offers cliff cruises and combo tickets.

The following ferry company services the islands year-round from Rossaveal, 38km west of Galway:

Aran Island Ferries (☎091-568 903; www.aranislandferries.com) Up to five return crossings daily in high season (three in low) to Inishmór and twice daily to Inishmaan and Inisheer. Shuttle bus available from Galway.

Alternatively you can pick up an eight-minute flight from Connemara airport at Inverin (also known as Minna airport), 27km west of Galway, on a nine-seater plane.

Aer Arann (☎091-593 034; www.aerarannislands.ie) Up to 25 return flights daily in high season (10 in low) to each of the islands. Seats cost €45 return.

---

that in many ways are more dramatic. On a clear day, Loop Head (Ceann Léime), Clare's southernmost point, has magnificent views south to the Dingle Peninsula crowned by Mt Brandon (951m), and north to the Aran Islands and Galway Bay. There are bracing walks in the area and a long hiking trail runs along the cliffs to Kilkee. A working **lighthouse** (complete with Fresnel lens) is the punctuation on the point.

The Drive » A scenic 40km drive north on the R467 brings you to the bustling local resort of Kilrush.

9 Kilrush

Kilrush (Cill Rois) is a small, atmospheric town that overlooks the Shannon Estuary and the hills of Kerry to the south. It has the western coast's biggest **marina** (www.kilrushcreekmarina.ie) at Kilrush Creek, and offers various opportunities to experience the bottlenose dolphins living in the Shannon.

The remarkable 'lost' **Vandeleur Walled Garden** (www.vandeleurwalledgarden.ie; ⏱10am-5pm Mon-Fri, 1-5pm Sat & Sun Apr-Oct) was the private domain of the wealthy Vandeleur family – merchants and landowners. The gardens are just east of the centre and have been redesigned and planted with colourful tropical and rare plants.

✖ p297

The Drive » After all that sea air and seafood you'll be ready for a straight 40-minute jaunt (on the N68) inland back to Ennis.

Eating & Sleeping

Ennis ❶

✗ Zest — Bakery, Cafe €
(Market Pl; meals €5-10; ⊙8am-6pm Mon-Sat)
A much-welcomed addition to Ennis' fresh food
scene, Zest combines a deli, bakery, shop and
cafe. Excellent prepared foods from the region
are offered along with salads, soups and much
more. It's ideal for a coffee or lunch.

Ballyvaughan ❷

✗ Monk's Bar & Restaurant — Seafood €€
(Old Pier; mains €10-20; ⊙kitchen noon-8pm)
Famed for its excellent seafood, Monk's is a
cheerful, spacious and comfortable place. Peat
fires warm in winter, while sea breezes cool
you at the outdoor tables in summer. The pub
is open late and there are trad sessions some
nights in high season.

⏋ Gregan's Castle Hotel — Hotel €€€
(☎065-707 7005; www.gregans.ie; r from €185;
P☎) This hidden Clare gem is housed in a
grand estate dating to the 19th century. The 20
rooms and suites have a plush, stylish feel with
just enough modern touches to keep you from
feeling you've bedded down in a waxworks. The
restaurant specialises in inventive fare sourced
locally, while the bar is the kind of place to let
hours roll away in genteel comfort. The grounds
are a fantasy of gardens and there's croquet.
The estate is some 6km south of Ballyvaughan
on the N67 at Corkscrew Hill.

Inishmór ❸

⏋ Kilmurvey House — B&B €€
(☎099-61218; www.kilmurveyhouse.com;
Kilmurvey; s/d from €65/110; ⊙Apr-Sep) On the
path leading to Dún Aengus is this grand 18th-
century mansion. It's a beautiful setting, and
the 12 rooms are well maintained. Hearty meals
(dinner €30) incorporate vegetables from the
garden, and local fish and meats. You can swim
at a pretty beach that's a short walk away.

Inishmaan ❹

⏋ Inis Meáin — Inn €€€
(☎086 826 6026; www.inismeain.com; r from
€250; ⊙Apr-Oct; @) A complete anomaly for
the island, where almost everything is as basic
as a rock – or is a rock – this posh boutique
inn has three sumptuous rooms crafted from
local materials (rocks). The restaurant (dinner
mains €15-35) serves a changing menu of
exquisite dishes made from local foods.

Inisheer ❺

⏋ Fisherman's Cottage & South Aran House — B&B €€
(☎099-75073; www.southaran.com; s/d €48/76;
⊙Apr-Oct; ☎) Slow-food enthusiasts run this
sprightly B&B and cafe that's a five-minute walk
from the pier. Food (lunch and dinner, mains
€13 to €20) is also available to nonguests and
celebrates local seafood and organic produce.
Rooms are simple yet stylish. Kayaking and
fishing are among the activities on offer.

Ennistymon ❼

⏋ Falls Hotel — Hotel €€
(☎065-707 1004; www.fallshotel.ie; s/d from
€59/100; P@☎) This handsome and
sprawling Georgian house, built on the ruins of
an O'Brien castle, has 140 modern rooms and a
large, enclosed pool. The view of the Cascades
from the entrance steps is breathtaking, and
there are walks around the 20 hectares of
wooded gardens. Welsh poet Dylan Thomas'
wife Caitlin once lived here.

Kilrush ❾

✗ Quayside Restaurant — Irish €€
(17 Frances St; meals €6-12; ⊙9am-5pm Mon-
Fri) Local gossip is dissected each morning
amid the smells of fresh coffee and baked treats
from the oven. Tables overlook the town's bustle
or boats moored out back.

Belfast & the North of Ireland

IRELAND'S NORTH IS MADE FOR ROAD TRIPS. Routes swoop from hard, stark hills to soft, sandy shores, and cliff-clinging roads snake into wild lands peppered with loughs, glens and bogs.

These epic routes link blockbuster sights. The Giant's Causeway, romantic castles and stately homes are just an exhilarating drive from surfing, hiking, or horseback riding across golden sand. And within easy reach are Belfast and Derry/Londonderry, once crippled by sectarian violence but now inspirational in their progress towards peace.

In this compelling corner of Ireland you might get a little lost, but that's more than made up for by what you'll find.

The Giant's Causeway (Trips 2, 29, 33, 34)
GARETH MCCORMACK/GETTY IMAGES ©

Belfast & the North of Ireland

Enniscrone Old seaweed baths (Trip 32)

DON'T MISS

Arranmore Island

Ancient pubs, turf fires and late-night music sessions make overnighting special. Do a Robinson Crusoe on Trip **29**

Glenariff Forest Park

Many visitors bypass this dramatic gorge. Let them. It will make your wander beside waterfalls even more tranquil on Trip **34**

Belfast

When previously warring communities have the courage to strive for peace, it's inspiring. Witness that transformation on Trips **29** **33**

Malin Head

Don't miss beachcombing for semiprecious stones near Ireland's most northerly point. Try your luck on Trip **31**

Enniscrone's Seaweed Baths

This Edwardian spa will have you steaming and soaking amid therapeutic seaweed on Trip **32**

Rock of Cashel
One of Ireland's true highlights

Classic Trip

Tip to Toe

28

If this trip was a film it would be a road epic. Sweep from mountain passes down cliffside roads past sandy shores to discover charismatic cities, big-name sights and hidden beaches.

TRIP HIGHLIGHTS

Mt Errigal

Glen Gesh Pass

7

Sligo

Galway

520 km

14

Cashel
Explore an ancient power base of churchmen and kings

1 START

0 km

Derry/Londonderry
Witness remarkable attempts to heal the sectarian past

160 km

Slieve League
Get thrillingly close to towering, multi-coloured sea cliffs

680 km

Kilkenny
Revel in the urban pleasures of vibrant Kilkenny

15

Kilmore Quay

FINISH

10 DAYS
950KM / 590 MILES

GREAT FOR...

BEST TIME TO GO

Spring and autumn are ideal; you'll miss the summer crowds.

ESSENTIAL PHOTO

Mountainous Glen Gesh Pass delivers a great 'did I really drive that?' snap.

BEST THREE DAYS

Stops 11 to 15 for party-town Galway, elegant Birr and iconic Rock of Cashel.

303

Classic Trip

28 Tip to Toe

This 10-day trip takes in so much. You'll bob on a boat beneath 600m cliffs, clamber castle ruins and marvel at massive seabird colonies. Scenery-rich routes link sites telling tales of rebellion, the Troubles, famine and faith. Memorable drives connect experiences rich in Irish culture, from lyrical poetry to pubs alive with traditional music. On this trip you'll really discover Ireland, tip to toe, head to heart.

TRIP HIGHLIGHT

1 Derry/Londonderry

Derry/Londonderry comes as a pleasant surprise to many visitors: a vibrant, riverside city, encircled by impressive, 17th-century fortifications. Like Belfast it has a past of bitter sectarian divisions, but here too a remarkable healing is under way. Get a true taste of both the enormity of the problems and the progress on our walking tour (p362). It'll see you strolling atop the city walls, passing Unionist strongholds and absorbing the powerful murals of the Republican Bogside district. En route, be sure to visit the **Tower Museum** (Union Hall Pl; adult/child £4.20/2.65; ⏰10am-5pm Tue-Sat), where audiovisual exhibits bring the city's rich and complex past to life.

The Drive ≫ Distance 12km. As the A2/N13 heads west out of Derry towards Letterkenny, road signs switch from mph to km/h: you've just entered the Irish Republic. At Bridgend follow signs left up to Grianán of Aileách, a dizzying ascent.

② Grianán of Aileách

This fort encircles Grianán Hill like a halo. Ducking in through its cavelike entrance and clambering up its tiered battlements reveals eye-popping views of Lough Swilly, with Inch Island plumb in the centre; Counties Donegal, Derry and Tyrone stretch out all the way around.

It's thought the site was in use in pre-Celtic times as a temple to the god Dagda, becoming the seat of the O'Neills between the 5th and 12th centuries. But it was demolished by Murtogh O'Brien, king of Munster, and most of these remains are a 19th-century reconstruction.

The Drive » Distance 50km. The N13 cruises west to traffic-choked Letterkenny

LINK YOUR TRIP

11 Wexford & Waterford

Scenic shorelines, bird life and fishing villages. Start where this trips stops: Kilmore Quay.

23 Mountains & Moors

Drive deep into romantic Connemara. Pick it up from, and return to, Galway city on this trip's route.

305

Classic Trip

(with handy accommodation options; see p314). There, climb north gradually on the N56 towards Dunfanaghy, with the distant Glendowan Mountains sliding into view. Once up in the high hills, take the R255 left to Glenveagh National Park and Glenveagh Castle.

- - - - - - - - - - - - -

3 Glenveagh National Park

Lakes shimmer like dew in mountainous **Glenveagh National Park** (Páirc Náisiúnta Ghleann Bheatha; www.glenveaghnationalpark.ie; ⊙10am-6pm mid-Mar–Oct), where knuckles of rock alternate with green-gold bogs and oak and birch forest. In delightfully showy **Glenveagh**

Castle (adult/child €5/2; ⊙10am-6pm mid-Mar–Oct) rooms combine stuffed stags with flamboyant furnishings, highlights being the tartan-and-antler-covered music room and the pink candy-striped room (formerly Greta Garbo's).

The exotic gardens are spectacular too, their terraces and Italianate style a marked contrast to the wildly beautiful landscape. A shuttle bus runs to the castle from the visitor centre, but the 3.6km walk is a better way to soak up the scenery.

The Drive » Distance 16km. Head west on the R251, an exhilarating, bouncing drive through cinematic scenery: the Derryveagh Mountains tower to your left, and the fast-approaching peak of Mt Errigal fills your windscreen ahead. At the hamlet of Dunlewey (Dún Lúiche), turn left to the lake.

DETOUR: LOUGHREA PENINSULA

Start: 4 Dunlewey

This leg's scenery is scenic enough, but if you fancy some sandy shores with your mountains, try this detour. Around 20km south of Dungloe, at Maas, instead of swinging left on the N56 to Glenties, peel right onto the coastal R261 which winds deep into beautiful Loughrea Peninsula. Next, take a minor road right to **Narin**, following signs to the **beach** (trá), a 4km spectacular, dune-backed, sandy stretch, where you can walk out to tiny **Iniskeel Island** at low tide.

Post-stroll, continue on the shoreside road, past Portnoo and Rossbeg, rejoining the R261, then the N56 at Ardara.

4 Dunlewey

Simply stepping out of your car in this mountain hamlet provides an insight into the isolated way of life this high in the hills. It's underlined at the **Dunlewey Lakeside Centre** (Ionad Cois Locha; www.dunleweycentre.com; adult/child €6/4; ⊙10.30am-6pm Mon-Sat, 11am-6pm Sun Easter-Oct), where the 30-minute tour of a thatched weaver's cottage reveals a huge loom, spartan bedroom (complete with chamber pot under the iron bedstead) and snug lounge warmed by a peat fire.

🛏 p314

The Drive » Distance 60km. The R251, then the N56, begin a slow descent south, bumping past crags and sudden loughs and bogs. Shortly after heritage-town Ardara turn right, following brown signs to Glen Gesh Pass. It's an ear-popping ascent up hairpin bends and past wayside shrines. Near the top, turn right into the walled parking bay.

- - - - - - - - - - - - -

5 Glen Gesh Pass

The Glen Gesh Pass is one of Donegal's most spectacular mountain views, and this parking spot is *the* place to take that holiday snap. The V-shaped valley sweeps away far below, while the Derryveagh Mountains line up far behind. The road you've just driven up is a tiny ribbon, snaking off into the distance. There's a picnic area immediately below the parking spot, ensuring an alfresco meal with a truly memorable view.

The Drive >> Distance 16km. Edging over the summit, a cluster of wind turbines spin into view. Descend gradually, past unfenced grazing (watch out for free-roaming sheep) and neat piles of drying peat. Suddenly, the sea around Glen Head appears. Head through Glencolumbcille (Gleann Cholm Cille) on the Malin Beg Rd; the Folk Village comes soon after.

6 Glencolumbcille

Glencolumbcille may feel like the middle of nowhere, but the three-pub village offers scalloped beaches, a strong sense of Irish identity and an insight into a fast-disappearing way of life. **Father McDyer's Folk Village** (www.glenfolkvillage.com; adult/child €3/2; ⏰10am-6pm Mon-Sat, noon-6pm Sun Easter-Sep) was set up in 1967 to freeze-frame traditional folk life for posterity. Its six thatched 18th- and 19th-century cottages are packed with everyday items, from beds and cooking pans to tools and open fires.

🍴🛏 p314

The Drive >> Distance 9km. The R263 snakes south, and soon reveals the massive mountain of Slieve League. Edge past it to Carrick (An Charraig), then follow brown Slieve League

---

DETOUR:
DONEGAL CASTLE

Start: 7 Slieve League

Midway between Slieve League and Sligo, riverside **Donegal Castle** (www.heritageireland.ie; Castle St; adult/child €4/2; ⏰10am-6pm Easter–mid-Sep) makes for a picturesque detour. The original 1474 castle was torched then rebuilt in 1623 along with a neighbouring Jacobean house. It's a deeply attractive spot: grassy lawns lead up to geometric battlements, and rooms are packed with fine furnishings and antiques.

The castle is in the centre of pretty Donegal town. Follow signs from the N56, and afterwards take the N15 to Sligo.

---

signs south beside the inlet to tiny Teelin (Tieleann).

TRIP HIGHLIGHT

7 Slieve League

The Cliffs of Moher may be more famous, but the ones at Slieve League are taller – the highest in Europe, in fact. This 600m, multicoloured rock face seems stark and otherworldly as it rears up from the Atlantic Ocean. A diminutive 12-seater boat, the **Nuala Star** (📞074-973 9365; www.sliabhleagueboattrips.com; from €20; ⏰Apr-Oct), sets off from Teelin to the foot of the cliffs. The trips are weather dependent and have to be booked. If the sea is too rough, you can drive or walk to the cliffs; see p352.

The Drive >> Distance 110km. The drive east from Carrick completes a gradual descent from wild, pitted hills

---

to smoother urban life; remote homesteads give way to garden-fronted houses. The N56 skirts Donegal town, from where the N15 heads south to Sligo.

---

8 Sligo Town

An appealing overnight base, vibrant Sligo town combines lively pubs and futuristic buildings with old stone bridges and a historic abbey. It also shines a spotlight on William Butler Yeats (1865–1939), Sligo's greatest literary figure and one of Ireland's premier poets. The **Sligo County Museum** (Stephen St; ⏰9.30am-12.30pm & 2-4.45pm Tue-Sat May-Sep) showcases his manuscripts and letters, along with sepia photos, a copy of his 1923 Nobel Prize medal and a complete collection of his poetic works.

🍴🛏 p314

GARETH MCCORMACK/GETTY IMAGES ©

EOIN CLARKE/GETTY IMAGES ©

WHY THIS IS A CLASSIC TRIP
BELINDA DIXON, AUTHOR

It's partly sensory overload: overwhelming scenery, tangy peat smoke, sweet strawberries, tingling sea spray, buzzing *céilidh* (sessions of traditional music and dancing) and soft, soft sand. It's emotional too: Derry's political murals are deeply disturbing, but also inspiring in their progress towards peace; don't miss our city walk (p362). And from the stark, sheep-dotted mountains in the north to the gentle lowlands of the south, this trip is one heck of a drive.

Top: Sligo town centre along the River Garavogue
Left: Gannet with chick: the Saltee Islands are home to an array of bird life
Right: Stream in Glenveagh National Park

GARETH McCORMACK/GETTY IMAGES ©

The Drive » Distance 32km. Take the N4 south, then the N17 (signed Galway). Soon the R293 meanders left through Ballymote and a deeply agricultural landscape. Make for Gurteen (also spelt Gorteen), following signs for the Coleman Irish Music Centre. It's the pink building right beside the main village crossroads.

❾ Gurteen

You've just explored poetry, now another mainstay of Irish culture: music. The **Coleman Irish Music Centre** (www. colemanirishmusic.com; admission free; ⏰10am-5pm Mon-Sat) champions melody and culture south-Sligo style, with multimedia exhibits on musical history, instruments, famous musicians and Irish dancing. The centre also provides tuition and sheet-music sales, and stages performances.

The Drive » Distance 60km. Continue south on the R293, an undulating ribbon of a road that deposits you in bustling Ballaghaderreen. There pick up the N5 west (signed Westport) for an effortless cruise through lowlands that are grazed by cattle and dotted with rounded hills. Some 55km later, signs point right for the National Museum of Country Life.

❿ Castlebar

Your discovery of Ireland's heritage continues, this time with a celebration of the ingenuity and self-sufficiency of the Irish

people. The **National Museum of Country Life** (www.museum.ie; Turlough Park, Turlough; admission free; ⏱10am-5pm Tue-Sat, 2-5pm Sun) explores everything from wickerwork to boat building, and herbal cures to traditional clothing. This historical one-stop-shop is a comprehensive, absorbing depiction of rural traditions and skills between 1850 and 1950.

🍴 🛏 p314

The Drive » Distance 80km. On the outskirts of Castlebar, the N84 heads south (signed Galway), bouncing beside scattered settlements before dog-legging through appealing Ballinrobe. This hummocky landscape of fields and dry-stone walls is replaced by bogs edged with peat stacks as you near Galway city.

---

⑪ Galway City

The biggest reason to stop in Galway city is simply to revel in its hedonistic, culture-rich spirit. Narrow alleys lead from sight to sight beside strings of pubs overflowing with live music.

Start explorations at the quayside **Spanish Arch** (1584), thought to be an extension of Galway's medieval walls. Next walk a few paces to the **Galway City Museum** (Spanish Pde; admission free; ⏱10am-5pm Apr-Oct) where exhibits trace daily life in the city through history; highlights include the smelly medieval era and photos of President John F Kennedy's 1963 visit to Galway. Then, stroll a few metres to the **Hall of the Red Earl** (www.galwaycivictrust.ie; Druid Lane; admission free; ⏱9.30am-4.45pm Mon-Fri), the artefact-rich archaeological remains of a 13th-century power base.

You can't leave Galway without experiencing a music session, so walk further up Quay St to nearby **Tig Cóilí** (Mainguard St), a gem of a fire-engine-red pub which stages two live *céilidh* a day.

🛏 p314

TOP TIP:
M6 TOLL

The recently completed M6 heading east out of Galway is a sleek, effortless drive. But like all shiny new things, it has to be paid for: have your €1.80 ready for the toll booth 20km east of Athenry.

The Drive » Distance 80km. Join the M6 towards Dublin for the hour-long, smooth motorway cruise to Athlone. Follow signs to Athlone West/Town Centre. Soon the River Shannon, bobbing with houseboats and pleasure cruisers, eases into view. Park by Athlone Castle, which appears straight ahead.

---

⑫ Athlone

The thriving riverside town of Athlone is an enchanting mix of stylish modern developments and ancient, twisting streets. **Viking Tours** (☎086 262 1136; www.vikingtoursireland.ie; 7 St Mary's Pl; adult/child €10/5; ⏱May-Sep) runs cruises from beside Athlone Castle, along the River Shannon aboard a replica Viking longship sailed by costumed crew. The best trip goes south to the stunning ruins at Clonmacnoise (see p79), allowing you a 90-minute wander there.

The Drive » Distance 45km. Continue through Athlone, picking up the minor N62 to Birr, which rises and dips past grazing livestock. Soon a boggy landscape takes over; look out for the swaths of exposed soil left by industrial-scale peat harvesting. At Birr, follow signs to the imposing, crenulated gateway of the Birr Castle Demesne.

---

⑬ Birr

Feel-good Birr is one of the Midlands' most attractive towns, with elegant pastel Georgian

DETOUR: ATHENRY

Start: ⑪ Galway City

Most people sweep past Athenry, but it actually boasts one of Ireland's most intact collections of medieval architecture. This amiable town features a restored, boxlike Norman **castle** (www.heritageireland. ie; adult/child €3/1; ⏱10am-5pm Easter-Sep), the medieval **Parish Church of St Mary's**, a 13th-century **Dominican Priory** (with superb masonry) and an original market cross.

Athenry sits beside the M6, and is signed off it.

---

buildings and a spirited nightlife buzzing with live music. It also boasts **Birr Castle** (www.birrcastle. com; adult/child €9/5; ⏱9am-6pm mid-Mar–Oct, 10am-4pm Nov–mid-Mar) where magnificent, 1000-species-strong gardens frame a large artificial lake. Don't miss the romantic Hornbeam cloister and the 12m-high box hedge, planted in the 1780s and now one of the world's tallest.

🛏 p315

The Drive ≫ Distance 74km. The N62 loops south through Roscrea towards Thurles, with the Silvermine Mountains' dark tops creeping up on the right. Then come Templemore's wide streets, before the N62 wiggles onto the M8 (head towards Cork); the Rock of Cashel is signed 13km later.

TRIP HIGHLIGHT

⑭ Cashel

The iconic and much-photographed **Rock of Cashel** (www.heritageireland.

com; adult/child €6/2; ⏱9am-6.15pm Jun-Sep, to 4.45pm Oct-May) is one of Ireland's true highlights – the Queen included it on her historic 2011 visit. The 'rock' is a fortified hill, the defences of which shelter a clutch of historical, religious monuments. The site has been a defensive one since the 4th century and its compelling features include the towering 13th-century Gothic cathedral, a 15th-century four-storey castle, an 11th-century round tower and a 12th-century Romanesque chapel.

The rock is a five-minute stroll along Bishop's Walk from appealing market-town Cashel.

The Drive ≫ Distance 67km. As you head north up the M8 (signed Dublin) you'll notice rounded field-chequered hills, backed by a distant smudge of mountains. At Urlingford, take the R693 into central Kilkenny.

TRIP HIGHLIGHT

⑮ Kilkenny

Kilkenny (Cill Chainnigh) is the Ireland of many people's imaginations, with its gracious medieval cathedral, tangle of 17th-century passageways, old-fashioned shopfronts and ancient live-music pubs. Make for **Kilkenny Castle** (www.kilkennycastle. ie; adult/child €6/2.50; ⏱9am-5.30pm Mar-Sep), a late-12th-century stone affair built by the son-in-law of Richard de Clare, the Anglo-Norman conqueror of Ireland (a man graced with the sobriquet 'Strongbow'). Forty-minute guided tours focus on the Long Gallery, an impressive hall with high ceilings, vividly painted Celtic and Pre-Raphaelite motifs and ranks of po-faced portraits.

✕ 🛏 p315

The Drive ≫ Distance 50km. Pick up the R700 southeast to New Ross. Hills feature again here, both in the rise and fall of the twisting road, and in the blue-black ridge of the Blackstairs Mountains far ahead. At New Ross make for the quay and the three-masted sailing vessel you can now see.

---

⑯ New Ross

In Ireland's Great Famine of 1845–51 a staggering three million people died or emigrated,

often to America and Australia. Many left in 'coffin ships', so called because of the appalling mortality rates on them. When you step aboard the replica **Dunbrody Famine Ship** (☏051-425 239; www.dunbrody.com; The Quay; adult/child €7.50/4.50; 🕙10am-6pm Apr-Sep, to 5pm Oct-Mar) you 'become' a migrant: you're allocated a living space and rations, while actors around you vividly re-create life on board. Expect cramped conditions, authentic sounds and smells and often-harrowing tales.

The Drive » Distance 32km. Head onto the N30 to Enniscorthy (initially signed N23 to Rosslare), a gentle, rural leg punctuated by frequents treats: roadside stalls selling sweet Wexford strawberries. As you head towards central Enniscorthy, the National Rebellion Centre is a sharp left, up the hill.

⑰ Enniscorthy

Enniscorthy's warren of steep streets descends from Augustus Pugin's cathedral to a riverside Norman castle. But the town is most famous for some of the fiercest fighting of the 1798 uprising against British rule, when rebels captured the town.

That story is told in the **National 1798 Rebellion Centre** (www.1798centre.ie; Mill Park Rd; adult/child €6/3.50; 🕙9.30am-5pm Mon-Fri, noon-5pm Sat & Sun Apr-Sep), where exhibits cover the French and American Revolutions that sparked Wexford's abortive revolt. It also chronicles what followed: the rebels' retreat and the massacre by English troops of hundreds of women and children.

🛏 p315

The Drive » Distance 19km. Carry on through Enniscorthy, crossing the river to pick up the N11, south, to Wexford. Then comes a long straight run, beside the River Slane and past more strawberry stalls, until the waters of Wexford Harbour glide into view.

⑱ Wexford Town

The sleepy port town of Wexford is a pleasing place to stroll through heritage-rich streets beside a wide estuary. Guided tours (€4) set out at 11am (March to October) from the **tourist office** (www.visitwexford.ie; 🕙9am-6pm Mon-Sat Apr-Oct), on the main Custom House Quay; it also provides maps. Or explore by yourself: head up Harper's Lane to North Main St and the 18th-century **St Iberius' Church** (where Oscar Wilde's forebears were rectors). A left up George St leads to Abbey St and

Selskar Abbey (Henry II did penance here after the murder of Thomas Becket); the 14th-century **Westgate** sits at the street's end.

🍴 p315

The Drive » Distance 20km. The N25 to Rosslare runs along Wexford's boat-lined waterfront. After more fruit stalls, the R739 turns right through a gentle landscape of trees and

GARETH MCCORMACK/GETTY IMAGES ©

Classic Trip

Glenveagh National Park The peak of Mt Errigal can be seen along the drive from Glenveagh

rich pastures – it feels a world away from the harsh, high hills at your trip's start. Soon the thatched cottages of Kilmore Quay appear.

- - - - - - - - - - -

🔟 Kilmore Quay

This tiny, relaxed port is the perfect finish to your trans-Ireland trip. Seafood restaurants, fishermen's pubs and B&Bs cluster around a boat-packed harbour. Just off shore, the **Saltee Islands** (www.salteeislands. info; ⊙11.30am-4pm) overflow with gannets, guillemots, kittiwakes and puffins; **Declan Bates** (☎053-912 9684, 087 252 9736; day trip €30) runs boat trips (booking required). If the weather scuppers that plan, stroll west from the quay to the 9km, wildlife-rich dunes of Ballyteigue Burrow, passing a memorial garden for those lost at sea, before reaching the Cull, a 4km sliver of land sheltering a slender inlet teeming with widgeon, oystercatchers, curlew and more.

✕ 🛏 p315

Classic Trip

Eating & Sleeping

Letterkenny

🛏 Station House   Hotel €€
(📞074-912 3100; www.stationhouseletterkenny.com; Lower Main St; s/d €79/99; P @ 🏠)
The 81 minimalist rooms here are immaculate, sporting rich red bedspreads, low lighting and glass-panelled bathrooms. The **Depot Café Bar** (mains €13-25) serves classic dishes.

Dunlewey ④

🛏 Glen Heights   B&B €€
(📞074-956 0844; www.glenheightsbb.com; s/d €50/€70; P) At this mountainside B&B the Donegal charm is in full swing. Rooms are simple and snug, while the breakfast table offers breathtaking views of Lough Dunlewey and Mt Errigal.

Glencolumbcille ⑥

🍴 An Chistin   Cafe €€
(mains €10-22; ⏰9am-9.30pm Easter-Oct) This cafe-restaurant attached to the Oideas Gael cultural centre serves up surprisingly gourmet fare to a soundtrack of mellow jazz.

🛏 Glencolumbcille Hill Walkers Centre   Hostel €
(📞074-973 0302; www.ionadsuil.ie; d €50; P) Overlooking sheep-filled paddocks, this smart place has pristine rooms. Breakfast isn't included but the self-catering kitchen is enormous and well kitted out.

Sligo Town ⑧

🍴 Ósta   Cafe €
(www.osta.ie; Hyde Bridge, Left Bank; light meals €6-13; ⏰8am-7.30pm Mon-Sat,

9am-6pm Sun) An array of preserved meats, seafood and Irish farmhouse cheeses accompany well-chosen wines in this intimate, quayside cafe-cum-wine bar.

🛏 Pearse Lodge   B&B €€
(📞071-916 1090; www.pearselodge.com; Pearse Rd; s/d €50/74; P @ 🏠) Welcoming owners Mary and Kieron not only maintain a stylish, cosy B&B but are also up on what's happening in town. Breakfasts include smoked salmon, French toast with bananas and homemade muesli.

Castlebar ⑩

🍴 Rua   Irish €€
(www.caferua.com; Spencer St; mains €7-13; ⏰9am-6pm Mon-Sat) With a gourmet deli downstairs and a buzzing cafe upstairs, this place champions artisan, organic produce: expect local duck eggs, Sligo pasta, Carrowholly cheese and Ballina smoked salmon. It's open for dinner on the last Friday of the month (three courses €40); don't miss it if you're in town.

🛏 Breaffy House   Hotel €€
(📞094-902 2033; www.breaffyhousehotel.com; r from €85; P 🏊 🏠) Set in a 19th-century country house, this grand hotel blends modernity with period charm. There's a pool and spa too. Breaffy House is 10 minutes east of Castlebar, off the N60.

Galway City ⑪

🛏 Skeffington Arms   Hotel €€
(📞091-563 173; www.skeffington.ie; Eyre Sq; r €65-160; @ 🏠) The Skeff eschews frills – pass through its arched, traditional entrance and you'll enter a minimalist haven. The air-con keeps you cool on hot summer nights with the

windows closed (muting the frolicsome masses roaming the streets below).

🛏 St Martins B&B
B&B €€

(📞091-568 286; 2 Nun's Island Rd; s/d from €50/80; @ 🛜) This beautifully renovated house has a flower-filled garden overlooking the River Corrib. Rooms have all the comforts, breakfasts are a cut above (the orange juice comes freshly squeezed) and owner Mary Sexton wins rave reviews.

Birr 🄓

🛏 Brendan House
B&B €€

(📞057-912 1818; www.tinjugstudio.com; Brendan St; s/d €55/85) Gloriously eccentric and packed to the gills with books, art and antiques, this Georgian town house is a bohemian delight. Rooms share a bathroom, but the four-poster beds and period charm more than make up for it.

Kilkenny 🄕

✗ Cafe Sol
Modern Irish €€

(📞056-776 4987; William St; lunch mains €9-15, dinner mains €17-25; ⏰lunch & dinner) Leisurely lunches stretch until 5pm at this much-loved restaurant. Local organic produce packs seasonal dishes, while bold flavours have a global feel.

🛏 Butler House
Hotel €€

(📞056-772 2828; www.butler.ie; 16 Patrick St; s €60-120, d €100-180; P @ 🛜) Once the home of Kilkenny Castle's builders, the earls of Ormonde, Butler House contains a boutique hotel with aristocratic trappings: sweeping staircases, marble fireplaces, an art collection and impeccably trimmed gardens.

🛏 Celtic House
B&B €€

(📞056-776 2249; www.celtic-house-bandb. com; 18 Michael St; r €70-90; P @) Artist Angela Byrne extends a warm welcome at her spick-and-span B&B. Some of the rooms have sky-lit bathrooms, others have castle views, while Angela's landscapes adorn many of the walls.

Enniscorthy 🄗

🛏 Old Bridge House
B&B €

(📞053-923 4222; www.oldbridgehouse.com; Slaney Pl; s/d from €35/60; 🛜) The Redmonds' comfortable guesthouse boasts bohemian artefacts, arty prints and a personable welcome. The River Slaney passes below the breakfast windows.

Wexford Town 🄘

✗ Greenacres
Deli €

(www.greenacres.ie; 7 Selskar St; ⏰9.30am-6pm Mon-Sat) Ireland's best cheeses, preserves, oatcakes, crackers and chocolates are beautifully displayed in this excellent food hall. The wine selection is the best south of Dublin; stock up for picnics.

✗ Jacques Bistro
French €€€

(📞053-912 2975; Selskar St; dinner mains €20-30; ⏰9.30am-10pm Mon-Sat) Top regional produce and seafood are prepared with French flair. By day enjoy a coffee or lunch special at an outside table, by night tuck into luscious local crab claws, cassoulet and more.

Kilmore Quay 🄙

✗ Silver Fox
Seafood €€€

(www.thesilverfox.ie; Kilmore Quay; mains €18-32; ⏰noon-10pm May-Sep) Fresh-from-the-ocean offerings here include a creamy fisherman's pie filled with prawns, monkfish, salmon and cod, plus a range of specials.

🛏 Mill Road Farm
B&B €€

(📞053-912 9633; www.millroadfarm.com; R739; s/d €45/70; P 🛜) This working dairy farm offers simple rooms and breakfasts featuring homemade bread and free-range eggs. You'll pass it on the R739 as you come into Kilmore Quay (about 2km north of the village).

🛏 Hotel Saltees
Hotel €€

(📞053-912 9601; www.hotelsaltees.ie; Kilmore Quay; s/d from €55/90; P) The rooms here may be typical motel-style, but they're generously sized and enlivened by painterly canvases and fresh colours.

Ballycastle *Set off from the habourside resort to see the coast's finest sights*

Classic Trip

The North in a Nutshell

29

The North's must-do trip takes in unmissable cities and big-name sights. It also heads off the tourist trail, revealing secret beaches, quaint harbours, waterfalls and music-filled pubs.

TRIP HIGHLIGHTS

455 km

Arranmore Island
A castaway island where music plays into the night

110 km

Giant's Causeway
An extraordinary outcrop of ancient, geometric rock

Horn Head

Mamore's Gap

13

17

Derry/Londonderry

4

Glencolumbcille
FINISH

1

START

Carrigart
Ride horseback across wide, golden sands

370 km

Belfast
Experience the transformed capital of the North

0 km

10 DAYS
470KM / 292 MILES

GREAT FOR...

BEST TIME TO GO

March to June and September means good weather but fewer crowds.

ESSENTIAL PHOTO

Crossing the Carrick-a-Rede Rope Bridge as it swings above the waves.

BEST FOR SCENERY

Stops 16 to 20 head into the heart of wild, wind-whipped Donegal.

On this road-trip-to-remember you'll drive routes that cling to cliffs, cross borders and head high into mountain passes. You'll witness Ireland's turbulent past and its inspiring path to peace. And you'll also explore rich faith, folk and music traditions, ride a horse across a sandy beach, cross a swaying rope bridge and spend a night on a castaway island. Not bad for a 10-day drive.

TRIP HIGHLIGHT

❶ Belfast

In bustling, big-city Belfast the past is palpably present – walk the city's former sectarian battlegrounds on our walking tour (p328), a profound way to start exploring the North's story. Next, take the M3 to the Titanic Quarter. Dominated by the towering yellow Harland and Wolff (H&W) cranes, it's where RMS *Titanic* was built. The new **Titanic Belfast** (www.titanicbelfast.com; Queens Rd; adult/child £14/7; ⏱9am-7pm Mon-Sat, to 5pm Sun Apr-Sep, 10am-5pm Oct-Mar) is a stunning multisensory experience: see bustling shipyards, join crowds at *Titanic's* launch, feel temperatures drop as she strikes that iceberg, and look through a glass floor at watery footage of the vessel today. Slightly to the west, don't miss the **Thompson Graving Dock** (www.titanicsdock.com; adult/child £6/4; ⏱10.30am-4pm) where you descend into the immense dry dock where the liner was fitted out.

The Drive ⟫ Distance 96km. As you drive the M3/M2 north, the now-familiar H&W cranes recede. Take the A26 through Ballymena; soon the Antrim Mountains loom large to the right. Skirt them, via the A44 into Ballycastle.

❷ Ballycastle

Head beyond the sandy beach and to the harbour at the appealing resort of Ballycastle. Here the pick of the high-speed boat tours offered by **Aquasports** (☎07962 309 670; www.aquasports.biz; £25) is a salt-sprayed, 1½-hour eco-trip around **Rathlin Island**, where you'll see seals, sea stacks and thousands of guillemots, kittiwakes, razorbills and puffins.

🛏 p327

LINK YOUR TRIP

33 **From Bangor to Derry**

Encounter seaside fun, a grand stately home and the Queen's official residence. Begin 20km east of Belfast at Bangor.

28 **Tip to Toe**

Take in the cream of Irish music and poetry; start where this trip stops: Glencolumbcille.

The Drive » Distance 10km. Next, pick up the B15 towards Ballintoy, which meanders up to a gorse-dotted coastal plateau where hills part to reveal bursts of the sea. As the road plunges downwards, take the right turn to the Carrick-a-Rede Rope Bridge.

❸ Carrick-a-Rede Rope Bridge

The **Carrick-a-Rede Rope Bridge** (www.ntni. org.uk; Ballintoy; adult/child £5.60/2.90; ⊙10am-7pm Jun-Aug, to 6pm Mar-May, Sep & Oct) loops across a surging sea to a tiny island 20m offshore. This walkway of planks and wire rope sways some 30m above the waves, testing your nerve and head for heights. The bridge is put up each year by salmon fishermen to help them set their nets, and signs along the 1km cliff-top hike

to the bridge detail the fascinating process.

The Drive » Distance 11km. The B15 then the A2 snake west along cliff tops past views of White Park Bay's sandy expanse. Next swing right onto the B146, passing Dunseverick Castle's fairy-tale tumblings, en route to the Giant's Causeway.

TRIP HIGHLIGHT

❹ Giant's Causeway

Stretching elegantly out from a rugged shore, the Giant's Causeway is one of the world's true geological wonders. Clambering around this jetty of fused geometric rock chunks, it's hard to believe it's not man-made. Legend says Irish giant Finn McCool built the Causeway to cross the sea to fight Scottish giant Benandonner. More prosaically, scientists tell us the 60-million-year-old rocks were formed when a flow of molten basaltic lava cooled and hardened from the top and bottom inwards; it contracted and the

hexagonal cracks spread as the rock solidified.

Entry to the causeway **site** (www.nationaltrust.org. uk; ⊙dawn-dusk) is free; car parks charge £5 to £6.

The Drive » Distance 16km. Continue west, through Bushmills, with its famous distillery (p370), picking up the A2 Coastal Causeway route, signed Portrush. You'll pass wind-pruned trees, crumbling Dunluce Castle and Portrush's long sandy beaches before arriving at Portstewart.

❺ Portstewart

Time for some unique parking. Head through resort-town Portstewart, following signs for the **Strand** (beach). Ever-sandier roads descend to an immense shoreline that doubles as a car park for 1000 cars. It's a decidedly weird experience to drive and park (£5) in an apparently endless expanse of hard-packed sand. It's also at your own risk, which doesn't deter the locals (but do stick to central, compacted areas). Nearby, a 1km **walking trail** meanders up a sand ladder, through huge dunes, past marram grass and occasional orchids.

📖 p327

The Drive » Distance 42km. Take the A2 west, through Coleraine towards Downhill. Some 1km after the Mussenden Temple's dome appears, take the Bishop's Rd left up steep hills with spectacular Lough

CAUSEWAY COAST WALKS

The official **Causeway Coast Way** (www.walkni.com) stretches for 53km from Ballycastle to Portstewart, but individual chunks can be walked whenever you feel like stretching your legs. Day hikes include the supremely scenic 16.5km section between Carrick-a-Rede and the Giant's Causeway – one of the finest coastal walks in Ireland. Shorter options also abound, including a 2km ramble around Portrush, a 1.5km stroll on sandy White Park Bay and a 300m scramble around ruined Dunluce Castle.

Foyle views. Descend, go through Limavady and onto the B68 (signed Dungiven); soon a brown Country Park sign points to Roe Valley.

6 Roe Valley

This beguiling country park is packed with rich reminders of a key Irish industry: linen production. The damp valley was ideal for growing the flax that made the cloth; the fast-flowing water powered the machinery. The **Green Lane Museum** (admission free; ⏰1-4.45pm Sat-Thu Jun-Aug), near the car park, features sowing fiddles, flax breakers and spinning wheels, while a free walking map from the nearby **Dogleap Centre** (⏰10am-5pm Jun-Aug, 1-5pm Sat & Sun Easter-May & Sep) pinpoints watchtowers, built to guard linen spread out to bleach in the fields, and Scutch Mills, where the flax was pounded.

The Drive » Distance 28km. Head back into Limavady to take the A2 west to Derry/Londonderry. Green fields give way to suburbs, then city streets.

7 Derry/ Londonderry

Northern Ireland's second city offers another powerful insight into the North's troubled past and the remarkable steps towards peace. It's best experienced on

TOP TIP: THE BORDER

Driving 20 minutes north out of Derry will see you entering another country: the Republic of Ireland. On road signs, be aware speed limits will suddenly change from mph to km/h, while wording switches from English to Irish and English. Stock up on euros in Derry or visit the first post-border ATM.

our walking tour (p362). Partway round, drop into the **Tower Museum** (Union Hall Pl; adult/child £4.20/2.65; ⏰10am-5pm Tue-Sat, plus 11am-3pm Sun Jul & Aug). Its imaginative **Story of Derry** exhibit leads you through the city's history, from the 6th-century monastery of St Colmcille (Columba) to the 1960s Battle of the Bogside.

🛏 p327

The Drive » Distance 11km. The A2 heads north towards Moville. Soon speed-limit signs switch from mph to km/h: welcome to the Republic of Ireland. Shortly after Muff take the small left turn, signed Iskaheen, up the hill; park beside Iskaheen church.

8 Iskaheen

It's completely off the tourist trail, but this church's tiny **graveyard** offers evidence of two of Ireland's most significant historical themes: the poverty that led to mass migration and the consequences of sectarian violence. One gravestone among many is to the McKinney

family, which records a string of children dying young: at 13 years, 11 months, nine months, and six weeks. It also bears the name of 34-year-old James Gerard McKinney, one of 13 unarmed civilians shot dead when British troops opened fire on demonstrators on Bloody Sunday, 1972.

The Drive » Distance 40km. Rejoin the R238 north. The R240 to Carndonagh climbs steeply left into rounded summits. After quaint Ballyliffin and Clonmany pick up the Inis Eoghain (Scenic Route) signs towards Mamore's Gap, before parking at the Glen House Tea Rooms.

9 Glenevin Waterfall

Welcome to Butler's Bridge – from here a 1km trail winds beside a stream through a wooded glen to the Glenevin Waterfall, which cascades 10m down the rock face. It's an utterly picturesque, gentle, waymarked route – the perfect leg-stretch.

🛏 p327

Classic Trip

DEIRDRE GREGG/GETTY IMAGES ©

STEPHEN SAKS/GETTY IMAGES ©

LOCAL KNOWLEDGE
JASON POWELL,
CAUSEWAY COAST
& GLENS TOURIST
BOARD

Giant's Causeway is my favourite place – 40,000 basalt columns, 400ft (122m) cliffs and magnificent views – while Rathlin Island has the largest seabird colony in Northern Ireland. For the best fish and chips try Morton's (22 Bayview Rd, Ballycastle). North West 200 (p324) delivers tension, adrenalin, revving bikes and thrilling noise.

Top: Portstewart Strand
Left: City Walls in Derry/Londonderry
Right: Arranmore Island lighthouse

TRISH PUNCH/GETTY IMAGES ©

The Drive >> Distance 37km. The Inis Eoghain snakes south up to Mamore's Gap – a high-altitude, white-knuckle mountain pass that climbs 260m on one-lane-only, twisting roads, past shrines to the saints. After a supremely steep descent (and glorious views) go south through Buncrana, and onto Fahan, parking beside the village church.

⑩ Fahan

St Colmcille founded a monastery in Fahan in the 6th century. Its creeper-clad ruins sit beside the church. Among them, hunt out the beautifully carved **St Mura Cross**. Each face of this 7th-century stone slab is decorated with a cross in intricate Celtic weave. The barely discernible Greek inscription is the only one known in Ireland from this early Christian period and is thought to be part of a prayer dating from 633.

The Drive >> Distance 50km. Take the N13 to Letterkenny, before picking up the R245 to Rathmelton (aka Ramelton), a 10km sweep north through the River Swilly valley. Turn off for the village, heading downhill to park beside the water in front of you.

⑪ Rathmelton

In this picture-perfect stop rows of Georgian houses and rough-walled stone warehouses curve along the River Lennon. Strolling right takes you to a string of three-storey, three-bay Victorian warehouses;

Classic Trip

walking back and left up Church Rd leads to the ruined **Tullyaughnish Church** with its Romanesque carvings in the eastern wall. Walking left beside the river leads past Victorian shops to the three-arched, late-18th-century Rathmelton Bridge.

🛏 p327

The Drive » Distance 11km. Cross the town bridge, turning right (north) for Rathmullan. The hills of the Inishowen Peninsula rise ahead, and Lough Swilly swings into view – soon you're driving right beside the shore. At Rathmullan, make for the harbour car park.

⑫ Rathmullan

Refined, tranquil Rathmullan was the setting for an event that shaped modern

Ireland. In 1607 a band of nobles boarded a ship here, leaving with the intention of raising an army to fight the occupying English. But they never returned. Known as the Flight of the Earls, it marked the end of the Irish (Catholic) chieftains' power; their estates were confiscated, paving the way for the Plantation of Ulster with British (Protestant) settlers. Rathmullan's harbourside **Flight of the Earl's Heritage Centre** (📞074-915 8131; admission €3; 🕙10am-6pm Mon-Sat, 12.30-6pm Sun Jun-Sep) explores the story. Beside the sandy beach, look out for the striking modern **sculpture**, depicting the earls' departure, waving to their distressed people as they left.

The Drive » Distance 74km. Head straight on from the harbour, picking up Fanad/Atlantic Dr, a roller-coaster road that surges up Lough Swilly's shore, round huge Knockalla,

past the exquisite beach at Ballymastocker Bay and around Fanad Head. It then hugs the (ironically) narrow Broad Water en route to Carrigart, with its village-centre horse-riding centre.

TRIP HIGHLIGHT

⑬ Carrigart

Most visitors scoot straight through laid-back Carrigart, heading for the swimming beach at Downings. But they miss a real treat: a horseback ride on a vast beach. The **Carrigart Riding Centre** (📞087 227 6926; per hour adult/child €20/15) is just across the main street from sandy, hill-ringed Mulroy Bay, meaning you can head straight onto the beach for an hour's ride amid the shallows and the dunes. Trips go on the hour, but it's best to book.

🛏 p327

The Drive » Distance 12km. Head south for Creeslough. An inlet with a creamy, single-towered castle soon pops into view. The turn-off comes on the plain, where brown signs point through narrow lanes and past farms to Doe Castle itself.

⑭ Doe Castle

You can't go inside early-16th-century **Doe Castle** (Caisleán na dTuath; Creeslough; 🕙10am-6pm), but you can wander the peaceful grounds, admiring its slender tower and crenellated

---

NORTH WEST 200 ROAD RACE

Driving this delightful coast can have its challenges, so imagine doing it at high speed. Each May the world's best motorcyclists do just that, going as fast as 300km/h in the **North West 200** (www.northwest200.org), which is run on a road circuit taking in Portrush, Portstewart and Coleraine. This classic race is Ireland's biggest outdoor sporting event and one of the last to take place on closed public roads anywhere in Europe. It attracts up to 150,000 spectators; if you're not one of them, it's best to avoid the area on the race weekend.

battlements. The castle was the stronghold of the Scottish MacSweeney family until it fell into English hands in the 17th century. It's a deeply picturesque spot: a low water-fringed promontory with a moat hewn out of the rock.

The Drive » Distance 25km. Near Creeslough, the bulk of Muckish Mountain rears up before the N56 to Dunfanaghy undulates past homesteads, loughs and sandy bays. Once in Dunfanaghy, with its gently kooky vibe, welcoming pubs and great places to sleep (see p327), look out for the signpost pointing right to Horn Head.

15 Horn Head

This headland provides one of Donegal's best cliff-top drives: along sheer, heather-clad quartzite cliffs with views of an island-dotted sea. A circular road bears left to the coastguard station – park to take the 20-minute walk due north to the signal tower. Next, hop back in the car, continuing east past Cnocasidh; around 1km later a viewpoint tops cliffs 180m high. There's another superb vantage point 1km further round – on a fine day you'll see Ireland's most northerly point, Malin Head.

The Drive » Distance 35km. The N56 continues west. Settlements thin out, the road climbs and the pointed peak of Mt Errigal fills more and more of your windscreen before the road

swings away. At tiny Crolly follow the R259 towards the airport, then turn right, picking up signs, for Leo's Tavern.

16 Meenaleck

You never know who'll drop by for one of the legendary singalongs at **Leo's Tavern** (☎074-954 8143; www.leostavern.com) in Meenaleck. It is owned by Leo and Baba Brennan, parents of Enya and her siblings Máire, Ciaran and Pól (aka the group Clannad). The pub glitters with gold, silver and platinum discs and is packed with musical mementos – there's live music nightly in the summer.

The Drive » Distance 25km. Continue west on the R259 as it bobbles and twists besides scattered communities and an at first boggy, then sandy shore. Head on to the pocket-sized port of Burtonport, following ferry signs right, to embark for Arranmore Island.

**DETOUR:
FINTOWN RAILWAY**

Start: 17 Arranmore Island

You've been driving for eight days now – time to let the train take the strain. The charming **Fintown Railway** (www.antraen.com; Fintown; adult/child €8/5; ☺11am-5pm Mon-Sat, 1-5pm Sun Jun-Sep) runs along a rebuilt 5km section of the former County Donegal Railway track beside picturesque Lough Finn. It's been lovingly restored to its original condition and a return trip in the red-and-white, 1940s diesel railcar takes around 40 minutes. To get to the railway, head east on the R252, off the N56 south of Dungloe. Then settle back to enjoy the ride.

TRIP HIGHLIGHT

17 Arranmore Island

Arranmore (Árainn Mhór) offers a true taste of Ireland. Framed by dramatic cliff faces, cavernous sea caves and clear sandy beaches, this 9km by 5km island sits 5km offshore. Here you'll discover a prehistoric triangular fort and an offshore bird sanctuary fluttering with corncrakes, snipes and seabirds. Irish is the main language spoken, pubs put on turf fires, and traditional music sessions run late into the night. To get the full castaway experience, stay overnight (book). The **Arranmore Ferry** (☎074-952 0532; www.arranmoreferry.com; return adult/child/€15/7) takes 20 minutes and runs up to nine times a day.

🛏 p327

The Drive ≫ Distance 45km. The R259 bounces down to Dungloe, where you take the N56 south into a rock-strewn landscape that's backed by the Blue Stack Mountains. After a stretch of rally-circuit-esque road, the sweep of Gweebarra Bay emerges. Next take the sharp right towards peaceful Narin (R261), following signs to the beach *(trá)*.

18 Narin

You've now entered the beautiful Loughrea Peninsula, which glistens with tiny lakes cupped by undulating hills. Narin boasts a spectacular stretch of sand: a 4km, wishbone-shaped Blue Flag beach the sandy tip of which points towards **Iniskeel Island**. You can walk out at low tide along a 500m sandy causeway. Your reward? An intimate island studded with early Christian remains: St Connell, a cousin of St Colmcille, founded a monastery here in the 6th century.

🛏 p327

The Drive ≫ Distance 14km. Continue south on the R261 through tweed-producing Ardara. Shortly after leaving town, take the right, signed 'Waterfall'; a road wedged between craggy hills and an increasingly sandy shore. In time, the Assarancagh Waterfall comes into view.

19 Assarancagh Waterfall

Stepping out of the car reveals just what an enchanting spot this is. As the waterfall streams down the sheer hillside, walk along the road (really a lane) towards the sea. This 1.5km route leads past time-warp farms; sheep bleat, the tang of peat smoke scents the air. At tiny Maghery head through the car park, down a track, over a boardwalk and onto a truly stunning expanse of pure white sand. This exquisite place belies a bloody past. Some 100 villagers hid from Cromwell's forces in nearby caves – all except one were discovered and massacred.

The Drive ≫ Distance 20km. Drive west through Maghery, a dramatic route that makes straight for the gap in the towering hills. At the fork, turn right, heading deeper into this remote headland, making for Glencolumbcille.

20 Glencolumbcille

The welcome in the scattered, pub-dotted, bayside village of Glencolumbcille (Gleann Cholm Cille) is warm. This remote settlement also offers a glimpse of a disappearing way of life. **Father McDyer's Folk Village** (www.glenfolkvillage. com; Doonalt; adult/child €3/2; ⏰10am-6pm Mon-Sat, noon-6pm Sun Easter-Sep) took traditional folk life of the 1960s and froze it in time. Its thatched cottages re-create daily life with genuine period fittings, while the Auld Craft Shop sells wines made from things like seaweed, as well as marmalade and whiskey truffles – a few treats at your journey's end.

🍴 🛏 p314

Eating & Sleeping

Ballycastle ②

🛏 Glenluce   B&B £

(📞028-2076 2914; www.glenluce.com; 42
Quay Rd; per person £25-40; P 🐾) Delightful
Glenluce features a luxurious lounge, a tea
shop and warm family atmosphere. Rooms are
spacious and comfortable and it's all only a few
minutes' walk from the beach.

Portstewart ⑤

🛏 York   Hotel ££

(📞028-7083 3594; www.theyorkportstewart.
co.uk; 2 Station Rd; s/d £90/120; P 🛜) The
York brims with boutique chic. Chocolate,
cream and cappuccino themed rooms come
with red leather chairs and spacious bathrooms;
breakfasts come with stunning coast views.

Derry/Londonderry ⑦

🛏 Merchant's House   B&B ££

(📞028-7126 9691; www.thesaddlershouse.
com; 16 Queen St; s £35-50, d £50-60; @🛜)
This Georgian-style town house is a real gem.
Expect an elegant lounge with antique furniture,
bedrooms with fluffy bathrobes, and breakfasts
with homemade marmalade.

Glenevin Waterfall ⑨

🛏 Glen House   B&B €€

(📞074-937 6745; www.glenhouse.ie; Straid,
Clonmany; s/d €60/90; P 🛜 🐾) Despite the
grand surroundings and luxurious rooms, prices
are reasonable. What's more, the walking trail to
the Glenevin Waterfall starts right outside.

Rathmelton ⑪

🛏 Frewin House   B&B €€

(📞074-915 1246; www.frewinhouse.com;
s €75-100, d €130-180) Prepare to enjoy antique

furniture, well-worn books and open fires at
this Victorian guesthouse. Dinner (€45) is
served communally and by candlelight, and the
gardens just beg to be walked.

Carrigart ⑬

🛏 Beach   Hotel €€

(Óstán na Trá; 📞074-915 5303; www.beachhotel.
ie; s/d €60/100; P) The bright, modern rooms
at this large family-run hotel come in calming
neutral tones; many have ocean views. You can
refuel in its restaurant (mains €12 to €26) or
bar (mains €9 to €14). It's in Downings, 4km
north of Carrigart.

Dunfanaghy

🛏 Corcreggan Mill   B&B, Hostel €

(📞074-913 6409; www.corcreggan.com;
Dunfanaghy; dm/s/d €17/40/55; P @ 🛜)
Spotless private rooms and dorms are tucked
away in this lovingly restored former mill.
Home-grown, organic veg goes into the soups
and stews (€5 to €10), while the breakfast
spread (€5 to €7) is a treat. It's signed off the
N56, just south of Dunfanaghy.

Arranmore Island ⑰

🛏 Claire's   B&B €€

(📞074-952 0042; www.clairesbandb.wordpress.
com; Leabgarrow; s/d €40/60; 🛜) This is the
perfect island getaway: simple, pretty rooms
handily near the ferry terminal.

Narin ⑱

🛏 Carnaween House   B&B €€

(📞074-954 5122; www.carnaweenhouse.com;
Narin; s/d €55/110; P 🛜) Luxury beach-house
style with minimalist, brilliant-white bedrooms
boasting subtle colour bursts; while the
restaurant (mains €14-21; 🕙 dinner Thu-Sun
Jun-Aug) serves excellent seafood and classic
Irish dishes.

STRETCH YOUR LEGS
BELFAST

Start/Finish Belfast City Hall

Distance 5km

Duration 3 hours

For decades Belfast's murals were powerful symbols of a violent sectarian divide. On this walk you'll see those passions painted large, but you'll also witness remarkable progress towards peace. Note that, although safe, this walk crosses West Belfast's Peace Lines (walls with gates), which are best avoided after dark.

Take this walk on Trips

2 | 29 | 33

City Hall

Start at the 1906 classical Renaissance **City Hall** (www.belfastcity.gov.uk; Donegall Sq), fronted by a dour Queen Victoria and framed by bronzes symbolising Belfast's textile and ship-building industries.

The Walk » Go up Donegall Pl, turning left on Castle St, which becomes the Falls Rd; you've entered Republican, Catholic West Belfast. After the huge murals of the Solidarity Wall, which champion global civil Rights Movements, stop at Sevastopol St.

Sinn Féin Headquarters

This red-brick building is the base of the Irish Republican party which is committed to ending British rule in Northern Ireland. It features a vast mural of Bobby Sands, the West Belfast MP who died on hunger strike in 1981.

The Walk » Pass the Royal Victoria Hospital, which developed expertise in treating gunshot wounds during the Troubles. The Cultúrlann McAdam Ó Fiaich comes soon after, on the left.

Cultúrlann McAdam Ó Fiaich

The welcoming **Cultúrlann McAdam Ó Fiaich** (Irish Cultural Centre; www.culturlann. ie; 216 Falls Rd; ⊙9am-9pm Mon-Fri, 10am-6pm Sat) features a shop selling Ireland-related books, crafts and CDs and a good cafe-restaurant.

The Walk » At nearby Islandbawn St the Plastic Bullet Mural commemorates 17 people, including eight children, killed by security service plastic baton rounds. Beechmount Ave is two streets on.

Beechmount Avenue

Absorbed by Beechmount Ave's murals, most visitors miss the hand-painted sign 'RPG Avenue' beside the street name. 'RPG' stands for 'rocket-propelled grenade', a nickname awarded because the street offered sight lines for IRA rocket attacks on security forces based nearby.

The Walk » Go back up Falls Rd, noticing dual Irish-English street names. After 1km, turn left into North Howard St and through the gate in the towering steel fencing. Turn left beside it, walking 150m.

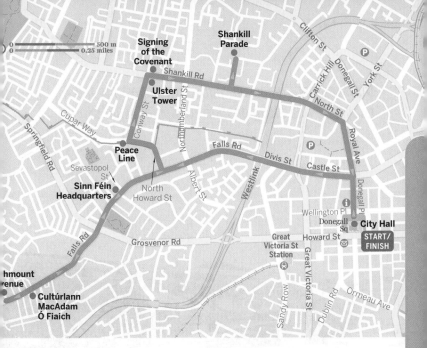

Peace Line

This imposing, 6m-high, 4km-long barrier has divided West Belfast's Catholic and Protestant communities for four decades. Now sections are a focus for reconciliation; here you'll find local peoples' testimonies and blank frames for adding your own peace message.

The Walk » Turn off the main road into pedestrianised, residential (unsigned) Conway St; you're now in Loyalist, Protestant West Belfast. Stop at the junction of Shankill Rd.

Ulster Tower

The huge mural depicting a creamy, poppy-fringed fort is the Ulster Tower, emphasising Protestant loyalty to Britain by highlighting Ulster regiments' catastrophic WWI losses.

The Walk » Cross Shankill Rd to the mural-filled courtyard beside the Rex Bar.

Signing of the Covenant

This shows a Unionist leader beside a table bearing the union flag; he's signing a mass 1912 petition against limited Irish self-government. An image from the border counties is nearby: a farmer's wife carries a gun, protecting her husband from Republican attacks.

The Walk » Head down Shankill Rd, passing batches of murals, English street signs and masses of red, white and blue. After the Gospel Hall, turn left into Shankill Pde.

Shankill Parade

Murals covering the entire gable-ends of houses pack this grass-fronted housing estate. The Protestant King William III rides a prancing white horse on the left; the (severed) **Red Hand of Ulster** is ahead. On the right sits **Remember, Respect, Resolution**; three metal columns representing the communities' willingness to embrace Northern Ireland's future.

The Walk » Shankill Rd crosses the dual carriageway. Head straight on, turning right down Royal Ave and on to City Hall.

Dunfanaghy *Chilled-out pubs, arty shops and the chance to ride along pristine sweeps of white sand*

Delights of Donegal

30

Supremely scenic (sometimes scary) roads lead from sandy shores to exposed mountains, taking in horse rides, boat trips and world-class art along the way.

TRIP HIGHLIGHTS

280 km

Dunfanaghy
Go for a gallop across soft, white sand

245 km

8

9

Tory Island
Discover Irish traditions on this rock outcrop

FINISH
Buncrana

12

Letterkenny

350 km

Glebe Gallery
Enjoy world-class art amid picture-perfect mountains and loughs

Ardara

Slieve League

2

Rossnowlagh
START

20 km

Donegal Bay
Delight in this charismatic town's scenic spot

7 DAYS
434KM / 269 MILES

GREAT FOR...

BEST TIME TO GO

Easter to October. Sights and activities are open; weather might be better.

ESSENTIAL PHOTO

Riding a horse across Dunfanaghy beach.

BEST TWO DAYS

From tweed town via mountain to classic Irish island: stops 6 to 8 deliver the essence of Donegal.

30

Delights of Donegal

This trip prompts diverse sensations: looming Mt Errigal is overwhelming; a beach horseback ride feels liberating; driving the high mountain passes is heart-in-the-mouth stuff. Relax on boat trips around Donegal Bay, to 600m sea cliffs and to an island, then encounter international art, Ireland's traditional industries and piles of hand-cut peat beside the road. On this trip you gain a true insight into delightful Donegal.

❶ Rossnowlagh

There's more to the happy-go-lucky resort of Rossnowlagh than its superb 3km sandy beach (p350). Deep in a forest (signed off the R231 south of town) a **Franciscan Friary** (franciscanfriary@eircom.net; admission free; ⊙10am-8pm Mon-Sat) offers tranquil gardens, a small museum and the Way of the Cross walk, which meanders up a hillside smothered with rhododendrons for spectacular views.

The Drive ❯❯ Distance 19km. The R231 heads north through a gently rolling landscape, onto the N15 for a smooth run into Donegal town. Head for the waterfront, parking near the pier.

TRIP HIGHLIGHT

❷ Donegal Town

With its handsome castle (see p307), waterside location and Blue Stack Mountains backdrop, Donegal town is a delightful stop. Drink in the beauty of Donegal Bay on the **Donegal Bay Waterbus** (www.donegalbaywaterbus. com; Donegal Pier; adult/child €15/5; ⊙ up to 3 daily Easter-Oct), a 1¼-hour boat tour that will see you gazing at historic sites, seal-inhabited coves, an island manor and a ruined castle.

The Drive ❯❯ Distance 32km. Take the N56 west. The Blue Stack Mountains retreat in your wing mirror, an open coast road unfurls and soon the wafer-thin St John's peninsula comes into view. Turn off left, heading out to its tip.

❸ St John's Point

This improbably thin finger of land pokes into

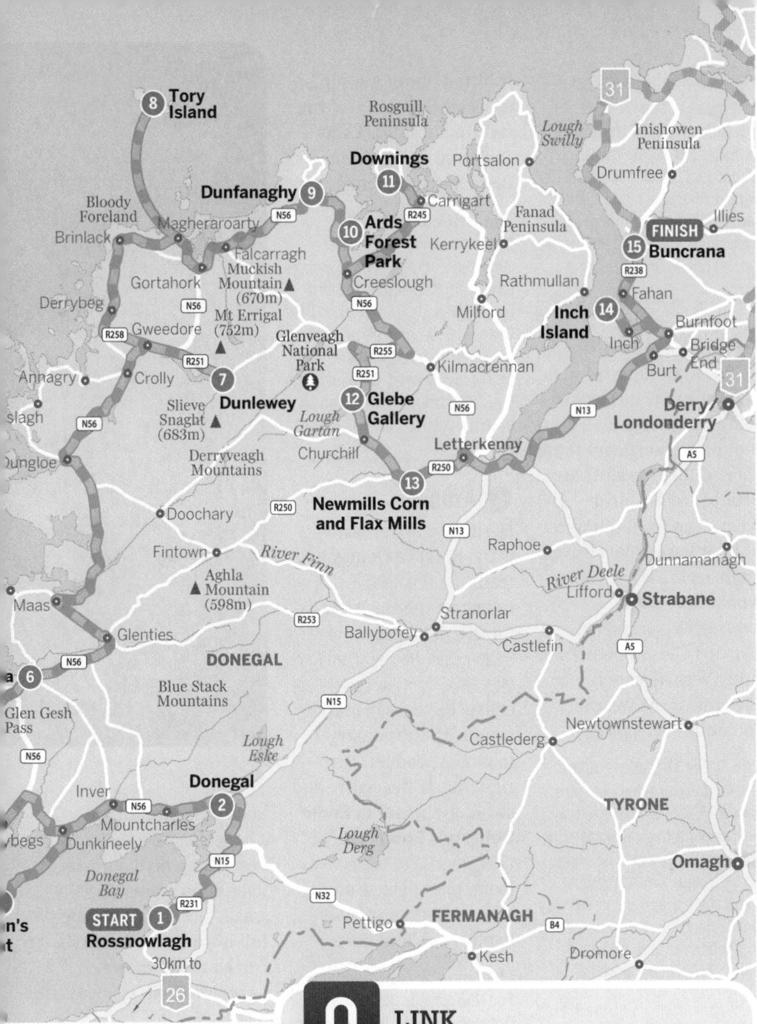

the sea, culminating at St John's Point. Driving the 11km lane to the tip feels like driving into the ocean; the point itself has a small sandy beach, rich bird and plant life, total tranquillity and (inevitably) remarkable, wrap-around views.

p337

LINK YOUR TRIP

26 **Sligo Surrounds**
A five-day meander through culture-packed Sligo. Head for Sligo town, 50km south of this trip's start.

31 **Inishowen Peninsula**
An exhilarating foray into a remote headland. Start in Derry/Londonderry, 20km east of this trip's finish.

The Drive ≫ Distance 34km. Continue west on the N56, then take the R263 through fish-scented Killybeggs. After its harbour full of trawlers, signs appear for Slieve League, the towering mountains looming ever-closer ahead. After Carrick, comes tiny Teelin (Tieleann).

4 Slieve League

So far, from the road Slieve League has looked like an impressive mountain range, but these sheer 600m sea cliffs are utterly awe-inspiring when seen from the water at their base. Boats leave from Teelin; book with **Nuala Star** (☎074-973 9365; www.sliabhleagueboattrips. com; from €20; ⏰Apr-Oct). For other ways to experience the cliffs if the weather's too rough, see p352.

The Drive ≫ Distance 12km. Back at Carrick, edge west on the R263, before turning left on the minor route signed Malin Beg (Málainn Bhig). It cuts behind Slieve League's massive peaks, threading through an increasingly remote landscape, dotted with isolated farms and scored by strips of hand-cut turf (peat).

5 Malin Beg

Malin Beg is one of Donegal's wildest spots which is quite something in a county crammed with them. An undulating sea-monster-like headland snakes in the waves, Sligo's coast appears, distant, to the south, a creamy lighthouse sits just offshore. The bay below

is bitten out of low cliffs; descend 60 steps to firm, red-tinged sand, a spot sheltered from Malin Beg's howling winds.

The Drive ≫ Distance 25km. Go north, through Glencolumbcille (Gleann Cholm Cille) with its sleeping options (p337), picking up signs for Glen Gesh Pass. A steep climb past bogs and wandering sheep leads to a plunging road, winding into the valley below. Next, go north onto the N56 to park in Ardara.

6 Ardara

Heritage town Ardara is the heart of Donegal's traditional tweed industry; the **Heritage Centre** (☎074-954 1704; Main St; admission free; ⏰10am-6pm Mon-Sat, 2-6pm Sun Easter-Sep) charts its transformation from cottage industry to global product. Turn right out of the centre and stroll up the hill to **Eddie Doherty's Shop** (☎074-954 1304; Front St) to see a vast loom, piles of rugs and rolls of cloth; staff will happily explain more.

The Drive ≫ Distance 70km. The N56 sweeps north towards Dungloe (signed Glenties). After Maas it narrows into a bucking, twisting road: subsidence amid bogs has created a suspension-testing ride. After Dungloe, Mt Errigal's pyramidal peak rears from a lough-studded landscape. Turn onto the R251, climbing steadily towards it and Dunlewey.

7 Dunlewey

Isolated, exposed loughside Dunlewey (Dún Lúiche) offers a true

taste of mountain life. The scenery overwhelms everything here; human habitation seems very small. Get the landscape's full impact on a boat trip run by the **Dunlewey Lakeside Centre** (Ionad Cois Locha; ☎074-953 1699; www. dunleweycentre.com; adult/child €6/4; ⏰11am-6pm Easter-Oct), as a storyteller expounds on ghoulish folklore.

🛏 p337

The Drive ≫ Distance 32km. Rejoin the N56, heading briefly west before taking the R258 around Bloody Foreland (Cnóc Fola), a spectacular shore so named because sunsets turn its rocks crimson. Turn towards the

Glen Gesh Pass Offering one of Donegal's most spectacular moutain views

tiny harbour (Magheraroarty) that eventually swings into view.

- - - - - - - - - - - -

TRIP HIGHLIGHT

8 Tory Island

Some 11km offshore, craggy Tory Island (Oileán Thóraí) is a fiercely independent community with its own Irish dialect, elected 'king' and style of 'naive' art, plus early Christian remains and 100 seabird species. The 35-minute crossing, with **Donegal Coastal Cruises** (Turasmara Teo; ☏074-953 1320; www. toryislandferry.com; adult/child return €26/13), can be wild.

The Drive » Distance 37km. The N56 undulates north past loughs to Dunfanaghy, a sheep-grazed landscape where the ever-present bulk of Muckish Mountain looms to the right. Once in Dunfanaghy, make for the central Arnold's Hotel.

- - - - - - - - - - - -

TRIP HIGHLIGHT

9 Dunfanaghy

Along with chilled-out pubs and arty shops, cheerful Dunfanaghy offers the chance to ride along pristine sweeps of white sand. The stables at **Arnold's Hotel** (☏074-910 0980; www.dunfanaghystables. com; per hour €30) are just across the road from

the beach; book for an unforgettable ride.

🍴 🛏 p337

The Drive » Continue east through Dunfanaghy; 5km later turn left into Ards Forest Park.

- - - - - - - - - - - -

10 Ards Forest Park

From the park's main **car park** (www.coillteoutdoors. ie; €4; ⏰10am-9pm Apr-Sep), pick up the trail that meanders east through ash and oak towards a Capuchin Friary. Follow the path further down still and you'll stumble upon first the exquisite Isabella's Cove, then

TOP TIP: GLENVEAGH NATIONAL PARK

Glebe Gallery sits beside the stunning **Glenveagh National Park** (Páirc Náisiúnta Ghleann Bheatha; www.glenveaghnationalpark.ie). This 16,500 sq km wilderness features forests, mountains, shimmering lakes and green-gold bogs, and makes for magnificent walking. The **visitor centre** (☺10am-6pm mid-Mar–Oct, 9am-5pm Nov–mid-Mar) provides free maps.

Lucky Shell Bay. Allow two hours return.

The Drive ›› Distance 24km. Rejoin the N56 east, before taking the R245 to Carrigart (Carraig Airt), an increasingly windy road backed by the rugged hills of the Fanad Peninsula. Head through amiable Carrigart to Downings.

⑪ Downings

The **beach** at Downings (or Downies) is simply superb: rolling green hills meet an immense curl of bright-white sand. It's also, unlike many local beaches, safe to swim here; the Atlantic makes for a chilly, but memorable, dip.

🛏 p337

The Drive ›› Distance 50km. Take the N56 towards Letterkenny, as the Derryveagh Mountains gather ahead. Turn onto the R255 (signed Glenveagh National Park), climbing towards those peaks. Turn left onto the R251; it descends revealing a glittering Lough Gartan; at the water's edge, follow Glebe Gallery signs right.

TRIP HIGHLIGHT

⑫ Glebe Gallery

This is a true treat: the top-notch artwork at **Glebe Gallery** (www.heritageireland.ie; adult/child €3/1; ☺11am-6.30pm daily Easter, Jul & Aug, Sat-Thu Jun & Sep) belonged to English painter, Derrick Hill. Works include those by Tory Island's 'naive' artists, plus Picasso, Landseer, Hokusai, Jack B Yeats and Kokoschka.

The Drive ›› Distance 11km. The R251 winds south through woodland, hugging the lough shore. Next turn onto the R250 to Letterkenny; soon you'll see the Newmills Corn and Flax Mills signed on your right.

⑬ Newmills Corn and Flax Mills

A whirring, creaking, gushing delight, this restored, three-storey, water-powered **corn mill** (www.heritageireland.ie; admission free; ☺10am-5pm late May-Sep) is full of in-motion grinding stones,

drive shafts, cogs and gears.

The Drive ›› Distance 53km. After Letterkenny (for sleeping options, see p337) join the N13 east towards Derry/Londonderry. The River Swilly uncurls to your left. Take the R238/239 turn, then the left to Inch Island (signed Wildfowl Reserve). Once over the causeway the (signed) road to Inch Pier snakes along tranquil, tree-lined lanes.

⑭ Inch Island

At Inch's tiny pier, park on the right (don't block the fishermen's track to the left). Few tourists make it to this compact crescent of sand. It's a place to rest, skim stones and watch waves.

The Drive ›› Distance 20km. The R238 sweeps north past a 5km sandy beach to Buncrana. By now Lough Swilly is stretching far ahead. Head for Buncrana's shoreline, parking beside the Leisure Centre.

⑮ Buncrana

Bustling Buncrana provides a fitting trip finale, courtesy of stunning sunsets; locals will tell you the ones over Lough Swilly are the best around. A path leads beside the waters to pint-sized, 1718 **Buncrana Castle**; it and neighbouring **O'Doherty's Keep** provide ideal sun-going-down vantage points.

🍴 🛏 p337

Eating & Sleeping

St John's Point ❸

🛏 Castle Murray   Hotel €€
(📞074-973 7022; www.castlemurray.com;
St John's Point; s/d €65/110; P 📶)
The small hotel at this fabulously romantic spot
has a superb French restaurant (four-course
lunch/dinner €32/45), simple rooms and
unbeatable sea views.

Glencolumbcille

🛏 Dooey Hostel   Hostel €€
(📞074-973 0130; d €30; 🕙 Feb–mid-Sep;
P) Partly carved out of the rock face, this
Independent Hotel Owners of Ireland hostel
features rustic, clean and comfortable doubles;
the views of ocean and hills are jaw-dropping.
Take the turning beside the Glenhead Tavern
for 1.5km.

Dunlewey ❼

🛏 Glen Heights   B&B €€
(📞074-956 0844; www.glenheightsbb.com; s/d
€50/70) Your breakfast may go cold here as you
feast on the breathtaking panorama of Lough
Dunlewey, Mt Errigal and the Poisoned Glen.
The unfancy bedrooms are cosy, the bathrooms
pristine and the Donegal charm is in full swing.

Dunfanaghy ❾

🍴 Muck 'n' Muffins   Cafe €
(Main Sq; snacks €4-10; 🕙 9.30am-5pm Mon-
Sat, 11am-5pm Sun, to 9pm Jul & Aug; 📶 ♿)
A 19th-century rough-stone grain store now
houses this waterfront cafe. Even on rainy
winter days, it's packed with locals tucking into
healthy sandwiches, quiches and hot specials,
tempting cakes and, of course, muffins.

🛏 Whins   B&B €€
(📞074-913 6481; www.thewhins.com; s/d
€50/74; P 📶) The colourful rooms at Whins

have patchwork quilts, quality furniture and a
real sense of character. A wide choice of superb
breakfasts is served in a room overlooking
scenic Horn Head. The B&B is about 750m
south of the village opposite the golf course.

Downings ⓫

🛏 Downings Bay   Hotel €€
(📞074-915 5586; www.downingsbayhotel.com;
s/d from €50/100; P 📶) Just footsteps from
the strand, rooms at this spacious, if slightly
austere, hotel have subtle checked and striped
fabrics. There are also a couple of bars (bar
food €10 to €20) and a decent restaurant, the
Haven (mains €15-22).

Letterkenny

🛏 Town View   B&B €€
(📞074-912 1570; www.townviewhouse.com;
Leck Rd; s/d €49/70; P @) The tastefully
decorated rooms here feature white linens,
splashes of colour, quality furniture and shining
bathrooms. There's an impressive array of
breakfast dishes and the owners are amicable.

Buncrana ⓯

🍴 Beach House   Seafood €€
(📞074-936 1050; www.thebeachhouse.ie; The
Pier, Swilly Rd; mains €6.50-26; 🕙 daily Jun-Aug,
dinner Wed-Sun, lunch Sat & Sun Sep-May) This
lough-view cafe-restaurant delivers deceptively
simple, supremely classy dishes; expect fillet
steak, crab claws and creamy bisques.

🛏 Caldra   B&B €€
(📞074-936 3703; www.caldrabandb.com;
Lisnakelly; s/d €50/80; P 📶 ♿) Impressive
fireplaces and gilt mirrors combine with tranquil
contemporary guest rooms. The garden and
patio overlook Lough Swilly and the mountains.

Malin Head *Tumbling cliffs and sparse vegetation on Ireland's most northerly point*

Inishowen Peninsula

31

This thrilling route heads deep into Ireland's wild lands. You'll encounter cliff-top hikes, shipwrecks, a fort and superb seafood, then return exhilarated to the comforts of town.

TRIP HIGHLIGHTS

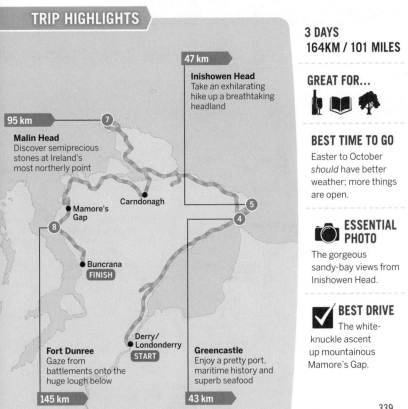

47 km

Inishowen Head
Take an exhilarating hike up a breathtaking headland

95 km

⑦

Malin Head
Discover semiprecious stones at Ireland's most northerly point

Mamore's Gap

Carndonagh

⑤

④

⑧

● Buncrana
FINISH

Fort Dunree
Gaze from battlements onto the huge lough below

145 km

Derry/
● Londonderry
START

Greencastle
Enjoy a pretty port, maritime history and superb seafood

43 km

3 DAYS
164KM / 101 MILES

GREAT FOR...

BEST TIME TO GO

Easter to October *should* have better weather; more things are open.

📷 ESSENTIAL PHOTO

The gorgeous sandy-bay views from Inishowen Head.

✓ BEST DRIVE

The white-knuckle ascent up mountainous Mamore's Gap.

339

This trip isn't about skimming Ireland's surface through big-name sights. Instead it's a route to the heart of the country's compelling narratives: faith; poverty; mass migration; territorial disputes; the Troubles. With unsigned, cliffside roads that look more like farm tracks, you'll probably get a little lost. But locals are helpful if you do – and asking for directions is a great conversation starter.

❶ Derry/ Londonderry

Kick-start your Inishowen trip by exploring the story of one of the coast's most famous victims: *La Trinidad Valenciera*. This Venetian trader was the second-biggest vessel in the Spanish Armada and was shipwrecked at Kinnagoe Bay in 1588 – a spot you'll see later. Derry/Londonderry's award-winning **Tower Museum** (Union Hall Pl; adult/child £4.20/2.65;

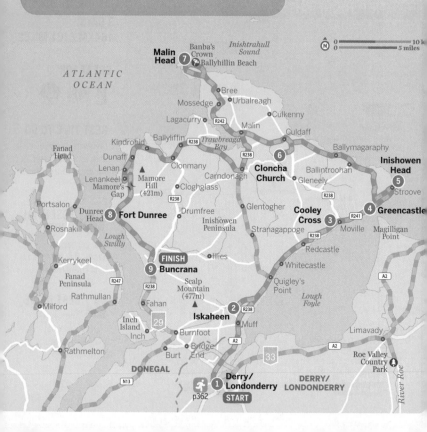

⊙10am-5pm Tue-Sat, plus 11am-3pm Sun Jul & Aug) tells the vessel's story and features poignant wreck finds: pewter tableware, wooden combs, olive jars, shoe soles. There are also impressive bronze guns. Look out for the 2.5-tonne siege gun bearing the arms of Phillip II of Spain, which show him as king of England – factually accurate because of his marriage to Queen Mary I, but perhaps also indicative of the ambitions that launched the Armada. Make time to explore vibrant, fascinating Derry, Northern Ireland's second city; see our walking tour, p362.

The Drive ≫ Distance 18km. Take the A2 north towards Moville. Derry's retail parks quickly give way to fields and mountain views; the silvery

LINK YOUR TRIP

29 **The North in a Nutshell**

The cream of the north in one glorious route; pick it up from this trip's end: Buncrana.

33 **From Bangor to Derry**

Belfast and the sight-packed Antrim Coast. It stops where this trips starts: Derry/Londonderry.

Lough Foyle emerges to your right. Soon, road signs switch from mph to km/h: welcome to the Republic of Ireland. Shortly after Muff, turn left to Iskaheen, head up the hill then park beside the village church.

- - - - - - - - - - - - - -

② Iskaheen

Head across the road, through the creaking gate and into the old graveyard. There you'll see evidence of spectres that have long stalked Ireland: poverty, high death rates and the Troubles. Among many gravestones recording multiple deaths, hunt out the broad memorial of the McKinney family. Its losses include a 24-year-old woman, a nine-month-old boy, and three girls, aged 13 years, 11 months and six weeks. It also commemorates 34-year-old James Gerard McKinney, one of 13 unarmed demonstrators shot dead by British troops in Derry on 30 January 1972 – Bloody Sunday.

The Drive ≫ Head back to the R238 drinking in the panorama of Lough Foyle as you go. Next comes a 15-minute, scenic shoreside cruise north to Moville. Just before town, take the left turn, signed Cooley Cross, which appears next to a small lay-by on the right.

- - - - - - - - - - - - - -

③ Cooley Cross

The 3m-high cross you've parked beside has an unusual ringed head – through it negotiating

---

parties are said to have shaken hands to seal agreements. The atmospheric tumbling of ruins beyond features the remnants of an early monastery founded by St Patrick. At the foot of the enclosure, set against some great lough views, sits the tiny, hutlike **Skull House**. This roofed, gabled structure is a tomb-shrine associated with St Finian, an abbot of the early monastery. Nearby Moville has good eating and sleeping options (p345).

The Drive ≫ Distance 5km. Rejoin the R238, heading left for the 10-minute drive along the shore to Greencastle. Opposite, Magilligan Point's sandy beaches curl into view. Soon after entering Greencastle, take the right to the Maritime Museum.

- - - - - - - - - - - - - -

TRIP HIGHLIGHT

④ Greencastle

Packed with boats and top seafood restaurants, the thriving port of Greencastle also boasts a fine **Maritime Museum** (www.inishowenmaritime.com; adult/child €5/3; ⊙9.30am-5.30pm Mon-Sat, noon-5.30pm Sun Easter-Oct). It reveals the part this area played in one of Ireland's most powerful stories: mass emigration to America and Australia. It started in 1718 and continued until 1939, but peaked in the mid-1800s; at one stage Derry was Ireland's premier emigration port, and the initial route those vessels took echoes your own – from the city, up the length of Lough Foyle to the sea.

✖ p345

The Drive ›› Distance 5km. Continue north. Just after the Fisheries College take the right signed Stroove. Houses thin out and the road narrows before the black-and-white Inishowen lighthouse edges into your windscreen. Park just beyond, beside Stroove Beach.

TRIP HIGHLIGHT

5 Inishowen Head

From Stroove Beach's curling sands, join the footpath that winds north, initially on the road, then onto a track, up towards Inishowen Head itself. This stiff 2.5km climb reveals spectacular views over Lough Foyle to the immense ribbon of sand framing Magilligan Point; on clear days you can spot Scotland's islands to the northeast. Edge high enough and you'll see the jagged rocks and golden sands of Kinnagoe Bay – where *La Trinidad Valenciera* came to grief.

The Drive ›› Distance 30km. Motor north, initially along your walk route, before curving left. Opposite the Maritime Museum turning, head up an unsigned, steep, narrow, roller-coaster road (it even has grass in the middle) to Culdaff. At Culdaff (for food and accommodation, see p345), take the R238 towards Gleneely. Turn right

1km along, opposite the modern church. Cloncha Church appears 1km later.

6 Cloncha Church

The towering gable-ends and huge windows of the roofless shell of 17th-century Cloncha Church frame views of the Donegal mountains. Inside sits the intricately carved tombstone of Scott Magnus MacOrristin – spot the carved writing sloping down the side, and the sword and hurling-stick motifs. Outside, a tall cross stands in a field; clamber down to decipher the depiction of the loaves and fishes miracle on its weathered face, amid ornate swirls and zigzags.

The Drive ›› Distance 25km. The R238/R243 leads from Culdaff to quaint Malin village, with its excellent sleeping options (p345). Next make for Malin Head, a spectacular drive through Trawbreaga Bay's lowlands, past massive dunes at Five Fingers Strand and the hulk of Knockamany. You emerge onto a rugged coast dotted with whitewashed cottages. Take the right, signed Banba's Crown.

TRIP HIGHLIGHT

7 Malin Head

Open your car door at Malin Head and step into a weather-battered landscape of tumbling cliffs and sparse vegetation – welcome to Ireland's most northerly point. The cliff-top tower

SIMON GREENWOOD/GETTY IMAGES ©

Donegal Shepherd with his flock

beside you was built in 1805 by the British admiralty and later used as a Lloyds signal station. WWII lookout posts are dotted around. To the west, a path leads to Hell's Hole, a chasm where the incoming waters crash against rock formations. Just to the east of the head sits Ballyhillin Beach – one of the best places locally to hunt for semiprecious stones.

The Drive » Distance 50km. From Malin village take the R238 through Carndonagh to Clonmany, then follow signs to Mamore's Gap, heading straight for the by now large-looming mountains. At the crossroads the Inis Eoghain (Scenic Route) goes up what looks like a farm track. Wayside shrines and another first-and-second-gear ascent follow, before a brake-burning descent. At the plain, head right to Dunree Head.

TRIP HIGHLIGHT

8 Fort Dunree

Dunree Head overlooks Lough Swilly, a highly strategic stretch of water that's been navigated by Norsemen, Normans, Ireland's fleeing aristocracy and part of Britain's WWI naval fleet. The 19th-century **Fort Dunree** (www.dunree.pro.ie; adult/child €6/4; ◷10.30am-6pm Mon-Sat, 1-6pm Sun

INISHOWEN'S TREASURES

Beachcombers love Inishowen's postglacial strand lines and raised beaches. They're littered with semiprecious stones such as agate and jasper. Ballyhillin Beach, just east of Malin Head, is a great hunting ground. From Banba's Crown car park, go back down the hill, take the rough farm track left towards a terracotta-coloured cottage and go over the ladder stile.

You can also buy the polished stones at **Malin Pebbles** (www.malinpebbles.com) in Greencastle.

Jun-Sep) commands the water. Along with some menacing artillery, films explore the fort's past, while an underground bunker conjures up daily life. The scenery and the bird life are stunning too.

The Drive » Distance 19km. Head south to Buncrana, past the mountains of Bulbin and Aghaweel, rising up to your left. The waters of Lough Swilly sweep off to the right, backed by the ranges of the Fanad Peninsula. At the appealing town of Buncrana head for the shore, initially signed Swilly Ferry, and park beside the leisure centre.

---

9 Buncrana

Take the path north for 20 minutes, leading across the grass, with Lough Swilly and the Fanad Peninsula's hills stretching out in front of you. John Newton, the composer of 'Amazing Grace', was inspired

to write his legendary antislavery song after his ship the *Greyhound* sheltered from a storm in these waters in 1748. It was a near-death experience that started his spiritual journey from slave trader to antislavery campaigner.

Make for **Buncrana Castle**, built in 1718. Wolfe Tone was imprisoned here following the unsuccessful French invasion in 1798. Beside the castle you'll find **O'Doherty's Keep**, a 15th-century tower built by the local O'Doherty chiefs, but burned by the English and rebuilt for their own use.

✕ ⊨ p345

Eating & Sleeping

Moville

✕ Rosato's   Italian €€

(Malin Rd, Moville; mains €9-12) This lively pub is
the best spot in town for pizza and pasta, plus
there's live music on Saturday nights.

⛏ Washington House   B&B €€

(☎074-938 5574; www.washingtonhousebandb.
com; Ballyrattan, Redcastle; s/d from €50/80;
☻mid-Apr–Sep; P) The spacious rooms of
this new B&B all have queen- or king-size beds
and pristine bathrooms, while the patio has
sweeping views of Lough Foyle.

Greencastle ❹

✕ Kealy's Seafood Bar   Seafood €€

(☎074-938 1010; The Harbour; lunch mains
€8-14.50, dinner mains €16-50; ☻lunch Sat &
Sun, dinner Wed-Sun) The catch here is so fresh
you almost have to fight the harbour seals for it.
It's an award-winning spot for a humble bowl of
chowder or a lobster extravaganza.

Culdaff

⛏ McGrory's of Culdaff   Hotel €€

(☎074-937 9104; www.mcgrorys.ie; s/d from
€59/89; P) Expect spiffy, contemporary
rooms at this raspberry red village landmark.
It also delivers classy bar food (€9 to €20 from
12.30pm to 8pm), live music in Mac's Backroom
and a **restaurant** (mains €14-22; ☻dinner
Tue-Sun, lunch Sun) serving the best Irish
cuisine for kilometres.

Malin Village

⛏ Malin Hotel   Hotel €€

(☎074-937 0606; www.malinhotel.ie; The Green;
s/d from €70/100; P ☎) Tucked in behind

Malin's old pub, this modern, boxlike hotel
boasts lavish rooms with designer wallpaper,
while the pub-restaurant (mains €10 to €22)
serves up good Irish standards.

⛏ Village B&B   B&B €€

(☎074-937 0763; www.malinvillagebandb.
com; The Green; s/d €45/70) Room choices
at this charming B&B range from traditional
(antique furniture and brocade armchairs) to
contemporary (white linen and floral patterns).
You can also cook a meal here and catch up on
some laundry.

Buncrana ❾

✕ Beach House   Seafood €€

(☎074-936 1050; www.thebeachhouse.ie; The
Pier, Swilly Rd; lunch mains €6.50-17.50, dinner
mains €16-26; ☻daily Jun-Aug, dinner Wed-Sun,
lunch Sat & Sun Sep-May; ♿) With plate-glass
windows facing the lough, this aptly named
cafe-restaurant projects an elegant simplicity.
Although the menu is simple, the quality is a cut
above the norm; 'surf 'n' turf' is fillet steak,
crab claws, langoustines and creamy bisque.

⛏ Tullyarvan Mill   Hostel €

(☎074-936 1613; www.tullyarvanmill.com;
Carndonagh Rd; dm/d €14/42; P) This excellent
purpose-built hostel, with great-value doubles,
is attached to Tullyarvan Mill, which hosts
regular cultural events and art exhibits. It's
signed off the R238 north out of town.

⛏ Westbrook House   B&B €€

(☎074-936 1067; www.westbrookhouse.ie;
Westbrook Rd; s/d €40/70; P ☎) A handsome
Georgian house set in beautiful gardens,
Westbrook offers old-world hospitality and
charm by the bucketload. Chandeliers,
antique furniture and cut glass give it a refined
sophistication, while the little trinkets make it a
much-loved home.

County Sligo Rugged and remote Atlantic coastline

Northwest on Adrenalin

32

This high-octane trip sees you surfing, hiking and gazing at 600m cliffs, driving through mountain passes and along remote, rugged roads – it's an action-packed, unforgettable drive.

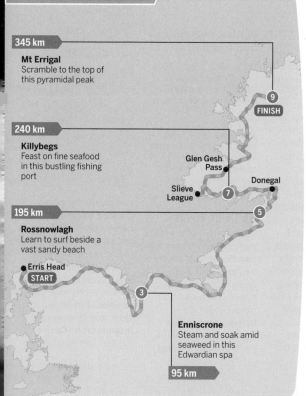

345 km

Mt Errigal
Scramble to the top of this pyramidal peak

240 km

Killybegs
Feast on fine seafood in this bustling fishing port

195 km

Rossnowlagh
Learn to surf beside a vast sandy beach

Erris Head
START

Enniscrone
Steam and soak amid seaweed in this Edwardian spa

95 km

Glen Gesh Pass

Slieve League

Donegal

9
FINISH

7

5

3

4 DAYS
345KM / 214 MILES

GREAT FOR...

BEST TIME TO GO
Easter to October means better weather and opening hours.

ESSENTIAL PHOTO
The 600m sea cliffs at Slieve League are a photographer's dream.

BEST FOR OUTDOORS
Stops 3 to 8 for surfing, clambering around cliffs and soaking in seaweed baths.

Northwest on Adrenalin

If you're after an Irish adventure, this trip delivers in spades. Along with adrenalin-fuelled surfing and hiking, you'll take in Donegal's highest mountain, Europe's biggest sea cliffs and the world's largest Stone Age monument. Other heritage crowds in too: an abbey, a castle and a seafaring past. And then there's the drive itself, from sand-dusted seaside lanes to exhilarating mountain roads – it's a roller-coaster ride.

❶ Erris Head

Where better to start a road trip than at the end of the road – literally. The parking area for Erris Head appears where the rough lane peters out. From there waymarks (black posts with purple arrows) direct you on a two-hour, 5km loop around this wind-buffeted headland. The path leads over footbridges and earth banks, across fields and along sheep tracks. The views from the high cliffs are spectacular, taking in islands, sea stacks and rock arches. **Belmullet Tourist Office** (☎097-81500; Main St) has free guides; to get to the lay-by, follow trailhead signs from Belmullet.

The Drive ≫ Distance 45km. Motor southeast across the narrow neck of land that fuses Belmullet to the rest of County Mayo. Soon, turn left onto the R314, towards Ballycastle. After it climbs a lush ravine and attaches itself to the coast, a wood and glass pyramid suddenly pops up on the right. It's your next stop: Céide Fields.

❷ Céide Fields

Céide Fields is the world's most extensive Stone Age monument; half a million tonnes of rock make up its field boundaries, houses and megalithic tombs. Today it's a barren, wind-blasted spot, but five millennia ago a thriving farming community lived here, growing wheat and barley and grazing sheep and cattle. Although important, this story is hard to tell engagingly (to the uninitiated the site could resemble tumbles of stone) but a sleek, award-winning **Interpretation Centre** (☎096-43325; www.heritage

ireland.ie; adult/child €4/2;
⊙10am-6pm Jun-Sep, to 5pm
Easter-May & Oct) cleverly
re-creates life in early
farming communities.
Better still, take a guided
tour of the site.

The Drive >> Distance 56km.
The R314 heads east, revealing
a vast sea stack at Downpatrick
Head. Gradually exposed hills
give way to rolling fields. After

§ LINK
YOUR
TRIP

28 Tip to Toe
Wind south to
Wexford, past the pick of
Ireland's historic sites.
Join it at stop 4, Sligo
town

30 Delights of
Donegal
Head further north for
exquisite beaches and
a sandy horseback ride.
Pick it up where this
trip stops: towering Mt
Errigal.

one-street Ballycastle comes congested Ballina where you take the N59 north (signed 'Sligo'). Soon the R297 peels off to Enniscrone. Drive up Main St, then follow the Hot Seaweed Baths signs left.

GARETH MCCORMACK/GETTY IMAGES ©

③ Enniscrone

Right beside Enniscrone's stunning 5km beach sits **Kilcullen's Seaweed Baths** (☎091-36238; www.kilcullenseaweedbaths.com; s/tw bath €25/40; ☉10am-8pm Jun-Sep, call for hours Oct-May). Step into this Edwardian spa and soon you'll be steaming away in a cedar cabinet then submerging yourself in a gigantic porcelain bath filled with orangey water and bits of seaweed. It's used to treat arthritis and rheumatism, but the baths' high iodine content means this traditional natural therapy also acts as an intense moisturiser. It's also a great way to recover from, and prepare for, this trip's adventures.

📖 p353

The Drive ≫ Distance 56km. You could head south back to the N59, but it's more fun to stay on the R297, as it bobbles and twists beside flat coastal fields. Eventually it rejoins the N59, to sweep east to Ballysadare. There take the N4 to Sligo; Sligo Abbey is signed from the ring road.

④ Sligo Town

Sligo town is an inviting stop: stone bridges frame the river; pedestrian streets are framed by attractive shops; pub music sessions overflow onto the pavement. **Sligo Abbey** (Abbey St; adult/child €3/1; ☉10am-6pm Easter– mid-Oct) sits in the centre, a Dominican friary founded around 1252. The abbey survived the worst ravages of the Tudor era and it has the only sculpted altar to survive the Reformation. The doorways reach only a few feet high at the abbey's rear – the ground around it was swollen by the mass graves from years of famine and war.

🍴 p353

The Drive ≫ Distance 53km. Heading north out of Sligo town on the N15 sees the mountains of Benbulben and Truskmore looming ever larger. At Ballyshannon take the R231 to Rossnowlagh. When sand starts edging onto the road, you know you're near the resort's Blue Flag beach. Make for the graffiti-art designs of Fin McCool's Surf School.

⑤ Rossnowlagh

Rossnowlagh's spectacular 3km-long beach is a wide, sandy stretch beloved by families, walkers and surfers throughout the year. The gentle rollers

Slieve League View from the spectacular polychrome sea cliffs

are great for learning to ride the waves, or to hone your skills. **Fin McCool Surf School** (☎071-985 9020; www.finmccoolsurfschool.com; ☺10am-7pm Easter-Oct) offers tuition (per two hours €35) and gear hire (per three hours €29); the waters of Donegal Bay offer an exhilarating ride.

✖ 🛏 p353

The Drive ❯❯ Distance 20km. From Rossnowlagh's sand-dusted road, the R231 winds north through rolling fields before rejoining the N15. This sweeps on towards Donegal town, with the Blue Stack Mountains now appearing

behind. On the roundabout on its fringes, pick up the signs for Donegal Castle.

- - - - - - - - - - -

❻ Donegal Town

Mountain-backed, pretty Donegal town was for centuries the stamping grounds of the chiefs who ruled northwest Ireland from the 15th to 17th centuries: the O'Donnells. They built **Donegal Castle** (www.heritageireland.ie; Castle St; adult/child €4/2; ☺10am-6pm Easter–mid-Sep) in 1474 and it served as the seat of their formidable power until 1607, when the English ousted

Ireland's chieftains. Rory O'Donnell torched his own castle before leaving for France in the infamous Flight of the Earls (p324). Their departure paved the way for the Plantation of Ulster by thousands of Scots and English Protestants, creating divisions still felt today. The castle was rebuilt in 1623 – it's a wonderfully atmospheric place to visit, with rooms furnished with French tapestries and Persian rugs.

✖ p353

TOP TIP: GAELTACHT

This part of Ireland is the Donegal Gaeltacht; one of many areas where Irish culture and language are championed. Initially, you'll notice it most in road signs; here they tend to be in Irish only (elsewhere it's Irish and English). We use English transliterations with Irish names included in brackets.

The Drive » Distance 30km. As the N56 heads west the Blue Stacks range to your right and more mountains shade the horizon ahead. For now though it's a gently rolling road that leads towards Killybegs. Take the R263 into town, the Maritime Museum is signed soon after the fishing-boat-packed harbour.

TRIP HIGHLIGHT

7 Killybegs

Killybegs is a sensory summation of the sea – the scent of fish hangs in the air, and seagulls wheel overhead in this, Ireland's largest fishing port. So a visit to the **Maritime and Heritage Centre** (www.visitkillybegs. com; Fintra Rd; admission €4; ⏰10am-6pm Mon-Fri, plus 1-5pm Sat Jul-Aug) is a must. You'll hear the personal accounts of local fishermen and see evocative sepia images of the industry's heyday. The best bit though is to step aboard the simulation of a fishing trawler wheelhouse, where you'll try navigating into port amid choppy seas –

driving seems easy after that.

🍴 🛏 p353

The Drive » Distance 16km. The R263 heads west, tracing the shore before cutting inland to a peak-lined landscape threaded with rough stone walls. Gradually, the brooding Slieve League mountains come to dominate the view. At Carrick turn left, signed Slieve League; nudge round the mountain edge to the lower car park.

---

8 Slieve League

The Cliffs of Moher get more publicity, but the spectacular polychrome sea cliffs at Slieve League are higher – the highest in Europe, plunging some 600m to the sea. From the lower car park, a path skirts up around the near-vertical rock face to the aptly named **One Man's Pass** – look out for two rocks nicknamed the 'school desk and chair'. Sunset can be stunning, with waves crashing dramatically far below and the ocean reflecting the day's last rays. It's a strenuous hike to the summit, and rain

and mist can appear unexpectedly, making conditions slippery. You can now drive all the way to the top; if you want to, be aware it can involve reversing up/down the steep, one-car-wide, cliffside road.

The Drive » Distance 83km. Pick up the (signed) Glen Gesh Pass, a long climb into a wild landscape that crests to reveal sweeping valley views. A dizzying, hairpin descent lurches to the N56 and towards Mt Errigal, the massive pointed peak that edges ever nearer. The R251 climbs through Dunlewey village; when Errigal is directly on your left, turn into the small, walled parking area.

TRIP HIGHLIGHT

9 Mount Errigal

Lowering Mt Errigal (752m) seemingly dares you to attempt the tough but beautiful climb to its pyramid-shaped peak. Watch the weather: it's a dangerous trek on misty or wet days, when visibility is minimal. The easiest path to the summit covers 5km and takes around three hours (two up, one back); The Dunlewey Lakeside Centre (p306) has full route details. Even if you don't climb, drink in this remarkably exposed, remote landscape of peaks, loughs and bogs.

🛏 p353

Eating & Sleeping

Enniscrone ❸

🛏 Ceol na Mara   B&B €€

(📞096-36351; www.ceol-na-mara.com; Enniscrone; s/d €50/80; 🅿🛜) With its crisp rooms and private path to the beach, this simple B&B makes for a calming sleep spot.

🛏 Seasons Lodge   B&B €€

(📞096-37122; www.seasonslodge.ie; s/d €65/110; 🅿🛜) Enniscrone's sunsets are legendary; enjoy them in the bright, spacious rooms of this charming guesthouse. Calm, neutral colour schemes and lots of thoughtful extras make it a wonderful place to stay.

Sligo Town ❹

🍴 Source   Irish €€

(📞071-914 7605; www.sourcesligo.ie; 1 John St; mains €15-20; 🕑9.30am-5pm Mon, to 9.30pm Tue-Sun) Source champions food traceability and local suppliers: portraits of its favourite fishermen, farmers and cheese producers grace the walls of the buzzy, ground-floor restaurant. In the more sedate **wine bar** (dishes €4-9; 🕑3-11pm Tue-Sun) tipples from the owners' French vineyard and Irish-style tapas are on offer.

Rossnowlagh ❺

🍴 Gaslight Restaurant   Irish €€

(📞071-985 1141; www.gaslight-rossnowlagh.com; mains €11-25) Set on the cliff top, Gaslight offers an extensive menu of well-cooked comfort food and spectacular views over the bay. The owners also run the **Ard na Mara** (📞071-985 1141; www.ardnamara-rossnowlagh.com; s/d €50/70; 🅿) guesthouse with its bright, sunny rooms.

🛏 Smugglers Creek   B&B €€

(📞071-985 2367; www.smugglerscreekinn.com; s/d €45/80; 🕑daily Apr-Sep, Thu-Sun Oct-Mar; 🅿) Perched on a hillside above the bay, this pub-restaurant-guesthouse is justifiably popular for its excellent food (mains €13 to €25) and sweeping views (the best are from the balcony of room 4). There's live music on summer weekends.

Donegal Town ❻

🍴 Old Castle Bar   Seafood €€

(📞074-972 1262; www.oldecastlebar.com; Castle St; mains €10-29; 🕑bar noon-8pm) This old-world boozer just off the central Diamond area serves upmarket pub classics such as venison pie, Donegal Bay oysters, Irish stew, seafood platters and good old bacon and cabbage. The restaurant opens at weekends and serves excellent seafood and steaks.

Killybegs ❼

🍴 22 Main Street   Seafood €€

(📞074-973 2876; www.22mainstreet.com; Main St; mains €13-25; 🕑dinner) Recently revamped, this Mediterranean-style bistro is undoubtedly the town's top table. Its speciality is excellent seafood, fresh off the trawlers, but the finest local meats sneak onto the menu too.

🛏 Tara Hotel   Hotel €€

(📞074-974 1700; www.tarahotel.ie; Main St; s/d from €65/80; 🅿@) This friendly, modern hotel overlooks the harbour. The rooms are minimalist but comfortable, while the gym, jacuzzi, sauna and steam room will soothe limbs tested by your adrenalin-fuelled adventures.

Mount Errigal ❾

🛏 Glen Heights   B&B €€

(📞074-956 0844; www.glenheightsbb.com; Dunlewey; s/d €50/70; 🅿) Your breakfast may go cold as you feast on breathtaking views of Lough Dunlewey, Mt Errigal and the Poisoned Glen. The rooms are simple but cosy, the bathrooms are pristine.

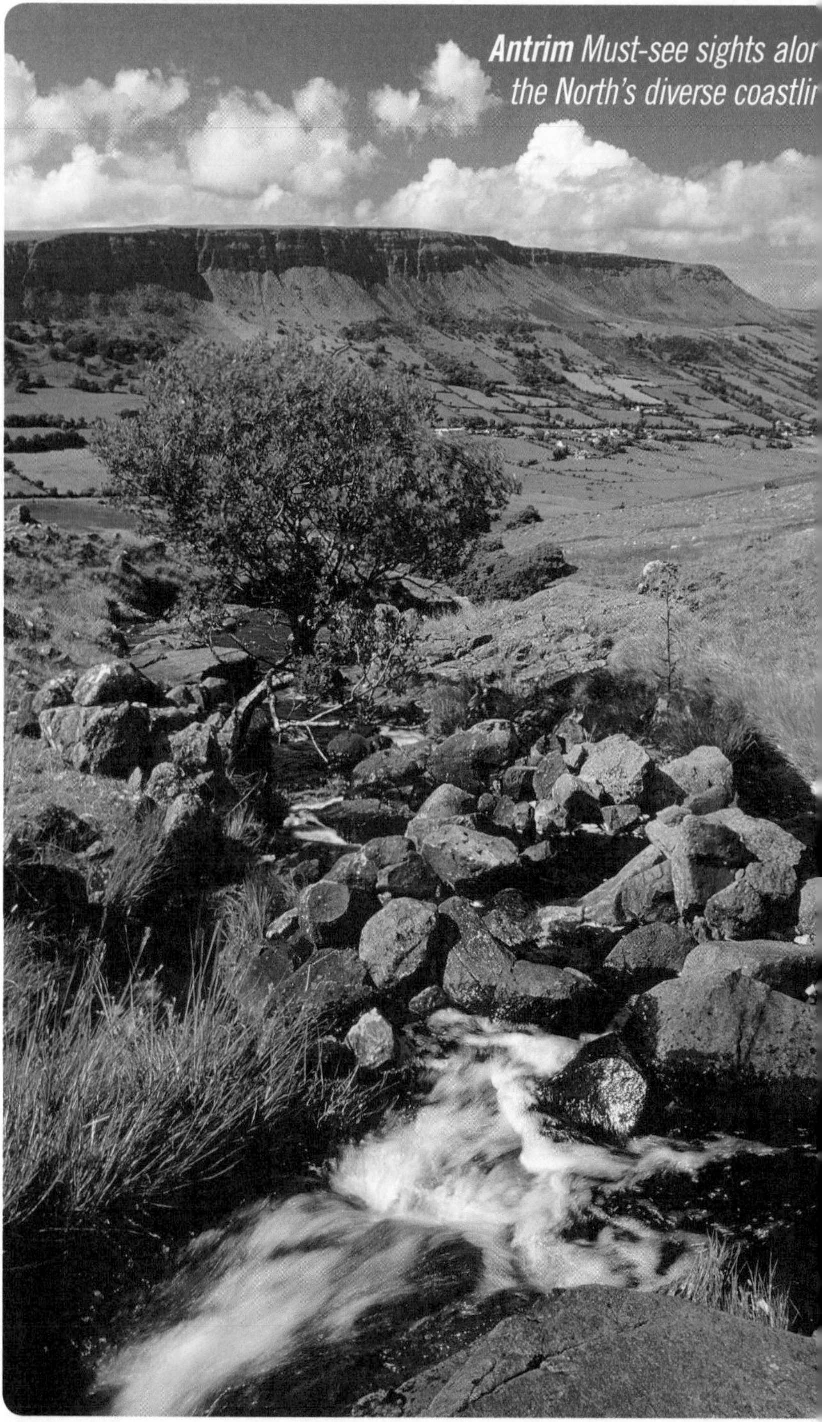
Antrim Must-see sights alor
the North's diverse coastlir

From Bangor to Derry

33

From seaside to mountainside, via ruined castles, stately homes, museums and the Giant's Causeway – this trip blends cracking coastal scenery with blockbuster historic sights.

215 km

Giant's Causeway
Clamber around on this extraordinary geological wonder

250 km

Downhill Demesne
Cliff-top gothic ruins with spectacular views

11 **8** **Portstewart** **Ballycastle**

Derry/
FINISH Londonderry

Glenariff Forest Park

75 km

Belfast
Witness the evolving peace process in this bustling city

4 **Bangor START**

2

Mt Stewart
Explore opulent interiors at this plush stately home

16 km

4 DAYS
330KM / 205 MILES

GREAT FOR...

BEST TIME TO GO

March to October brings better weather; avoid August to dodge holiday crowds.

ESSENTIAL PHOTO

The spectacular Giant's Causeway: your must-have north-coast snap.

BEST TWO DAYS

Stops 8 to 11 take in the Causeway, castles, ruins and golden sands.

355

33 From Bangor to Derry

This drive delivers a true taste of Ireland's gloriously diverse north: the must-see stops of the Giant's Causeway and Carrick-a-Rede; castles and historic homes at Mt Stewart, Hillsborough, Dunluce and Downhill; and superb scenery, from Slemish to sea-sprayed cliffs and immense sand dunes. While in Belfast and Derry/Londonderry, you'll experience two vibrant cities progressing beyond a painful past.

① Bangor

Start your journey through the north's scenic and historic highlights at a stop with a pop-culture twist. Pedal round the ornamental lake at Bangor's kitsch-rich **Pickie Family Fun Park** (Marine Gardens; per ride £1.50; ⊙10am-10pm Easter–Sep) in one of its famous swan-shaped boats. Then do a road trip warm-up by putting a track full of electric cars through their paces.

The Drive » Distance 16km. From Bangor's pastel-painted seafront terraces, pick up the A21 south to Newtownards. From there the A20 runs south towards Mt Stewart (initially signed Portaferry). Soon the vast, island-dotted Strangford Lough emerges to your right; the road clings to its winding shore.

TRIP HIGHLIGHT

② Mount Stewart House

Magnificent, 18th-century **Mount Stewart House** (www.ntni.org.uk; adult/child £7/3.50; ⊙house noon-6pm, garden 10am-6pm mid-Mar–Oct) is one of Northern Ireland's grandest stately homes. Lavish plasterwork combines with antiques and artworks that include a painting of the racehorse Hambletonian by George Stubbs. Garden highlights include griffin and mermaid statues on the Dodo Terrace, and the **Temple of the Winds** (⊙2-5pm Sun mid-Mar–Oct), a mock Gothic ruin with great views of the Strangford Lough.

The Drive » Distance 50km. Head north, back along the A20 beside scenic Strangford into Newtownards. There, take the A21 south through Comber. Soon, the B178 to Hillsborough cuts off to the right, across a

ATLANTIC
OCEAN

SCOTLAND

0 — 20 km
0 — 10 miles

Rathlin
Island

Ballintoy

**Giant's
Causeway** 8

**Carrick-a-Rede
Rope Bridge** 7

Ballycastle

Portrush
Portstewart 10 9 Bushmills

Downhill 11 **Dunluce
Castle**

**Downhill
Demesne** Coleraine

Armoy
Knocklayd
(514m)

Cushendun

North Channel

Ballymoney

29

Slievanorra
(511m)

Waterfoot

6 **Cushendall**

Limavady

Newtown
Crommelin

A43

Roe Valley
Country Park

A54

Garvagh

Clogh
Martinstown

**Glenariff
Forest
Park** Carnlough
Glenarm

ERRY/
ONDERRY

Dungiven

Kilrea

B94

Broughshane

A42

aghmore
(554m)

A6

Portglenone

Ballymena

**Slemish
Mountain** 5

Ballygally

Larne

Portmuck

n Mountains

Maghera

Gracehill

Kells

Draperstown

Randalstown

A26

ANTRIM

Ballyclare

Ballynure

Whitehead

Slieve
Gallion ▲
(528m)

Magherafelt

Antrim

Carrickfergus

Moneymore

M2

Newtownabbey

Belfast
Lough

A505

Coagh

eggan

Cookstown

Crumlin

Lough
Neagh

Bangor 1

Donaghadee

Millisle

p328

Belfast 4

A21

Newtownards

A2

neroy

Coalisland

Dunmurry

Comber

2 **Mount
Stewart
House**

Ballywalter

Dungannon

Lisburn

M1

B178

Lisbane

A20

allygawley

Moira

Saintfield

Strangford
Lough

Portaferry

Aughnacloy

Portadown

Lurgan
Craigavon

3 **Hillsborough**

A21

Ballynahinch

Strangford

ARMAGH

Dromore

DOWN

A1

---

lush landscape of fields, woods
and farms.

3 Hillsborough

Set in elegant
Hillsborough, the
rambling, late-Georgian
Hillsborough Castle
(www.nio.gov.uk; Main St;
guided tours adult/child
£6/3.50, grounds only £3/2;

**LINK
YOUR
TRIP**

29 **The North in a
Nutshell**

Head west to wild
Donegal for sandy shores,
live-music sessions and
a castaway island. Pick
it up at this trip's end:
Derry/Londonderry.

31 **Inishowen
Peninsula**

Drive north into a remote
headland boasting
exquisite scenery,
shipwrecks and white-
knuckle drives. Start in
Derry.

⊙10.30am-4pm Sat May, Jun & Aug) is the Queen's official residence in Northern Ireland. You'll see opulent state drawing and dining rooms, and the Lady Grey Room, where former UK prime minister Tony Blair and former US president George W Bush had talks on Iraq. Garden delights include yew and lime tree walks, an ice house and a lake.

✕ 🛏 p361

The Drive ➤ Distance 16km. Head north on the A1, then join the M1 for Belfast. Exit onto the A55/Outer Ring, then follow signs for Queens University, Botanic Gardens or your destination: Ulster Museum.

TRIP HIGHLIGHT

❹ Belfast

Bustling Belfast has big-city appeal. As well as taking our Stretch Your Legs walk (p328) through its former sectarian strongholds, drop by the **Ulster Museum** (www.nmni.com/um; Stranmillis Rd; admission free; ⊙10am-5pm Tue-Sun). Recently reopened after a major revamp, it's now one of the North's don't-miss attractions. Highlights of its beautifully designed displays are the Armada Room; Takabuti, a 2500-year-old Egyptian mummy; the Bann Disc; and the Snapshot of an Ancient Sea Floor. See also p29.

✕ p361

The Drive ➤ Distance 67km. Head into Belfast, passing the Grand Opera House (which was bombed by the IRA in the 1990s). Take the M2 north, then the A26 to Ballymena, then the A42 to Broughshane. There, turn right after James McNeil Hardware, following the hard-to-see sign to Slemish. Follow another sign, which points left almost immediately, before the mountain itself emerges, an immense, hump-topped plateau of rock.

❺ Slemish

Craggy Slemish (438m) is where Ireland's patron saint St Patrick is said to have tended goats. On St Patrick's Day, thousands make a pilgrimage to its summit. It's a steep but pleasant 30-minute climb that's rewarded with fine views.

The Drive ➤ Distance 32km. Head back to Broughshane then peel off right onto the B94 towards Clogh. Next take the A43 north towards Waterfoot. In time, the road suddenly rises, settlements thin out and you're in the glens: sweeping ridges of steep-sided hills. After a steep valley descent, emerge onto the coast to go north to Cushendall, parking beside its beach.

❻ Cushendall

From Cushendall's beach, walk 1km north, scrambling up the coast path to the picturesque ruins of **Layde Old Church**. Here views stretch as far as the Scottish coast. Founded by the Franciscans, Layde was used as a parish

church from the early 14th century. Today the picturesque ruins have grand memorials to the MacDonnells (earls of Antrim from 1620) in the graveyard, and an ancient, weathered ring-cross by the gate.

🛏 p361

The Drive ➤ Distance 25km. The A2 heads north, through pretty Cushendun (p367), before climbing steeply up to open heathland. At the holiday resort of Ballycastle, pick up the B15, which winds beside fields and windswept cliffs to the Carrick-a-Rede Rope Bridge.

❼ Carrick-a-Rede Rope Bridge

A wobbling bridge is an unusual spot to stretch your legs, but it's unforgettable none the less. The **Carrick-a-Rede Rope Bridge** (www.ntni.org.uk; Ballintoy; adult/child £5.60/2.90; ⊙10am-6pm Mar-May, Sep & Oct, to 7pm Jun-Aug) is a 20m-long, 1m-wide contraption of wire and planks that stretches 30m above rock-strewn water. It sways and bounces beneath your feet before you emerge onto a tiny island dotted with reminders of its past as a salmon fishery.

The Drive ➤ Distance 10km. Rejoin the B15, then the A2 before turning right onto the scenic B146, which clings to the coast, passing ruined Dunseverick Castle en route to the Giant's Causeway.

PATRICK HORTON/GETTY IMAGES ©

Belfast Bar with ornate glass, tile and wooden interior

TRIP HIGHLIGHT

8 Giant's Causeway

The **Giant's Causeway** (www.nationaltrust.org.uk; admission free; ☼dawn-dusk) is this coast's must-see sight: a remarkable, ragged ribbon of regular, closely packed, hexagonal stone columns that dips gently beneath the waves. The spectacular rock formation is Northern Ireland's only Unesco World Heritage site and is one of Ireland's most impressive and atmospheric landscape features. Car parks charge from £5 to £6 per stay.

The Drive ≫ Distance 8km. Head through Bushmills, with its historic distillery (p370) and great sleeping options (p361), onto the A2 to Portrush. Soon sea views flood in, then Dunluce Castle's ragged ruins spring suddenly into view. Be aware: the castle turn-off comes immediately afterwards, down a sloping track on the right.

9 Dunluce Castle

The atmospheric remains of **Dunluce Castle** (www.causewaycoastandglens.com; adult/child £4/2; ☼10am-6pm) cling to a dramatic basalt crag. Built between the 15th and 17th centuries, it was once the coast's

✓ TOP TIP:
GIANT'S CAUSEWAY

The causeway is stunning but it can get overwhelmed by sheer visitor numbers. If you can, visit midweek or out of season to experience it at its most evocative. Sunset in spring and autumn is the best time for photographs.

finest castle and the seat of the powerful MacDonnell family. A narrow bridge leads from the mainland courtyard across a dizzying gap to the main fortress, where you can roam the shells of buildings and listen to the sea pounding on the cliffs.

The Drive » Distance 6km. Taking the A2 towards Portrush, you're soon sandwiched between creamy cliffs and a huge golden beach far below. At Portrush, sand dunes dotted with golf courses take over; head for the central East (Curran) Strand car park.

⑩ Portrush

You can't leave the Antrim coast without a post-drive head clearance beside the sea. The East Strand car park borders the 3km Curran Strand, a dune-backed golden ribbon of sand that makes for a glorious walk. Or make for nearby **Troggs Surf School** (☎07748 257717; www.troggssurfshop.co.uk;

East Strand Car Park; 2hr lessons £25; ⊙10am-6pm). It runs lessons (bookings advised) and hires out bodyboards/surfboards (per day £5/10) and wetsuits (per day £7).

✖ ⏚ p361

The Drive » Distance 24km. The A2 heads west, passing through seaside Portstewart and shop-packed Coleraine. Next the cupola of Downhill Demesne's Mussenden Temple eases into the windscreen. Go past the Bishop's Gate entrance, turning off into the Lion's Gate.

TRIP HIGHLIGHT

⑪ Downhill Demesne

In 1774 the eccentric Bishop of Derry built himself a palatial, cliff-top home, **Downhill Demesne** (www.ntni.org.uk; adult/child £4.50/2.25, parking £4; ⊙temple 10am-5pm Apr-Sep, grounds dawn-dusk year-round). It burnt down in 1851, was rebuilt in 1876, and was finally abandoned after WWII. Today it features follies

(ornamental buildings), mausoleums and a giant, ruined house. Trails lead past a dovecote onto a grassy headland and the elegant **Mussenden Temple**. From inside, the cliff-edge views are extraordinary, from Portrush (where you strolled on the sand) round to the shores of Lough Foyle (where you're headed).

The Drive » Distance 41km. The A2 continues west, through the fertile lowlands that frame Lough Foyle, and onto the city of Derry.

⑫ Derry/Londonderry

Northern Ireland's second city surprises some with its riverside setting and impressive, 17th-century walls. The best way to explore them, and the city's inspiring progress beyond sectarian violence, is on our Stretch Your Legs walk (p362). En route, make sure you drop into **St Columb's Cathedral** (www.stcolumbscathedral. org; London St; ⊙9am-5pm Mon-Sat). This stately church was completed in 1633, making it Derry's oldest building. In the porch, look for the hollow mortar shell fired into the churchyard during the Great Siege of 1688; inside the shell were the terms of a surrender that never came.

✖ ⏚ p361

DERRY OR LONDONDERRY?

Derry/Londonderry is a town with two names. Nationalists/Republicans (mostly Catholics who want the north to be part of the Irish Republic) use Derry, Unionists/Loyalists (mostly Protestants who want to preserve the union with Britain) use Londonderry, which is still the city's official name. Northern Ireland road signs point to Londonderry, while Republic road signs point to Derry – as you drive you might well see the 'London' part of the name defaced. Politics aside, the city's often shortened to Derry in everyday speech.

Eating & Sleeping

Hillsborough ❸

✗ Plough Inn   Bistro ££
(☏028-9268 2985; www.theploughhillsborough.
co.uk; 3 The Square; mains bar £6-12, restaurant
£13-23; ☺bar food noon-2.30pm, restaurant
6-9.30pm) This fine old pub, with a dim,
mazelike interior full of wood-panelled nooks
and crannies, has been offering 'beer and
banter' since 1758. Gourmet bar lunches
include tempura of pheasant, and wild duck with
sesame, ginger and Asian leaves.

🛏 Fortwilliam   B&B ££
(☏028-9268 2255; www.fortwilliamcountry
house.com; 210 Ballynahinch Rd; s/d £50/70;
P @ �) Fortwilliam's luxurious rooms
come replete with vintage wallpaper, antique
wardrobes and garden views. Home-laid eggs
and home-baked bread grace the breakfast
table. Book well in advance.

Belfast ❹

✗ Café Conor   Cafe, Bistro ££
(www.cafeconor.com; 11A Stranmillis Rd; mains
£9-12; ☺9am-11pm) Directly opposite the
Ulster Museum, this laid-back bistro offers a
range of pastas, salads, burgers and stir-fries.
Endearingly, the breakfast menu (think waffles
with bacon and maple syrup) is served till 5pm.

Cushendall ❻

🛏 Village   B&B ££
(☏028-2177 2366; www.thevillagebandb.com;
18 Mill St; s/d £38/60; ☺Apr-Sep; P) Bang
in the middle of town, the Village offers three
spotless rooms with private bathrooms and
huge hearty breakfasts. And it's just across the
road from McCollams, the best local pub for
traditional music.

Bushmills

🛏 Bushmills Inn   Hotel £££
(☏028-2073 3000; www.bushmillsinn.com;
9 Dunluce Rd; s/d from £158/178, ste £298;
P @ ☰) This is one of Northern Ireland's most
atmospheric hotels. Expect an old coaching inn
with peat fires, gas lamps, a round tower and a
secret library.

Portrush ❿

✗ 55 Degrees North   International ££
(☏028-7082 2811; www.55-north.com;
1 Causeway St; mains £10-18; ☺5-9pm Mon-Sat,
to 8.30pm Sun) One not to miss: this is one of
the area's most stylish restaurants. A wall of
floor-to-ceiling windows offers a spectacular
panorama of sand and sea, while excellent food
concentrates on clean, simple flavours and
unfussy presentation.

🛏 Clarmont   B&B ££
(☏028-7082 2397; www.clarmont.com; 10
Landsdowne Cres; d £70-90) With its polished
pine floors and period fireplaces, the Clarmont
tastefully mixes Victorian and modern styles. Ask
for a room with a bay window overlooking the sea.

Derry ⓬

✗ Halo Pantry & Grill   International ££
(☏028-7127 1567; 5 Market St; mains lunch
£6-10, dinner £9-22; ☺pantry noon-10pm, grill
5-10pm) This arty converted shirt factory dishes
up light meals and snacks (including superb
homemade lasagne) in the Pantry, and more
formal dinners (from steak to seafood) in the
upstairs Grill. Bookings advised.

🛏 Saddler's House   B&B ££
(☏028-7126 9691; www.thesaddlershouse.
com; 36 Great James St; s £35-50, d £50-60;
@ ☰) Centrally located within a five-minute
walk of the city walls, this friendly B&B is set in
a gorgeous Victorian town house, where you'll
enjoy a huge breakfast in the family kitchen.

STRETCH YOUR LEGS
DERRY

Start/Finish Butcher's Gate, City Walls

Distance 3km

Duration 3 hours

In winding along 17th-century city walls and past former sectarian battlegrounds, this walk reveals a vivid history, startling political murals and the inspiring steps being taken towards peace.

Take this walk on Trips

28 29 31 33

Butcher's Gate

Derry/Londonderry's immense **city walls** (www.derryswalls.com) were built in 1619 to secure the settlement of immigrant Protestants. In 1688 they helped residents repel a 105-day siege by Catholic forces. The Protestants' slogan, 'No Surrender', remains a Loyalist battle cry today.

The Walk » Climb the gateside steps, walking downhill along the top of the walls, high above the streets, to the first corner.

Magazine Gate

The **Tower Museum** (Union Hall Pl; adult/child £4.20/2.65; ⊙10am-5pm Tue-Sat) rears up to the right. On the left, the red-brick, neo-Gothic **Guildhall** (Guildhall Sq; ⊙9am-5pm Mon-Fri) was formerly home to the Londonderry Corporation, which institutionalised anti-Catholic discrimination over housing and jobs.

The Walk » After the next corner, the wall-top walk climbs steeply, passing bastions occupied by huge cannons. As you near the crest of the rise, look down left over the wall.

Fountain Housing Estate

You're now looking onto the last significant Protestant community on the River Foyle's western bank. Immediately obvious is the massive slogan: 'West Bank Loyalists Still Under Siege. No Surrender'. Looking closer reveals kerb-stones and lamp posts painted in Unionist (British) red, white and blue.

The Walk » After more bastions and massive cannons, the walls widen, revealing a plinth that's been empty since the IRA blew up a statue of one of Derry's siege-era governors. Go down the Butcher's Gate steps, through the arch, into Waterloo St.

Peadar O'Donnell's

Time to refuel. **Peadar O'Donnell's** (63 Waterloo St) is done up as a typical Irish pub-cum-grocer. It's alive with traditional music on weekend afternoons (and every night) too.

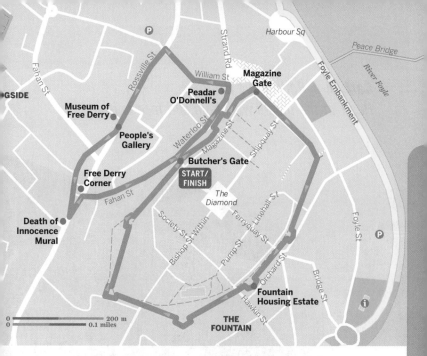

The Walk » William St cuts left to Rossville St, a junction dubbed Agro Corner, where security forces and residents of the Catholic Bogside housing estate routinely clashed. Some 120m on, the Bloody Sunday Memorial commemorates where British soldiers shot dead 13 unarmed demonstrators in 1972.

People's Gallery

The huge murals you can now see are part of the People's Gallery and were painted by three Bogsiders who lived through the Troubles. Ahead is a huge monochrome **Civil Rights** mural, behind you a rioter and armoured car clash in **Saturday Matinee**.

The Walk » Cut between these murals, into the Museum of Free Derry.

Museum of Free Derry

This **museum** (www.museumoffreederry. org; 55-61 Glenfada Park; adult/child £3/2; ⏰9.30am-4.30pm Mon-Fri year-round, plus 1-4pm Sat Apr-Sep) chronicles the Bogside's history, the Civil Rights Movement and the events of Bloody Sunday.

The Walk » Pass more murals: the sledgehammer drama of *Operation Motorman; Bloody Sunday*, where a priest tries to shepherd one of the dying to safety; and a boy in a gas mask (*Petrol Bomber*). Look to the left.

Free Derry Corner

The roundabout contains a house remnant bearing the words 'You Are Now Entering Free Derry'. This stems from the late 1960s, when Bogsiders declared themselves independent of the authorities and barricaded the streets.

The Walk » Continue down Rossville St, looking back up to the gable ends to your right.

Death of Innocence Mural

This mural depicts 14-year-old Annette McGavigan, who was killed in crossfire between the IRA and the British Army in 1971. The downward-pointing, broken rifle symbolises the failure of violence; the butterfly symbolises the peace process.

The Walk » From Free Derry Corner, head up Fahan St, back to Butcher's Gate.

Carrick-a-Rede Rope Bridge
Heart-in-the-mouth walk from cliff face to island

The Antrim Coast

34

This trip encompasses Antrim's big sights (causeway, rope bridge, distillery) and some surprises: a hideaway island, a gorgeous glen and a cliff-top walk where you'll hardly see another soul.

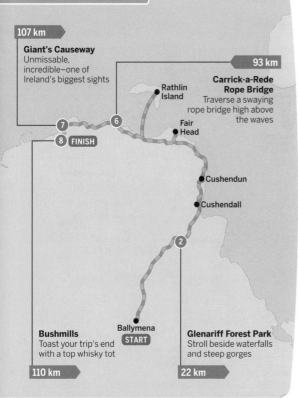

TRIP HIGHLIGHTS

107 km

Giant's Causeway
Unmissable, incredible—one of Ireland's biggest sights

93 km

Carrick-a-Rede Rope Bridge
Traverse a swaying rope bridge high above the waves

Rathlin Island

Fair Head

7

8 FINISH

6

Cushendun

Cushendall

2

Bushmills
Toast your trip's end with a top whisky tot

Ballymena
START

110 km

Glenariff Forest Park
Stroll beside waterfalls and steep gorges

22 km

---

3 DAYS
110KM / 68 MILES

GREAT FOR...

BEST TIME TO GO
Avoiding August means less-crowded sights; Easter to July and September should mean brighter days.

 ESSENTIAL PHOTO
You standing on the Giant's Causeway's basalt columns.

✓ **BEST FOR SOLITUDE**
Stops 4 and 5 see you well away from the crowds.

34 The Antrim Coast

Many visitors belt around the Antrim coast, cramming the big-name sights into a day. But this trip can be taken slowly. The reward? In-depth explorations of those big-name attractions, but also the chance to marvel at less-obvious sights. From a thought-provoking museum to alpine-esque trails; from white-knuckle headland drives to overnighting on an island – you'll discover an Antrim many people miss.

1 Ballymena

Start exploring the Antrim coast with the superb potted history offered by the **Braid Museum** (www.thebraid. com; 1-29 Bridge St; admission free; ◷10am-5pm Mon-Fri, to 4pm Sat). Here interactive, audiovisual displays evoke a rich history stretching from the county's prehistoric inhabitants to the present. Prepare for stories of Irish chiefs, the mass settlement of Scottish and English Protestants (called

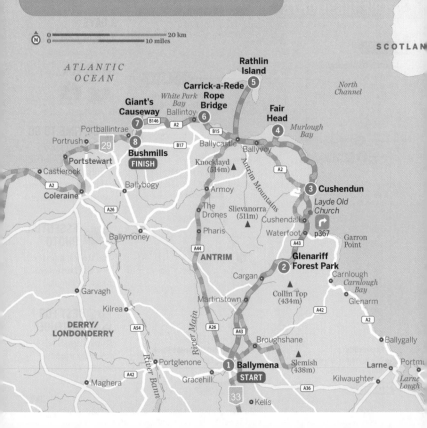

Plantation) and the historic events behind the island's political banners – both Unionist/Loyalist (mostly Protestants who want to preserve the union with Britain) and Nationalist/Republican (mostly Catholics who want the north to be part of the Irish Republic). The *Modern Times* film montage is another highlight, encompassing the *Titanic*, WWI, the Depression, Civil Rights, footballer George Best and former US president Bill Clinton.

The Drive » Distance 23km. As the A43 heads north towards Waterfoot, the Antrim Mountains rise closer. Suddenly, there's a landscape shift: houses peter away, the road climbs and trees thin out, revealing rock ridges and plunging valleys. Turn right, into Glenariff Forest Park, onto a track that winds between

LINK YOUR TRIP

29 The North in a Nutshell

Head west to Donegal's wild, beach-fringed coast. Begin where this trip ends: Bushmills.

33 From Bangor to Derry

Take in seaside fun, history-rich Belfast and two stately homes. Start 60km southeast of Ballymena, at Bangor.

DETOUR: LAYDE OLD CHURCH

Start: ② Glenariff Forest Park

In a coast full of big sights it's worth hunting out some hidden delights. In central Cushendall, turn right to park beside its beach. Then walk 1km north up the coast path, enjoying views across to the Scottish coast. The path leads to Layde Old Church. Founded by the Franciscans, it was in use from the early 14th century until 1790. The graveyard features grand memorials to the MacDonnells (earls of Antrim from 1620), and an ancient, weathered ring-cross, much older than the 19th-century inscription on its shaft.

dense conifers. The trees clear abruptly, exposing plummeting hills.

TRIP HIGHLIGHT

② Glenariff Forest Park

The pick of the trails at Glenariff Forest Park is the Red Waterfall Walk. From the car park (surely one of the north's most scenic; parking £4.50), this 3km, waymarked, circular trail goes beside the Glenariff River and past the Ess-na-Larach and Ess-na-Crub waterfalls, along paths cut into the sheer gorge sides, up stairways and along boardwalks set on stilts on the water. The forest is a mix of native species (look out for oak, elm and hazel) and introduced trees, notably pine and Douglas fir. You've a fair chance of spotting red squirrels, hen harriers and Irish hares darting among the trees. The tea house beside the car park

offers the chance to refuel, and more stunning gorge views.

✗ p371

The Drive » Distance 17km. Continue on the A43, descending steeply via hairpin bends into a wide, U-shaped glacial valley with suddenly revealed sea views. Follow the A2 north along the shore, through the busy resort of Cushendall to Cushendun's main car park.

③ Cushendun

To best explore pretty Cushendun, head across the road to the beach. Follow the sandy shore to the right skirting the front of the Cushendun Hotel. After about 800m you come to a pocket-sized, pebbly beach, where the sea has sculpted minicaves out of porous-looking rock. Head back along the seafront and over the bridge, this time going straight on to the village itself. Its central

GARETH MCCORMACK/GETTY IMAGES ©

cluster of Cornish-style cottages was built between 1912 and 1925, and designed by Clough Williams-Ellis, the architect of Portmeirion in north Wales. They were commissioned by Lord Cushendun and his Cornish wife Maud. Her grave in the village churchyard bears the inscription 'To a Cornish woman who loved the Glens and their people'.

✗ ⊨ p371

The Drive ≫ Distance 16km. Pick up the (signed) Torr Head Scenic Route, a heart-in-the-mouth route of winding first-gear gradients that clings to increasingly stark cliffs. Ignore the Torr Head turn-off, and instead peel off right to Murlough Bay, passing a National Trust welcome sign before reaching a car park 300m further on.

------

4 Fair Head

By now the 180m-high basalt cliffs of Fair Head rear to your left. Walk towards them, following a 1km moderate cliff-top path (waymarked by yellow circles) to the top. Once there, look out for rock climbers (this is one of the region's best climbing sites)

Fair Head The view to Rathlin Island

and the spectacular gully bridged by a fallen rock, called Grey Man's Path. A stunning panorama sweeps from Rathlin Island in the west to Scotland's Mull of Kintyre in the east. Keep an eye out, too, for whales and dolphins swimming offshore.

The Drive » Distance 20km. Heading west on the A2, the landscape becomes steadily less rugged. Soon golf courses replace sheep-grazed hills and sandy beaches replace that precipitous shore. At the cheery resort of Ballycastle, park in a harbourside, free, long-stay bay (some have time limits, so double-check).

- - - - - - - - - - -

⑤ Rathlin Island

Time to leave the car behind and overnight on **Rathlin Island** (Reachlainn; www.rathlincommunity. org), a 6.5km by 4km windswept slab of rock, 6km offshore. From mid-April to August it's home to hundreds of seals and thousands of nesting seabirds; the Royal Society for the Protection of Birds' **West Light Viewpoint** (www.rspb.org. uk; admission free; ⏰11am-3pm Apr-Aug) provides extraordinary views of sea stacks thick with guillemots, kittiwakes, razorbills and puffins.

Scottish hero Robert the Bruce hid here in 1306 after being defeated by the English. Inspired by a spider's determined web-spinning, he subsequently triumphed at Bannockburn. His cave is beneath the East Lighthouse.

Between April and September, 10 **ferries** (☏028-2076 9299; www. rathlinballycastleferry.com; adult/child return £11.20/5.60) a day make the 25- to 45-minute crossing (five daily from October to March). Book in advance.

🛏 p371

The Drive ⟫ Distance 19km. From the Rathlin Island ferry terminal, the B15 climbs north towards Ballintoy. As Rathlin Island recedes behind you, a coastal plateau of rugged heathland unfurls. The plateau runs along then steeply down to the Carrick-a-Rede Rope Bridge turn on the right.

TRIP HIGHLIGHT

6 Carrick-a-Rede Rope Bridge

The **Carrick-a-Rede Rope Bridge** (www.ntni. org.uk; Ballintoy; adult/child £5.60/2.90; ⏰10am-7pm Jun-Aug, to 6pm Mar-May, Sep & Oct) is a 20m-long, 1m-wide assemblage of wire rope and planks that sways 30m above rock-strewn water. It spans a chasm between cliffs and a tiny island that has sustained

a salmon fishery for centuries; fishermen use the bridge to stretch their nets out from the island's tip to intercept migrating salmon. The fishermen still put the bridge up every spring as they have done for the last 200 years.

It's a heart-in-the-mouth walk across the bridge. Once on the island, the panorama includes your overnight stop, Rathlin Island, and the site of your walk the day before: the sheer cliffs of Fair Head.

The Drive ⟫ Distance 11km. Heading west, the B15 then the A2 deliver more bursts of rugged coastal driving – the golden beach unfurling below is White Park Bay. Turn onto the B146, getting even closer to the shore. This road glides past ruined Dunseverick Castle en route to the coast's big draw: the Giant's Causeway.

TRIP HIGHLIGHT

7 Giant's Causeway

When you first see it you'll understand why the ancients believed the **causeway** (www.national trust.org.uk; ⏰dawn-dusk) couldn't be a natural feature. The spectacular expanse of regular, closely packed, hexagonal stone columns dipping gently beneath the waves looks for all the world like the handiwork of giants. It's a sloping 1km walk to the causeway. Once you've clambered around on the geometric rocks, don't

miss the stack of pipelike basalt columns known as the **Organ** – access them on the lower coastal path that heads towards the **Amphitheatre Viewpoint** at Port Reostan.

Visiting the causeway itself is free, but the main, often overcrowded, National Trust car park charges £6 per car. Overflow car parks ring the attraction.

The Drive ⟫ Rejoin the A2 for a 3km uphill drive inland to the small town of Bushmills. Signs point towards the world-famous distillery on its western edge.

TRIP HIGHLIGHT

8 Bushmills

What better way to finish a trip full of the flavour of the Antrim coast than with a true taste of Ireland – Bushmills Irish Whiskey. **Old Bushmills Distillery** (www.bushmills. com; Distillery Rd; adult/child £6/3; ⏰9.15am-5pm Mon-Sat year-round, plus 11am-5pm Sun Jul-Sep, noon-5.30pm Sun Mar-Jun & Oct) is the world's oldest legal distillery. During ageing, the alcohol content drops from around 60% to 40%; the spirit lost through evaporation is known as 'the angels' share'. A free sample follows the tour, and four lucky souls get a testing session comparing Bushmills with other brands (if you fancy it, make sure you're first to volunteer).

🍴 🛏 p371

Eating & Sleeping

Glenariff Forest Park ②

✕ Laragh Lodge   Irish ££

(☎028-2175 8221; 120 Glen Rd; mains £10-15; ⏰11am-9pm, food noon-9pm) A renovated Victorian tourist lodge with assorted bric-a-brac dangling from the rafters, the Laragh dates from 1890 and serves hearty pub-grub-style meals: beef-and-Guinness pie, fish and chips, sausage and mash. It's signed off the A43, 3km northeast of the main park entrance.

Cushendun ③

✕ Mary McBride's   Pub £

(2 Main St; mains £6-10; ⏰12.30-8pm Apr-Sep, to 7pm Oct-Mar) The original bar here is the smallest in Ireland (2.7m by 1.5m). The pub grub is good and there's Guinness on tap, as well as occasional live music on weekends.

⊨ Cloneymore House   B&B ££

(☎028-2176 1443; ann.cloneymore@btinternet. com; 103 Knocknacarry Rd; s/d £40/50; P 🛜) A traditional family B&B, Cloneymore has three spacious and spotless rooms named after Irish and Scottish islands – Aran is the biggest. It's on the B92 road, 500m southwest of Cushendun.

⊨ Villa Farmhouse   B&B ££

(☎028-2176 1252; www.thevillafarmhouse. com; 185 Torr Rd; s/d from £35/60; P @) This lovely old whitewashed farmhouse is set on a hillside, 1km north of the village, with great views over the sea and down to Cushendun Bay. The owner is an expert chef and breakfast will be a highlight of your stay (featuring arguably the best scrambled eggs in Northern Ireland). Evening meals by arrangement.

Rathlin Island ⑤

⊨ Manor House   B&B ££

(☎028-2076 3964; www.rathlinmanorhouse. co.uk; Church Quarter; s/d £42/72) Restored and run by the National Trust, the 18th-century Manor House, on the north side of the harbour, is the island's best place to stay. All rooms have sea views. The **restaurant** (mains £12-18, lobster £27; ⏰10.45am-5.30pm Mon, to 11pm Wed-Sun May-Sep) is open to nonresidents (bookings necessary).

⊨ Coolnagrock   B&B ££

(☎028-2076 3983; Coolnagrock; s/d £35/60) This well-appointed guesthouse is in the eastern part of the island, with great views across the sea to Kintyre. It's a 15-minute walk from the ferry, but you can arrange for the owner to pick you up.

Bushmills ⑧

✕ Bushmills Inn   Irish ££

(www.bushmillsinn.com; 9 Dunluce Rd; mains £11-22; ⏰12.30-9pm) The Bushmills Inn's excellent restaurant has intimate wooden booths set in the old 17th-century stables. It specialises in fresh Ulster produce and serves everything from sandwiches to full à-la-carte dinners.

⊨ Bushmills Inn   Hotel £££

(☎028-2073 3000; www.bushmillsinn.com; 9 Dunluce Rd; s/d from £158/178, ste £298; P @ 🛜) One of Northern Ireland's most atmospheric hotels, the Bushmills is an old coaching inn complete with peat fires, gas lamps and a round tower with a secret library. The luxury bedrooms are all modern, in the Mill House complex next door.

ROAD TRIP ESSENTIALS

Ireland Driving Guide

The motorway system makes for easy travelling between major towns, but the spidery network of secondary and tertiary roads makes for the most scenic driving.

DRIVING LICENCE & DOCUMENTS

EU licences are treated like Irish ones. Holders of non-EU licences from countries other than the US or Canada should obtain an International Driving Permit (IDP) from their home automobile association.

You must carry your driving licence at all times.

INSURANCE

All cars on public roads must be insured. Most hire companies quote basic insurance in their initial quote.

If you are bringing your own vehicle, check that your insurance will cover you in Ireland. When driving your own car, you'll need a minimum insurance known as third-party insurance.

HIRING A CAR

Compared with many countries (especially the USA), hire rates are expensive in Ireland; you should expect to pay around €250 a week for a small car (unlimited mileage), but rates go up at busy times and drop off in quieter seasons. he main players:

Avis (www.avis.ie)

Budget (www.budget.ie)

Europcar (www.europcar.ie)

Hertz (www.hertz.ie)

Sixt (www.sixt.ie)

Thrifty (www.thrifty.ie)

Driving Fast Facts

- ➡ **Right or left?** Drive on the left
- ➡ **Manual or automatic?** Manual
- ➡ **Legal driving age** 18
- ➡ **Top speed limit** 120km/h (motorways; 70mph in Northern Ireland)
- ➡ **Best radio station** Newstalk 106-108

The major car-hire companies have different web pages on their websites for different countries, so the price of a car in Ireland can differ from the same car's price in the USA or Australia. You have to surf a lot of sites to get the best deals. **Nova Car Hire** (www.novacarhire.com) acts as an agent for Alamo, Budget, European and National, and offers greatly discounted rates.

Other tips:

➡ Most cars are manual; automatic cars are available, but they're more expensive to hire.

➡ If you're travelling from the Republic into Northern Ireland, it's important to be sure that your insurance covers journeys to the North.

➡ The majority of hire companies won't rent you a car if you're under 23 and haven't had a valid driving licence for at least a year.

➡ Some companies in the Republic won't rent to you if you're aged 74 or over; there's no upper age limit in the North.

➡ Motorbikes and mopeds are not available for hire in Ireland.

Local Expert: Driving Tips

Conor Faughnan, Director of Consumer Affairs with the Automobile Association, shares his tips for hassle-free driving in Ireland:

➡ The motorway network is excellent, but there aren't nearly enough rest areas so check that you have a full tank of fuel before setting off. Off the motorway network there is a good supply of service stations, often open 24 hours, but less so in more remote areas.

➡ The real driving fun is on Ireland's network of secondary roads, where road conditions vary – make sure you're equipped with a good map along with your sat-nav, and beware of potholes, poor road surfaces and corners obscured by protruding hedges! You may also encounter farm machinery and even livestock on rural roads.

➡ Although it rarely snows, winter conditions can be testing (particularly with ice).

➡ A driver may flash their hazard lights once or twice as an informal way to say 'thank you' for any kind of road courtesy extended to them.

BRINGING YOUR OWN VEHICLE

It's easy to take your own vehicle to Ireland and there are no specific procedures involved, but you should carry a vehicle registration document as proof that it's yours.

MAPS

You'll need a good road map; we recommend getting one even if you have a sat-nav system.

Michelin's 1:400,000-scale Ireland map (No 923) is a decent single sheet map, with clear cartography and most of the island's scenic roads marked. The four maps – North, South, East and West – that make up the Ordnance Survey Holiday map series at 1:250,000 scale are useful if you want more detail. Collins also publishes a range of maps covering Ireland.

The Ordnance Survey Discovery series covers the whole island in 89 maps at a scale of 1:50,000.

These are all available at the **National Map Centre** (📞01-476 0471; www.mapcentre.ie; 34 Aungier St, Dublin), through www.osi.ie and at many bookshops around Ireland.

ROADS & CONDITIONS

Irish road types and conditions vary wildly. The road network is divided into the following categories:

Regional Roads Indicated by an R and (usually) three numbers on a white background,

these are the secondary and tertiary roads that make up the bulk of the road network, generally splintering off larger roads to access even the smallest hamlet. Blind corners, potholes and a width barely enough for two cars are the price for some of the most scenic routes in all of Ireland; whatever you do, go slow. In Northern Ireland, these are classified as B-roads.

National Roads Indicated by an N and two numbers against a green background, these were, until the construction of the motorway network, the primary roads in Ireland. They link most towns and are usually single lane in either direction, widening occasionally to double lane (usually on uphill stretches to allow for the overtaking of slower vehicles). In Northern Ireland, these are classified as A-roads.

Motorways Indicated by an M and a single digit against a blue background, the network is limited to the major routes and towns. Most motorways are partially tolled. Motorways in Northern Ireland are not tolled.

ROAD RULES

A copy of Ireland's road rules is available from tourist offices. Following are the most basic rules:

➡ Drive on the left, overtake to the right.

➡ Safety belts must be worn by the driver and all passengers.

- ➡ Children aged under 12 aren't allowed to sit on the front seats.
- ➡ Motorcyclists and their passengers must wear helmets.
- ➡ When entering a roundabout, give way to the right.
- ➡ Speed limits are 120km/h on motorways (70mph in Northern Ireland), 100km/h on national roads (60mph in Northern Ireland), 80km/h on regional and local roads (60mph in Northern Ireland) and 50km/h (30mph in the North) or as signposted in towns.
- ➡ The legal alcohol limit is 80mg of alcohol per 100ml of blood or 35mg on the breath (roughly two units of alcohol per day for a man and one for a woman).

PARKING

All big towns and cities have covered short-stay car parks that are conveniently signposted.

- ➡ On-street parking is usually by 'pay and display' tickets available from on-street machines or disc parking (discs, which rotate to display the time you park your car, are available from newsagencies). Costs range from €1.50 to €5 per hour; all-day parking in a car park will cost around €26.
- ➡ Yellow lines (single or double) along the edge of the road indicate restrictions. You can usually park on single yellow lines between 7pm and 8am, while double yellow lines means no parking at any time. Always look for the nearby sign that spells out when you can and cannot park.
- ➡ In Dublin, Cork and Galway, clamping is rigorously enforced; it'll cost you €85 to have the yellow beast removed. In Northern Ireland, the fee is £100 for removal.

FUEL

The majority of vehicles operate on unleaded petrol; the rest (including many hire cars) run on diesel.

Cost In the Republic, petrol costs range from €1.60 to €1.80 per litre, with diesel usually €0.10 cheaper. Fuel is marginally more expensive in

Road Distances (Km)

	Athlone	Belfast	Cork	Derry	Donegal	Dublin	Galway	Kilkenny	Killarney	Limerick	Rosslare Harbour	Shannon Airport	Sligo	Waterford
Belfast	227													
Cork	219	424												
Derry	209	117	428											
Donegal	183	180	402	69										
Dublin	127	167	256	237	233									
Galway	93	306	209	272	204	212								
Kilkenny	116	284	148	335	309	114	172							
Killarney	232	436	87	441	407	304	193	198						
Limerick	121	323	105	328	296	193	104	113	111					
Rosslare Harbour	201	330	208	397	391	153	274	98	275	211				
Shannon Airport	133	346	128	351	282	218	93	135	135	25	234			
Sligo	117	206	336	135	66	214	138	245	343	232	325	218		
Waterford	164	333	126	383	357	163	220	48	193	129	82	152	293	
Wexford	184	309	187	378	372	135	253	80	254	190	19	213	307	61

Driving Problem-Buster

What should I do if my car breaks down? Call the service number of your car-hire company and a local garage will be contacted. If you're bringing your own car, it's a good idea to join the Automobile Association Ireland, which covers the whole country, or, in Northern Ireland, the Royal Automobile Club (RAC), which can be called to breakdowns any time.

What if I have an accident? Hire cars usually have a leaflet in the glovebox about what to do in case of an accident. Exchange basic information with the other party (name, insurance details, driver's licence number, company details if the car's a rental). No discussion of liability needs to take place at the scene. It's a good idea to photograph the scene of the accident, noting key details (damage sustained, car positions on the road, any skid markings). Call the police (☎999) if required.

What should I do if I get stopped by police? Always remain calm and polite: police are generally courteous and helpful. They will want to see your passport (or valid form of ID), licence and proof of insurance. In the Republic, breath testing is mandatory if asked.

What if I can't find anywhere to stay? If you're travelling during the summer months, always book your accommodation in advance. If you're stuck, call the local tourist office's accommodation hotline.

How do I pay for tollways? Tolls are paid by putting cash in the bucket as you pass.

Dublin. In Northern Ireland, petrol costs between £1.25 and £1.35 per litre, but diesel is more expensive (between £1.35 and £1.45 per litre).

Service Stations These are ubiquitous on all national roads, usually on the outskirts of towns. They're increasingly harder to find in cities, and the motorway network has only three or four spread across the entire system. In the North, the big supermarket chains have gotten into the fuel business, so you can fill your car as you shop. There are service stations along the North's motorway network.

SAFETY

Although driving in Ireland is a relatively pain-free experience, hire cars and cars with foreign registrations can be targeted by thieves looking to clean them of their contents. Don't leave any valuables, including bags and suitcases, on display. Overnight parking is safest in covered car parks.

RADIO

The Irish love radio – up to 85% of the population listens in on any given day. Following are the national radio stations:

Newstalk 106-108 (106-108FM) News, current affairs and lifestyle.

RTE Radio 1 (88.2-90FM) Mostly news and discussion.

Ireland Playlist

Virtually every parish and hamlet has a song about it. Here are our favourites:

Carrickfergus Traditional Irish folk song

Galway Girl Steve Earle

Raglan Road Luke Kelly

Running to Stand Still U2

The Fields of Athenry Paddy Reilly

The Town I Loved So Well The Dubliners

RTE Radio 2 (90.4-92.2FM) Lifestyle and music.
RTE Lyric FM (96-99FM) Classical music.
Today FM (100-102FM) Music, chat and news.

Regional or local radio is also very popular, with 25 independent local radio stations available, depending on your location.

In Northern Ireland, the BBC rules supreme, with BBC Radio Ulster (92.7-95.4FM) flying the local flag in addition to the four main BBC stations.

ROAD TRIP WEBSITES

Automobile Associations

Automobile Association (AA; www.aa ireland.ie) Roadside assistance and driving tips.

Royal Automobile Club (RAC; www.rac. co.uk) Roadside assistance, route planner and accommodation.

Road Rules

Road Safety Authority (www.rotr.ie) Rules, tips and information in case of accident.

Conditions & Traffic

AA Roadwatch (www.aaireland.ie) Up-to-date traffic info.
Traffic Watch Northern Ireland (www.trafficwatchni.com) Traffic news, maps and live cameras.

Maps

AA Route Planner (www.aaireland.ie) Map your route for the whole island.

Ireland Travel Guide

GETTING THERE & AWAY

AIR

Ireland's main airports:
Cork (ORK; ☎021-431 3131; www.corkairport.com)
Dublin (DUB; ☎01-814 1111; www.dublinairport.com)
Shannon (SNN; ☎061-712 000; www.shannonairport.com)

Other airports in the Republic with scheduled services from Britain:
Donegal (CFN; ☎074-954 8284; www.donegalairport.ie; Carrickfinn)
Kerry (KIR; ☎066-976 4644; www.kerryairport.ie; Farranfore)
Knock (NOC; ☎094-936 8100; www.irelandwestairport.com)
Waterford (WAT; ☎051-875 589; www.flywaterford.com)

Northern Ireland's airports:
Belfast International (BFS; ☎028-9448 4848; www.belfastairport.com) Flights from Britain, Continental Europe and the USA.
Derry/Londonderry (LDY; ☎028-7181 0784; www.cityofderryairport.com)
George Best Belfast City (BHD; ☎028-9093 9093; www.belfastcityairport.com)

Car hire firms are well represented at all major airports. Regional airports will have at least one internationally recognised firm as well as local operators.

SEA

The main ferry routes between Ireland and the UK and mainland Europe:
➡ Belfast to Liverpool (England; 8½ hours)
➡ Belfast to Stranraer (Scotland; 1¾ hours)
➡ Cork to Roscoff (France; 14 hours)
➡ Dublin to Liverpool (England; fast/slow four/8½ hours)
➡ Dublin and Dún Laoghaire to Holyhead (Wales; fast/slow 1½/three hours)
➡ Larne to Cairnryan (Scotland; 1½ hours)
➡ Larne to Fleetwood (England; six hours)
➡ Rosslare to Cherbourg and Roscoff (France; 20½ hours)
➡ Rosslare to Fishguard and Pembroke (Wales; 3½ hours)

Competition from budget airlines has forced ferry operators to discount heavily and offer flexible fares, which can translate into great bargains at quiet times of the day or year. For example, the popular route across the Irish Sea between Dublin and Holyhead can be had for as little as €80 for a car plus up to four passengers.

The main operators include the following:
Brittany Ferries (www.brittany-ferries.com)
Irish Ferries (www.irishferries.com)
Isle of Man Steam Packet Company/ Sea Cat (www.steam-packet.com)
Norfolkline (www.norfolkline.com)
P&O Irish Sea (www.poirishsea.com)
Stena Line (www.stenaline.com)

A very useful online tool is www.ferry booker.com, a single site covering all sea-ferry routes and operators out of the UK (the mainstay of sea travel to Ireland).

Practicalities

➡ **Smoking** Smoking is illegal in all indoor public spaces, including restaurants and pubs.

➡ **Time** Ireland uses the 12-hour clock and is on Greenwich Mean Time (GMT), aka Universal Time Coordinated (UTC).

➡ **TV & DVD** All TV in Ireland is digital terrestrial; Ireland is DVD Region 2.

➡ **Weights & Measures** In the Republic, both imperial and metric units are used for most measures except height, which is in feet and inches only. So at a market you might buy a pound of potatoes and half a kilo of apples, but wherever you are you're still five feet nine inches tall. When measuring distance, though, it's all about kilometres, even if people still talk in miles colloquially. It's less confusing in the North, imperial all the way.

DIRECTORY A–Z

ACCOMMODATION

Accommodation options range from bare and basic to pricey and palatial. The spine of the Irish hospitality business is the ubiquitous B&B, but in recent years they have been challenged by a plethora of midrange hotels and guesthouses. Online resources for accommodation include the following:

Daft.ie (www.daft.ie) Online classified paper for short- and long-term rentals.

Elegant Ireland (www.elegant.ie) Specialises in self-catering castles, period houses and unique properties.

Family Homes of Ireland (www.family homes.ie) Lists (you guessed it) family-run guesthouses and self-catering properties.

Gulliver (www.gulliver.ie) Fáilte Ireland and the Northern Ireland Tourist Board's web-based accommodation reservation system.

Irish Landmark Trust (www.irishland mark.com) Not-for-profit conservation group that rents self-catering properties of historical and cultural significance, such as castles, gate lodges and lighthouses.

Stay in Ireland (www.stayinireland.com) Lists guesthouses and self-catering options.

B&Bs & Guesthouses

Bed and breakfasts are small, family-run houses, farmhouses and period country houses with fewer than five bedrooms. Standards vary enormously, but most have some bedrooms with private bathroom at a cost of roughly €35 to €40 (£20 to £25) per person per night. In luxurious B&Bs, expect to pay €55 (£38) or more per person. Off-season rates – usually November through to February – are usually lower, as are midweek prices.

Guesthouses are like upmarket B&Bs but bigger – the Irish equivalent of a boutique hotel. Facilities are usually better and sometimes include a restaurant.

Other tips:

➡ Facilities in B&Bs range from basic (bed, bathroom, kettle) to beatific (whirlpool baths, LCD TVs, wi-fi) as you go up in price.

➡ Most B&Bs take credit cards, but the occasional rural one might not have facilities; check when you book.

➡ Advance reservations are strongly recommended, especially in peak season (June to August).

➡ If full, B&B owners may recommend another house in the area (possibly a private house taking occasional guests, not in tourist listings).

Camping & Caravan Parks

Camping and caravan parks aren't as common in Ireland as they are in Britain or on the Continent. Some hostels have camping space for tents and also offer house facilities, which makes them better

Book Your Stay Online

For more accommodation reviews by Lonely Planet authors, check out http://hotels.lonelyplanet.com. You'll find independent reviews, as well as recommendations on the best places to stay. Best of all, you can book online.

A 'Standard' Hotel Rate?

There is no such thing. Prices vary according to demand, and there are different rates for online, phone or walk-in bookings. B&B rates are more consistent, but virtually every other accommodation will charge wildly different rates depending on the time of year, the day, festival schedules and even your ability to do a little negotiating. The following price ranges have been used in our reviews of places to stay. Prices are all based on a double room with private bathroom in high season.

Budget	Republic	Northern Ireland
Budget (€/£)	< €60	< £40
Midrange (€€/££)	€60–€150	£40–£100
Top end (€€€/£££)	> €150	> £100

value than the main camping grounds. At commercial parks the cost is typically somewhere between €12 and €20 (£7 to £10) for a tent and two people. Prices for campsites in this book are for two people unless stated otherwise. Caravan sites cost around €15 to €25 (£11 to £15). Most parks are open only from Easter to the end of September or October.

Hostels

The prices quoted in this book for hostel accommodation are for those aged over 18. A dorm bed in high season generally costs €10 to €25 (£6 to £15). Many hostels now have family and smaller rooms.

The following is a list of the relevant hostel associations:

An Óige (www.anoige.ie) Hostelling International (HI)–associated national organisation with 26 hostels scattered around the Republic.

HINI (www.hini.org.uk) HI-associated organisation with six hostels in Northern Ireland.

Independent Holiday Hostels of Ireland (IHH; www.hostels-ireland.com) Eighty tourist-board-approved hostels throughout all of Ireland.

Independent Hostel Owners of Ireland (IHO; www.independenthostelsireland.com) Independent hostelling association.

Hotels

Hotels range from the local pub to medieval castles. In most cases, you'll get a better rate if you go online or negotiate directly with the hotel, especially out of season. The explosion of bland midrange chain hotels (many Irish-owned) has proved a major challenge to the traditional B&B or guesthouse: they might not have the same personalised service, but their rooms are clean and their facilities generally quite good.

ELECTRICITY

120V/60Hz

FOOD

Irish cuisine has come on in leaps and bounds in recent decades, and you can now eat as well in Ireland as in any European country. Reservations are only necessary in the more upscale restaurants or in trendy, city-centre eateries. You have your choice of eateries:

Restaurants From cheap 'n' cheerful to Michelin-starred, Ireland has something for every palate and budget.

Cafes Ireland is awash with cafes of every description, many of which are perfect for a quick, tasty bite.

Hotels Even if you're not a guest, most hotel restaurants cater to outside diners. Top hotels usually feature good restaurants with prices to match.

Pubs Pub grub is ubiquitous; it's mostly of the toasted-sandwich variety. However, a large number of pubs also have full-menu service, with some of them being as good as any top restaurant.

Irish eating habits have also changed over the last couple of decades, and there are differences between urban and rural practices.

➡ **Breakfast** An important meal given the Irish tendency towards small lunches. It's usually eaten before 9am (although hotels and B&Bs will serve until 11am Monday to Friday and to noon on weekends in urban areas), as most people rush off to work. Weekend brunch is popular in bigger towns and cities, although it pretty much copies traditional rural habits of eating a large, hearty breakfast late in the morning.

Price Ranges

Our cafe and restaurant listings appear in order of price, with the cheapest appearing first. We've used the following price indicators, which represent the cost of a main dish:

€/£	less than €10/£10
€€/££	€11–€20/£11–£20
€€€/£££	more than €20/£20

➡ **Lunch** Once the biggest meal of the day, lunch is now one of the more obvious rural/urban divides. Urban workers have succumbed to the eat-on-the-run restrictions of nine to five, with most eating a sandwich or a light meal between 12.30pm and 2pm (most restaurants don't begin to serve lunch until at least midday). On weekends, especially Sunday, the midday lunch is skipped in favour of a substantial mid-afternoon meal (called dinner), usually between 2pm and 4pm.

➡ **Tea** No, not the drink, but the evening meal – also confusingly called dinner. For urbanites, this is the main meal of the day, usually eaten around 6.30pm. Rural communities eat at the same time but with a more traditional tea of bread, cold cuts and, yes, tea. Restaurants follow international habits, with most diners not eating until at least 7.30pm.

➡ **Supper** A before-bed snack of tea and toast or sandwiches, still enjoyed by many Irish, although urbanites increasingly eschew it for health reasons. This is not a practice in restaurants.

GAY & LESBIAN TRAVELLERS

Ireland is a pretty tolerant place for gays and lesbians. Bigger cities like Dublin, Galway and Cork have well-established gay scenes, as do Belfast and Derry in Northern Ireland. That said, you'll still find pockets of homophobia throughout the island, particularly in smaller towns and rural areas. Resources include the following:

Gaire (www.gaire.com) Message board and info for a host of gay-related issues.

Gay & Lesbian Youth Northern Ireland (www.glyni.org.uk)

Gay Men's Health Project (☑01-660 2189; www.hse.ie) Practical advice on men's health issues.

National Lesbian & Gay Federation (NLGF; ☑01-671 9076; www.nlgf.ie) Publishes the monthly *Gay Community News* (www.gcn.ie).

Northern Ireland Gay Rights Association (Nigra; ☑028-9066 5257)

Outhouse (☑01-873 4932; www.outhouse. ie; 105 Capel St, Dublin) A gay, lesbian and transgender community centre.

HEALTH

No jabs are required to travel to Ireland. Excellent health care is readily available. For minor, self-limiting illnesses, pharmacists can give valuable advice and sell over-the-counter medication. They can also advise when more specialised help is required and point you in the right direction.

EU citizens equipped with a European Health Insurance Card (EHIC), available from health centres or, in the UK, post offices, will be covered for some medical care – but not nonemergencies or emergency repatriation. While other countries, such as Australia, also have reciprocal agreements with Ireland and Britain, many do not.

In Northern Ireland, everyone receives free emergency treatment at accident and emergency (A&E) departments of state-run NHS hospitals, irrespective of nationality.

INTERNET ACCESS

With the advent of 3G and wi-fi networks, internet cafes are increasingly disappearing from Irish towns. The ones that are left generally charge up to €5/£5 per hour.

If you'll be using your laptop or mobile device to get online, most hotels and an increasing number of B&Bs, hostels, bars and restaurants offer wi-fi access, charging anything from nothing to €5/£5 per hour.

Otherwise, most hotels and hostels in larger towns and cities have internet access via a desktop for customer use.

MONEY

The currency in the Republic of Ireland is the euro (€); Northern Ireland uses the pound sterling (£). Although notes issued by Northern Irish banks are legal tender throughout the UK, many businesses outside of Northern Ireland refuse to accept them and you'll have to swap them in British banks.

ATMs

Usually called 'cash machines', ATMs are easy to find in cities and all but the smallest of towns. Watch out for ATMs that have been tampered with; card-reader scams ('skimming') have become a real problem.

Tipping Guide

You're not obliged to tip if the service or food was unsatisfactory (even if it's been automatically added to your bill as a 'service charge').

Hotels Only for bellhops who carry luggage (€1/£1 per bag).

Pubs Not expected unless table service is provided, then €1/£1 for a round of drinks.

Restaurants For decent service, 10%; up to 15% in more expensive places.

Taxis 10% or rounded up to the nearest euro/pound.

Toilet attendants €0.50/50p.

Credit & Debit Cards

Visa and MasterCard credit and debit cards are widely accepted in Ireland. American Express is only accepted by the major chains, and very few places accept Diners or JCB. Smaller businesses, like pubs or some B&Bs, prefer debit cards (and will charge a fee for credit cards). Nearly all credit and debit cards use the chip-and-PIN system, but if your card isn't PIN enabled you should be able to sign in the usual way.

Taxes & Refunds

Non-EU residents can claim Value Added Tax (VAT: a sales tax, 21% of the purchase price of goods, except for books, children's clothing or educational items) back on their purchases as long as the store operates either the Cashback or Taxback refund program (it should display a sticker). You'll get a voucher with your purchase that must be stamped at the *last point of exit* from the EU. If you're travelling on to Britain or mainland Europe from Ireland, hold on to your voucher until you pass through your final customs stop in the EU; it can then be stamped and you can post it back for a refund of the duty paid.

VAT in Northern Ireland is 20%; shops participating in the Tax-Free Shopping refund scheme will give you a form or invoice on request to be presented to customs when you leave. After customs has certified the form, it will be returned to the shop for a refund and the cheque sent to you at home.

Travellers Cheques

Safer than cash but hardly ever used, travellers cheques have become increasingly rare as credit/debit cards have become the method of choice. They are rarely accepted for purchases, so to get cash you'll still have to go to a bank or a change bureau.

OPENING HOURS

Hours in both the Republic and Northern Ireland are roughly the same. Throughout this book we don't list opening and closing hours unless they differ significantly from those listed here:

Banks 10am to 4pm Monday to Friday (to 5pm Thursday)

Offices 9am to 5pm Monday to Friday

Post offices Northern Ireland: 9am to 5.30pm Monday to Friday, 9am to 12.30pm Saturday. Republic: 9am to 6pm Monday to Friday, 9am to 1pm Saturday. Smaller post offices may close at lunch and one day per week.

Pubs Northern Ireland: 11.30am to 11pm Monday to Saturday, 12.30pm to 10pm Sunday. Pubs with late licences open until 1am Monday to Saturday, and midnight Sunday. Republic: 10.30am to 11.30pm Monday to Thursday, 10.30am to 12.30am Friday and Saturday, noon to 11pm Sunday (30 minutes 'drinking up' time allowed). Pubs with bar extensions open to 2.30am Thursday to Saturday. All pubs close Christmas Day and Good Friday.

Restaurants Noon to 10.30pm; many close one day of the week.

Shops 9am to 5.30pm or 6pm Monday to Saturday (until 8pm on Thursday and sometimes Friday), noon to 6pm Sunday (in bigger towns only). Shops in rural towns may close at lunch and one day per week.

Tourist offices 9am to 5pm Monday to Friday, 9am to 1pm Saturday. Many extend their hours in summer, and open fewer hours/days or close from October to April.

PUBLIC HOLIDAYS

Public holidays can cause road chaos as everyone tries to get somewhere else for the break. It's wise to book accommodation in advance around these times.

The following are public holidays in both the Republic and Northern Ireland:

New Year's Day 1 January

St Patrick's Day 17 March

Easter (Good Friday to Easter Monday inclusive) March/April

May Holiday 1st Monday in May

Christmas Day 25 December

St Stephen's Day (Boxing Day) 26 December

The St Patrick's Day and St Stephen's Day holidays are taken on the following Monday when they fall on a weekend. In the Republic, nearly everywhere closes on Good Friday even though it isn't an official public holiday. In the North, most shops open on Good Friday but close the following Tuesday.

Northern Ireland

Spring Bank Holiday Last Monday in May

Orangemen's Day 12 July

August Holiday Last Monday in August

Republic

June Holiday 1st Monday in June

August Holiday 1st Monday in August

October Holiday Last Monday in October

SAFE TRAVEL

Ireland is safer than most countries in Europe, but normal precautions should be observed.

Northern Ireland is as safe as anywhere else, but there are areas where the sectarian divide is bitterly pronounced, most notably in parts of Belfast, the interface areas of north Belfast particularly. It's probably best to ensure your visit to Northern Ireland doesn't coincide with the climax of the Orange marching season on 12 July; sectarian passions are usually inflamed and even many Northerners leave the province at this time.

TELEPHONE

Phone Codes

In this book, area codes and individual numbers are listed together, separated by a hyphen (unless it's a mobile phone number). Area codes in the Republic have three digits and begin with a 0, eg ✐021 for Cork, ✐091 for Galway and ✐061 for Limerick. The only exception is Dublin, which has a two-digit code (✐01). Always use the area code if calling from a mobile phone, but you don't need it if calling from a fixed-line number within the area code.

In Northern Ireland, the area code for all fixed-line numbers is ✐028, but you only need to use it if calling from a mobile phone or from outside Northern Ireland. To call Northern Ireland from the Republic, use ✐048 instead of ✐028, without the international dialling code.

Mobile phone numbers in the Republic usually begin with 085, 086 or 087; in Northern Ireland, as with the rest of the UK, mobile numbers start with a five-digit prefix beginning with 07.

Other codes:

➡ ✐1550 or ✐1580 – premium rate (costs up to €2/£2 per minute)

➡ ✐1890 or ✐1850 – local or shared rate (standard rate)

➡ ✐0818 – calls at local rates, wherever you're dialling from within the Republic

➡ ✐1800 – free calls

Free call and lo-call numbers are not accessible from outside the Republic. Prices are lower during evenings after 6pm and on weekends.

Mobile Phones (Cell Phones)

➡ Ireland uses the GSM 900/1800 cellular phone system, which is compatible with European and Australian, but not North American or Japanese, phones.

➡ SMS ('texting') is a national obsession – most people under 25 communic8 mostly by txt.

➡ Pay-as-you-go mobile-phone packages with any of the main providers start at around €40

and usually include a basic handset and credit of around €10.

➡ SIM-only packages are also available, but make sure your phone is compatible with the local provider.

Pay phones & Phonecards

➡ If you can find a public phone that works, local calls in the Republic cost €0.30 for around three minutes (around €0.60 to a mobile), regardless of when you call. From Northern Ireland local calls cost about 40p, or 60p to a mobile, although this varies somewhat.

➡ Prepaid phonecards can be purchased at both newsagencies and post offices, and work from all pay phones for both domestic and international calls.

Directory Enquiries

For directory enquiries, a number of agencies compete for your business:

➡ In the Republic, dial ✐11811 or ✐11850; for international enquiries it's ✐11818.

➡ In the North, call ✐118 118, ✐118 192, ✐118 500 or ✐118 811.

➡ Expect to pay at least €1/£1 from a landline and up to €2/£2 from a mobile phone.

International Calls

To call out from Ireland dial ✐00, then the country code (✐1 for USA, ✐61 for Australia etc), the area code (you usually drop the initial zero) then the number.

TOURIST INFORMATION

In both the Republic and the North there's a tourist office in almost every big town; most can offer a variety of services including accommodation and attraction reservations, currency-changing services, map and guidebook sales, and free publications.

In the Republic, the tourism purview falls to **Fáilte Ireland** (✐1850 230 330 in the Republic, 0800 039 7000 in the UK; www.discoverireland.ie). It also has seven regional offices:

Cork & Kerry (✐021-425 5100; Cork Kerry Tourism, Áras Discover, Grand Pde, Cork)

Dublin (✐01-605 7700; www.visitdublin.com; Dublin Tourism Centre, St Andrew's Church, 2 Suffolk St, Dublin)

East Coast & Midlands (✐044-934 8761; East Coast & Midlands Tourism, Dublin Rd,

---

Important Numbers

Country code (✐353 Republic, 44 Northern Ireland)

Emergencies (✐999)

Roadside assistance (✐1800 667 788 in the Republic, 0800 887 766 in Northern Ireland)

Mullingar) For Kildare, Laois, Longford, Louth, Meath, North Offaly, Westmeath and Wicklow.

Ireland North West & Lakelands
(☑071-916 1201; Temple St, Sligo) For Cavan, Donegal, Leitrim, Monaghan and Sligo.

Ireland West (☑091-537 700; Ireland West Tourism, Áras Fáilte, Forster St, Galway) For Galway, Roscommon and Mayo.

Shannon Region (☑061-361 555; Shannon Development, Shannon, Clare) For Clare, Limerick, North Tipperary and South Offaly.

South East (☑051-875 823; South East Tourism, 41 The Quay, Waterford) For Carlow, Kilkenny, South Tipperary, Waterford and Wexford.

In Northern Ireland, it's the **Northern Ireland Tourist Board** (NITB; ☑head office 028-9023 1221; www.discovernorthernireland. com). Outside Ireland, Fáilte Ireland and the NITB unite under the banner Tourism Ireland. More information about offices around the world can be found at www. discoverireland.com.

TRAVELLERS WITH DISABILITIES

All new buildings have wheelchair access, and many hotels have installed lifts, ramps and other facilities. Others, especially B&Bs, have not adapted as successfully so you'll have far less choice. The Fáilte Ireland and Northern Ireland Tourist Board accommodation guide (www.gulliver.ie) indicates which places are wheelchair accessible.

In big cities, most buses have low-floor access and priority space on board, but the number of kneeling buses on regional routes is still relatively small.

Trains are accessible with help. In theory, if you call ahead, an employee of Iarnród Éireann (Irish Rail) will arrange to accompany you to the train. Newer trains have audio and visual information systems for visually impaired and hearing-impaired passengers.

The **Citizens' Information Board** (☑01-605 9000; www.citizensinformationboard. ie) in the Republic and **Disability Action** (☑028-9066 1252; www.disabilityaction.org) in Northern Ireland can give some advice to travellers with disabilities. Travellers to Northern Ireland can also check out the website www.allgohere.com.

VISAS

If you're a European Economic Area (EEA) national, you don't need a visa to visit (or work in) either the Republic or Northern Ireland. Citizens of Australia, Canada, New Zealand, South Africa and the US can visit the Republic for up to three months and Northern Ireland for up to six months without a visa. They are not allowed to work unless sponsored by an employer.

Full visa requirements for visiting the Republic are available online at www.dfa.ie; for Northern Ireland's visa requirements, see www.ukvisas.gov.uk.

To stay longer in the Republic, contact the local *garda* (police) station or the **Garda National Immigration Bureau** (☑01-666 9100; www.garda.ie; 13-14 Burgh Quay, Dublin). To stay longer in Northern Ireland, contact the **Home Office** (UK Border Agency; ☑0870-606 7766; www.ukba. homeoffice.gov.uk).

Language

Irish (Gaeilge) is the country's official language. In 2003 the government introduced the Official Languages Act, whereby all official documents and street signs must be either in Irish or in both Irish and English. Despite its official status, Irish is really only spoken in pockets of rural Ireland known as the Gaeltacht, the main ones being Cork (Corcaigh), Donegal (Dún na nGall), Galway (Gaillimh), Kerry (Ciarraí) and Mayo (Maigh Eo).

Ask people outside the Gaeltacht if they can speak Irish and nine out of 10 of them will probably reply, '*ah, cupla focal*' (a couple of words), and they generally mean it – but many adults also regret not having a greater grasp of it. Irish is a compulsory subject in schools for those aged six to 15. In recent times, a new Irish curriculum has been introduced cutting the hours devoted to the subject but making the lessons more fun, practical and celebratory.

Irish divides vowels into long (those with an accent) and short (those without), and also distinguishes between broad (a, á, o, ó, u) and slender (e, é, i and í), which can affect the pronunciation of preceding consonants. Other than a few clusters, such as mh and bhf (both pronounced as w), consonants are generally pronounced the same as in English.

Irish has three main dialects: Connaught Irish (in Galway and northern Mayo), Munster Irish (in Cork, Kerry and Waterford) and Ulster Irish (in Donegal). Our pronunciation guides are an anglicised version of modern standard Irish, which is essentially an amalgam of the three – if you read them as if they were English, you'll be able to get your point across in Gaeilge without even having to think about the specifics of Irish pronunciation or spelling.

BASICS

Hello.
Dia duit.   deea gwit

Hello. (reply)
Dia is Muire duit.   deeas moyra gwit

Good morning.
Maidin mhaith.   mawjin wah

Good night.
Oíche mhaith.   eekheh wah

Goodbye. (when leaving)
Slán leat.   slawn lyat

Goodbye. (when staying)
Slán agat.   slawn agut

Yes.
Tá .   taw

No.
Níl.   neel

It is.
Sea.   sheh

It isn't.
Ní hea.   nee heh

Thank you (very) much.
Go raibh (míle)   goh rev (meela)
maith agat.   mah agut

Excuse me.
Gabh mo leithscéal.   gamoh lesh scale

I'm sorry.
Tá brón orm.   taw brohn oruhm

Do you speak (Irish)?
An bhfuil (Gaeilge) agat?   on wil (gaylge) oguht

I don't understand.
Ní thuigim.   nee higgim

What is this?
Cad é seo?   kod ay shoh

Want More?

For in-depth language information and handy phrases, check out Lonely Planet's *Irish Language & Culture*. You'll find it at **shop.lonelyplanet.com**, or you can buy Lonely Planet's iPhone phrasebooks at the Apple App Store.

Signs

Dúnta	Closed
Fir	Men
Gardaí	Police
Leithreas	Toilet
Mná	Women
Ná Caitear Tobac	No Smoking
Oifig An Phoist	Post Office
Oifig Eolais	Tourist Information
Oscailte	Open
Páirceáil	Parking

What is that?
Cad é sin? kod ay shin

I'd like to go to ...
Ba mhaith liom baw wah lohm
dul go dtí ... dull go dee ...

I'd like to buy ...
Ba mhaith liom ... bah wah lohm ...
a cheannach. a kyanukh

another/one more
ceann eile kyawn ella

nice
go deas goh dyass

MAKING CONVERSATION

Welcome.
Ceád míle fáilte. kade meela fawlcha
(lit: 100,000 welcomes)

Bon voyage!
Go n-éirí an bóthar leat! go nairee on bohhar lat

How are you?
Conas a tá tú? kunas aw taw too

I'm fine.
Táim go maith. thawm go mah

... please.
... más é do thoil é. ... maws ay do hall ay

Cheers!
Slainte! slawncha

What's your name?
Cad is ainm duit? kod is anim dwit

My name is (Sean Frayne).
(Sean Frayne) is (shawn frain) is
ainm dom. anim dohm

Impossible!
Ní féidir é! nee faydir ay

Nonsense!
Ráiméis! rawmaysh

That's terrible!
Go huafásach! guh hoofawsokh

Take it easy.
Tóg é gobogé . tohg ay gobogay

DAYS OF THE WEEK

Monday	*Dé Luaín*	day loon
Tuesday	*Dé Máirt*	day maart
Wednesday	*Dé Ceádaoin*	day kaydeen
Thursday	*Déardaoin*	daredeen
Friday	*Dé hAoine*	day heeneh
Saturday	*Dé Sathairn*	day sahern
Sunday	*Dé Domhnaigh*	day downick

NUMBERS

1	*haon*	hayin
2	*dó*	doe
3	*trí*	tree
4	*ceathaír*	kahirr
5	*cúig*	kooig
6	*sé*	shay
7	*seacht*	shocked
8	*hocht*	hukt
9	*naoi*	nay
10	*deich*	jeh
11	*haon déag*	hayin jague
12	*dó dhéag*	doe yague
20	*fiche*	feekhe
21	*fiche haon*	feekhe hayin

BEHIND THE SCENES

SEND US YOUR FEEDBACK

We love to hear from travellers – your comments help make our books better. We read every word, and we guarantee that your feedback goes straight to the authors. Visit **lonelyplanet. com/contact** to submit your updates and suggestions.

Note: We may edit, reproduce and incorporate your comments in Lonely Planet products such as guidebooks, websites and digital products, so let us know if you don't want your comments reproduced or your name acknowledged. For a copy of our privacy policy visit lonelyplanet.com/privacy.

AUTHOR THANKS

FIONN DAVENPORT

A big thanks to my fellow authors Belinda, Catherine and Oda for their skills and forbearance. Big *bualadh bos* to Laura Stansfeld, Anna Metcalfe and Diana Von Holdt in Melbourne, and Clifton Wilkinson in London – without your expert advice and patience this book would never have happened. At home, as always, a big thanks to Caroline Clarke for her wit, chilli and tea.

BELINDA DIXON

Huge thanks to Cliff and Fionn (for guidance), Catherine (for conveying composure) and Oda (for invaluable moral support). The National Trust's Barry Crawford and Maurica Lavery, and the Belfast Visitor Bureau's Eve O'Neil provided sound advice.

Engaging conversationalists included Brendan Rohan (Dunfanaghy; politics), Georgina O'Connor (Wexford; books!) and Eamonn Cunniss (Galway; ballroom dancing).

CATHERINE LE NEVEZ

Sláinte to Julian, and to my trips coauthors Fionn, Oda and Belinda, and *Ireland* coauthors, as well as the locals, fellow travellers and tourism professionals in the southwest for insights and great craic. *Sláinte*, too, to Cliff, Laura, Di and all at LP. As ever, *merci encore* to my family.

ODA O'CARROLL

Thanks to my ever-patient co-authors Belinda, Catherine and Fionn, and to our Olympian editor Cliff. Gratitude to both Lauras and Di at LP HQ for their endless help. On the ground, a big shout to Mrs O, Charlotte, Jane, Ger, Eibhlin, Julie and Meabh for keeping the little ones at bay, and to Eoin, Ésa, Mella and Minnie for being 'the bomb'.

PUBLISHER THANKS

Climate map data adapted from Peel MC, Finlayson BL & McMahon TA (2007) 'Updated World Map of the Köppen-Geiger Climate Classification', *Hydrology and Earth System Sciences*, 11, 163344.

Cover photographs
Front (clockwise from top): Slieve League, Simon Greenwood/ Getty Images; Temple Bar, Dublin, Eoin Clarke/Getty Images; Fox's Pub in County Wicklow, Destinations/Corbis
Back: Dunguaire Castle, Gareth McCormack/Getty Images.

THIS BOOK

This 1st edition of Lonely Planet's *Ireland's Best Trips* guidebook was researched and written by Fionn Davenport, Belinda Dixon, Catherine Le Nevez and Oda O'Carroll. It was commissioned in Lonely Planet's London office, and produced by the following people:

Commissioning Editor Clifton Wilkinson **Coordinating Editors** Michelle Bennett, Anne Mason **Coordinating Cartographer** Corey Hutchison **Coordinating**

Layout Designer Jessica Rose **Managing Editors** Sasha Baskett, Kirsten Rawlings, Angela Tinson **Senior Editors** Catherine Naghten, Susan Paterson **Managing Cartographer** Diana Von Holdt **Managing Layout Designer** Chris Girdler **Assisting Editors** Janet Austin, Anne Mulvaney, Charlotte Orr **Assisting Cartographers** Hunor Csutoros, James Leversha, Gabriel Lindquist, Jolyon Philcox, Andy Rojas, Cameron Romeril, Chris Tsismetzis **Cover Research** Timothy O'Hanlon

Internal Image Research Aude Vauconsant **Language Content** Branislava Vladisavljevic **Thanks to** Anita Banh, Jennifer Bilos, Laura Crawford, Janine Eberle, Ryan Evans, Jennye Garibaldi, Joshua Geoghegan, Jane Hart, Liz Heynes, Laura Jane, Jennifer Johnston, David Kemp, Anna Metcalfe, Wayne Murphy, Trent Paton, Anthony Phelan, Martine Power, Raphael Richards, Mik Ruff, Julie Sheridan, Rebecca Skinner, Luna Soo, Laura Stansfeld, Matt Swaine, John Taufa, Gerard Walker, Juan Winata

INDEX

Catherine Le Nevez My wanderlust kicked in when I road-tripped across Europe aged four. I've been hitting the road at every opportunity since, completing a Doctorate of Creative Arts in writing, a Masters in professional writing and post-grad qualifications in editing and publishing along the way. With Celtic connections including Irish and Breton heritage (and a love of Guinness!), I've travelled throughout every county in the emerald isle, and covered 20 of them for various Lonely Planet titles.

My Favourite Trip `15` **Dingle Peninsula** This trip ticks all the boxes: perfect breakers, fresh-as-it-gets seafood, phenomenal scenery and a poetic soul.

Oda O'Carroll From the far-flung reaches of Midwest Ireland, I upped sticks and moved to Dublin to study communications. After a stint as a TV researcher I went on to direct short films and TV documentaries in between travel writing for Lonely Planet and other (lesser!) publications. I've worked on titles like *Britain, France, Corsica, Ireland* and *Dublin* and now live in Dublin with my husband and three daughters.

My Favourite Trip `21` **Best of the West** It's hard to beat this coastline for sheer scenic diversity: windswept beaches, great stretches of mountains and super-friendly towns.

OUR WRITERS

OUR STORY

A beat-up old car, a few dollars in the pocket and a sense of adventure. In 1972 that's all Tony and Maureen Wheeler needed for the trip of a lifetime – across Europe and Asia overland to Australia. It took several months, and at the end – broke but inspired – they sat at their kitchen table writing and stapling together their first travel guide, *Across Asia on the Cheap*. Within a week they'd sold 1500 copies. Lonely Planet was born.

Today, Lonely Planet has offices in Melbourne, London and Oakland, with more than 600 staff and writers. We share Tony's belief that 'a great guidebook should do three things: inform, educate and amuse'.

Fionn Davenport It's funny how you can least know that which is most familiar to you. Irish-born, bred and raised, I've lived in and out of Ireland all of my life. But it was only when I began writing about it 20 years ago that I began to really get to know it – and this

Belinda Dixon I first visited Northern Ireland 20 years ago, when armed soldiers patrolled the streets. Witnessing the transformative power of the peace process in Belfast and Derry on this research trip has been inspiring. But what is also always appealing is the cliff-clinging